Patrons and Adversaries

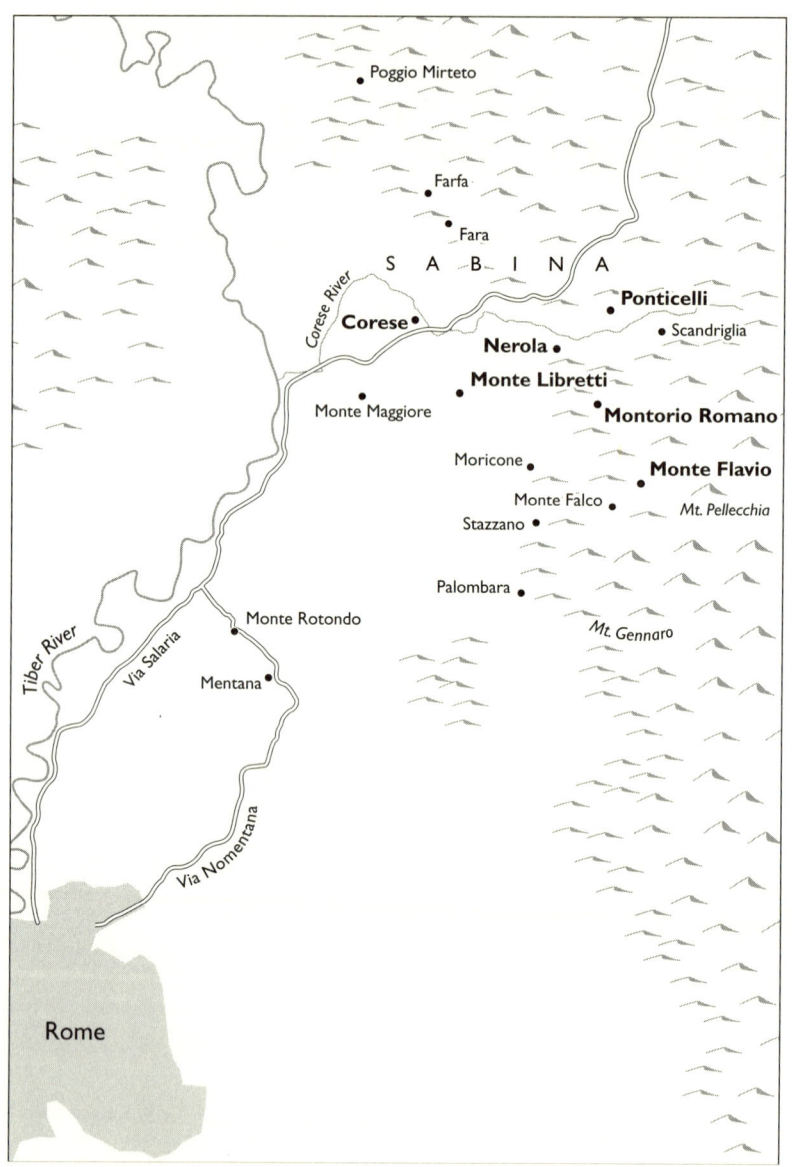

The Roman Countryside near the Stato of Monte Libretti. Villages in the Stato are in boldface type.
In this map and in this book, I employ the early modern rather than the modern spellings of the villages.

Patrons and Adversaries

Nobles and Villagers in Italian Politics, 1640–1760

CAROLINE CASTIGLIONE

UNIVERSITY PRESS

2005

OXFORD
UNIVERSITY PRESS

Oxford   New York

Auckland   Bangkok   Buenos Aires   Cape Town   Chennai
Dar es Salaam   Delhi   Hong Kong   Istanbul   Karachi   Kolkata
Kuala Lumpur   Madrid   Melbourne   Mexico City   Mumbai   Nairobi
São Paulo   Shanghai   Taipei   Tokyo   Toronto

Published by Oxford University Press, Inc.
198 Madison Avenue, New York, New York 10016

www.oup.com

Oxford is a registered trademark of Oxford University Press

Library of Congress Cataloging-in-Publication Data
Castiglione, Caroline.
Patrons and adversaries : nobles and villagers in Italian politics, 1640–1760 /
Caroline Castiglione.
p. cm.
Includes bibliographical references and index.
ISBN-13 978-0-19-517386-4; 978-0-19-517387-1 (pbk.)
ISBN 0-19-517386-4; 0-19-517387-2 (pbk.)
1. Barberini family 2. Monte Libretti (Italy)—History.
3. Nobility—Italy—Rome—History. 4. Feudalism—Italy—Monte Libretti—
History. 5. Villages—Italy—Monte Libretti—History. 6. Rome (Italy)—Politics
and government—1420–1798. 7. Papacy—History—1566–1799. I. Title.
DG803.6.B37C37 2004
320.945'63'09031—dc22   2004045577

Portions of chapters 1, 5, 6, and the conclusion are reprinted, with permission, from
"Adversarial Literacy: How Peasant Politics Influenced Noble Governing of the Roman
Countryside during the Early Modern Period," *AHR* 109, no. 3 (June 2004): 783–804.

Portions of chapter 2 and the introduction are reprinted from "Political Culture
in Seventeenth-Century Italian Villages," *Journal of Interdisciplinary History* 31 (2001): 523–552,
with the permission of the editors of *The Journal of Interdisciplinary History* and the MIT Press,
Cambridge, Massachussetts. © 2001 by the Massachussetts Institute of Technology
and The Journal of Interdisciplinary History, Inc.

1 3 5 7 9 8 6 4 2

Printed in the United States of America
on acid-free paper

For Samuel

Joy amidst chaos

ACKNOWLEDGMENTS

This book placed me in the company of some fascinating historians and writers, some of whom I have had the pleasure to meet, many of whom I would like to thank here, none of whom is responsible for the shortcomings in this work.

One of the benefits of spending so much of one's time on the road has to be the contribution of audiences and commentators to the process of writing. I would like to thank a few exceptionally insightful commentators at conferences, especially John Marino and Edward Muir, who have generously continued the dialogue initiated at those meetings. Audiences at the American Historical Association, the American Society for Eighteenth Century Studies, the Sixteenth Century Studies Conference, Trinity University, the Erasmus Institute, and the New York Area Faculty Seminar on Modern European History had a profound impact on the book. I greatly benefited from specific suggestions offered at those settings by Jeffrey Merrick, Brad Gregory, Sarah Hanley, Giovanna Benadusi, and John Martin. John deserves special thanks for a conversation that has endured for over two decades.

To the readers who endured very early versions of this project when it was centered on the nobility as a governing class, I owe a special debt of gratitude. Nina Safran, Ben Westervelt, David Bush, Michael Prokopow, James Hankins, Simon Schama, Laurie Nussdorfer, Maureen Miller, Charles Maier, and Myron Gutmann waded through that study and probably never anticipated the way in which it would be hijacked by village sources and village issues. Early inspiration on the history of the Roman countryside came from Renata Ago, Mirka Beneš, and the late Jean Coste. On Mirka's expertise and advice I have long relied.

At the University of Texas the circle of readers and writers in the departmental works-in-progress seminar sharpened my thinking and challenged my standard set of assumptions about this project. Without the intellectual support and thoughtful editing of Jim Sidbury and Judy Coffin this book and its author would both be in a truly regrettable state. I appreciate the time they took from their own work to venture into the strange territory of early modern Rome. Ken Ward and Ian Brown provided invaluable research assistance.

Susan Ferber has encouraged and inspired me in the writing of this book for several years. I thank her and the readers and staff at Oxford for giving such a great effort to improving it. I am especially grateful to the owner of the beautiful painting by Passeri who allowed me to use it for the cover illustration.

The friendship and readership of Janet Davis and Denise Spellberg ameliorated my life in Austin. Mike Rose, Sonja Rajkovich, and Iris Farias gave long-distance inspiration. Sara Hurd, Carolyn Bates, and Beth Hyde remain among the wisest women I know, and I would rather not think about where I would be without their insights. The Castiglione-Martinez dynasties of San Antonio and Los Angeles remain a network of support. I am grateful to my sister Virginia Castiglione, who sorted out computer formatting problems too complex for my limited abilities and enabled me to see why they, along with countless other disasters, were actually funny. Adrienne Gracia tended my son while we traveled in Italy and made the time for him and me more delightful. My friend Courtney Bensch did two similar Italian tours for which I am grateful to her. Tommaso, Luisa, and Veronica Clemente, Marcella Iafrate, Sister Angela Perego, and Sister Maria Argentino help make Italy feel like home to me.

Librarians, archivists, and mayors in the Roman countryside endured more questions about their resources than must have seemed necessary. I would like to thank the librarians and staff members of the Vatican Library for their kind assistance, especially the late Father Leonard Boyle, Dr. Luigi Fiorani, Elvio Buriola, Dr. Christine Grapfzinger, Dr. Massimo Ceresa, and Antonio Schiavi. In the Roman countryside I thank especially the mayor of Montelibretti, Pasqualino Imperi.

Funding for this project was provided by the American Council of Learned Societies, the Gladys Krieble Delmas Foundation, the University of Texas at Austin, and the University Cooperative Society Subvention Grant.

I would not have written this book without the loving camaraderie of Robert Martinez. Born in the same working-class neighborhood separated by 1,500 miles of Interstate 10, we have been marveling at the world beyond it ever since. This book is dedicated to our son, Samuel, who does his own writing in singsong beside me, drawing new worlds on the pages of the old drafts of this book, reminding me that I write best when looking backward and forward at the same time.

CONTENTS

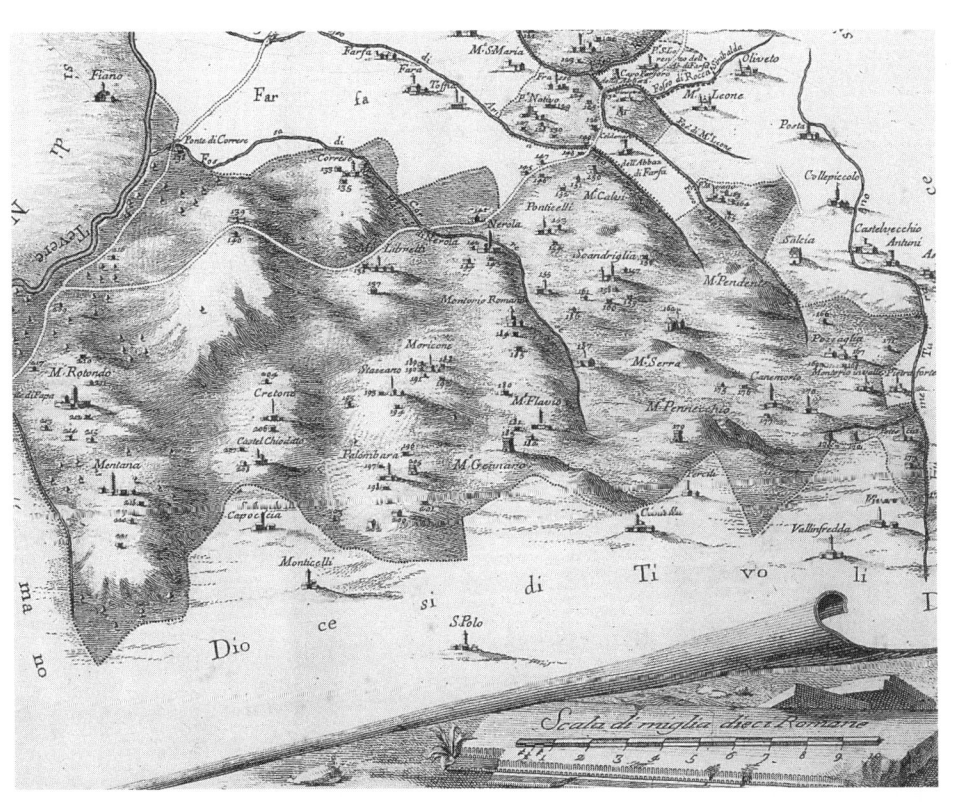

Angelo Sani, Carta Geografica e descrizzione della diocesi di Sabina. Rome, 1759. Copyright Vatican Library, Stampe Geografiche, S. 45. Shown here is a detail of the southern portion of the map, near Rome.

Patrons and Adversaries

Introduction

View of a village on a hillside. Anonymous, circa 1630. Photo copyright Vatican Library, Barb. Lat. 9910, f. 17.

In the winter of 1811–1812, Innocenzo Campanelli, a notary and sometimes employee of the Barberini family, sent a description of his native village to Prince Maffeo Barberini, the new owner of the *stato* of Monte Libretti. The *stato* was an extensive territory northeast of Rome comprising six villages, one of which was Campanelli's village of Nerola. In Campanelli's obviously biased geography, Nerola was "the most celebrated village of the province of Sabina," and the Sabina was the most ancient (and therefore most important) province of Italy. Campanelli combined his historical assessment with a survey of the village's most impressive sons (and one exceptional daughter), notable buildings, and potential for agricultural and industrial development. The author courted Maffeo as a patron—a potential benefactor who could address some of the village's problems—its abandoned houses, declining families, and stubborn residents who were committed to following the "deadly example" of their ancestors by quitting the perfect air of Nerola to do agricultural work in the malaria-ridden valleys below. Maffeo Barberini could help make a different future for down-and-out Nerola, building on its strengths to restore its ancient glories. Campanelli's assessment of Nerola since antiquity inscribed in prose what eighteenth-century Italians throughout the peninsula commemorated in stone about their local communities. The self-made historian memorialized in part for political aims, hoping to focus the attention of a governing authority in Rome on what could be done for his village.[1]

Campanelli's work as notary and noble employee also brought him into contact with the bureaucrats of the papal government, a potential rival of the Barberini rule of Nerola. Typically the history of the Roman countryside has been understood as a site of contestation between these two rivals for its rule. The elective theocracy of the Papal States, staffed exclusively by clerics at its highest echelons, supposedly undermined the political role of great baronial families like the Barberini. In this model, the clerics also imposed a crushing burden of taxation on the peasants from which the latter, in theory, lacked the means to escape. Campanelli's active life in government, his list of who's who in the village of Nerola, and his appeal to the Barberini suggest dynamism at the local level that belies the characterization of the passive political role of country inhabitants and Roman nobles. Campanelli thought his text might remake Nerola, and by that act of faith, he located himself in a long stream of individuals from his and neighboring villages who thought that by writing for political purposes they might achieve the same. While some writers advocated for local needs, others composed thinly veiled threats against authorities in Rome in order to keep them out of local affairs and to keep their hands off of local resources. Politics for them was best left to the villagers. The volume and the complexity of what partisans of a variety of political opinions left behind beckons us out of urban archives and urban-centered politics. "Grace us with your presence,"

Campanelli urged Maffeo Barberini. This book answers that invitation, although now it is only by means of those texts that the journey can be taken, and the journey's purpose, of course, is rather different from what the nobleman and the early nineteenth-century notary turned historian had in mind.

Campanelli's history of Nerola is a mere fourteen folios in what was once a mountain of paper in the Roman countryside. Unlike those Braudellian barriers of early modern geography, this mountain was man-made and built to connect rather than divide the worlds which stood on either side of it. It attempted to shape the relations between noble and villager, and miraculously, parts of it survive in a place where threats to it were many. Human inhabitants in the village had their own reasons for wanting it to disappear. If eighteenth-century rats were a risk to wooden furniture, then they alone were a considerable adversary to this cartulary landscape. Fires, like the one that destroyed nearly the entire archive of the village of Monte Flavio in a single day, are the worst enemy of village records. And since the nineteenth-century (until very recently) the centralizing state was no friend to the little, the local, the particular, in sum all that these country archives embodied.[2]

The poet Eavan Boland has marveled at the tenacity of twentieth-century writers to pursue historical figures now nearly irretrievable due to the lack of sources: "What act of love or corruption makes us turn to a past full of obstruction and misinformation?" Historians have, with good justification, avoided this potential quandary for villagers by working on better surviving serial sources, such as the records of births, deaths, marriages, prices, and property sales. The precariousness of their economy and the heartbreaking facts of their demography are now clearer to us as a result. But their political ideas remain obscure, due to the far spottier survival of village communal records. Among the six villages of Monte Libretti, most of the records of the village *consiglio* are gone, most of the letters written by the villagers to the Barberini, gone. We can only surmise what the villagers wrote, for the most part, from the noble family's replies. Two villages of the *stato*, however, Monte Libretti and Nerola, had a rather miraculous survival of their communal records, especially their communal assembly records. Combining what we can learn from these sources with the evidence in the Barberini archives, testimony from lawsuits, and assessments of the villagers by the papal bureaucrats, a more comprehensive, if not complete analysis of rural political culture becomes possible.[3]

This book wrestles with what remains of what was once a vast source base in order to understand what it can tell us about rural politics in the *stato* of Monte Libretti. Village documents are evaluated here in the larger context of archival collections that have been remarkably well preserved, especially the papers of the Barberini, the noble family that attempted to rule the territory between the mid-seventeenth and mid-eighteenth centuries, and the archive of the Buon Governo, the papal bureaucracy devoted to reforming communal institutions in the villages of the Roman countryside.

In their attempts to intervene in village politics, four generations of the Barberini frequently found themselves in a tangle of local customs, village assembly decisions, and inhabitants as stubborn as members of the noble family. Disputes between nobles and villagers combined the gracefulness of a tug-of-war with the honesty of a tavern card game. The villagers, even when they lost their battles with the Barberini, sometimes emerged the de facto winners nonetheless. That they endured to fight the noble family again demonstrates the vitality of their politics and explains why we have any documentation at all in the village. A lot of paper had to be sent from Rome to convince the losers that the most recent defeat was truly the final word on the subject, while in the village the words or deeds that denied the finality of the loss often continued unabated, despite the proclamations of authorities in Rome.

The residents of Monte Libretti scarcely appeared capable of challenging either a powerful noble family like the Barberini or the expanding papal bureaucracy. They lived in small villages ranging in population from 200 to 800 individuals, perched on the foothills of the Sabine mountains. In the Middle Ages the Roman barons had battled for control of the countryside through domination of these fortified towns. Within the villages, however, a different medieval legacy had a profound impact on country life: the village commune. Its officials were chosen by lot and in its meetings heads of households debated controversies and decided issues by vote. Successive generations of the Barberini family took ever greater interest in controlling these local governing bodies and each generation of villagers grew more sophisticated in its participation in the commune and in its responses to Barberini attempts to influence village institutions.

In part this century-long relationship is the story of village resistance to noble attempts to usurp peasant rights. But it is, like all historical inquiry, also a more complicated tale. Noble authority in these rural communities was also respected and even sought after when villagers turned to the Barberini to help them resolve long-standing local conflicts and to find and keep priests, doctors, and schoolteachers in their local communities. The same family, even the same person, could be both a patron and an adversary from the perspective of the villagers. Further complicating the dynamic between nobles and villagers was the eighteenth-century extension of the papal bureaucracy into the Roman countryside. Papal bureaucrats could be allies in village struggles against noble families, but they were also adversaries in their own right: They attempted to impose new taxes, audited communal records, and intervened in communal affairs.

Patrons, adversaries, mediators, meddlers: Nobles and bureaucrats appeared in a number of guises in the village world. This book illuminates what made

Monte Libretti's exquisitely tangled choreography work and how its complexity contributed (often unintentionally) to the villagers' increasingly sophisticated political savvy. It explores why, even in the Papal States, a region of Europe long characterized as an "absolutist" government badly run by clerics, the laity was profoundly interested in participating in politics. This is an especially surprising feature of the countryside around the eternal city, since Roman nobles were supposed to be committed only to the "inexorable gilded decadence" of their urban lives, and villagers were supposed to have slipped without protest under the increasing tax burdens imposed by the papacy.[4]

One of the common assessments about the politics of nobles during the long eighteenth century is that they acquiesced to the centralizing state, abandoning their periodic participation in the unrest in Europe between 1500 and about 1650. During the relative tranquility that characterized Europe between the mid-seventeenth and late eighteenth centuries, nobles drew a number of benefits both financial and social from integrating themselves in the state, and the eighteenth century has been characterized as the "aristocratic century," suggesting that there was considerable success intertwined with their surrender. Co-opted by the state, they in turn co-opted it to their advantage. Critics of the process, then and now, observed that they were also emasculated by it, since royal institutions usurped some of their prior judicial and governing functions. France and its historiography tell this story best, and it clearly has application to other parts of Europe, including the Roman countryside. At the level of the village, however, Roman nobles could theoretically still exercise considerable authority, more judicial authority, for instance, than their French counterparts. Did they? Did nobility in other parts of Europe retreat from their village role in government, public order, and justice, as did the French nobility? Such accusations were leveled even at the great aristocratic families of the Roman countryside, although the Barberini family's trajectory in the eighteenth century was completely contrary to this pattern.[5]

The region around Rome we know today as Latium is an excellent area in which to examine baronial jurisdictions. The pope's power, it was observed, declined the closer one got to the eternal city. These numerous baronial communes were considered "indirectly subject" to the pope through noble families like the Barberini. In these 282 baronial communes, nobles could exercise considerable jurisdiction over their "vassals" by attempting to control key areas of village life: monitoring the affairs and participants in communal government; maintaining public order; overseeing the administration of justice. Attention to one's jurisdiction also implied a concern for the economic and religious well-being of noble "vassals" in the countryside.[6]

The enduring power of the Roman nobility can be glimpsed in the texts recording their "possession" of the various territories. In the last days of April

1729, Pietro Felice Paulini, priest and "special procurator" for Cornelia Costanza and Giulio Cesare Barberini, traveled to the fiefs of Monte Libretti in
order to take "true, real, corporal, and actual possession" of the villages for the
next generation of the Barberini family. Throughout the *stato* Paulini followed
a practice much like the one recorded for the village of Nerola. From the villagers assembled there, he required an oath of fealty and their pledge to pay the
rents and dues owed to their lords. The "vassals" present at the *possesso* swore an
oath of loyalty to the new rulers, giving their word to "obey their orders . . .
and to offer the obliged reverence, obedience, and service . . . [the vassals]
promised in all things to be faithful." In return Paulini accepted the local *statuto*
in the name of Cornelia Costanza and Giulio Cesare and received from the priors the "keys" to the village. Paulini, along with the priors and the other villagers, then proceeded to the gate of Nerola, which he opened and closed as a
sign of the "true possession" of the fief by the Barberini family. Returning to
the Barberini palace, Paulini conceded the keys to the priors, entrusting them
to the village officials for the duration of their office.[7]

Historians caution against interpreting these ceremonies of lordship as a
meaningful reflection of the relations between nobles and "vassals" in the eighteenth century. Although the *possesso* reaffirmed the superiority of the noble
family's authority in the governing of the village (the priors, after all, received
the keys to the village from the emissary of the noble family, a symbolic rep-
resentation of the source of village political power), noble control of village
government was challenged in the seventeenth century by the judicial possibilities offered to the villagers by the papal courts, and in the eighteenth century,
by those same courts as well as the Papal Congregation of the Buon Governo,
the papal bureaucracy that began to interfere in the affairs of the communal
government. A number of historians have assumed that such interference effectively broke the hold of the barons on the rural communes directly subject to
them; it was, in other words, the institutional equivalent of the proliferation of
the power of the intendants in France.[8]

The usurpation of the political role of the nobles in the countryside is a
deeply held assumption about European history, with a particular vitality in
the area around Rome. Nineteenth- and early twentieth-century historians
concerned with the history of the nobility and the Roman countryside after
the sixteenth century placed considerable emphasis on the "decadence" of
both urban landowners and the lands and villages around Rome. Even the bi-
ographer of the Barberini family, Pio Pecchiai, wrote disparagingly of the Barberini after their arrival in Rome where they became, as he put it, "Roman to
the roots of their hair." A typical Roman nobleman, according to such historiography, was an absentee landlord, living decadently in the city, indifferent to
his fiefs and vassals in the countryside. He rented his properties to "merchants

of the countryside," and he appointed and then ignored the governors who managed his jurisdiction. This sixteenth-century shift from direct administration to a reliance on officials and renters transformed the once independent Roman nobility into a "court nobility" and according to the legal historian Giovanni Curis, "broke every connection between lords and vassals."[9] This interpretation has proved to be remarkably tenacious, although individual authors vary the relative culpability of nobles, popes, and "merchants of the countryside" in transforming the area around Rome from grain cultivation to pasture land, from a land of "thriving" villages to desolate and abandoned farmlands.[10]

This study shifts the focus from the "abandoned" countryside around Rome to the villages in the hills around that countryside, where most of the people in the region actually resided. Historians of the Roman nobility have only recently examined noble participation in governing.[11] In order to assess the nature of noble jurisdiction in the countryside, its reliance on absenteeism, and its challenges (real and perceived) from papal bureaucrats, we have to look at it on the level of the village. It is only in that world that we can start to understand the realities of noble jurisdiction, and only by considering that jurisdiction across many decades, that we can assess its actual transformation. Is noble jurisdiction truly in decline between the seventeenth and eighteenth centuries? Evidence in the Barberini archive suggests that the family was inspired by the expansion of the Papal Congregation of the Buon Governo, rather than merely threatened by it. Because the papal bureaucracy failed to limit aristocratic control of village participation in communal government, and because that bureaucracy relied heavily on the noble families to monitor communal finances, the "triumphant" state remained conspicuously indebted to noble knowledge and noble resources to achieve its goals in the countryside. The Barberini, for instance, were increasingly obsessed by issues of communal government in the eighteenth century. The family's interest in these issues, already present in the seventeenth century, only intensified in the eighteenth century, when thousands of letters flowed from the noble family to their officials in the countryside, in the hopes of securing tighter control over village affairs.

What did any of these "outsiders" (nobles or bureaucrats) in Rome really have to do with village political life? While political authority in the Roman countryside is usually analyzed as a struggle between these two competing rulers, records related to village communal governments, especially the notes from the meetings of village assemblies, suggest that this bifurcated view of power in the countryside obscures the realities of its governance in the early modern period. Much of the world revealed in the letters of the Barberini implies that whatever the generation of villagers recited for Paulini in 1729, they and their descendants never stuck very consistently to the text. Cornelia Costanza, for instance, referred to the "arrogance" of her vassals, and during a disturbance in 1775, she solicited suggestions from the governor in Monte Libretti to secure the "tranquility and the subordination owed in vassalage not only to this Government but also to our officials." Although we have far fewer sources with which to analyze it, the track record of their ancestors was scarcely better.[12]

Cultivating subordination in the countryside remained the quixotic quest of the noble family until the end of the eighteenth century. Yet the vassals of Monte Libretti seem docile enough—they, after all, never rebelled violently against the noble family during more than a century of Barberini lordship. Monte Libretti's mere "disturbances" could be dismissed as minor and apolitical. A half-century of scholarship focused on peasant uprisings in early modern Europe has tended to characterize most of those movements as conservative or lacking in political ideology, since they did not demand the overthrow of the entire social order.[13]

A few scholars have proposed that we recognize the political content of a broader range of peasant behaviors, including griping, stealing, and petition writing, to name only a few. Wayne Te Brake has asserted that we should conceptualize politics as "an ongoing bargaining process between those who claim governmental authority . . . and those over whom that authority is said to extend," a definition that calls for a reassessment of peasant demands during ordinary times as well as during rebellion. In early modern Italy, rural unrest was relatively rare, and its absence has often been explained by the peasants' hopelessly low status vis-à-vis cities and lords. Alternatively, the rarity of peasant rebellion has been attributed to their "better opportunities for political organization rather than because they were unusually repressed." Such a theory fits well with current research on Italian state development: Allegiance to early modern Italian states was built through their success in acting as mediators between conflicting class and corporate interests in society. The historian John Marino made this point convincingly for southern Italy, and historians of northern Italian states have emphasized that a similar process characterized state development there as well.[14]

In rural Italy, the state mediated disputes between lords and villagers through the judicial system. Although the institutional mechanisms of this process are now better understood, we know little about the political ideas of the villagers who used the state to address their grievances. By contrast, urban political culture, especially in northern and central Italy, has a rich and controversial historiography. The political scientist Robert Putnam's analysis of Italy's uneven development in the twentieth century underscored the long-lasting impact of civic traditions that emerged with the rise of the medieval urban commune—what he called "horizontal solidarity." Historians of early modern Italy have taken issue with this model, raising concerns both about its historical accuracy and its relevance to the rest of Italy, especially rural Italy, where local political culture is still largely unknown.[15]

Although Italian history after the Renaissance emphasizes the demise of urban communal institutions and the rise of seigneurial regimes under the tutelage of a ruling family, evidence from the central Italian countryside suggests that the communal tradition survived outside an urban setting, even in territories like the *stato* of Monte Libretti, where the Barberini claimed considerable authority as lords. Here I focus on village civic traditions made by the male heads of household who participated in the *consiglio* (assembly) or who held other communal offices. Through such participation, these individuals organized themselves politically, debated alternate possibilities for managing village resources or meeting village needs, oversaw the payment of papal taxes, negotiated with the Barberini lord, and in some cases challenged the lord's edicts, judicial practices, or demands on village labor or goods. These men were the segment of village society that has left the best records about the political ideas circulating in the village in the early modern period. As was the case in the town in central Italy that the anthropologist Sydel Silverman studied in the twentieth century, politically active villagers demonstrated pride in their village, its history, and its communal government. This does not mean, however, that they were cohesively united in every undertaking, since the records of the village assembly suggest considerable animosity among participants, as can be seen most clearly in chapters 3 and 5. However, it was through their participation in the village commune that villagers were able to exploit the paradoxes inherent in the Old Regime, often to their benefit. Male heads of household were simultaneously, citizens of the village, with the right to participate in the village assembly and serve in village offices, vassals of their lords, who still claimed extensive jurisdiction over them; and subjects of the pope, whose temporal government wrestled with their inclusion in the eighteenth century. Village politics is thus multifaceted, and only a few of its aspects are captured in the texts studied here.[16]

I acknowledge but do not explore in detail the inevitable animosities among villagers because in the struggle of villagers against aristocrats, the unifying characteristics of village politics were more important and ultimately more effective against such adversaries. Communal loyalty was of course, a constructed, rather than an innate characteristic of village life, and it required both the disciplining of the village by the communal government and the success of that village commune in cultivating allegiance through providing services for the village and through litigating effectively against village adversaries. How villagers were able to do this through their participation in the commune, especially in the village assembly, is one of the contributions of this book. I agree with the historian Peter Blickle, that neither nostalgia nor excessive pessimism about communal politics is helpful for understanding its impact on early modern history. Even a quick survey of village politics in early modern Europe underscores the potential richness and variety of its expression. In central Italy that included a thriving communal tradition that merits further scrutiny than it has hitherto received. Village political ideas, regardless of the specific motivations of the actors using them, constituted a rural intellectual patrimony to which other villagers could turn during conflict with the noble family, some of whose members came to regret the longevity and the vitality of rural political culture.[17]

Villagers in the area around Rome, in contrast to those of Germany, did not control the administration of justice, an aspect of governing that in the *stato* of Monte Libretti remained in the hands of the noble family. Such power also distinguished Barberini seigneurialism from French seigneurialism, since the Roman aristocratic family had the right to issue edicts and practiced this right throughout the era covered by this study. Perhaps as a result of facing considerable seigneurial power, communal politics in this region remained coherently organized throughout this period against possible encroachments by the lord, and resistance to Barberini edicts could only be accomplished through the efforts of the commune. While no rural study can encompass all the issues of governance faced by villagers, those issues raised in the communal politics of Monte Libretti seemed relevant enough to inhabitants that they returned to them, sometimes across several decades, and frequently committed communal resources or raised taxes on specifically affected individuals in order to pursue such controversies through the papal courts. Such pressure points are useful sites for intense scrutiny of village politics. They generated more controversy and thereby more sources.[18]

The texts studied here have long awaited systematic scrutiny by historians. Village *consiglio* records are among the rarest documents related to the political history of Europe. Although they certainly do not provide the "hidden transcript" of the villagers' views of power, they are one of the few sources for the political ideas of the supposedly tranquil villagers of the early modern Roman countryside. The records of the village meetings offer new perspectives on village politics, although they often contain considerable gaps, and their content does not immediately dazzle researchers. The *consiglio* often focused upon what might be called the politics of everyday life: finding and paying schoolteachers and village doctors, repairing church steeples, renting communal property, maintaining food and water supplies, negotiating controversies over animal grazing and agriculture, and avoiding tax demands from Rome. But they also contain the other side of rural politics, the extraordinary skirmishes between villagers and their rulers in Rome that kept controversial issues alive from one generation to the next. Combined with the village testimony that reached Roman law courts, it has been possible to piece together a sense both of village politics, and the local political culture that was necessary to sustain it.[19]

Village politics is analyzed here in relationship to one kind of village literacy, what I have named adversarial literacy, or the practices of political reading and writing that sustained nonviolent resistance by ordinary Europeans between the mid-seventeenth and mid-eighteenth century. In the villages of Monte Libretti, adversarial literacy in the seventeenth century developed though the reading of the village constitution and notarial records, the contents and significance of which were "taught" in meetings of the village *consiglio*. By the eighteenth century, villagers were making their own sources, pushing the interpretations of old ones, and challenging the textual monopoly that dictated that only those in Rome should be able to make or interpret written records. The historian R. A. Houston's recent survey of early modern literacy underscores the current skepticism about the possibility of literacy changing rural society, where, he argues, family, community, religion, and magic were more important, and sophisticated political concepts unknown. Certainly all of the standard attributes of early modern society apply to the *stato* of Monte Libretti, but I will show that many of its residents were capable of manipulating rather sophisticated political ideas. While most historians of literacy have focused on the formal acquisition of learning through the school, here the focus will be on the social practices of literacy among politically active adults. Literacy studies of early modern Europe have emphasized how villagers read literary and religious texts, clearly important questions. Here I focus instead on the reading of political and legal texts, and the place of those texts in village political culture. That state expansion explicitly and implicitly fueled literacy is indisputable, but how literate practices developed in the village in response to judicial opportunities offered by the state is less well understood and will receive close attention here, especially in chapters 2 and 6. Such a focus brings the politics of Monte Libretti into current debates among historians of political culture, who analyze the lines of influence between state and society in the great variety of political regimes that characterize early modern Europe.[20]

Many subtleties of village politics doubtless remain outside the written record. Even villagers whose politics left documentary traces were not consistent in their conceptual choices. They grabbed the ideas that worked and bent them to their purposes, a long-maligned and potentially dangerous practice employed by many politicians. Consequently, in order to discuss their views, I have occasionally imposed a consistency to their thought that seems more necessary for our comprehension than it was for theirs. "Politics is language," as a historian of early modern England recently reminded us, and in the villages around Rome it had many dialects—regional, communal, seigneurial, bureaucratic, religious, with the latter especially concerned with issues of social justice, which comes to be increasingly important in the eighteenth century. The articulate villagers navigated them all, often within the same text. The primary method employed here is to analyze the ideological and linguistic tools the villagers returned to again and again, or, as the historian David Sabean has suggested, to focus on repetitions in the language that might provide a clue as to the main features of the villagers' conceptual landscape. Wherever possible, the reported activities of the villagers have been incorporated into the analysis of village ideas, especially where the sources were rich in such details, or where village activities seemed to shed light on the political ideas of the villagers whose views are otherwise poorly represented in the written sources.[21]

In *Patrons and Adversaries* microhistories of particular conflicts and negotiations are situated in a larger narrative of the political evolution of nobles and villagers during the long eighteenth century. It examines both the extraordinary politics of conflict between nobles and villagers as well as the politics of everyday life in which they cooperated with one another to provide basic services to the villages. This comparative political history of nobles and villagers in Monte Libretti begins in the 1640s with the Barberini purchase of the *stato* and ends in the early 1760s, when a forty-year cycle of intensive record keeping on the part of the Barberini came to a close, curtailing the possibility of a comparative view of noble and village politics.[22]

Because I have integrated the relevant details of the history of the Barberini family with the story of their rule in Monte Libretti, I will not provide here a detailed overview of the family's complex history. My study focuses on the governing of these generations of the Barberini family: briefly, on the rule of Taddeo (1603–1647) and more closely on the efforts of Maffeo (1631–1686). In the generation of the spendthrift Urbano (1664–1722), his brother, Cardinal Francesco Junior (1662–1738), expended more effort in the governing of Monte Libretti, and hence receives closer scrutiny. Finally, the long reign of Cornelia Costanza (1716–1797) and her husband Giulio Cesare Colonna di Sciarra (1708–1787) provides most of the documentation for the rule of the family between the 1730s and 1760s.

The first chapter introduces the Barberini and the *stato* of Monte Libretti, explaining how a Florentine family made a future in Rome by writing a Roman history for itself in which governing the countryside figured prominently as a source of social and political identity. The effort by the Barberini to become lords of the countryside illuminates the importance for the nobility of possessing and governing prestigious territories in the countryside around Rome, and why a territory like Monte Libretti would have had particular appeal for the Barberini family. Although lordship was easy to buy and sell in Rome, the villagers were an unpredictable "commodity" with their own ideas about the relevant historical context that defined their rights and obligations vis-à-vis the Barberini family. They provided the noble family with important lessons in the limitations on their governing of the countryside.

Chapters 2 and 3 examine issues relevant to the lordship of Maffeo Barberini from the 1650s through the 1670s. Chapter 2 focuses on a dispute between the inhabitants of Nerola and Maffeo Barberini over his claim to hold a monopoly on hunting and fishing rights in the village. The conflict provides a rare glimpse into peasant political culture, as revealed in the record of the village *consiglio*. While the papal government and the nobles attempted to extend their power in the Roman countryside, villagers remained remarkably autonomous, demonstrating the greatest political allegiance to the *consiglio*. Their level of political sophistication and free-spirited attitude toward both the state and the nobility underscores the importance of studying peasant political ideology beyond the moments of violent rural rebellion.

Chapter 3 shifts the focus from extraordinary politics to the politics of everyday life and examines the circumstances under which residents of the neighboring village of Monte Libretti found it useful to have Maffeo's occasional interference in communal affairs. Why Maffeo, who disparaged and meddled in the politics of Nerola, chose to interfere so little in the politics of Monte Libretti, even at the villagers' request, suggests an explanation for the long-term survival of the communal tradition in the countryside. Although Maffeo subjected the *consiglio* to occasional attack in Nerola, his interests were better served by its independent functioning in Monte Libretti, a bifurcation of strategies that underscores his role as a sometimes reluctant patron and sometimes enthusiastic adversary of communal politics.

Chapter 4 chronicles the expansion of the greatest new institutional challenge to noble governing in the countryside—the eighteenth-century extension of the authority of the Papal Congregation of the Buon Governo to the fiefs subject to baronial jurisdiction. This chapter analyzes how the Barberini, having been immersed in a dynastic crisis during the decades of the Buon Governo's expansion, finally addressed the threat the Buon Governo posed to their authority in the *stato* of Monte Libretti. In the 1720s, they proceeded haltingly, using methods from the seventeenth century, but by the 1740s, the family had established tighter control over its rural officialdom and had more intensely inserted itself into the many aspects of communal government by a relentless letter-writing campaign to its officials in the countryside. While the family and the Buon Governo competed to control rural tax collection, villagers in Monte Libretti took note of their efforts, but remained skeptical of the importance of either the taxes or the more carefully monitored means of collecting them.

In addition to addressing the bureaucratic rivalry of the Buon Governo, the Barberini's enormous epistolary output attempted to promote the legitimacy of their obsessive rule of the *stato* in terms of the religious paternalism they claimed to show their "vassals." Chapter 5 demonstrates the centrality of this concept to the noble family's sense of identity and its role in the villages during the eighteenth century. While religious paternalism clarified for nobles the purpose of their activities in the countryside, its reception in the village *consiglio* was considerably less favorable, and its core notion (the love the Barberini bore their vassals) increased the villagers' scrutiny of Barberini behavior. While the Barberini intervened more than ever in village affairs, they were increasingly required to take the villagers' opinions into consideration. Even in the formerly friendly village of Monte Libretti, the noble family faced an increasingly adversarial dynamic that it could not ignore if it wished to govern effectively.

The final chapter considers new forms of political reading and writing that made both everyday and extraordinary exchanges between the villagers and the nobles more adversarial in the eighteenth century, and that called into question the legitimacy of the Barberini's religious paternalism. While the villagers of the *stato* had long been adept at utilizing written sources to sustain or expand their rights, the possibilities for village resistance to seigneurial obligations were more limited when the written sources and the papal government failed to support the peasants' point of view. Villagers and political leaders in Monte Flavio tackled these and other textual and legal barriers in order to reject the payment of some seigneurial dues during the mid-eighteenth century. In Monte Flavio, the villagers elaborated new ways of interpreting existing sources and manufactured new ones, a level of adversarial literacy that enabled village resistance despite the obstacles created by older historical records and accepted judicial interpretations of sources.

This political history of Monte Libretti brings unexpected historical actors into prominent roles—a reorientation in the historiography the final implications of which are only now being integrated into the history of politics and political culture. Alternate political arenas and alternate archival sources yield new ways of understanding the old problems of governing in early modern Europe. Noble archives and village archives suggest dimensions to governance that are little revealed by the archives of the state. Nobles and villagers were sometimes allied, and increasingly at odds with each other in the Roman countryside, and their tangled relations suggest the villagers had as much to do with the formulation and orientation of noble politics as did the centralizing state. Through the village *consiglio*, villagers sustained a political tradition and shaped the practices of the noble governors of their territory. Having backed themselves into the corner of religious paternalism, nobles and clerical magistrates were forced by the villagers to deal with the political contradictions of such values. By such tactics villagers won short-term gains for themselves and by the combined similar efforts of peasants elsewhere in western Europe, they helped to undermine the legitimacy of the seigneurial system of which they were a part.

I

The Barberini Buy a Piece of Paradise While They Descend into Hell

The Castello of Nerola, in the village of Nerola. Photograph by the author.

A little more than a month after the death of his uncle Pope Urban VIII in July 1644, Taddeo Barberini finalized his purchase of the *stato* of Monte Libretti from the Orsini family for 1,160,000 scudi. Northeast of Rome on the road to Rieti, its farmland in the gentle valley of the Tiber was dry and deserted in the August heat. September rains would bring it back to life, renew it with natural pasture, and tempt the shepherds and their flocks back down again from the Sabine mountains. The *stato*'s hilltop villages were encircled by vineyards, olive groves, and the last remnants of their old and obsolete walls. The fortified towers of their baronial palaces were their most striking feature from afar, but up close, the villages were centers of humble houses, tiny churches, and the new owner's "vassals," including a resident hermit, who, no doubt, could no more resist this earthly paradise than could Taddeo Barberini.[1]

Monte Libretti was a purchase befitting the dignity and honor to which the papal nephews had been raised during the spectacular twenty-year reign of their uncle. Its six communities and the *tenuta* of Monte Maggiore had been tied together administratively by the Orsini in the late sixteenth century. All but one of the villages were fortified by walls, around which the Barberini residents gathered at the end of their day: peasants, millers, bakers, guards, brick makers, weavers, and day laborers. The security of those defensive walls would have been especially attractive to the inhabitants since the fragile tranquility of the countryside had been recently shattered by Urban's disastrous War of Castro. His foreign mercenaries still wandered in the countryside in the summer of 1644, nominally under the command of Taddeo, still General of the Church and Prefect of Rome during the interregnum.[2]

Monte Libretti was on the fringes of the Roman *campagna*, in the province of Sabina. It belonged to the "third ring" of estates around Rome. The first ring comprised the vineyards prized by the inhabitants of the city and required for citizenship, the second contained the large farms called *casali*, which mostly belonged to the princes of the church, and the third ring, to which Monte Libretti belonged, contained the fiefs in the hill towns, grouped around fortified castles. They were perched at a higher elevation since medieval times for both defensive and health reasons, the lower lands being considered more dangerous on account of malaria.[3]

One anonymous seventeenth-century description (possibly written to promote the sale of the territory) presented Monte Libretti as basking in wealth and tranquility. Its author considered it a paradise in the riches of the Mediterranean: grain, wine, olives, and fruit. Individual villages claimed their glory in products as varied as the production of woolen cloth and maiolica pottery. The inhabitants of the *stato*, usually described as industrious, sometimes described as obedient and loving, also occupied an important part of the author's account of Monte Libretti. The presence of a religious community near the *castello* of Ponticelli resembles, in this description, a heavenly paradise on earth on account of its holiness and its success in leading the people to confession and communion. The inhabitants of Monte Flavio helped satisfy the great demand for snow water and ices by hauling snow from Mount Pellecchia to Rome. Despite this arduous labor, they were said to live to an extreme old age. The greatness of Monte Libretti, according to the author, rested in this mixture of sanctity and industry, religious devotion and excellent trout fishing. In Rome the character of the inhabitants was considered as important as the agricultural assets, since the former could easily affect the yield of the latter, and have a serious impact on the quantity and the quality of the administrative attention the potential lord would have to lavish on the territory.[4]

The Barberini were not unique in their attempt to secure an earthly paradise for themselves in Latium. Purchasing land around Rome was a common practice among the families of popes and cardinals in this period. A previous papal family, the Borghese, had invested vast sums of money to acquire fiefs throughout the Roman *campagna* and the Sabina, eventually establishing themselves as the largest landowners in the city. The *stato* of Monte Libretti, however, was in a different category of purchase from the acquisition of various individual fiefs. With a single purchase the Barberini created a concentration of landholding along the Tiber in an area north of Rome where they already owned some property. Its cost also set it apart. One million scudi was an enormous sum; for Taddeo's father had paid only 575,000 scudi for Palestrina, and it had conferred a prestigious princely title. One historian of the nobility has asserted that it was the largest amount of money spent in Rome for a land purchase during the seventeenth century.[5]

Why did the Barberini push forward such an extravagant purchase in the last days of Urban VIII's papacy? Monte Libretti was a bold gesture, and one typical in many ways of the family, who had, until the 1640s, so successfully stretched the accepted norms of Roman society to their limits. To remain near the pinnacle of Roman society, the Barberini had to have territory to govern after the papacy had slipped through their hands. Becoming lords of a substantial territory in the countryside enabled the family to make the transition from ruling family to subjects of the new pope and yet remain rulers of their fiefs. This chapter will analyze how the acquisitions of the Barberini show that the rule of the territory was more important to the Barberini than its economic value, and it will show how in pursuing this priority the family was forced to learn two important lessons about being members of the aristocracy governing the countryside. The first they would learn from their Roman aristocratic peers, who had apparently long waited to teach the upstart family to be less ambitious in its claims to power. The second lesson they would learn from the vassals of Monte Libretti, who probably knew little of the family's grand attempts to Romanize itself by becoming lords of the semi-independent territories of the countryside. Villagers were long acquainted with the language of vassalage employed by Roman barons. But as they would repeatedly prove willing to teach the noble family, vassals spoke in constitutions, and they continued to do so until they got what they wanted. The dimensions of the territory and the grandness of the baronial family's status in Rome made no difference. In sheer commitment to worldview, the Barberini met their peers in the humble villages of Monte Libretti. Roman aristocrats would settle their differences with the family in 1653. In the countryside, however, the conflicts had only barely begun.

Newcomers in a "Patchwork
City of Strangers"

The Barberini established themselves at the highest level of Roman society through the election of Maffeo Barberini to the papacy in 1623. He took the name Urban VIII to emphasize his attachment to the city of Rome, but he had been born in Florence to a modest noble family that had risen in wealth and status through their activities in the wool trade. The family established itself in Rome through Urban's uncle Francesco, who became apostolic protonotary and who brought Maffeo to Rome in 1584. With Francesco's help, the young Maffeo began a brilliant career in the church, rising steadily through the hierarchy, and eventually receiving several important papal appointments, including apostolic nuncio in 1604 to the new French king, Henry IV. Maffeo was popular at the French court, and he cultivated close ties to France, which he maintained throughout his papacy and which would prove essential to his family after his death. In 1606 he was made a cardinal and five years later he became the papal legate to Bologna, a position so prestigious, according to Pecchiai, that it raised the recipient to the ranks of the "papabili."[6]

Maffeo's election to the papacy was the result of changes in the electoral practices and a serious stalemate created by factionalism among the cardinals. A deadlock in the conclave meant increasing violence in the city and countryside, as occurred during any interregnum. The situation was complicated in 1623 by an outbreak of malaria among the cardinals. Maffeo emerged as the compromise candidate between the factions, though his election was considered unusual given his age (he was only 55), and because, as the art historian Judith Hook has argued, "Even by contemporary standards, the rise of the Barberini to power, fame, and fortune was meteoric." Most other newcomers to Rome spent at least several generations, if not more, attempting to secure the highest office.[7]

As pope, Urban VIII struggled to defend and enhance the papacy's diverse cultural, political, and territorial inheritance. The pope was both the spiritual leader of Catholicism, as well as the head of an Italian state. In many ways, Urban VIII was a man well suited to the peculiar demands of the papacy. A great patron of the arts, he promoted the young artist Bernini, making him the most favored artist of his reign as well as his personal friend. Throughout his papacy Urban was concerned not only with completing the work begun under his predecessors to beautify the city and complete the decoration of Saint Peter's, but he was also committed to modernizing the fortifications of the Papal States. He was inspired in this effort by the power of the medieval papacy, though the reality of the seventeenth-century papacy was much changed since the medieval triumphs he commemorated in the decoration of St. Peter's. In the international arena the papacy's influence and prestige had seriously declined. Urban VIII could no longer influence even those disputes closest to the Papal States, like the war of succession in Mantua, or the dispute between the French and the Spanish over the control of the mountain fortresses in Valtellina. By and large his diplomacy was unsuccessful, and neither side paid much attention to the papacy, now caught both between these two warring Catholic countries, as well as between battling both the Turks and the Protestants. Urban, however, did his best to maintain as much military power and diplomatic influence as possible in the tangled affairs of the 1620s and 1630s. He succeeded at least in creating an impressive image of the papal court and the Catholic Church.[8]

Urban ruled a city that was increasingly important in Italy itself, where the pope had become the most powerful bishop in Italy, controlling a vast number of benefices, offices, and the supervision of the papal debt. By 1600, though still an international city, Rome was more Italian in its population than it had been a century before, due in part to the increasing tendency of Italian families to seek the cardinalate for one of their members and to establish a branch of the family in Rome. Rome's influence in Italy also expanded with the growing centralization of the Papal States. As capital of the Catholic Church and as a political capital, Rome offered many possibilities for advancement to Italians, who were constantly pulled toward the papal court.[9]

The modesty of the family's origins in Florence may have made it more difficult for Roman society to accept the Barberini. The Barberini's insecurity about their status may have inspired some of the family's grandest artistic patronage. The Barberini were certainly obsessed with size, as is evident from the scale of any of their projects, including land purchases. However, they were in a city characterized by parvenus, many of relatively modest origins compared to the antiquity of the Roman nobility. The parvenus were attracted to Rome because they could integrate themselves into Roman society on a level and at a speed which would have been impossible in other cities. The opportunities for advancement in the papal hierarchy expanded rapidly in the sixteenth century, when the number of cardinals increased from thirty-five to seventy, the sale of venal office dramatically accelerated, and a rapidly increasing system of public and private loans turned Rome into one of the principal money markets in Europe. Newcomers arriving in Rome to take advantage of these possibilities intermarried so extensively with the older baronial nobility that by the mid-sixteenth century the college of cardinals was an intricately interconnected web of families, a kind of "nationalized" elite.[10]

Unfortunately this hybrid aristocracy was riddled with serious financial difficulties. As one seventeenth-century observer noted, the old families had an abundance of glory, but they also had a cash deficit to balance it. The noble lifestyle was becoming an increasingly expensive endeavor for a nobleman, given the more sumptuous lifestyles of the nobility during the sixteenth century. Building became a passion for Roman elites, and both the urban palace and the villa became essential expenditures for noble families. While the sheer number of household members declined in importance as a status symbol, twenty attendants was considered the minimum number required for a cardinal, and Pope Clement VIII (ruled, 1592–1605) was willing to provide his cardinals with the funds necessary to help sustain this lifestyle. New symbols of status replaced the old, including ownership of a large number of carriages, collections of antiquities and art work, and rich furnishings for the urban and rural residences.[11]

So much splendor required a steady flow of cash or credit, which old noble families like the Orsini were having an increasingly difficult time maintaining. As one seventeenth-century observer, Theodor Amayden, noted, the head of the Orsini family had inherited more than just the honor of the family history; a good deal of debt came with the lineage. These older noble families, the first to suffer from an overextension of resources, were rescued from their indebtedness by the papacy. Pope Sixtus V (ruled, 1585–1590) provided the solution to their increasing indebtedness in 1585, offering them the possibility of securing loans or *monti*, guaranteed by the Apostolic Chamber. But as Amayden reminds us, not all of the newer families did so well either, considering the Aldobrandini (Clement VIII), "also extinct their Riches, dissolve[d] into the Families of the Borghese, and Pamphilj." By the seventeenth century even the Farnese family, perhaps the greatest of the sixteenth-century papal families, had to borrow over 900,000 scudi in just five years. Similarly, the family of Sixtus V, who had created the system of loans to save the nobility, was in financial trouble within a decade of their papacy. Despite the best efforts of gravely indebted nobles, the sale of noble lands moved forward at an astonishing pace, not only in the area around Rome, but throughout the Papal States.[12]

The old nobility had forged its power prior to the papacy's attempt to establish its hegemony in the countryside during the fifteenth century. From their castles in the Roman *campagna* and their towers in the city, families like the Orsini, Savelli, Colonna, and Conti had controlled territory, vied for power, and dominated Roman society, especially while the papacy was temporarily located in Avignon during the fourteenth century. After Rome became the permanent center of Catholicism during the fifteenth century, the popes were faced with the challenge of taming this nobility in both the city and the countryside. As the rapidly growing center of the Catholic Church, Rome attracted an increasing number of foreigners, especially the families of cardinals (who came overwhelmingly from northern Italy), as well as important financiers on whom the papacy had depended since the fourteenth century. While domesticating the older nobility was done with whatever means were necessary, the "newer," often "papal," nobility in Rome slowly but surely both co-opted and copied the older one as it intermingled and intermarried with it. Copying the old nobility meant appropriating their claims to be rulers of substantial amounts of the Roman countryside. To be among the greatest aristocratic families, one needed some share in this semi-autonomous rule that was the hallmark of the Roman aristocracy.[13]

Well into the seventeenth century, new families in Rome continued to solicit ties to the descendants of medieval times long after the older nobility experienced severe economic difficulties. The lure of their former political power remained. Either through the purchase of one of their territories, or through marriage with one of their daughters (or in the case of the Barberini, both), a newer family to the city "Romanized" itself and its heirs through a connection to Rome's surviving aristocracy.[14]

The insecurity of the Barberini, intensified perhaps by the rapidity of their rise and the humility of their origins compared with Roman noble families, was not unique among the Roman nobility. Insecurity about the present and future status of a family seemed to be a permanent part of noble life in the city. These families faced the difficult task of maintaining a delicate balance of qualities necessary for successive generations to flourish in Roman society. The past political power of the old aristocratic families continued to have its own kind of value in the scramble for prestige and rank in Rome. Money alone was not enough to make a great family (though it certainly did not hurt). A cardinal's hat in the family, or better still, the papacy itself, could move a family very quickly forward. The Barberini lacked sufficient connections to the old Roman aristocratic families, best secured by purchasing some of their significant properties before Urban died. They attempted to secure that past for themselves and then legitimate its usurpation through public presentations of their rural acquisitions. The buying and the presenting were both necessary efforts for the Barberini, each containing perils contributing to the family's demise in the 1640s.[15]

Making Appear Real What in Fact
Was Feigned: The Barberini and
Their Acquisitions in the Countryside

In the 1620s and the 1630s, the Barberini seemed to be moving smoothly toward establishing the delicate balance required of Roman nobility. Urban VIII showed a deep commitment to his family, whether individual members wanted to accept his generosity or not. His brother Antonio, a humble Capuchin, resisted Urban's offer to become a cardinal. When at last he accepted, he walked barefoot from Florence to Rome. His nephews, younger and immersed in the culture of Rome since their youth, adapted more easily to the privileges provided by their uncle, and eventually were placed in important positions at his side. In keeping with a practice by then well established in the papacy, he made his oldest nephew Francesco a cardinal in the first year of his papacy; as Secretary of State, Francesco became his most important advisor, diplomatic representative, and confidant. Less acceptable to Roman society was his raising of a second nephew to the cardinalate in 1627. Only 19, Antonio was thought too young and too wild for such an office; raising a second nephew was also seen as excessive, though Clement VIII had also promoted more than one nephew. A third nephew, Taddeo, was to carry on the secular line of the family, and he was awarded with the office of Prefect of Rome in 1631, largely a ceremonial title, though one whose prestige and honors Taddeo does not seem to have shunned.[16]

Carlo Barberini, Urban's brother and the father of Francesco, Taddeo, and Antonio, began building a patrimony and a future for the secular branch of the family in the 1620s through purchasing estates around Rome, acquiring Monte Rotondo from the Orsini in 1624, and Roviano from the Colonna in 1625. Carlo also initiated the purchase of Palestrina from Francesco Colonna in 1627, and finally succeeded in buying it from the financially ruined but proud owner in 1630. Francesco Colonna was one of the nobles who had proved himself a valuable soldier in the armies of the King of Spain, though significant financial rewards for his service never materialized. The family became increasingly insolvent in the late 1620s, forcing Francesco at last to agree to sell Palestrina, the oldest Colonna possession, which Pius V had elevated to a principality in 1571. After the Barberini purchase of Palestrina in 1630, Urban VIII extended the title of principality to a remaining Colonna estate, Carbognano, in order to leave this ancient noble family with one title. Two years later, Francesco Colonna had the bones of his ancestors transferred from Palestrina to the Basilica of Santa Maria Maggiore, cutting the final bond between the family and the fief.[17]

With Carlo's death in 1630, Palestrina, as well as the management of the rest of the estates passed to the young Taddeo. Taddeo's marriage in 1627 to

Anna Colonna, daughter of the Conestabile of Naples, a collateral branch of the famous Roman Colonna family, helped to link them with the oldest families in Rome, and legitimate the Barberini's new ownership of Palestrina, which had for centuries been the most prized possession and residence of the Colonna family. The Barberini's new family palace in the Quirinal, completed in 1633, became an elegant and carefully controlled setting for presenting the family's new land acquisitions. Not surprisingly, one of the purchases the Barberini chose to emphasize first in the palace was the purchase of the Principality of Palestrina, perhaps the most impressive acquisition of the Barberini papacy.[18]

Although the Barberini were now distantly tied by marriage to the former owners, a wall mural by Pietro da Cortona, called *The Founding of Palestrina* (1632) offered the seventeenth-century visitor additional, mythological arguments about the legitimacy of Barberini ownership. Located in the Barberini palace apartment of Anna Colonna, the mural suggested links between a mythological story about the winning of legitimacy and acceptance and the contemporary struggle of the Barberini to do the same:

> In the fresco, Caeculus, the mythical founder of Palestrina (Praeneste), offers as proof of his divine lineage the fiery sanction of his father, Vulcan. This sign of heavenly favor won for Caeculus the numerous followers who had earlier doubted his claims to godly descent but who thereafter became the loyal inhabitants of Palestrina—a significant allusion for the newly arrived Barberini prince.[19]

As the closest female relative of the pope, Anna Colonna played a central role in receiving visitors to the pope. The symbolism of "her" apartments then was also an important public statement about the Barberini, emphasizing the legitimacy of their ownership and suggesting parallels between themselves and the previous divine rulers of Palestrina. Palestrina reminded Roman society how far a modest noble family from Florence had come and visitors could get the point without ever leaving Rome to see Palestrina for themselves.[20]

Palestrina tied the Barberini to antiquity, to a long-established pattern of leaving the city in the hottest months of the year (*villeggiatura*), and to an old, though now financially troubled Roman family. Three years prior to its purchase, the Barberini had achieved control of another property, the Abbacy of Farfa, an extensive territory, which included ten *castelli*, just north of Rome on the Via Flaminia. The Orsini family had controlled the abbacy up to the mid sixteenth century, then it had passed to the Farnese family and remained with them until the reign of Urban VIII. In 1627 Francesco Barberini had received it as a benefice *in commendam*, which in keeping with the practices of the time meant that he could keep the income of the benefice until his death and name his own successor to the rich prize, who not surprisingly turned out to be his nephew. As was the case with Palestrina, the Barberini chose to present their control of this vast territory in their urban palace on the Quirinal. Farfa became the setting for a famous intermezzo in one of the operas performed in the Barberini palace, *Chi soffre, speri*. The Barberini were enthusiastic sponsors of elaborate opera productions in their palace. In the early 1630s these were performed in a large hall but by carnival time in 1639 the Barberini had completed a new theater building adjacent to the palace. While performances of plays and operas were not uncommon in private palaces, the building of the theater was unique in Rome. It supposedly could accommodate as many as 3,000 spectators; its cost of over 5,000 scudi was divided unequally among the three Barberini nephews.[21]

Francesco, Antonio, and Taddeo participated actively in the life of the theater under their patronage, personally hosting the productions. This proved to be particularly challenging for the first production in the newly completed theater, *Chi soffre, speri* in 1639. The Modenese envoy Massimiliano Montecuccoli reported to his duke that in the midst of the chaos involved in seating everyone Francesco went from bench to bench greeting with courtesy as many people as merited it. Antonio meanwhile was seen beating with a stick a well-dressed young man he accused of insolence, demonstrating his princely arrogance with a personal touch.[22]

Chi soffre, speri was first performed in 1637 and expanded to five hours for the production in 1639. The music was by Virgilio Mazzocchi and Marco Mazzaroli and the libretto by Giulio Rospigliosi, the future Clement IX (ruled, 1667–1669). It caused a sensation in its re-creation of the natural world. A rising and setting sun, lightening, thunder, hail, and a reproduction of the garden of the Barberini palace beyond the theater dazzled the spectators. The efforts to reproduce the natural world through the use of background perspective paintings and special lighting, along with more dramatic techniques, was viewed, according to Bernini, as the main goal of these productions: "the point of these Comedies and Sets consisted in making appear real what in fact was feigned." The most spectacular scene by far in this production was the Fair of Farfa, designed by Bernini, which included "carriages, horses, litters, pillotta-players, and spectators," a spectacular setting that brought the glory of the Roman countryside (and the Barberini presence there) alive for the audience at the opera.[23]

If the Barberini stick failed to persuade the insolent visitor, the play and the intermezzo were the dramatic carrot designed to remind him and everyone else of the appropriateness of Barberini rule of rural territory. Barberini operas were often attended "by visiting heads of state and ambassadors, as well as by all variegated households that comprised the papal court." News of the Barberini productions extended beyond the city to a broader European audience. Familiarity with these operas was spread in part through the distribution of the libretti. Almost 4,000 copies of the libretto of *Chi soffre, speri* were printed for the performance. A copy of the libretto might have been handy for following the plot, which like other operas of the period, lacked "linear logic," character development, and plot subtlety, but offered instead a series of "exempla" of a particular theme. The *concetto* that unites *Chi soffre, speri*, is that of "deprivation and its rewards." Based loosely on the story of the Decameron by Boccaccio, the opera recounts the story of Egisto, an impoverished nobleman in love with the wealthy widow Alvida. She mistrusted his affections and refused to see him. When she at last agrees to visit him, he kills his beloved falcon because it is all he has to offer her to eat. She has come, however, to ask for the falcon for her dying son, who desired to see the bird as his last request. When she realizes what a sacrifice Egisto has made for her, she recognizes his love for her; in the bird was found a heliotrope that cured her ailing son, allowing the play to end happily for all concerned.[24]

Although the contortions of the plot may have been difficult, if not unnecessary for the viewer to follow, it is remarkable how many motifs, expanded or added to Boccaccio's text, reflected the issues and concerns of the Roman nobility: the poverty of the nobleman, and yet his stubborn refusal to sell his remaining family property; the tower, another symbol of the power of the older nobility, which he agreed to destroy since it was displeasing to Alvida; the salvation, both sentimental and financial, which could be found through marriage to a wealthy widow. All of these themes must have had a certain resonance with Roman audiences, who were probably touched emotionally, if they disagreed pragmatically, with Boccaccio's notion that the nobility of Egisto's spirit mattered more than his loss of the trappings of a noble lifestyle.

While these familiar thematic tangles of Roman society and theater passed before the viewer, the opera used decidedly less subtle imagery to remind those in the audience that much in this imagined world referred directly to their energetic hosts. At one point, the stage opened to the outside world, on to the Barberini gardens. The intermezzo created by Bernini, the Fair of Farfa, filled the theater with a scene from the Roman countryside where artisans and traders had gathered to sell their wares at the fair. Farfa, like the Barberini palace gardens, once again referred to the family and their control of the territory since 1627.

Francesco's household, like the household of Egisto in the play, was supplied with goods from the fair. If one theme of the play is deprivation, then Farfa was constructed to reveal its opposite; it was bursting with an abundance of products offered at cheap prices by the singers/sellers of the scene: ribbons, crystal glasses, basins, games, combs, mirrors, veils, hats, pendants, and a variety of game birds, pies, ravioli, cakes, and wine. The music reveals a competition of voices, each hawking a product. The interweaving of the voices of the vendors describing the virtues of their products is eventually eclipsed by that of the persistent Neapolitan peddler of an elixir which not surprising can cure all.[25]

The countryside suggested here through a mixture of voices, of dialects, and of goods suggests a rough prosperity and a merry view of rural life, though it does end in a mock battle. It was also one image of popular life cherished in Roman society at this time. It embraced the vision of the contented poor, which was reflected in the paintings of the *Bambocccianti*, genre painters who flourished in Rome in the first half of the seventeenth century. Their visual ideas about the poor found literary expression in a book published in Rome in 1650 by Daniello Bartoli, a Catholic priest. He stressed the greater happiness of the poor in comparison with the rich, noting that their poverty "arouses the pity and piety of others." This seemingly innocuous idea would remain central to Catholic piety, and in the hands of the villagers it would later become the source of considerable difficulty to the noble family. But in the seventeenth century this view of the poor, whether in painting or in theater, was to show them in the best possible light: "Visibly contented: Peasants dancing the saltarello before their humble cottages; merry grape-gathering women; vagabonds who gamble their only penny at the roulette in the hopes of winning a ring-shaped cake." The image of the Fair of Farfa was a pleasant voyage into the rural world beyond Rome, a world whose violent and volatile aspects were only hinted at by the end of the intermezzo. Farfa reminded those attending the opera that the Barberini's family power extended from Rome to the countryside. Its juxtaposition of an elegant palace setting and a humble but delightful and comfortably familiar rural world emphasized the rightfulness of Barberini control of public life in the city and in the fiefs in the countryside. Just as they were described in Monte Libretti's sales advance, the theatrical and the rural poor were merry, industrious, and harmonious in their subjugated state. Unfortunately for the Barberini the residents of their own fiefs would undermine this euphoric vision of country residents.[26]

The Charcoal Seller, the Hunter, and the Priest

Given the enthusiasm with which the Barberini had displayed their control of prestigious territories to Roman society, it is perhaps not surprising that in the 1640s the Barberini nearly ruined themselves, and then hoped to redeem themselves by acquiring a significant piece of property. During that decade the family was immersed in their war with the Farnese family over the Duchy of Castro, a territory they had hoped to acquire through a marriage alliance. In creating their Roman dynasty the Barberini hoped to surpass the greatness of the Farnese family, which had controlled the papacy about a hundred years before (Alessandro Farnese, ruled 1534–1549). The magnificent Barberini *salone* with its ceiling painting by Pietro da Cortona had to be larger than the famous ceiling by Carracci at the Farnese palace. Urban moved the funeral monument of the Farnese pope, Paul III, so that it would be adjacent to his own. The Farnese were the first papal family to make an extraordinary splash in the city and the Barberini set their aspirations high.[27]

Odoardo Farnese's financial troubles helped pave the way for the Barberini's plans. The Barberini offered him money for the Duchy of Castro, and the promise of a marriage alliance during his visit to Rome in late 1639. Odoardo definitively and rudely refused. When he left Rome in January 1640, he further insulted the family by refusing to pay his respects to Cardinal Francesco before he left the city.[28]

Due to decreasing agricultural yields from the Duchy of Castro, Odoardo was no longer able to make the interest payments on the loans he had borrowed against the duchy. After the unpleasantness of Odoardo's visits to Rome, Urban VIII restricted his right to export grain, effectively limiting the income he required in order to make the interest payments on his loans. In response, Odoardo readied the duchy for war, something which Urban VIII ordered him to stop. In the following months of 1640, Urban and Odoardo each made demands the other ignored; Odoardo continued his preparations and courted French support for his cause. By the fall of 1641 Urban was ready to declare war with his vassal over his armaments, and over about a million and a half scudi that Odoardo was unable to pay his creditors. By October papal troops had captured the duchy. To the surprise of the Barberini, Odoardo managed to secure the financial backing of Florence, Venice, and France and in 1642 prepared to fight to regain Castro. He portrayed his struggle as a battle against the Barberini, rather than against the papacy. The war proved to be an extremely unsuccessful venture for the Barberini; Odoardo's troops pillaged their way toward Rome, to the terror of the Romans. Papal fortifications, troops, and the military leadership of the Barberini nephews had all proved useless against the combined troops of Venice, Florence, and Modena. In Rome the war created shortages, higher taxes, and endless grumbling against the Barberini, who, it was muttered, were making money off the war, even if they were not winning it.[29]

A disastrous campaign in March 1644 against the Venetians and the increasing costs of battle at last made the Barberini realize the futility of continuing the war. In the peace settlement of March 31, 1644, the Barberini agreed to return Castro and the other Farnese possessions they had confiscated while Odoardo agreed to surrender the lands he had captured. The war and the peace settlement were a humiliating end to the Barberini papacy.[30]

While the Barberini's aspirations were without a doubt grandiose, to say the least, they were not particularly out of keeping with the bellicose popes of the sixteenth century, though they were perhaps out of touch with the realities of the seventeenth-century papacy. However, if we imagine how a map of Latium might have looked to the ambitious Taddeo Barberini, it is easy to see both the temptation of the Duchy of Castro as well as the possibilities of Monte Libretti. Rather than pursue piecemeal acquisitions of territory (the strategy of their most successful land-purchasing predecessors, the Borghese), the Barberini focused on larger, more prestigious *stati* in the last years of Urban VIII's papacy.[31]

To understand the attractions of the duchy and the *stato* of Monte Libretti, we have to take into account the political importance of purchasing a *stato*, even one of the humblest of the ten semi-independent territories. The word *stato*, with its associations with the great states of Italy, the nationalizing states of Europe, and the political musings of Machiavelli, may have seemed a rather grand title for a relatively small area. Barbara Hallman, however, uses the expression *"un bello stato"* to describe the "temporal sovereignty" cardinals sought in the late sixteenth century to help secure their family an established place among the Roman nobility. However, not all estates were described as *stati*, and the term was used more narrowly to define independent territories that enjoyed varying degrees of sovereignty within the Papal States. These lands were the *terrae mediate subiectae*, not directly governed by the papal administration, even though they were within the pope's dominion. In order of decreasing autonomy, the geographer Lando Scotoni identified ten such territories: Duchies of Ferrara, Urbino, Castro, Bracciano, and Paliano; the Marchesates of Castiglione del Lago and the *stato* of Monte Libretti, the *stato* of Torri, and the republics of Bauco and Cospaia. These autonomous territories covered a fourth of the area and a fifth of the population of the Papal States.[32]

One of the more impressive among these "states" was the Duchy of Castro, which had been carved out of the patrimony of Saint Peter's by Paul III for his son Pierluigi Farnese in 1537, along with the Duchy of Parma and Piacenza. The Barberini had hoped that in connecting themselves to the Farnese through marriage, they could eventually acquire the Duchy of Castro. Creating an autonomous state for their heirs, as the Farnese had done, was the one thing the Barberini had not been able to achieve, and the Duchy of Castro was their best and quickest possibility for adding such a valuable territory to the growing Barberini patrimony. But with the Duchy of Castro no longer within their grasp, the Barberini set their sights on Monte Libretti, securing the papal bull granting permission for the Orsini to sell only three days before Urban VIII died; they finalized the sale about one month later. Purchasing the *stato* of Monte Libretti allowed the Barberini to draw on another sixteenth-century work of consolidation, which had been carried out by the Orsini family. The *stato* of Monte Libretti had been created by the Orsini of S. Gemini through a unification of six separate villages, Monte Libretti, Corese, Montorio, Monte Flavio, Nerola, Ponticelli, as well as the *tenuta giurisdizionale* of Monte Maggiore. During the sixteenth century, the Orsini family had united these villages by putting them under a common set of edicts and under one jurisdiction under the direction of an *auditore generale*, their chief judicial magistrate.[33]

The Barberini might have had greater ambitions for Monte Libretti. Although individual estates on the *stato* of Monte Libretti held titles, such as a duchy (Monte Libretti), principality (Nerola), or marquisate (Montorio), the Barberini may have acquired the *stato* with the hope of securing for it at some point a more prestigious title through a papal bull. Although Urban VIII was quite ill when he authorized the sale, the Barberini may have hoped to push the sale through and secure a grander title for the whole *stato* before he died.[34]

The location of the *stato* was probably also attractive to the Barberini. It was just north of Monte Rotondo, and adjacent to the abbacy of Farfa, which was already held as a benefice by Francesco and could potentially remain controlled by the family indefinitely. Did the Barberini hope to add territory to these purchases and to unite them into a single *stato*, thus securing an autonomous dynastic territory that might rival the Duchy of Castro and other greater semi-independent *stati* in the Papal States?

Even without the attainment of these ambitions during the papacy of Urban VIII, Monte Libretti was essential to a family that realized they were in their last months as rulers of Rome and the Papal States. As the seventeenth-century decrees for Monte Libretti issued by the Orsini make clear, noble families were "rulers" of their *stati*. The inhabitants of Monte Libretti, for instance, were referred to as the vassals of the noble family. The Orsini (and later the Barberini) wrote the laws that applied in Monte Libretti. A noble official administered justice in the territory, and as one of the Orsini edicts made clear, his Excellency, in the end, was the final arbiter of the meaning of the law in his *stato*: "And in the *capitoli* and aforesaid decrees, if anyone claims that there is any ambiguity or obscurity, the free will to interpret them according to his wishes is reserved for His Illustrious Excellency." Noble officials also meddled in the affairs of the communal governments of each village, attempting to control who could participate in them as well as what village assemblies could discuss or decide. Once among the most lawless people in Roman society, aristocrats threw themselves into securing "law and order" in the countryside, joining the popes in their campaign to criminalize almost all ordinary behaviors believed to support banditry, a source of rural unrest the aristocrats had formerly supported. After Urban VIII's death, the Barberini would have to participate in this coalition on the aristocratic side, as subjects of the pope, but lords, they hoped, of a semi-independent territory that would leave them some political autonomy with in its borders. In 1644, were the Barberini still dreaming, perhaps, of that elusive Duchy of Castro? It is impossible to say, now, how their minds might have turned this way and that over the map of Latium, planning perhaps a Duchy of Monte Libretti, not quite the desirable Castro, but not a terrible consolation prize after all—closer to Rome, along the Tiber, and with beautiful views of the city in the distance which they had once ruled.[35]

After the death of their uncle at the end of July 1644, the Barberini entered a peculiar type of Roman hell. Once they had justified their ambitions in Rome by suggesting an affinity between themselves and the descendants of Vulcan. Now they were to be forged in the fire. The months following the death of the pope were always particularly tense ones for a former papal family, one in which the papal nephews were in the most dangerous positions of their lives, facing possible persecution by the succeeding papal family. The situation was especially grave for the Barberini, considering the lengthy duration of Urban's papacy, the rewards they had reaped from it, and the resentment against the family over their alleged profiteering during the war of Castro.[36]

The situation was complicated by the turn of events in the papal conclave, where Francesco and Antonio battled for the election of someone sympathetic to the Barberini, but found themselves entangled in the struggle between the French party (which they also headed) and the Spanish party. Because of an outbreak of malaria among the cardinals, which eventually affected even Francesco, and the refusal of the Spanish to budge on their opposition to the French candidate, the Barberini found themselves supporting Giambattista Pamphilj, the Spanish candidate, in exchange for the promise that in the event the French should react badly to the election of Pamphilj, the "Barberini would be assured of Spain's protection." The election of Pamphilj, who took the name Innocent X, outraged Mazarin, who withdrew his support of the Barberini, while rumors were spreading in Rome about an impending investigation of the Barberini in connection with their handling of the war of Castro.[37]

In this seemingly hopeless situation, the Barberini were not without possibilities for salvation through the French, due mostly to Mazarin's increasing fury with Innocent X for refusing to promote his brother to the cardinalate and for naming eight pro-Spanish cardinals. Antonio was the first to gamble on the support of the French; he fled in September 1645, claiming at first to be on his way to Monte Rotondo, but leaving Rome disguised instead as a charcoal seller, arriving in Santa Marinella where he took a small boat for Genoa. After being forced ashore at Livorno by a storm, Antonio disguised himself as a sailor and managed to reach the coast of Provence. Within a month Taddeo and Francesco had hung the arms of the French king on their palaces, and the anticipated investigation had been launched. Although the Barberini agreed to hand over their records, they were too fearful of what was to come to remain in Rome. They accepted Mazarin's offer of asylum and in January 1646 Cardinal Francesco, Taddeo, and his four children also left Rome, with the cardinal disguised as a lowly priest and Taddeo as a huntsman.[38]

During their papacy the Barberini had been fearless and brilliant in constructing a suitable place for themselves in Roman society. When they entered what was always the darkest hour for a papal family, they panicked. Like Zanni, a *commedia dell'arte* character in the Fair of Farfa intermezzo, the Barberini had decided that, "In such affairs it appears the finest thing is to be a coward." The Barberini fell from power in a dramatic way, collapsing from the pinnacle of their dignity and urban prestige into the anonymity of disguise and inglorious flight through the countryside. While a return to a less ostentatious "private" life was an inevitable part of the end of a family's papacy, fleeing disguised as a hunter, charcoal seller, and priest was a particularly dramatic transformation. They exited Rome as though they were entering the set of the Fair of Farfa, stripped of their former grandeur, and in the costume of vassals who sang in their palace theater or who inhabited their country estates.[39]

Their flight only fanned the flames of rage now burning against them in Rome: All their goods so lavishly and proudly gathered during the papacy were sequestered. Their palaces were protected by entrusting them to the French crown, but the rest of their lands were at the mercy of Innocent X. "The Pope has taken all of your possessions," Taddeo's wife Anna Colonna wrote desperately to the family now safely in France: "All of your lands, Palestrina, Valmontone, Lugnano, San Gregorio, Cas'Ape, Montelanico, Monterotondo and Montelibretti, the estate of the Signori Orsini which isn't yet completely paid for." Pragmatic and brave Anna Colonna, left behind to defend the family patrimony, reminded the Barberini men not only of their losses, but of their yet incomplete financial obligations. The Barberini men, it seems, had handled their success better than they could handle their failure.[40]

Taddeo never returned from his exile in Paris. He died in November 1647, with his children and his brothers gathered round him but his wife far away in Rome struggling to hold together the family's patrimony. According to Pastor, it was only her protests to Innocent X that kept the Barberini's confiscated property from being sold to compensate the papal treasury for revenue lost when Urban VIII's hated tax on flour was abolished. After her successful intercession, Anna too, went to Paris in April 1646, to wait out the Pamphilj storm. She returned to Rome in June 1647, a few months before her husband's death.[41]

The Barberini benefited both from Anna's tenacity and the cunning of Cardinal Mazarin, who, as protector of the family in Paris, tied their return to Roman society to his militancy against the Spanish power in Italy. Mazarin pursued his machinations against the pro-Spanish Innocent X throughout 1646, pushing for a cardinalate for his brother and a favorable papal policy toward France. His bullying was successful on all counts, including the guarantee of a safe homecoming for the Barberini. Francesco was allowed to return to Rome in February 1647. As early as January 1647, the *stato* of Monte Libretti was officially returned to the Barberini family. An inventory prepared in the first days of that month accounted for the most important assets of the *stato*, including livestock and the contents of the *stato's* palaces, mills, ovens, and granaries. In April 1647 the final payments to the Orsini for the *stato* were arranged, and Monte Libretti was at last firmly in the hands of its new owners.[42]

The practical matters related to resuming life as Roman barons and landowners were thus underway at the time of Taddeo's death in November 1647. The Barberini, however, had yet to return to Rome. Anna was home, but Cardinal Francesco, despite the pope's permission, remained in Paris. It was Anna Colonna who took formal possession of the *stato* of Monte Libretti when her husband died in November. She acted as guardian for her son Carlo, 16 years old at that time. In Monte Libretti Anna Colonna was the steward of the Barberini's interests. From Rome she oversaw a variety of activities, including the sale of agricultural products; she replied to letters from villagers asking her to forgive their penalties for hunting violations; she reminded ministers in the *stato* not to undertake any work there "however minimal, except in the case of the greatest urgency."[43]

In February 1648 her brother-in-law Cardinal Francesco came back to Rome. He resumed both his ecclesiastical duties and helped supervise the Barberini's future in Rome. His brother Antonio did not return to Rome until 1653, and by that time, the former outcasts had made their peace with the Pamphilj. Anna's oldest son Carlo renounced the Barberini primogeniture in order to pursue an ecclesiastical career. Innocent X made him a cardinal in 1653. Maffeo, the second eldest, became the heir to the family's fortune and was married to the pope's niece, Olimpia Giustiniani, that same year. Appropriately, an opera celebrated this symbolic uniting of old adversaries. *Dal male, il bene* (The good which can result from evil) was performed in 1654 in the Barberini palace to honor the newlyweds. In true Roman fashion, it portrayed a convoluted series of misunderstandings that end in a happy state of clarity and reconciliation for all parties concerned. Such were the more charming possibilities of Roman life on and off stage.[44]

Speaking in Constitutions: The Villagers
Talk Back to Their New Lords

While the Barberini survived the death of Urban VIII and returned to their proper place in urban aristocratic society, the countryside presented them with an ongoing set of challenges. They were supposed to rule as "lords" of their territory, by extending the limits of their jurisdiction and deriving as much income as possible from the *stato*. The first decades of Barberini ownership were marred both by financial difficulties and challenges to the family's desire to make whatever laws they wanted regardless of the wishes of the villagers. Fortunately for the villagers of the *stato*, the papacy supported limits on the Barberini's ability to increase what they could demand from villagers or significantly change village law. Since the early sixteenth century, papal law had prohibited proprietors of lands near the Tiber from charging more than one-sixth of the harvest total in the form of rent. Everywhere in the Roman countryside seigneurial dues were permanently fixed by the terms written in village constitutions. Thus, although the Barberini were in some sense the largest "owners" of land in the *stato*, there were tight legal restrictions on the payments that they could require on their lands. Second, the villagers were de facto owners of a large amount of land in the *stato* (especially in the hills), even though they owed fixed seigneurial dues on those lands to the noble family.

Seventeenth-century documents draw a clear distinction between lands belonging "to the Barberini" and lands belonging to *"particolari"* or individuals in the *stato*. Payments owed on all lands were extremely complex, but certain patterns emerge. Lands attributed to "direct" ownership by the Barberini were subject both to a rent per rubbio and to a payment which amounted to a payment on a percentage of the harvest. Lands that belonged to *"particolari"* were subject to the latter, but not to the rents based on the surface area of land under cultivation. The villagers could sell these properties but only to other villagers and restrictions on the sale of these lands indicate that this was not yet "true" private property for the villagers, though it was recognized as a form of it by all parties involved. On these lands villagers paid fixed seigneurial dues to the Barberini, amounts set by law and not subject to change by the noble family. Papal law and papal courts sustained and supported the fixed payments guaranteed in village *statuti* (the summaries of customs and practices compiled in villages beginning in the thirteenth century). The Barberini were obliged to loan seed to the villagers to cultivate these lands. The inhabitants were free to work any lands in any village they wished, and wherever they could find available lands. The low population around Rome meant that renters, rather than land, were in short supply.[45]

The Barberini owned "directly" many of the lands of the *stato* situated in the Tiber valley, including the lands of the *tenuta*, or farm, of Monte Maggiore, and also the lands of the village of Corese and half of the lands of the village of Monte Libretti. These areas correspond to the portion of the *stato* that most resembled the *campagna romana*. Even here the low population prevented the Barberini from charging much more than the going local rates on land for these properties, simply because there were too few people to work them. Since the

Barberini (like other Roman landowners) did not "modernize" the agrarian techniques used in the *stato*, there were also limits on how much they could expand cultivation (or pasture) even in the relatively fertile areas of the Tiber valley. The system was already in delicate balance, as testimony regarding land use in the seventeenth century makes clear. Lands that were subject to cultivation more frequently than quadrennial rotation (the norm in Monte Libretti) exhausted the soil and the low yield produced made it "hardly worthwhile for the cultivator." Increasing the use of lands for pasture was not really a way to make higher profit either, since quadrennial rotation already allowed for the rental of pasture for two consecutive years, and the rental fees paid during the second year were substantially lower than the first one. At the end of two years' use as pasture, it was time to plow and cultivate the soil again in order to revitalize it for use as pasture two years later.[46]

The income records suggest that during the decades following the purchase of Monte Libretti, the Barberini, even with their vast territory, earned much less from the *stato* than they had expected when they bought it. At the time of the sale, its yearly income had been estimated as high as 26,000 scudi per year; this was the figure that was to determine the agreed upon price for the *stato*. (The yearly income of 26,000 was supposed to represent 2.25 percent of the total value of the *stato*.) Balance sheets were rarely compiled for the *stato* of Monte Libretti, but the one from 1662 indicates that the Barberini were in trouble: Total revenue was only 16,566.83 1/2 scudi and expenses for the year were 4,677.70 scudi. The figures from 1685 illustrate similarly low revenues: 16,425.41 scudi of income and 4,036.37 1/2 scudi of expenses. This low net income of just over 12,000 scudi during these two decades was substantially below what the Barberini had anticipated at the time of purchase.[47]

What explains Monte Libretti's relatively low income? Its terrain, especially as one moved further eastward, was very rough. Some of the lands of Monte Flavio were unreachable during the winter when it snowed. Monte Libretti's expansiveness was part of its prestige, but it also meant that it inevitably contained many acres little suited for agriculture. It was estimated that half of all of the *stato*'s more than 30,000 acres were either *macchie* or mountainous regions. These were valuable for pasturing animals or gathering wood, but were not useful for grain cultivation. So in terms of economic logic of purchase, the Barberini would have been better off with scattered purchases in the countryside that helped them avoid less productive lands. But that had not been their aim in acquiring Monte Libretti. It was for reasons of rule, not economics that led them to its purchase when the plans for Castro failed.

The misrule of the villagers would be the second painful surprise to the Barberini's first years of governing in the countryside northeast of Rome.[48] The vassals of Monte Libretti had sworn oaths of loyalty to the family when a new generation of Barberini took charge of the *stato;* they were subject to the lord's justice; they courted the Barberini as patrons and as mediators of local crises, especially during the seventeenth century. They had, however, as each generation of the Barberini family would notice, a tendency to define their status as vassals in their own terms, or to insist, at a minimum, that the noble family impose on them no more than was outlined in their village *statuti,* or constitutions. The latter lesson in local politics had to be taught to the Barberini repeatedly during the seventeenth century by the citizens of the *stato.* The first rulers of the territory tried to rule simply by issuing decrees through their officials, typically through their chief judicial magistrate, the *auditore,* or through governors who assisted the *auditore* in publicizing and enforcing Barberini law. In the 1640s, the Barberini had a particularly aggressive official who issued edicts first and asked questions later. He challenged what villagers of the *stato* considered to be established local practices, many of which were described in the village *statuti.* Perini had an authoritative swagger particularly odious to the locals. While the Barberini may have come to regret this bureaucratic attribute, they supported Perini's actions through lawsuits, so evidently his views represented theirs. In the village of Nerola, Perini issued edicts that imposed corporal punishment for offenses previously only penalized by monetary fines. He also challenged the villagers' right to hunt and fish in the lands of Nerola. He tried to swap the measuring cup used at the olive mill to collect dues owed to the Barberini, in effect, an attempt to raise Barberini revenue by surreptitious means. Village participants in the *consiglio* of Nerola rejected Perini's tactics in the 1640s, and initiated lawsuits and protests that their children successfully later concluded with the noble family in the 1680s.[49]

Another of Perini's village blunders was resolved more quickly, and it also illustrates the way in which the village constitution was central to village politics and to legal support for village claims. Perini insisted that the villagers of the territory were obliged to carry the grain they owed the noble family to the Tiber river, in preparation for its eventual transport to Rome. While the villagers of Nerola and Monte Libretti became the leaders in the protest of this claim, an anonymous letter written from Monte Flavio, the most remote village of the territory, suggests that news of Perini's demands had reached even the periphery of the *stato.* The threatening letter from Monte Flavio makes clear that at least some villagers knew the difference between religious devotion and seigneurial obligations. "The community does not want to be subject to doing any manual labor for the lords whatsoever ... even if in past years we did so in order to supply with water [the convent of] Madonna delle Grazie of Ponticelli, this was done for charity, and for the love of God." When it came to defending local rights, the distinction between God's kingdom and the Barberini kingdom was well understood.[50]

Perini did successfully intimidate some villagers into hauling the grain they owed the Barberini to the Tiber river in 1645. During harvest time, Perini told Pietro Securantia, the *auditore* of the *stato* to order the villagers to do so. The *auditore* protested, and Perini, along with other minor officials of the noble family, unanimously asserted that "since the time of the Orsini (the previous owners of the territory) the vassals had carried the grain to the port [on the Tiber] free, and without any payment whatsoever." Securantia offered his version of the events in 1646 (one year later), by which time the villagers had already lodged their protests with a papal official of the Camera Apostolica, an act that served as a point of first entry for villagers into the system of papal courts. These assertions about the villagers' labor (especially whether it was "free" or "paid" labor) entangled the Barberini and the Orsini in two decades of lawsuits, since the villagers refused to accept that they were obliged to labor for free. As a result, the Barberini found their territory's net income (used as the basis for the sale price) had been overestimated, since it included the not insignificant cost of paying for the transport of the grain.[51]

How were the villagers able to support their cause? Organized village protest against this labor obligation began in the fall of 1645. In October of that year, the priors of the village of Monte Libretti offered testimony that contradicted the declaration in the bill of sale that the vassals were obliged to carry the grain to the Tiber river. The testimony of the three men offered another interpretation of the meaning of such an activity. They testified that in the times of the Orsini, the villagers carried the grain to the ports on the Tiber, but not out of any "obligation" or "duty" but "out of courtesy for the many favors that we received from those Excellent Lords, indeed, while we were carrying the grain we owed to the port, we were given food, that is bread, wine, and cheese, on the orders of the aforementioned Excellent Orsini Lords." Testimony collected during a *consiglio* meeting in Nerola in October 1645 specified that if the villagers did not receive "lunch" then "[the lords] gave us so much per person for lunch," that is, they paid in cash, rather than kind. The remainder of the village testimony in Nerola also articulates the difference between an obligation and an act performed out of "courtesy" for the "services" rendered by the noble family. Testimony provided in the following spring of 1646 by two of the three priors in Monte Libretti reiterated the villagers' position. They testified before the Barberini lawyer about a number of controversies between the villagers and the noble family, including the "obligation" to carry the grain to the river, which, they emphasized, the "Community or people [of the village] collectively and individually were united in saying [that the villagers] were not now, nor had they ever been, under obligation to carry or to have carried at their expense." The priors' testimony of 1646 was less focused on the exchange of courtesies, and more specific about excluding the possibilities of villagers being obliged to carry anything, anywhere, especially to the Tiber. Testimony from participants in the village government was consistent with this interpretation.[52]

Testimony in support of the Orsini's position proved to be useless in their cause, since it was all collected after the villagers had lodged their complaint with papal magistrates in 1645. Judges in a number of courts who heard the case consistently ruled that such testimony did not substantiate Orsini claims about the legitimacy of labor obligations. The Orsini failed to produce any evidence prior to 1646 that could verify their claims, and consequently, the original decision by the *luogetenente* of the Camera Apostolica in 1646, in favor of the villagers, was never overturned by the two other papal tribunals that were eventually called upon to revisit the case. Some villagers had, in 1644–1645, been forced to do the labor, but because they had been bullied with fines and imprisonment. The papal courts determined that a one-year-old extortion of village labor did not validate the noble's claims on that labor.[53]

In anthropological terms the lunch in exchange for grain hauling could be described as a ritualized exchange of "courtesies" both of which were obligatory (or neither was obligatory if the other were not). The anthropologist Marcel Mauss refers to this as "gift-payment"—we do something for the lords, because they give something specific to us, a repetitive reciprocity of giving and receiving. This distinguishes the hauling from an obligation on the part of the villagers to give their lord "one labor," as specified in the *statuto*, for instance, if he wanted to rebuild the lime-kiln or repair the walls in his castle. The villagers' version bears the closest resemblance to the language of the *statuti*, or the village constitutions, in which dues and services owed to the lord were enumerated.

When the Barberini took formal possession of the territory in 1644, the family's representative accepted the village *statuti* in the name of the noble family. The villagers made an oath of fealty to the Barberini, promising to pay dues and to render assistance to their lords when necessary. While this formal possession of the territory symbolized the subjugation of the villagers, it also represented noble recognition of their rights, since those too were outlined in the *statuto*, and villagers insisted that members of the noble family had to uphold those rights, even if it meant that periodically the villagers had to cart the *statuto* to Rome to remind them of that obligation.[54]

Village testimony related to the labor controversy echoed the language of the *statuto* of Nerola, which specifically stated that the villagers received monetary compensation for hauling the grain ("pro quolibet Rubro solidos quinque"). However, village testimony omitted the portion of the *statuto* that allowed the noble family to impose a fine on the villagers who refused to do the hauling, a qualification that underscores the nature of the exchange as "gift payment."

Although few records from the 1640s for the *consiglio* of Monte Libretti survive, it is clear from such records in the village of Nerola that the *statuto* was the crucial touchstone of village politics. Admittedly, very few of the villagers could read the *statuti*, written mostly in Latin, but in Nerola its contents were discussed in the *consiglio*. The *consiglio* thus became the site for adversarial politics, with the *statuto* as the primary text. Readings in it were certainly "selective," but villagers showed they knew what to do with it.[55]

The villagers would deliver this rude awakening to the Barberini repeatedly during the reign of Maffeo. They would remind the Barberini that what you could say in Rome and what you could do in the countryside were profoundly different. The next chapter explores the willingness of the villagers to make that point repeatedly to the noble family through the 1680s. Roman aristocrats applied quick and brutal sanctions upon one another to bring overly ambitions families like the Barberini back into line with seventeenth-century realities. Villagers lacked the political clout to deliver such blows. But using the support offered by their constitutions and the papal courts, villagers of Nerola continued to speak in constitutions and to rely on their communal institutions, to challenge the noble family when it overstepped the boundaries of its lordship in the countryside.

2

Before It Was a Dirty Word

Politics in the Roman Countryside, 1640s–1680s

View of the countryside from Nerola. Photograph by the author.

That Antonio, Taddeo, and Francesco could successfully traverse the Roman countryside disguised as a charcoal seller, a hunter, and a lowly priest was not as impossible as it might seem. The true identity of visitors to the countryside could be difficult to discern. At the Fair of Farfa in the spring of 1645, residents of Nerola believed that they were paying the village tax burden to a real papal tax collector. But charlatans peddled many wares at Farfa—and this one offered counterfeit receipts in exchange for village taxes. A few days later the villagers learned that both the tax collector and the receipts were fakes, and that papal officials still expected the prompt payment of what the villagers had paid the impostor.[1]

Both papal officials and new "lords" of the countryside like the Barberini exported edicts and officials to the countryside in an attempt to secure money, obedience, fealty, or goods from their subjects. Distinguishing the fake demands from the legitimate ones was a familiar dilemma in rural life. The Barberini, like other Roman noble families, kept their demands before the villagers through their officials in the village, occasional visits, as well as letters and edicts. In the seventeenth century, many villagers showed considerable willingness and commensurate skill to challenge the declarations of both papal representatives and Barberini officials. While the Nerolani fell victim to the Fair of Farfa swindle, they were typically more savvy regarding the demands made upon them by their would-be Roman rulers.

Noble landowners prized purchases like the *stato* of Monte Libretti because such properties made them "rulers" of the prestigious semi-independent territories of the Papal States. This chapter examines how Barberini rule looked to the residents who were legally their "vassals." In the decades following the Barberini purchase of the *stato*, the villagers challenged a number of the Barberini claims on village resources. Villagers attempted to expose the "fakeness" of noble demands for "more" use rights and to underscore the legitimacy of their own position, sometimes challenging the noble family legally in court. One such challenge over hunting and fishing rights in the village of Nerola between the 1640s and 1680s is especially revealing of village political culture. During the lengthy controversy, the Nerolani elaborated a number of ideas during *consiglio* meetings that suggest the level of adversarial literacy of the villagers—including the village sources upon which it was based.

Although the villagers of Nerola were "vassals" of their Barberini lords, the tax-paying men resident there were also "citizens" of the village, with the right to participate in the village assembly and serve in village offices during the seventeenth century. They were simultaneously subjects of the pope, whose temporal government, most historians believe, was weaker than the governing authority of the popes. Political authority there is usually analyzed as a struggle between the popes and the great noble families. Records from village communal governments, especially the notes from the meetings of village assemblies, suggest that this bifurcated view of power in the countryside obscures the realities of its governance in the early modern period. Village sources illuminate the tripartite nature of this political power and undermine the argument that either noble or papal authority mattered more than village politics in the Roman countryside.[2]

Many characters appear in the detailed narratives that follow—Maffeo Barberini, part of a relatively new landowning noble family, anxious to control his jurisdiction in the countryside; the intervening magistrates, whose legal decisions the villagers pursued, but whose opinions they ignored when it suited them; beleaguered officials of the noble family, surrounded by uncooperative villagers and disloyal fellow officials. The villagers, however, are the central figures. Their level of political sophistication and free-spirited attitude toward their Roman rulers can best be grasped in conflicts that "cut them to the quick," as a Barberini official noted in 1685. Legally, the villagers of Nerola and the rest of the *stato* were at the bottom of a political hierarchy that gave nobles the right to make laws and papal magistrates the role of interpreting them. This chapter explains how the Nerolani challenged this view of who governed the Roman countryside, using texts and ideas that had been brought to the village for other purposes.

Uncovering Village Politics

Late in July 1685, two naked men ran from the Corese river and vanished into the countryside north of Rome. They were residents of the nearby village of Nerola, a fief belonging to the Barberini family. In 1685, the *padrone* of the family was Maffeo Barberini, who jealously guarded his rights as "lord" of all the villagers (naked or otherwise). Cristiano Leggiardi and Mariano Angelonio fled without most of their clothes after they were spotted by a guard of the Barberini family. He claimed that what the two men were doing down in the Corese river was fishing, or, to put it in criminal terms, poaching the precious trout reserves, which the Barberini declared belonged only to the noble family but which the villagers argued were rightfully their own.[3]

The guard turned the matter over to his superior, the "*auditore generale*," or chief judicial magistrate of the Barberini family. His role was to investigate the alleged crime, collect testimony from the witnesses, interrogate the accused, and in the case of minor offenses, decide the punishment. He admitted in a letter of August 1685 that he had little to offer Maffeo Barberini in this regard, since he and his subordinates had failed to collect anything but the fishermen's clothes. The *auditore* claimed that the two men were fishing with their hands (*con le mani*), which suggests that these two must have been as quick with their hands as they were on their feet—since no one succeeded in catching the fisherman after they ran away.[4]

Two other villagers hauled before the *auditore* admitted that while the *auditore* was away in the neighboring village of Monte Rotondo, Cristiano (one of the accused) showed up in the piazza of Nerola and recounted the story of his ill-fated fishing expedition. Neither witness knew where he was. The *auditore* admitted in his letter to Maffeo Barberini that "better evidence," as well as the accused, were impossible to produce because the issue of who had the right to the fish in the Corese river "cuts the villagers of Nerola to the quick."[5]

The naked fishing expedition occurred at the end of four decades of conflict between the villagers and the Barberini family. From the 1640s to the 1680s, a number of controversies arose between the noble family and the Nerolani about labor obligations, hunting rights, and seigneurial dues. The villagers challenged the grandiose claims of the Barberini in the meetings of the village *consiglio*, in which all heads of household could participate, and which the whole village might attend when the matter under discussion was sufficiently serious.

The villagers of Nerola (or at least the men eligible to participate in the *consiglio*) were probably more political than the citizens of the average American city today, where the lines at the polls get shorter each election year. By contrast an adult head of household in a village like Nerola during the 1640s and 1650s was called to participate in the general *consiglio* meetings about six times per year, a bit more often during years in which a number of important issues were pending. A second type of *consiglio* also met, the *consiglio delli* [*sic*] *dodici* or the council of the twelve. During the 1640s and 1650s, it met two or three times a year, often during the times of greatest agricultural activity when it was probably difficult to gather enough people to call the *consiglio generale*. In 1645, for instance, 114 different individuals attended one of the eleven *consiglio* meetings called that year. For a village of about 400 people, this is an astonishing level of public participation. However, if we consider attendance at the general *consiglio* meetings for that year (eight in all), on average villagers attended only three or four of those meetings per year. Participating in a village *consiglio* was not always a pleasant affair, since villagers had to state their vote aloud and explain their differences with any of the options presented. In particularly difficult decisions, a small number of villagers refused to take a stand at all, voting instead "with the majority." Politics then and now is a risky, messy business and even in Nerola it suited some people's tastes much more than others. A few dozen individuals participated consistently in village affairs and made most of the remarks recorded for the village deliberations.[6]

Village debates were written down by either the village secretary, or the vice-governor, or occasionally, an unidentified (and rough) hand. The spelling and grammar of the meeting notes demonstrate the influence of the local dialect and the scribal limitations of those who took them (I do not update or correct their language in my transcriptions in the endnotes). The notes are flawed too, insofar as it may have been in the village piazza or at the tables of one of the local inns that the most honest opinions about local politics were given and the frankest lessons in power passed from one generation to the next. But the *consiglio* meeting records are the closest surviving source for understanding village political culture.

The village of Nerola had three executive officers, called the priors, who were chosen by lot to serve the village for two years. The priors were the first to interact with the officials of the Barberini family and the first to deal with other outsiders as well. Papal tax collectors, visiting clergy, and officials of other villages, usually first consulted the priors of the village. The priors called the *consiglio* if they wanted advice about how to approach an unusual situation (a request for charity) or whenever they wanted to spend money beyond the usual amounts (to pursue a lawsuit in Rome, for instance). The priors set the agenda for the meetings and sometimes made suggestions about how to resolve a particular problem. To lead in the village meant more than managing disagreements between the villagers and the lord: It also meant wrestling with the demands of the papal government. Although Nerola and the other villages of the *stato* of Monte Libretti were part of a semi-independent territory not directly governed by the papal administration, the villagers still had to pay some papal taxes, and raising those taxes was an issue often discussed in the *consiglio*. The papal bureaucracy, however, could also be an ally in the struggle with noble lords: Villagers could petition papal tribunals to settle controversies like the one between the villagers of Nerola and the Barberini about fishing rights. Such disputes about rural resources were common in the seventeenth century, and they often spilled over into the law courts of the papal government. To those law courts the villagers took issues like the dispute over fishing and hunting rights that could not be resolved by local means or appeals to the Barberini prince.[7]

Failed Possession: Nerola
and the Recovered Statuto

As the new owners of Nerola, the Barberini became the proprietors of about half of the village lands and the lords of its inhabitants, with significant judicial and legal jurisdiction in the village. To confirm their ownership of Nerola, the Barberini would either have gone to the village or (more likely) sent one of their officials to extract an oath of fealty from their vassals. This formal visit, the *possesso* of the village by its new lords, became an important part of the political ideology of the villagers. For the villagers of Nerola, the political meaning of the *possesso* was embodied in the *statuto* or constitution of the village. The recovery and interpretation of this document was one of the acts of the *consiglio* that made it possible for the villagers to argue that they were not only the vassals of the Barberini, but as participants in the *consiglio* of Nerola, political actors in their own right.

Detailed records from the first *possesso* by the Barberini have not survived, but lengthy descriptions from an early eighteenth-century *possesso* in Nerola and other seventeenth-century evidence suggest some of the things that must have happened in 1644. The eighteenth-century *possesso* required the men who could participate in the *consiglio* to swear that they would be the "true and faithful vassals" of the Barberini, that they would pay the rents and dues owed to the new noble family, and that they and their heirs would assist the new "lords" in any way they could.[8] The documents describing the *possesso* elaborate these oaths in a number of ways, creating a lengthy legalistic inventory of village subjugation.

The oath of vassalage also outlined the reciprocity between lords and villagers in the Roman countryside. The *consiglio* participants accepted the Barberini as lords, and the Barberini official accepted a copy of the *statuto* of the village. According to the language of the *possesso*, the Barberini emissary "accepted [the *statuto*] in the place and in the name of the prince."[9] Probably written down in the early fifteenth century at the request of Francesco Orsini, the *statuto* was in Latin, although some text added after the fifteenth century was written in Italian. Descriptions of the condition of the *statuto* in the village *consiglio* meetings of the 1640s and 1650s suggest that in the summer of 1644, the *statuto* was probably no more than a bundle of papers in fragile condition.[10]

The copies of Nerola's *statuto* that exist today illustrate the comprehensive nature of such a document. It summarized criminal and civil law in the village; it fixed the punishments for violating those laws; it specified the payments that the villagers owed to the lord; it described local agrarian practices; it provided an overview of village government; and it listed the rights (like hunting rights) that belonged to the villagers and those belonging to the lord. Statutes in the Roman countryside were not systematically collected until, between the fifteenth and the eighteenth centuries. As late as 1746 the priors of Ponticelli claimed the village had no statutes of its own, but rather it followed those of Nerola. Ponticelli was the exception in the *stato* of Monte Libretti, since the other five villages all had a written *statuto*. Both nobles and villagers referred to the statutes in their disputes, sometimes calling them the *fondamento* of their particular rights.[11]

The *statuto* was supposed to clarify rights and obligations in the village world. After the arrival of the Barberini, however, it was up to the villagers to try to bring interpretive clarity and political legitimacy to the document. As the conflicts continued with the Barberini officials, a number of *consiglio* meetings raised the importance of the *statuto* as the essential political document supporting the claims of the villagers against their new lords. The villagers' attempt to "recover" and interpret the *statuto* was an important foundation for their political views, prompted, in part, by what villagers perceived as challenges from the new lords to undermine village practices.

The official representing the Barberini's interest in the village was the *auditore*, who, in addition to acting as a judge, issued edicts in the name of the noble family, and was required to represent the lord's interests at the meeting of the *consiglio*. Certainly his most controversial role in Nerola was issuing edicts. Noble edicts added to existing local and papal laws, sometimes repeating previous laws and sometimes modifying them to the benefit of the noble family. Since Popes and their ministers also issued edicts, and many villages had their own *statuti*, legal jurisdictions in the countryside were quite complex, a phenomenon similar to the situation in the city of Rome and in the Papal States in general.[12]

In 1644, Marco Perini, the *auditore*, posted an edict on the village gate that said that the *danni dati* (fines) for livestock trespassing on property would be increased from a monetary penalty to "corporal punishment," regardless of whether the culprit trespassed on the property of the Barberini or on the property of an individual villager. Since local agriculture was a mixture of olive groves, vineyards, grain fields organized in an open field system, and animal husbandry, accidental livestock wanderings were not unusual. In such cases, the *auditore* would typically impose a small monetary fine and the relevant payment of damages.[13]

Villagers were quick to notice when edicts deviated from their local customs or the text of the *statuto*. The priors immediately noted the discrepancy between current penalties for livestock trespassing and those of the Barberini edict in 1644. They reported in the *consiglio* meeting that the *auditore* had dismissed their concerns "with his usual elegant phrases" and that he had defended the edict by saying that it was "to frighten people and that he wouldn't revoke it." In a typical *consiglio* meeting like this one, the priors first provided an overview of the situation, and then one or two individuals offered solutions to the problem. Subsequent speakers agreed with the first speaker, qualified his position, or offered a different solution altogether.[14]

On this occasion Ser Artilio Granci gave a very thoughtful speech that gained the approval of all those present. He observed that "in the time of the past lords [the Orsini] . . . no new practices detrimental to the *comunità* or the *statuto* were ever introduced." For that reason, he urged the priors to petition the *auditore* to withdraw and to impose only the penalties for trespassing required by the *statuto*. If the petition failed, Granci suggested that the priors appeal directly to the lord "or to whom it might be necessary, especially since they had just sworn their oath of vassalage according to what the *statuto* required of them." Granci did not mention the physical presentation of the *statuto* to the Barberini official, but his speech (and the unanimous vote supporting it) indicate general agreement in the *consiglio* that it was the *statuto* that defined the terms of their vassalage and its terms could not be changed unilaterally by the lord.[15]

Perini was also involved in a controversy early the next year over the payments owed by the villagers for the olive oil harvest. The priors convened the *consiglio* because Perini was trying to use a new measuring cup to determine the fees for the use of the noble family's olive press. Instead of the cup with the Orsini seal formerly used to measure these debts, Perini produced a different and clearly larger one, thereby effectively raising the payments. Discussion between the priors and Perini again yielded nothing: "with elegant phrases he was dragging out the resolution of this matter—in so doing he does great damage to the people [of the village]." The priors noted in the *consiglio* that Perini's actions deviated from the *statuto* and violated the accepted process for changing that document ("the other times we called the *consiglio* if we wanted to adjust the *statuto*"). They advised that the *consiglio* vote on their plan to approach Perini one last time to "ask him to conclude this matter in order not to annoy His Excellency" (the Barberini lord). Should they not prevail, the priors wanted permission to travel to Rome to ask the Barberini to rectify the situation.[16]

As tensions between the villagers and the Barberini continued, concerns were raised in the *consiglio* about the condition of the *statuto* itself. During a meeting in March 1646, the priors explained to the *consiglio* that the village copy of the *statuto* had a number of problems. They advised that this precious source had to be protected, since "it was very old and in disarray." They wanted to know whether they should make a handwritten copy of it or whether they should have it printed. The priors also suggested that the copy of the *statuto* be carried to the *padroni* (the Barberini) so that the noble family could "sanction it by clear order [impressing upon their officials] that it should be observed inviolate, particularly the parts which favor our *comunità*." [17]

One villager, Battista Ferrazoli, supported the priors' recommendation for, as he put it, an "authentic copy" (probably meaning a notarized copy) of what they had which they could send it out to be printed. He also urged that they keep the original and the copy in a chest with three keys, one for each prior. Alternatively, he suggested that they could put the original in the archive of "San Pietro Vaticano." By preserving and copying the *statuto* so that it could be presented again to the Barberini, the members of the *consiglio* hoped to impress upon the noble family the importance of the moment in the *possesso* when Barberini officials recognized and accepted the *statuto* from the villagers. This was the significant moment of the *possesso* for the Nerolani.[18]

The relevant text of the *statuto* supports the villagers' claim that they had the right to hunt in Nerola. But the two sides exchanged paper in the mid-1640s, each trying to justify who had the hunting and fishing rights in the village. At a meeting of the *consiglio delli dodici* in 1645 the participants were asked to address five statements from Perini, the *auditore generale*, related to the growing disputes between the villagers and the Barberini. One was about hunting, specifically whether the lords had ever sold the rights to it, to which the *consiglio* participants responded in the negative. In April 1646, the priors swore before a Barberini official that the villagers had the right to hunt in the territory of Nerola. In June that same year, the *auditore generale* issued an edict prohibiting hunting in the *stato* of Monte Libretti. In February 1648 the *auditore* arrested some men for hunting violations, "despite the fact that the *statuto* says that one can hunt in Nerola," as it was argued in the *consiglio* shortly after the incident.[19]

The villagers enjoyed a brief respite from this matter at the end of the 1640s because the Barberini family was having more serious troubles in Rome with their successors to the papal throne, the Pamphilij family. Only in the early 1650s did the Barberini return their attention to villages like Nerola. Without outside pressures from the noble family, the matter of copying the *statuto* was set aside and no longer discussed in the *consiglio*. When it was raised again in a *consiglio* meeting in 1652, the *consiglieri* agreed once more that a good copy of the *statuto* had to be made, "whatever the cost."[20]

The Barberini were firmly reintegrated into Roman society after their Parisian exile and turned once again to administering their territory in 1653. That year they "renewed a ban on hunting," which they claimed the previous owners, the Orsini, had promulgated in 1613. This last edict was discussed in the *consiglio* about a week after it appeared on the village gate. Pietro Granci argued that the priors should "ask his Excellency to observe the *statuto* which the *comunità* has recovered . . . [the *statuto*] which was lost during the time of Duke Giovanni Antonio Orsini." Granci urged the priors to travel to Rome to present it to the Barberini "or to whomever necessary and to hire an attorney . . . for the service of our *comunità*."[21]

In 1653, it appears the priors had either gone to Rome, or written to the prince, or possibly had their lawyer make a visit to the Barberini palace, because they presented a letter in the *consiglio* from Maffeo Barberini, "who would be greatly pleased if someone would tell him what the *comunità* claims regarding hunting, since a few individuals have been harassed for hunting." Giovanni Nicola Portasacco, the main speaker, insisted that the priors take the *statuto* to the prince to remind him of his appropriate behavior in this case—"to attend to these things as a father and as a *padrone* [would] and to return to his benignity."[22]

Two aspects of this conflict during the 1640s and 1650s are important for understanding the villagers' political culture of the villagers. The first is the obvious way in which the *statuto* became the embodiment of village interests, a text with near-sacred status, and a source of community solidarity. Such a view was encouraged by papal bureaucrats. During the hunting and fishing controversy, a papal bureaucrat wrote a letter admonishing the inhabitants of Nerola to "make another Archive," that is, to find a new location for the village records. The priors and the *consiglio* members complied by renting a better room for them. The garbled nature of this request, as recorded in the village *consiglio* meetings, suggests that villagers were not too familiar with the papal official (his title, for instance, does not seem to have been understood). Nonetheless, the papal bureaucrat reinforced the villagers' desire to preserve important documents. The quest to "archive" the *statuto* properly in a chest with three keys or to lock it up in "San Pietro Vaticano" originated in a conflict with the Barberini family, but it was also encouraged by papal bureaucrats trying to pry their way into the semi-independent territories, mostly in order to tax them more effectively.[23]

The second aspect of the conflict was the attempt to show the *statuto* to the relevant person or persons (especially the Barberini) and to instruct those people in how to read it. The villagers had to make sure that the parts favorable to the Nerolani were noted and "affirmed" by the noble family. Sending the priors or employing a lawyer in Rome was crucial in this regard, and, evidently, many representatives from Nerola and the neighboring villagers of Monte Libretti traveled to Rome to appeal to the Barberini after they purchased the *stato* in 1644. A Barberini edict of 1648 prohibited priors from traveling to Rome to talk to their new lords, which suggests that enough villagers did so to annoy the noble family and their officials. The edict was decreed in the name of reducing village expenses, but considering how many matters were contested by the villagers, it seems more likely that it was issued as a way to reduce the number of unwelcome visitors to the Barberini palace. According to the records of the *consiglio* meetings of the early 1650s, it is unlikely anyone in the village paid much attention to the edict—no mention of it was made when a trip to Rome was urged on the part of the priors. The priors probably did call upon the Barberini in 1653, carrying the copy of the *statuto* to present to one of the members of the Barberini court in Rome, if not to a member of the noble family itself. So far as the villagers were concerned, the *possesso* ritual had to be repeated during the 1640s and 1650s until the *padroni* understood its meaning.[24]

The *statuto*, however, was not the only document that discussed their rights or inventoried their obligations. Nobles liked edicts and defended their role in both making and interpreting them. As one of the edicts of Giovanni Antonio Orsini phrased it in the early seventeenth century: "If in the . . . aforesaid decrees, anyone claims that there is any ambiguity or obscurity, the free will to interpret them according to his wishes is reserved for His Illustrious Excellency."[25] When nobles issued edicts in the sixteenth and seventeenth centuries, they added to an established body of laws, sometimes repeating papal edicts, sometimes repeating parts of the *statuti*, and sometimes modifying language from both sources in order to issue edicts to their benefit.

When considered together as a compilation of edicts, noble laws appear highly problematic as tools for governing the countryside. The aforesaid grand claim by Giovanni Antonio Orsini was part of a compendium of edicts that his *auditore* compiled in the 1620s, probably for the use of future *auditori* in the *stato* of Monte Libretti. The edicts related to banditry are a good example of how flawed this kind of early modern lawmaking could be. As was the case with papal laws on banditry, the Orsini edicts held the families of bandits responsible for the crimes of their relatives, even to relatives of the fourth degree. Another edict required inhabitants to keep their bandit relatives out of village. How the relatives were supposed to hold their wayward kin at bay while still obeying another edict prohibiting any contact with bandits is not explained in the edicts. Relatives were also required to notify noble officials of the arrival of bandit relatives, an action which would have amounted to turning themselves in for not keeping their relatives out of the territory in the first place. The inconsistencies are obvious when the edicts are read together, but they were surely also noticeable when posted individually on the village gate. They probably contributed to village skepticism about whether or not noble laws should be taken seriously at first posting.[26]

The villagers of Nerola clearly had their own opinions about whether or how an edict posted on the village gate applied to them. As debates in the *consiglio* of Nerola show, edicts posted on the village gate were subject to deliberation, and their stature as village law was lower than that of the *statuto*. The *consiglio* became an important arbiter for what would be accepted as local "law." Barberini officials occasionally used "*belle parole*" or the elegance of good manners to smooth the reception of the edicts in the village. But the *consiglio* meeting notes suggest that the *auditore*'s civility was viewed suspiciously. It was not impressive enough to deter the villagers' from protest.[27]

In 1653, Pietro Granci argued that the *statuto* was, in effect, the safeguard for village rights. Now that the villagers had "recovered" it (as he put it), it had to take precedence over later noble edicts. The implication of Granci's argument is that the only reason Giovanni Antonio Orsini got away with issuing the edict against hunting in 1613 was because the *statuto* had been "lost"; otherwise the villagers would have discussed the edict in the *consiglio* and contested it with the Orsini family. The recovered *statuto* (his logic goes) clearly showed that the right to hunt belonged to them and could not be revoked by a Barberini edict.

The conflict created by the discrepancies between the *statuto* and the noble edicts was not resolved in the 1660s and 1670s. Villagers apparently continued to ignore the edicts on fishing and hunting periodically issued by the Barberini. As the Barberini *auditore* found out in the early 1680s, such edicts were impossible to enforce without generating village protest. In this later phase of the conflict, lawyers took the controversy to papal tribunals for adjudication. However, the conflict in the 1680s cannot be studied with the same detail at the village level as the conflict of the 1640s and 1650s because almost all of the *consiglio* records have disappeared for that decade. A lengthy letter from a Barberini official in the countryside reveals what the villagers did, but not what they said. Letters and other sources indicate, however, the villagers' continued skepticism about noble hunting "rights." They also document villagers' reaction to papal authority as it was represented in the decisions of the tribunals that became entangled in this case in the 1680s.

"To Listen to These Hill-Folk, You'd Think Every One of Them Was a Lawyer"

Maffeo Barberini reissued edicts prohibiting hunting in 1660, 1672, 1677, and 1678 in order to assert his claim to a monopoly on hunting rights in the *stato.* The recalcitrance of the Nerolani during the prosecution of one of their fellow villagers for poaching in 1676 suggests that they continued to reject such claims by the Barberini lord. Benedetto Gattani, a weaver in the wool industry in Nerola, was accused both of poaching and of engaging in a brief shoot-out with the Barberini *bargello* and *sbirro* late one evening in May 1676. While standing in the piazza of the neighboring village of Monte Libretti, the Barberini officials saw three men harvesting grain in a nearby field. The men quit their work and made their way toward the adjacent woods carrying arquebuses, presumably for hunting purposes. The *bargello* and the *sbirro* pursued them to the woods, calling for them to stop in the name of the Barberini court. The poachers answered with gunfire and the Barberini officials responded in kind. The *bargello*'s testimony emphasized the gravity of the gunfight, noting that the three men were "resisting the Court [of the Barberini]" and that it was only by the "grace of God" that neither he nor the *sbirro* were injured.[28]

Both Barberini officials identified Gattani, and although they were unable to name the other two men, they professed with certainty that they were "people of Nerola." They gave their testimony to the *auditore*, who interviewed four more witnesses from the village of Monte Libretti also present in the piazza that night. Since the villagers of Monte Libretti ventured no further than the piazza, they were too far from the incident to identify any of the accused poachers. In the village of Nerola the *auditore* pressed nine people to testify, and although he doubled his investigative efforts, he received little useful information about an event that must have come to the attention of many in the village. Nor did he learn the location of a suspect who, to avoid arrest, loitered in the village church for several days before he disappeared altogether for the rest of the summer.[29]

The Nerolani he interrogated admitted little knowledge of the case. Some villagers were openly hostile in response to the most basic inquiries. When asked to state his "profession," Francesco Galloni replied, "My trade is staying home and minding my own business." The remainder of his testimony continued in this vein—Galloni was sick in bed the day of the incident, and only claimed to know anything about it on the basis of what others had told him. He (along with the rest of the villagers) had all seen Gattani standing in or near the church, leaning against its walls, but had not bothered to ask the accused weaver turned reaper turned poacher the reason for his newfound piety, or why he now lingered on the church steps, instead of his usual hang-out in the village piazza. Camillo Rizzoli "imagined" it must be because Gattani was a suspect, but he did not pursue the matter any further.[30]

Gattani finally reappeared in the village in mid-August 1676 and was questioned by the *auditore* about the incident. He gave a detailed account of his movements in Nerola that day, but insisted that he had been at home the night of the attempted poaching and shoot-out. Gattani noted that he had "the necessary respect for the court of his Excellency" and observed that villagers from Fara and Moricone hunted frequently in Barberini territory, but not he. He conceded that he had retreated to the church when he learned he was a suspect, but only to avoid the fate of another villager, Andrea Orfeo, who, although innocent, had recently been jailed for twelve days by the *sbirri*. The *sbirri*, Gattani noted, "could say whatever they liked because they were disgraceful people, who, in order to make it appear they were doing their job say that they recognized me, when, on no account was I ever in that place."[31]

The failed attempt to prosecute Gattani was one of a number of efforts by the *auditore* to protect Barberini hunting rights in the *stato*. Maffeo Barberini followed some of these cases carefully, especially the prosecution of Domenico Eugeni, from the village of Monte Libretti. Eugeni, alias Minichella, was an incorrigible poacher and a crafty storyteller, who explained the vast discrepancies between his accounts and those of the witnesses with an observation similar to Gattani's, "anyone can say whatever he likes." In February 1678 Maffeo Barberini wrote to the *auditore* to give his judgment on what should be done to Minichella, in light of the fact that he had been accused for the third time of hunting violations.[32]

Because Minichella had actually confessed during the second case against him (and then was apparently pardoned) and since he had subsequently renewed his illegal hunting practices, the Barberini prince told the minister to use corporal punishment on Minichella. If the accused could make no "relevant" case in his own defense, then the Barberini ordered the official to inflict torture, specifically, the *strappado*. Maffeo indicated that if Minichella was found guilty this third time, he should be "attached to the rope," raised off the ground but without jerking his body upward.[33]

The cases of Gattani and Minichella were unusual because they were "natives" of the *stato*. Usually the *auditore* prosecuted "foreigners," who lacked the knowledge or the village allies to avoid getting caught.[34] Gattani's charge that Barberini rights were defended by "vile" individuals (the *sbirri*) and that the innocent were wrongfully imprisoned reflected poorly on the system of justice in the *stato*. Maffeo Barberini addressed judicial practice in his territory in an edict of 1681. The stated motivation for Maffeo's edict was his desire "to see that justice for the vassals be administered promptly," that is, that the "innocent be quickly freed, and criminals quickly punished." He asked his *auditore* to keep him better informed about all the cases they were prosecuting. He chastised his officials for not transmitting information according to his specific guidelines. Maffeo wanted the information about judicial prosecutions in a "column" form that would allow the Barberini prince the room "to note in one column the decisions which will be taken by us." One copy was to be returned to village governors, and the other copy the Barberini intended to keep in their secretary's office in Rome. This latter record, according to the edict, would be necessary to respond to the appeals of the inhabitants, indicating that the Barberini expected petitions and intended to handle such matters directly from Rome.[35]

While the Barberini prince expressed general interest in the quality of justice in his territories, letters and testimony from inhabitants suggest that in practice the guards' enforcement of the bans on hunting were the most rigorously enforced aspect of local law. In a letter of 1681 the priors of the village of Monte Libretti asked for permission to hunt the *palombacci* nesting in great numbers in the thickets of the village. The priors expressed fear of the guards of the Barberini family, noting that they would not dare hunt one of these birds without his excellency's permission. As a one time "favor" to the villagers, Maffeo agreed to let them kill the birds, provided the villagers gave him every bird they caught the first night of the hunting.[36] In Monte Libretti the Barberini must have succeeded in convincing the villagers of the noble monopoly of hunting, since in 1687 they agreed to rent that right back from the noble family and continued to do so during the eighteenth-century.[37]

The Nerolani responded differently to the Barberini family's increasing attempts to enforce their monopoly over hunting and fishing rights in the village. A letter sent to Maffeo Barberini in 1682 explained that the *auditore* of Nerola caused an uproar in the village by "making an edict prohibiting fishing and hunting with rigorous penalties even imprisonment." A letter written on behalf of the villagers to Maffeo Barberini in 1682 also noted that the same *auditore* refused to attend the *consiglio* even though he had been asked twice to do so by the priors. The whole village was so "oppressed" by the edict that the *consiglio* was called (even without the presence of the *auditore*), and the congregated "*popolo*" declared "*viva voce* that the priors should go to Rome to His Excellency to make known to him the recalcitrance of the *auditore*." The prince must be informed that "the *Comunità* and *popolo* of Nerola had the free right (*jus libero*) to hunt and fish and so the *auditore* had no right to make such an edict." The villagers' petition to the Barberini was probably intended to be, and received as, a threat to noble hegemony in the village. But along with this threat the villagers' offered a face-saving alternative that could help both sides avoid a legal battle. The villagers intertwine the language of village rights with the language of deference in the letter to the lord: "This people . . . intends to be most faithful to his Excellency and to proceed with the appropriate reverence, and they hoped that the great benignity and honorable conscience of his Excellency would not permit him to do anything damaging to this people nor to their rights." The villagers clearly hoped that that their reverence would be reciprocated by noble recognition of village hunting and fishing rights. The reminder failed to have the intended effect, however, and the fishing controversy eventually went from the village to the papal courts.[38]

A reply to the villagers, briefly outlined at the bottom of their letter of 1682 and signed by Maffeo Barberini, instructed the *auditore* to enforce the past edicts (including those prohibiting hunting and fishing in Nerola) and told him to avoid "innovations of any kind." Although both the villagers and the noble family stress the importance of not allowing "innovations," their positions were incompatible. Each side recognized different documents as having preeminent status in the village. For the nobles their own edicts took precedence; for the villagers, the *statuto* did.

Maffeo Barberini's answer failed to satisfy the villagers. The controversy between the Nerolani and the noble family remained unresolved throughout the fall and winter of 1682–1683. In anticipation of the matter coming before a papal tribunal, both sides began to collect testimony during the spring of 1683 from rural inhabitants regarding the status of hunting rights in Nerola. The villagers' lawyer also approached a magistrate of the Apostolic Chamber who concurred in 1684 that the villagers' evidence (mainly the *statuto*) was admissible and that the issue should be presented formally to a Roman court. As was the case in the 1640s and 1650s, the *statuto* remained the document that the villagers relied upon to support their claims.[39]

The Barberini lawyers rejected this view of the relevance of the *statuto* and argued before a magistrate of a papal court (the Segnatura) that because many edicts had been issued by the Orsini and the Barberini prohibiting hunting, and because the testimony of local inhabitants (especially those who resided outside of Nerola) supported the noble claim that these edicts had been enforced, the Barberini had the right to prohibit hunting. Witnesses were an important element of the Barberini case, since they supported the Barberini version of what had happened in the village. Two elderly men, aged 75 and 76, claimed to remember prosecutions even during the time of the Orsini, who by the 1680s had been gone for forty years. They demonstrated the reliability of their memories by naming some of those accused: "I remember that a guy nicknamed 'the Sausage' was definitely given the rope [corda, the Italian expression for the strappado]." Such specificity was valued in oral testimony. No witness supporting the villagers' position chose to match the details of the two men testifying for the Barberini. Since Nerolani who gave too many particulars about their own fishing expeditions could find themselves prosecuted if the villagers lost their case, village testimony did little more than assert that hunting and fishing were local rights.[40]

The Barberini lawyers also claimed that the absence of village protest (after the Orsini edict of 1613, for instance) indicated that the Barberini bans on hunting were a valid and accepted local practice. The Barberini lawyers acknowledged the passages in the statuto that described the villagers' hunting and fishing rights, but the evidence since the statuto was written clearly indicated that hunting violations had been prosecuted as "a serious crime . . . like homicide."[41]

The lawyer for the Nerolani emphasized the discrepancies between the claims of the Barberini witnesses and other evidence. For example, witnesses from outside Nerola testified that the Nerolani had always been free to hunt; four decades before the lawsuit, the priors of Nerola had sworn before a Barberini lawyer the very same thing. The statuto evidence clearly had to be given the greatest weight in order to settle the case fairly. These were the same arguments made by participants in the consiglio in the 1640s and 1650s. Although the villagers' lawyer agreed that there was one section of the village lands (an area called Licineto) where the Nerolani did not have the right to hunt, elsewhere the right to hunt was a "free right of the people," over which the lords did not have jurisdiction. He also referred to hunting as "an ancient right which they preserved regardless of noble edicts." Finally, the lawyer for the Nerolani reminded the papal tribunal that the statuto was useless if it could be undone by the lord, whose task, by Roman law, was to preserve the statuto itself.[42]

The magistrate of the Segnatura who reviewed the case in 1684–1685 found the Barberini lawyers' arguments and evidence more persuasive. In 1685 he decreed that the Barberini had the right to prohibit or allow hunting and fishing, and (anticipating the possibility of future disputes) he noted that even if the Barberini allowed the villagers to hunt and fish in Nerola, these activities did not belong to them as a "right." It remained the jurisdiction of the lord to grant or withdraw this privilege. The villagers and their lawyer refused to accept this decision and appealed the case to another tribunal, the Court of the Sacra Rota. While the lawyers in Rome continued to debate the legal dilemmas posed by discrepancies between the *statuto* and the edicts, the relations between the Barberini's *auditore generale* and the Nerolani deteriorated. In the summer of 1685, two men violated the Barberini ban on fishing and fled before they could be prosecuted.[43]

The Barberini had won their case in the legal system, but it was not accepted in the village, where the runaway fishermen remained hidden and the villagers hostile to the noble family's claims. The letter from the *auditore* states this clearly. Despite the local obstacles facing the *auditore* when he tried to enforce the Barberini edicts, he was optimistic about the possibility of the noble family having enough proof "to continue in the near possession of the right to prohibit hunting."[44]

The remainder of his report to Maffeo Barberini, however, suggests that it would be a considerable struggle to do so. The *auditore* notes that the Nerolani were not the only ones putting up walls of silence and subterfuge to protect the men and thwart the Barberini's enforcement of their supposed rights. The "*capo della pesca*," the warden charged with protecting the Barberini monopoly on fishing rights, was apparently rather casual in his stewardship of the Barberini trout reserves. He allowed one Vincenzo Castigliano to fish whenever he liked, despite the fact that the *auditore* had declared Vincenzo in violation of Barberini law for his excursions to Nerola's ichthyofauna. Vincenzo sent some of his illegal bounty to the governor of the neighboring village of Fara, as well as to Giovanni Battista Raimondi, renter of the Barberini inn in Nerola. Raimondi found himself so well supplied with stolen fish that when "foreigners" came to visit prisoners in the Barberini jail in Monte Rotondo,

> Raimondo sent [the visitors] as a gift four beautiful trout, which were eaten in the house of the archpriest, and another trout of about two pounds was presented by Raimondi to me, in the name of the aforementioned Vincenzo, but I didn't accept it [but rather] sent it back to him so that he couldn't say I approved of his breach of fishing [bans].[45]

In the summer of 1685, the Barberini won the lawsuit and lost the village. Even a local priest enjoyed the illegal bounty from the Corese river. The Barberini *auditore* was very much alone in trying to protect the noble family's "right" to prohibit hunting and fishing. Wayward fishermen, silent villagers, and negligent Barberini employees were finding their own way to interpret the law. The innkeeper's "betrayal" in particular was a serious blow to the ability of the noble family to protect its jurisdiction in the countryside. The innkeepers of Monte Libretti were often involved in the administration of justice in the *stato*.

Rural inns were a congregating point for villagers, officials, travelers, and suspicious n'er-do-wells. Innkeepers were in charge of relaying the noble family's edicts to seasonal workers and other visitors, reporting their suspicions about potential poachers to *stato* officials, and maintaining decorum and cleanliness described in a number of edicts in the *stato*.[46] The rural inn might also include a chapel, although in Monte Libretti the inn was more frequently used as a Barberini jail than as a center of spiritual devotion. Animals confiscated for grazing violations were deposited for safekeeping with the innkeeper. Barberini guards frequently brought poaching suspects into the inn in order to collect testimony in support of their arrest: "I swear the guard came in with a suspect dressed like a hunter who had a gun and a dead bird in his bag." Without the cooperation of local innkeepers, the Barberini officials would have considerable difficulty protecting the noble family's jurisdiction in the village.

The *consiglio* records from the 1640s and 1650s show that noble edicts were subject to deliberation. The Barberini official's letter demonstrates that in the 1680s, the villagers rejected both the noble edicts on fishing and hunting and the papal tribunal's decision in favor of the Barberini family. The Barberini had to enforce the papal tribunal's decision, but, as the letter indicates, it was nearly impossible to do so. The local interpretation of hunting and fishing rights must certainly have been a factor in the resolution of the situation by the spring of 1686. In early April of that year, the priors of the village held a *consiglio*, bringing together most of the inhabitants of the village for "a full *consiglio* . . . in sufficient number . . . the majority and most healthy part of the population notwithstanding [not including] children, the sick, and the absent." Fifty-one names were recorded for the meeting, the largest number for any seventeenth-century *consiglio* meeting on record. At issue was whether or not the villagers should agree to a settlement (a *concordia*) with the Barberini family about the villagers' right to hunt and fish.[47]

The *concordia* presented in the April *consiglio* would have been attractive to the Nerolani. In it they retained the right to hunt and fish almost anywhere in the territory of the village except one specific area—essentially all of the hunting area that their lawyer claimed for them during the lawsuit. Although the *concordia* did not technically reverse the decision of the Segnatura court, it must have looked like a victory at the village level. The Barberini had to grant to the Nerolani what the villagers insisted was theirs. The Barberini "right" to "allow" hunting seemed to be the only part of the Segnatura decision recognized in Nerola.

Another factor motivating the noble family to settle the matter in favor of the villagers was the effort of the *comunità*'s lawyer to appeal the case to another papal tribunal, the Rota. Hence the Barberini would have to defend their "right" to prohibit hunting and fishing yet another time and hope for the same decision. Nor would another decision in the noble family's favor necessarily produce better results in the village. Further, the Barberini family had other matters requiring their attention. By the spring of 1686, Maffeo Barberini had died, and his son, Urbano Barberini, had other fish to fry—he was fond of gambling, traveling, and women. To the consternation of his family, he seems to have been the stereotypical dissolute noble: He had trouble with debt and even more trouble with his mother.[48]

According to the surviving copy of the village *consiglio* meeting of April 1686, the villagers unanimously accepted the terms of the *concordia* as it was presented to them that day by the priors of the village. At the same *consiglio* meeting, they also unanimously accepted a second *concordia*. It resolved the controversy about the measuring cups used to determine the payments owed to the Barberini on the olive oil produced in the village. One measuring cup with the Barberini seal would be left at the olive press; one would be left with the Barberini *auditore*; and one cup would be deposited at the village archive. The two agreements had to be formally accepted by representatives of the villagers, whose task was to go before the Barberini lord in Rome "to reach an agreement with His Excellency to do, say, and to execute everything declared [in the village *consiglio*]." The defeat of the summer of 1685 turned into a victory by the following spring. The fishing must have continued more openly as the representatives of the village made their way to the meeting with the Barberini lord.[49]

Concordia documents related to these two affairs still exist in the Barberini archives. The terms of the olive oil *concordia* are largely the same as the terms presented to the villagers at the April *consiglio* meeting. This *concordia* states that the three priors, all named, and Urbano agreed to abide by the stipulations of the document, thus ending a forty-year long conflict between the Nerolani and the Barberini.

A text of a *concordia* about the hunting and fishing controversy also survives, but it appears to be an incomplete document, or a draft. Its truncated form suggests that the two parties were unable to reach an accord. Names and dates are conspicuously absent. For instance, the document gives no date for the *consiglio* that approved it, although a blank space is left for it. Nor are the names of the priors provided, although a blank space is left for them as well. These omissions indicate that either this *concordia* was never officially approved by either party, or that this is an earlier draft of a document that no longer survives in its final form. Since the Barberini kept multiple copies of many important documents, it is unusual that they only preserved an incomplete version of such an important text.[50]

The text reveals a great deal about how the Barberini and their officials saw the controversy and village politics. Not surprisingly, the Barberini draft of the *concordia* reaffirms that the noble family had the right to prohibit hunting. It states that the origin of the disagreement between the villagers and the Barberini was "recent." There is no mention of the conflict going back to the 1640s, illustrating either noble ignorance or an intentional recasting of the long-standing significance of the issue for the Nerolani. Likewise, the hunting and fishing controversy from the perspective of the Barberini *concordia* was the work of "a few individuals," who began the legal suit against Maffeo Barberini "in the name of the *comunità*." Such an interpretation suggests that many years of concern by the villagers about the potential loss of their hunting and fishing rights was the work of a "few," and by implication a sinister few.

The evidence in village sources contradicts the nobleman's theory that only a small number of people cared about the issue. Attendance at the *consiglio* in the 1640s and 1650s was at its highest levels when hunting and fishing rights were the focus of the meeting. A few individuals could not launch the legal suit without wider support among the participants in the *consiglio*, since those participants had to approve of the additional costs of sending representatives to talk to the Barberini, or hiring a lawyer to present the case to a papal magistrate. Widespread concern over the issue seems to have continued in the 1680s; a very large number of Nerolani showed up for the *consiglio* in April 1686 to hear the Barberini proposal for resolving the conflict. Moreover, the villagers threw a cloak of secrecy over the naked fishermen. It is unlikely that no one knew where they were. If Cristiano stepped into the piazza of Nerola the same day the Barberini *auditore* was out of town, he could not have been far away (and was probably in the village itself). According to the *auditore*, the fishing issue "[struck] a nerve with the villagers of Nerola," so the struggle itself could scarcely have been the work of a "few individuals" or if it were, these few articulate individuals had to win the approval of many others in the *consiglio* about how best to proceed against the Barberini on this matter.[51]

Historians have stressed the critical role of village elites, especially notaries, in organizing or facilitating village protest against lords. Notaries and literate individuals certainly aided villagers in their struggles with the Barberini. But we should not overestimate the extent to which such individuals single-handedly guided village affairs. Did the Nerolani resist the Barberini because they had notaries, or did Nerolani resistance and determination to exist as a political entity organized around the *consiglio* drive the demand for, and enhance the presence of, notaries and notarial culture? In Nerola, the level of participation in the *consiglio* and the village response to the judgments of the papal tribunal demonstrate that there was a symbiotic relationship between the *consiglio* political culture and the contribution of notarial culture. Adversarial literacy, or the tactics of resistance through the effective use of written sources, was widespread among ordinary people by the seventeenth century and was tied tightly in Nerola to politics. Notaries were useful allies in its practices, but it took the organization, the informal education, and the financing made possible by the village *consiglio* to fuel sustained and successful resistance to the Barberini.[52]

The description of the villagers' attitudes in the Barberini *concordia* emphasizes by contrast their subjugated status as vassals. The text of the draft states that both in Rome and during Urbano Barberini's first visit to Nerola, the villagers expressed "their very humble feelings and their reverent obedience" to the Barberini prince. It also stipulates that Urbano "allowed them" to go hunting and fishing, "so highly pleased was he by their act of obedience and their submission to his will." His granting of these rights was a sign of his "pleasure in their obedience and his own fatherly affection."[53]

The villagers also speak this language of lordship. They used it in the *consiglio* during the 1640s and 1650s, and even more elaborately in the letter of 1682 written to the Barberini to protest the "new" edicts on hunting. Completely absent from the *concordia* is any mention of the villagers' hunting and fishing rights as described in the *statuto*, or the claim of the villagers in the letter of 1682 to the Barberini lord that hunting was their "free right" (*jus libero*). Worse still from the villagers' point of view, this *concordia* was more about fatherly deception than it was about fatherly affection.

The Barberini description of where the villagers could hunt is essentially the same as that in the village *consiglio*, except for certain restrictions placed upon their hunting. Specifically, the Barberini *concordia* prohibits the killing of certain animals, namely, partridges, gray partridges, wild boar, and wild goats.[54] This prohibition would be unwelcome in the village world, where people hunted mostly for food or to protect crops from destruction. These terms clearly deviated from the *consiglio* agreement, which had imposed no restrictions on the type of game that the villagers could pursue.

Given the importance of the hunting and fishing controversy, and the existence of a completed *concordia* document for the olive oil measuring cup, it is odd that no completed copy of the *concordia* concerning the fishing dispute survives. This suspicious lacuna in the archive suggests that the priors (even if they showed the requisite humility in the presence of Urbano's "fatherly affection") may have walked away from Urbano without agreeing to the terms of a *concordia* so clearly different from the consensus about village rights in Nerola. The priors would scarcely have been able to take back to the village *consiglio* a *concordia* with such restrictive terms. While subjects of the Barberini lord, they were also citizens of the village, and, apparently, they owed greater allegiance to village institutions.

Although the villagers (including the notaries and other local "elites") seemed insignificant politically in a world where nobles claimed the right to make laws and papal tribunals had the role of interpreting them, participants in the *consiglio* were the arbiters of what would become recognized locally as law.

From their discussions in the village *consiglio* during the 1640s and 1650s about the legitimacy of noble edicts to their protection of the runaway fishermen and open defiance of a papal tribunal in the 1680s, the villagers of Nerola appeared to be remarkably autonomous in their relationship to governing authorities, more autonomous even than the common people of Rome, who were also active politically even in the capital city of the "absolutist" popes.[55]

By the late seventeenth century, the strategies of adversarial literacy in the hillside village of Nerola had proliferated to a considerable extent, surely encouraged, by the judicial avenues offered by the papal government, purchased through the services of lawyers, and directed against the claims of the noble family. In the papal government the villagers were supposed to find an ally against the Barberini, although, in this case, the ally did not rule in their favor. The conflict about hunting and fishing rights in Nerola requires a reconsideration of village allegiance to noble or papal authority in the late seventeenth century.

The papacy was building alliances in the Roman countryside by offering legal opportunities for sorting out class conflicts, one of the cornerstones of European and Italian state development. Subjects were supposed to voluntarily acquiesce to state power in exchange for these judicial possibilities. The Nerolani seem remarkably undisciplined in this regard and the Papal States, by this measure, particularly weak. This weakness in the countryside closest to Rome has been attributed to the great power still wielded there by the Roman nobility, but in Nerola's hunting and fishing controversy, even that form of authority in the village was subject to local scrutiny. In Nerola, the noble family could make laws, interpret them, and successfully win papal support for them, without winning the compliance of the village. Local allegiance to would-be rulers (whether noble or papal) was still limited, in this regard, whereas villagers' political culture, or as the political scientist Robert Putnam called it, their local social capital, as nourished through the *consiglio*, was relatively high. Their greatest "collective discipline," to use the historian Pierangelo Schiera's term, inclined toward the decisions of the *consiglio*, rather than any outside power.[56]

Whoever left that old copy of the *statuto* in Nerola or nailed to the village gate the first in a long series of edicts, did so to admonish, and to cultivate deference on the part of the villagers. But these acts were also invitations to join the empire of paper and to make room in the village for the words and the things (like the measuring cup) that gave a legitimate historical and legal justification for what villagers claimed were their "free rights." Nobles like the Barberini might try to refashion village political culture with words, but they could not ignore it in practice. Aristocrats and bureaucrats encouraged a local political culture that they could not control, and inadvertently nurtured the development of adversarial literacy, a form of local advocacy that would continue to evolve in the eighteenth century as the Barberini extended their control of village politics. In seventeenth-century Nerola the villagers did not confine their ambitions to the level of vassals, notaries, or lawyers. In their independent interpretation of noble edicts and papal court decisions they acted more like magistrates. Zora Neale Hurston, an American novelist and anthropologist, captured the attitude of such seemingly powerless people this way: Wherever they gathered—in the inn, or in the *consiglio*, or (in the case of her fictional world) in the doorways of their houses—they "became lords of sounds and lesser things. They passed nations through their mouths. They sat in judgement."[57]

3

The Adversary as Patron

Inviting the Barberini into Village Politics, 1660–1685

Village of Monte Libretti, with crenellated tower of castello near center of photograph. Photograph by the author.

Standing up to the Barberini necessitated a politically constructed unanimity about the meaning of the village constitution in Nerola. However, not all the disputes within the neighboring village of Monte Libretti produced such a coherent vision. Villagers in Monte Libretti who disagreed with each other had the additional burden of facing their adversaries on a regular basis in the village piazza. While the Nerolani unanimously supported the clarity of hunting rights promised in the *statuto*, residents in the neighboring village of Monte Libretti struggled with a number of dilemmas for which the *statuto* provided no answers. One key issue for villagers was access to medical care and education, but experts in both were in short supply and their salaries sometimes beyond what strained communal finances could afford. Other dilemmas required participants in the *consiglio* to wrestle with what constituted the "public good" for Monte Libretti. Those trying to define in material terms this abstract concept were mostly illiterate or semi-literate people whose work lives were centered in the agricultural and pastoral economy of the region. They were among the most poorly educated people in early modern society, and yet they were actively engaged in one of its most challenging forms of government, representative government, although the ordinary dilemmas it encountered at the village level have received little historical scrutiny and the key terms of its debates have not received extensive analysis.

To subdue the messy politics of everyday life, some villagers of Monte Libretti turned occasionally to their lord, Maffeo Barberini. But what insights or assistance could a Barberini prince provide for their dilemmas? Scattered clues suggest that he would have avoided such interventions if possible, but politically minded villagers were insistent that he should be involved when it came to solving the villagers' difficulty in finding a schoolteacher or a physician, or sorting out the competing notions of the "public good" of Monte Libretti. In cultivating Maffeo's interference in their affairs, they were quite different from the villagers of the neighboring Nerola. An anonymous seventeenth-century observer also remarked on the singularity of Monte Libretti's villagers who, he wrote, "loved their lord with all their hearts and in a way adored him." His description also noted, however, that while they obeyed his edicts and his officials, they also complained a lot about doing so. The Monte Librettians were as effusive in their complaints about fellow villagers whom they thought had interfered with the rightful order of the village. As this chapter will show, one person's promotion of the public good was another's pursuit of private interest or passion. Limited communal resources added to the acrimony of this debate. Some villagers thus courted Maffeo as a potential patron who could settle these irreconcilable differences of interpretation.[1]

Maffeo was unable to avoid completely the long-standing conflicts conceptualized in these terms. As was evident in his conflict with Nerola, Maffeo was clearly interested in influencing rural life through issuing edicts, monitoring the activities of his village officials, or occasionally visiting the *stato*. By these means Maffeo hoped to shape the *stato* to his ideals and to promote his own financial and jurisdictional interests there. Priors and other concerned citizens of Monte Libretti brought him the thornier problems by letter or through a personal visit to the Barberini palace. Some aspects of his personal intervention were the direct result of these villagers' requests. Maffeo's granddaughter, Cornelia Costanza, and her husband, Giluio Cesare, later took Maffeo's standards of noble engagement in the countryside to unprecedented levels. But even in the generation of Maffeo Barberini, noble intervention played a role in village politics. The intersection of Maffeo Barberini's practice of lordship and the everyday politics in the village of Monte Libretti between the 1660s and 1680s suggest that residents there were more willing to accept their status as vassals of his illustrious noble family, and less inclined to threaten his authority to the degree the villagers of Nerola had done. But for such deference the Monte Librettians demanded solutions to the everyday issues that seemed beyond the resolution of their *consiglio*.

Taxes Paid and Houses Open: Citizens in the Countryside

The "Magnificent Community" of Monte Libretti fulfilled a variety of functions in the village. Since the Middle Ages villagers in the Roman countryside delegated the supervision of their grazing and gathering rights as well as the coordination of agricultural and pastoral activities to the institution of the village commune. The coordination of agricultural and pastoral activities was another motivation for the foundation of rural communes. In seventeenth-century Monte Libretti, such practices occurred year to year without much controversy, and, as a result, they were very rarely discussed in the *consiglio*. As the conflict over hunting and fishing rights in Nerola showed, it was through the efforts of the communal government that villagers could challenge the authority of the barons in the papal law courts. For the papal bureaucracy, the communal governments of the villages were the administrative centers through which taxes could be demanded, and hopefully even paid. At the village level, however, the officials of the communal government found that local politics had other dimensions, many of which had to be discussed in the *consiglio* before participants voted on the issue.[2]

In Monte Libretti the *consiglio* that convened most frequently was the "public and general *consiglio* with one man representing each household." Citizens of the village were defined as those men who had paid their taxes and who currently resided in the village (whose houses were open, in their words). Scholars have asserted that in the seventeenth-century Roman countryside the *consigli* became more restricted, composed of an elite core of citizens, whose membership was sometimes controlled by the lord. In Maffeo Barberini's compendium of edicts issued in 1658, a restricted *consiglio* of forty men is mentioned, although the edict acknowledged that it did not exist in every community. In the *consiglio* of Monte Libretti, the number attending ranged from as few as twenty to as many as thirty-seven, but no name is ever given to their meetings except the "public and general *consiglio*." A more restricted *consiglio* does not seem to have existed—no notes from its meetings survive, no lists defining its membership exist, and no control of such membership is mentioned in letters to or from the Barberini family. One village in the *stato* of Monte Libretti that seemed to have a restricted *consiglio* was Monte Flavio, where, in 1687, a request was made to the Barberini to allow the priors to name the "fifty good men" who would be eligible to participate in the *consiglio*. A variant of the general *consiglio* also existed in Nerola, where periodically the *consiglio* of the twelve, rather than the general *consiglio*, convened. But, even in Nerola, the general *consiglio* was very active, and about two-thirds of all the *consigio* meetings in Nerola in the 1640s and 1650s were meetings of the general *consiglio*. The widespread development of a restricted *consiglio* came later in the *stato* of Monte Libretti, during the 1720s, when lists of those eligible to participate in the *consiglio* began to be controlled by the Barberini.[3]

Not all of the daily tasks of governing the countryside could be handled by the *consiglio*, although it was the most powerful political institution within the village. A number of communal officers and employees had more specialized tasks. As was the case in Nerola, the priors of Monte Libretti were the executive officers who convened the *consiglio* to address the pressing concerns of the village. They had to secure the approval of the *consiglieri* for additional expenditures not covered by the communal budget. From the *consiglio* participants a *depositario* was chosen to handle village income. The village *consiglio* elected two *sindici* to put together the lists of the "suitable persons" (*"persone idonea"*) who would comprise the *bussola* from which potential priors and *depositari* could be chosen, thus making these village officials indirectly elected by the *consiglio*.[4]

The schoolteacher, who was one of the parish priests, received a portion of his salary from communal revenues. The priors carefully monitored his employment. The *consiglio* had more direct input in the selection of the surgeon and the physician, whose appointments were put to a vote in the *consiglio*. Within the city of Rome, the village sometimes retained a lawyer to tend to communal affairs, not only in the case of disputes with the noble family but also for entanglements with neighboring villages or private individuals who were the debtors or creditors of the communal government.[5]

The meeting records of the *consiglio* of Monte Libretti suggest the range of subjects that participants in the *consiglio* discussed. The *consiglio* addressed issues related to communal officials and employees (especially those whose service left something to be desired). Occasionally the village government was left with surplus grain, and *consiglio* members debated what should be done with it if it could not be sold, whether it should be dispersed by household or offered only to those unable to work. Shortages of grain or oil within the village were also a concern for the *consiglio*. Disputes with the Barberini family were subject to debate in the *consiglio*, although such controversies were relatively rare in Monte Libretti. During the 1670s *consiglieri* there discussed controversies between the noble family and the village on only three occasions, whereas in Nerola such conflicts were debated at thirteen different *consiglio* meetings between the mid-1640s and mid-1650s.[6]

Local institutions and individuals approached the *consiglio* regularly for financial support. Priests asked for donations for the parish church and the local confraternity of San Nicola requested sponsorship of the festivities for the patron saint's feast day. The communal government regularly paid the cost of providing the village with a Lenten preacher, although how such money was to be raised was debated at *consiglio* meetings. A musically ambitious resident, Bartolomeo Simeoni, even approached the *consiglio* for a loan of 5 scudi for a trombone. When he could not make the payments on the loan a few months later, he volunteered to play for free for the village church for one year to make good his debt. Bartolomeo sweetened the deal by offering the services of his musician buddies along with his own, although he noted that the band would expect to be paid extra for special feast days. *Consiglio* members thought this was a good offer and accepted it for the "dignity of the church and the divine faith," as one *consigliere* put it. In February 1676, the priors suggested to the *consiglieri* that the commune spend 25 to 30 giulij on a drum for the schoolchildren to use to keep time while they practiced their dancing. The *consiglieri* also agreed to this small investment in the musical life of the village, provided the drum was purchased as inexpensively as possible.[7]

Acting within the *consiglio*, villagers of Monte Libretti could be patrons of the arts, financial supporters of the church and its activities, and charitable donors to the poor or the disabled in their own community (when the circumstances were right). These issues were relatively straightforward to address, while others generated more controversy. Many of the notes from the *consiglio* meetings are devoted to the problems that resurfaced without definitive resolution: keeping a physician and surgeon regularly working and living in the village; selecting those eligible to hold the office of prior or *depositario*; finding suitable renters for communal properties; and the refurbishing of the village bell (a project which took several decades due to various difficulties with materials, craftsmen, and cash). The *comunità* of Monte Libretti had economic assets not all the neighboring villages enjoyed, but these too could inspire lengthy debate in the *consiglio*. Monte Libretti owned an inn, but the terms granted to the renters for this property occasionally fostered intense disagreements among *consiglieri*.

These were the usual causes for controversial speeches and divisive votes in the *consiglio*. For some villagers, Barberini patronage provided a potential solution to these local concerns, although the Barberini could be problematic allies. When the Barberini spontaneously stepped into village affairs, they sometimes did so with different issues in mind. The task of the priors and occasionally, the *consiglio* members, was to turn the Barberini prince's attention to matters the villagers perceived to be most important, and to persuade the prince of the sincerity of their devotion both to their lord and to the public good.

Petitioning the "First Citizen" to Be
the Noble Patron of Monte Libretti

Sometimes what the villagers needed most was the financial and social prestige of their lords in Rome. Letters to the Barberini from villagers and the speeches in the *consiglio* indicate the areas of village life where the patronage of the noble family was most useful. Although surviving letters are few (only about thirty for the late seventeenth century), references in the *consiglio* record suggest more frequent contact between the villagers and the Barberini family than this scant epistolary evidence would indicate. In the few surviving letters the priors refer to themselves as the "vassals" or "most beholden servants" or "humblest sons" of the Barberini prince, whom they addressed as their "Most Illustrious and Excellent Lord and Most Venerated *Padron.*" Most of the letters were written in Monte Libretti and are in a ragged and at times illegible hand. A few were dictated in Rome, perhaps to a secretary or official of the Barberini family. Most of these letters are short, about one page. Almost all of them are from the priors, but a few are written in the name of the *consiglieri* or the "men and individuals" of Monte Libretti. Regardless of the status of the writer, all the letters address the prince in a gentle and deferent style, inviting him to intervene in a pressing matter or simply informing him of recent events (apparently as a prelude to requesting his intervention later).[8]

Even without their requests, Maffeo occasionally intervened in village matters on his own. One area of interest to him was the physical condition of the surroundings of his most important "allies" in the village, namely, the school and the church. On a visit to the village in 1669, he expressed his dissatisfaction with the room allocated for the use of the schoolteacher. He took interest in providing the church with a new bell, a decade-long project that became bogged down. He offered a modest amount of material support for the project, donating 85 pounds of metal for the 1,150 pound bell in 1674. At about the same time he donated a crucifix for the church. Occasionally princely interest in the physical condition of the church was actively cultivated by the archpriest. In March 1678, Maffeo visited Monte Libretti, and, at the urging of the archpriest, called the priors' attention to the many basic things the parish church was missing. Maffeo asked the villagers to address this shortcoming in the *consiglio* and suggested to them that they vote to offer additional support to the church from the communal finances. The Barberini patron urged the *consiglieri* to be better patrons themselves.[9]

Some *consiglio* members remained skeptical about the appropriateness of this suggestion, even though it emanated from the prince himself. Anibale Morgante suggested that since no one in the village had been notified in advance, then no more than the usual support allotted for the parish from the commune be offered (1 giulio per household, which was the "old practice" in the village). He also hypothesized that "His Excellency's concern over this detail was due to his being informed in a sinister way," implying the archpriest had misinformed the lord about the shortcomings in the church. The *consiglieri* unanimously voted to offer the archpriest the usual allotment of 1 giulio per household. A year later the archpriest again pressed the priors for additional money for the church. He suggested that they divert some of the communal money set aside for the feast of the Purification of the Virgin (February 2) to buy something "more necessary for the benefit of the church and the sacristy." The resolution passed, with the caveat that the parish priest was obligated to note the provenance of such items in the inventory (i.e., to note that they were bought with donations from the commune) and to call the donation to the attention of the sacristans.[10]

The *consiglio*'s contribution to the practice of religion in the village could be independent of the suggestions of their clerical and noble "superiors." *Consiglieri* focused more on ritual practices and a little less on the sacramental accoutrements of the faith. The *consiglieri* as a group were consistently supportive of the confraternity of San Nicola, who was the patron saint of the village. They met the expenses of the confraternity's trip to Rome for the Holy Year in 1675. When low participation in the confraternity threatened the celebration of the saint's day, members of the *consiglio* voted to pay 10 scudi from communal funds for the masses and candles to celebrate the solemnity. There were those, of course, who wanted to do more (Ottavio Pellone hoped the commune would donate money to the congregation every time funds were available) and there was one villager who wanted to do nothing at all, but for most *consiglieri*, support for the confraternity was a shared commitment. Similarly, the communal support for the Lenten preacher remained unwavering. It was only a topic of discussion when communal funds were insufficient to meet his salary. In 1674, when the failure of the Orsini to pay the interest on their loans jeopardized the funds for many basic services in the village, the priors informed the *consiglio* that no money remained to pay the Lenten preacher that year. One *consigliere* suggested paying the preacher through the levy of an additional tax by household, but his solution was only supported by nine other votes. Seventeen *consiglieri* voted against the measure and that year, it seems, no Lenten preacher came to Monte Libretti.[11]

Village participants in the *consiglio* had to pick and choose among expenditures for religious purposes, balancing demands in that area with other needs in the community. They too, like the Barberini, thought the refurbishing of the church bell an important expenditure, but the lengthy process required had to be managed amidst other dilemmas. To rebuild the bell tower required buying the house of one of the villagers whose dwelling stood in the way of the project. Refurbishing the bell also required the building of a small structure for the bell maker to work in, but he was willing to build the structure for free, provided the commune would cover his living expenses. While the villagers wrestled with the dilemma of where to raise the funds for the metal to recast the bell, Maffeo Barberini worried more about who would have the key to the room where the bell maker would be working. The first bell created was a disaster, visibly defective in the handle. The prince noticed it during his visit to the village in December 1673 and commanded that the defect be remedied, with the commune and the bell maker splitting the cost of its refurbishing. The villagers scarcely needed the prince to point out the problem with the bell; they had debated almost two weeks earlier in the *consiglio* how to negotiate with the bell maker. Finally, in 1674, the bell was installed in the church. "If it is pleasing to the prince," the priors wrote, they planned to install the bell and ring it for Easter.[12]

While the villagers still faced the problem of paying the loans taken out by the commune for the metal for the bell (Maffeo Barberini had not even provided a tenth of what was needed), the project was at last completed. The bell rang in Monte Libretti until March 1679, when it fell to the ground, and the villagers were faced with the prospect of starting again, this time with entirely new materials. Suggestions for raising the money were few, and the one adopted would scarcely produce sufficient funds to take on the project again. An alms box was put in church to collect donations to replace entirely the ill-fated bell, but as a communal project it seemed beyond their reach in the late seventeenth century, and the issue was never raised again in the *consiglio* in the 1680s.[13]

Villagers were more consistently worried during these decades about keeping a schoolteacher in the village, and occasionally sought the advice and financial support of the Barberini family to achieve this goal. The schoolteacher, or *canonico*, was a parish priest who was paid an additional stipend by the village commune to educate the boys in the village. The priors exercised considerable control over his services—they could terminate him at will, as they did in December 1662, when they discharged Don Aurelio for "the sake of the tranquility of this populace." The priors also exercised considerable autonomy in hiring new schoolteachers. After the death of the schoolteacher in January 1670, the priors hired Giuseppe Ricci. The priors replaced Ricci in turn in 1674 when he "abandoned" the school and "never wanted to open it again." They wrote to "various places" to find a suitable replacement, who "though young in years, was old in judgement and learning."[14]

The difficulties with the schoolteacher returned in the late 1670s. In May 1676, the conduct of Don Pietro Maioli was discussed in the *consiglio* because he had quit teaching before the end of his contract, inspiring complaints and "suffering in the village since the boys were forgetting the little bit they had learned." Later that same year, the schoolteacher vanished "without letting anyone know" of his departure, further inconveniencing the villagers by leaving them only one mass for Christmas. According to the priors the *canonico* was in the habit of taking his salary and disappearing for entire months. The priors, however, had two new possible candidates, one of them, interestingly enough, Giuseppe Ricci, whom they had wanted to replace two years before for not wanting to open the school.[15]

While the priors could hire and fire the schoolteacher, their letters to the prince sought his approval of their choices. Finding suitable candidates was a difficult task, and the priors saw Maffeo Barberini as a potential patron in that challenge. When Don Marco Romano died in 1669, the priors requested the prince to name a suitable successor, "to instruct our little sons, whom we want to become fearful of God." A month later when he visited Monte Libretti, the prince did more than suggest a successor, he ordered the priors to find a new room for the school. It seems that the school was held temporarily in a house normally rented to the physician, for which the community paid half the rent. The priors wanted to make this the permanent site for the school, but the physician refused and they could find no other physician to take his place on these terms. The priors requested the prince to write a *memoriale* ordering the physician to accept these terms. They pointed to the scarcity of houses as a reason for having such difficulty in providing a permanent room for the school.[16]

In addition to the problems with the school's location, the priors had difficulty paying the schoolteacher enough to inspire his loyalty to his duties. The village could afford a schoolteacher in the first place because Monte Libretti had some important properties it could rent, including the village inn, and some interest-producing loans, including one to the Orsini family that was supposed to produce 200 scudi per year in communal revenues. The latter was especially important in meeting the wages of the schoolteacher. Whenever the Orsini failed to make the interest payments, however, the salary for the schoolteacher was jeopardized. In 1663, the schoolteacher threatened to leave the village at a time when it was also without an archpriest. The *canonico* "would have already left if his charity and piety had not hindered him from leaving us like animals, without Divine help," the priors explained in a letter to Maffeo Barberini in 1663. The *canonico* Don Fammiano Fiammiani di Zinato wanted to leave because the communal investments from which he derived his salary "no longer produced any income." The remaining 30 scudi that the community gave him was not enough for him to support himself. In this financially strapped situation the priors "ran to the Clemency of [His] Excellency," requesting that the prince purchase the community's loan investments (the *censi*) for which it was no longer receiving interest payments. The prince ordered his secretary in Rome to "write a letter to the priest of Monte Libretti and exhort him to attend to the parish, and to reply to the *comunità* that we will do everything that it asks."[17]

The replies of Maffeo Barberini to the priors' letters, as well as his concern about the school's location on one of his rare visits to Monte Libretti, show that he recognized the centrality of the schoolteacher to village life. But the school survived primarily because of the initiative of the priors and the commitment of the *consiglio* to the hiring and maintenance of the schoolmaster. The priors worried about their "sons being lost" or their smattering of catechism being forgotten if the schoolteacher deserted his post. No *consiglio* debate or letter to Maffeo Barberini indicates any controversy over the expenditure, only anxiety about the absence of the teacher. No alms box was set up to raise the money for his pay. It simply had to be found and presumably it was. Maffeo Barberini was cultivated as a patron in this matter in the hopes that he might help find a suitable candidate (at a time when suitable candidates were difficult to find) and that he might provide the promise of financial backing to convince a restless priest to stay.

*The Prince as Mediator: Medical
Controversies in Monte Libretti*

A more frequent and controversial subject of debate was the hiring of the village surgeon and physician. The priors kept the prince informed in the hopes he would throw weight in on their side, in the event of a dispute over candidates. Those who summoned the Barberini to intervene in such scenarios demonstrated more respect for his role as mediator (biased in their favor, of course) than they did for the decisions of the village *consiglio*. Medical controversies dominated the *consiglio*, which had to approve the hiring of the physician and the surgeon. These offices were put on the agenda by the priors at nearly half of the seventy-two meetings that took place in the 1670s. In comparison, the schoolteacher's employment, although occasionally inconsistent, especially in the 1660s, flowed relatively smoothly in the 1670s and was the subject of discussion in the *consiglio* only twice during that decade. In both those cases the *consiglieri* made a unanimous decision. By contrast, when the physician and surgeon were discussed in the meeting, the *consiglieri* frequently disagreed about what should be done; about a third of those meetings resulted in split votes in the *consiglio*.

A number of issues complicated the hiring of the men to serve these roles in Monte Libretti. As was the case with the schoolteacher, the villagers did not seem to have a wide variety of choices among doctors and surgeons, and although dissatisfied with some people's services, they resorted to them again when they found no other candidates. Another issue fuelling debate in the *consiglio* revolved around the question of whether a physician, in addition to a surgeon, was even necessary for the village. Strained communal finances created difficulties in funding both salaries, and the physician could sometimes cost twice as much as the surgeon (80 scudi, as opposed to 40). There was, however, enough support for the presence of the physician in the village to keep the issue alive, even if it remained divisive.

Of these two communal employees, the surgeon proved to be more reliable. Records pertaining to him have survived in greater number for Monte Libretti and the neighboring village of Nerola. A contract between Marco Pangrazio and the village of Nerola in 1645 specified that Pangrazio, as "surgeon and barber," was required to tend to all the sick or wounded in the village of Nerola. He was also required to cut hair and shave the beards of the men in the village, and the manner of collecting the revenue for his pay was structured to reflect this aspect of his work in the village (men paid more than women in fees to fund his salary). Pangrazio was required to be resident in the village and to get the permission of the priors before he left the village.[18]

Nerola pursued the surgeon by offering him a salary based on a collection of funds made by individuals. In Monte Libretti, the surgeon was almost always paid a salary from communal funds. One surgeon in particular, Giacinto Bravetti, was frequently the village surgeon between the 1660s and the 1680s. *Consiglio* records and surviving letters to the noble family related to Bravetti's career provide important insights on the politics of medical care in the Roman countryside. Bravetti first appears in the mid-1660s during a struggle between the priors and some members of the *consiglio* over whether Monte Libretti needed a physician. As reported in a letter from the priors to the prince, Bravetti hoped to be the sole person employed by the commune to tend to the medical needs of Monte Libretti in 1665. Other villagers were also unconvinced that the costs associated with hiring a physician were necessary. The priors, however, were in favor of hiring a physician in addition to a surgeon, and they brought the matter to the attention of Maffeo Barberini, suggesting a way the commune might pay the physician's salary. Since the contract of the village organist had come to an end, the priors hoped to allocate those funds to hire a physician. The Barberini prince wrote his *auditore* in May 1665 to get more information on this matter. The prince thought the idea might work, provided the funds would suffice; otherwise, the commune would have to make up the difference. In June 1665, the priors were evidently sufficiently convinced that medical needs outweighed musical ones. They wrote the prince proposing that a physician from Scandriglia named Troilo be hired for 60 scudi per year. Their letter requested permission from the Barberini prince to call the *consiglio* to decide the matter, but it also noted that it was difficult to convene the *consiglio* at that time (probably due to the harvest, although this reason is not stated). In the interim, they hoped the prince would sanction their bringing the physician to the village without a contract. A letter from the priors at the end of July 1665 chronicles Troilo's inauspicious beginning as physician in Monte Libretti. He arrived in the village and immediately became ill "with a fever" due to the change in air. He returned home to get well, and then came back to Monte Libretti to resume the duties of his office.[19]

Some people in Monte Libretti were apparently less than thrilled to see Troilo. During the *consiglio* in which he was confirmed, arguments against hiring the physician were made by Giacinto Bravetti, the surgeon, who wanted to be "the only one to treat the ill" in the village, and the *canonico* Fabiano Fabiani, who protested losing the 30 scudi per year for the organist. Apparently Fabiani had accosted the physician the previous Wednesday and told him he would never be paid because he would never be confirmed by the *consiglieri*. Troilo, according to the priors, would have quit immediately if they had not assured him he would be paid for his short, preliminary visit. They encouraged him to wait out the *consiglio* until the *rinfrescata* (until more of its members returned to the village) at which time the prince could hear the different sides and resolve the question to his liking, meaning, according to the priors, that he would order those who disagreed to "tend to their own affairs" so that the community did not "lose a physician, especially during these terrible times, when it was scarcely possible to find someone for 100 scudi or more."[20]

Giacinto Bravetti apparently gave up the fight against the new physician and quit in November 1665. Anibale Morgante went to Rome at that time to find out from the Barberini what the community should do in this case. Bravetti's competitor, however, was apparently unreliable. By 1668 the priors were once again trying to replace the physician, since Troilo's successor, Felli, had left. An undated letter, probably from that same period, mentions the physician Felli. The letter informed the prince that due to the departure of Felli, the "poor Community" finds itself, "in the worst time of the year," abandoned by the physician who was going to Fara regularly over the last two months and spending the night there, something that the *consiglio* had explicitly prohibited.[21]

Felli seems to be the physician who drove the priors to reorder communal priorities. In a letter from July 1668, the priors explained to the prince that they wanted to take the money the community would have paid a physician and use it instead to refurbish the bell and the bell tower. More agreement could be found among the villagers at that time regarding divine rather than medical intervention. The *consiglio* found a new solution to the problem of securing a physician for the community by drawing up a list of individuals in the village who are obliged to pay, some more, some less, according to their wishes," in order to bring a physician once a week to Monte Libretti to treat the sick. Like the Nerolani in the 1640s, the Monte Librettians opted for a semi-private solution to bringing a physician to the village. Such a solution had limited success however, and the debate over hiring a physician with communal funds returned to the agenda of the *consiglio*.[22]

While a number of physicians came and went over the next two decades, Bravetti returned to Monte Libretti and remained its surgeon for many years. In the 1660s, he lost the fight to be the village's only health care provider, but he turned the situation to his advantage a decade later by insisting that Monte Libretti maintain a physician, and that limitations be placed accordingly on what he was required to do. In the mid-1670s the priors of Monte Libretti unsuccessfully pursued several physicians to help care for the sick in the village. Their efforts were complicated by the failure of the *depositario* to pay an outgoing physician his salary. Between the fall of 1674 and the summer of 1680, the village rarely had regular access to the services of a physician. Some physicians declined the office due to the pay; others promised to show up but never arrived. In 1676, during the summer and fall when illness was typically at its peak, the surgeon Bravetti managed the care of the ill alone. He petitioned the *consiglio* for extra money for what he regarded as his extraordinary efforts to care for sick of Monte Libretti. The following spring, he pointed out that there should be limits to what he was doing in the village. Specifically, he wanted to be paid more money to treat those injured in brawls or accidents. In the fall of 1677 (a year after his first complaint) Bravetti was still petitioning the *consiglio* for more money, in light of the fact he worked alone in the village during the especially difficult months when there were many "ill with fever, whom he assiduously visited every morning." (If Monte Libretti had a midwife who also dispensed medical advice and care, Bravetti failed to mention her.) Some in the village were not satisfied with his work in Monte Libretti. In a meeting in March 1679, Biagio Piergentile complained that Bravetti "badly served" the community of

Monte Libretti. Finally in July 1679, Bravetti was rewarded for his hard work earlier in the decade with a new contract offering him a 5 scudi raise.[23]

Giacinto Bravetti emphasized in his pleas the heavy burden he bore for the sick of the village during the summer and the fall, seasons when the topic of medical care in Monte Libretti was usually raised in the *consiglio*. Bravetti's vague reference to widespread illness ("the many ill with fever") in the fall of 1677 and the timing of most debates in the *consiglio* suggest the impact of malaria (or relapse into malaria) in the village. Harvesting in the late spring and sowing in the early fall sent villagers to lands at lower elevation in the Tiber valley, where malaria had been a recurrent, if not lethal, problem. If the physicians had access to the quinine promoted by the Jesuits as an effective treatment for the disease, the results would have been noticeable in the village, and the desire for a physician regularly employed and residing in the village was an understandable, if not an achievable goal. The choice between physician and surgeon in the village also intersected with the rising status of physicians vis-à-vis surgeons. Bravetti was clearly being pushed in the direction of becoming merely the barber and occasional assistant to the physician, rather than also the village blood-letter, and performer of "light surgery." Village politics were complicated by the declining status of the barber and rising expectations about what a physician could do for the villagers. Not everyone accepted that the physician, a relative newcomer to village life, was worth the cost.[24]

This hesitancy on the part of some villagers was probably related to the seasonal nature of illness in the village. At certain times of the year his presence was less necessary, and if communal finances were already strained, the expenditure probably seemed superfluous. As the typical ailments of summer and fall returned (malaria, and in August, probably also the plague) then the services of a physician became more attractive, and the necessity of having him reside in the village more important. What good was a physician if one had to go many miles to Fara to fetch him in the middle of the night? And would he not be as busy there during the same times of the year? In the neighboring village of Nerola, debates over hiring a physician were few, but when the issue was raised in the *consiglio*, the residency of the physician was the most important issue. In 1649, the Nerolani debated whether to accept a physician who insisted on residing elsewhere, but who promised to come two times per week and as often as called to the village in times of need. The villagers rejected his offer on the grounds that residency was an essential element of the contract. A couple of years later, at the urging of Cardinal [Francesco] Barberini, they relented on this requirement, provided the physician recommended by the cardinal came two times per week and agreed to stay overnight when necessary.[25]

As the priors of Monte Libretti noted in their letter to Maffeo Barberini in 1665, it was difficult to find a physician willing to serve and reside in the village for the salary the community could pay him. Not everyone agreed that having a physician resident in the village, paid from communal funds, was worth the cost, so some villagers eventually turned to contracting his labor for one day a week for those individuals within the village who desired (and could afford) such services. Even this private solution must have proved inadequate, since the struggle to find a physician to serve as a public employee continued to be a subject of debate in the *consiglio*. News of controversies related to health practitioners in the village reached the prince as late as the 1680s. In 1682, after the death of Bravetti (who, the priors eulogized, had "served the public with love and charity for twenty-seven years"), a particularly contentious meeting took place to choose his successor. Later Maffeo ordered a *consiglio* meeting at which the votes for the new surgeon be taken by secret ballot, an extremely rare practice in seventeenth-century village politics, and a sign of the clearly divisive place such decisions held in village politics.[26]

To secure the steady employment of teachers, surgeons, and doctors, the priors and the members of the *consiglio* saw Maffeo Barberini as a resource for ideas about potential candidates, or as additional "muscle" to convince hesitant candidates to stay, while the commune found the financial resources to meet the employee's demand. These were some of the most important reasons for the priors to pull the Barberini into village affairs. The priors hoped that noble involvement in the dispute over the physician Troilo in 1665 would overcome village resistance to their choice of him. In their letter of 1665, outlining their reasons for hiring him over the wishes of the surgeon and the parish priest, the priors clearly counted on the Barberini as a crucial ally in the struggle. As they recounted in their letter to Maffeo, Troilo would have left if they had not reassured him that the Barberini prince would pay his salary for his short preliminary visit. Their letter invited the Barberini prince to delay the potentially controversial meeting of the *consiglio* until the fall, when the prince himself could come to the village, meet the new physician and "listen ... to the parties concerned and then ... resolve the issues as [His Excellency] saw fit, and ... to command the aforementioned individuals to mind their own business, so that we do not lose the physician ... we rely for the rest upon your prudence and your justice." While the letter's closing suggests the priors' willingness to submit to the Barberini prince's "prudence and justice," the rest of the letter leaves no doubt about the just choice in this case. The "aforementioned individuals" refers not to the two opposing parties, but rather to those who oppose the priors' plans for Troilo's employment in Monte Libretti. "Minding one's own business" meant staying out of the *consiglio* debate if a villager disagreed with the priors on this issue. The priors' letter pointed to a clear role for the prince in the village: silencing those who opposed the view of the executive officers. Here was a role the noble patron seemed to suggest for himself when he issued edicts for the villages of his territory. In those edicts, including the important compendium of edicts related to communal affairs, issued in 1658, Maffeo Barberini reserved the right to interfere as he wished in village life, to add to the law "anything he deemed necessary." Those edicts refer to him as the "first Citizen of every place where he holds Jurisdiction." The peculiar term suggests the ambiguous role of a noble lord in the representative institution of the village, the *consiglio*, where each vote counted the same. The existence of a first citizen would suggest that one voice, even without voting, would be louder than the rest. The priors invited the Barberini to exercise these grand claims, to undermine, if necessary, the legitimacy of the *consiglio* to resolve long-standing conflicts in village politics.[27]

Private Interest Versus Public Good

In times of conflict, the priors had good reason to think Maffeo Barberini could be more than just a patron with desirable financial and social clout. He was the only outside authority who operated as mediator in seventeenth-century politics. Although an entirely new papal Congregation had been established in the late sixteenth century to monitor communal affairs (the Congregation of the Buon Governo), it failed to reach into villages under noble jurisdiction until its authority was extended in 1704. While Roman nobles and papal bureaucrats are typically viewed by historians as adversaries in the struggle to govern the countryside, relations between them were more peaceful in the seventeenth century than they had been in the sixteenth century. In the Barberini family the relations were as personal as the bonds between brothers: Maffeo, administrator of family fiefs, and his brother Carlo, cardinal and bishop of Palestrina, lived in the same palace in Rome and moved in similar circles. Although we cannot know whether difficulties in rural jurisdictions were subjects they discussed over dinner in the Barberini palace, it does seem that an exclusively competitive relationship between barons and papal bureaucrats needs reconsideration. By the seventeenth century, both regimes found much to support and reinforce in the other. Maffeo's edicts of 1658, for instance, cite the edicts of the Buon Governo, sometimes merely restating them, substituting the prince's name in the place of the Congregation's.

Although Maffeo's role in the village was more important than that of the Buon Governo, his edicts on good government emphasized many of the concerns of the papal Congregation. Such concerns were not always shared by the villagers. The thirty-one Barberini edicts of 1658 placed particular importance on the communal budgets (six edicts) and issues related to debtors to the commune (four edicts). The communal budget was supposed to assist the nobleman in monitoring village governments. Budgets were to be sent to Rome, and a handful seem to have arrived there. In Rome they were rewritten in a beautiful secretarial hand, signed by the Prince, and returned to the villages to be posted in the room where the *consiglio* met. Such oversight was scarcely sufficient to monitor communal affairs successfully, however, since so few of Monte Libretti's budgets arrived in Rome, and almost no seventeenth-century budgets exist in the Barberini archives for the other villages in the *stato*. The Barberini therefore relied on their traveling accounting emissaries to settle disputes about communal finances. They left behind more edicts that were to inspire village officials to be tidier and truer in their accounts. Special auditors went out in 1658, 1684, and 1699. The number of disputes about debts owed to the communes of the *stato* was very high, as the visit of Mario Callisto in 1699 illustrates. In every village of the *stato* there were fifteen to seventeen different disputes, except in the village Monte Flavio, which had twenty-nine pending financial controversies that Callisto tried to resolve.[28]

The Barberini understood the importance of the *depositario* in village government and tried to tie his work explicitly to the monitoring of the village budget. The few surviving copies of budgets for Monte Libretti contain addenda from Maffeo that instruct the governor to hold the *depositario* accountable for the income and expenditures outlined in the budget. The four budgets from 1662, 1665, 1672, and 1682 present a rather hypothetical view of village finances, in which the commune was always in the black, sometimes, as in 1672, ahead as much as 100 scudi. That year the *depositario* was reminded by the prince to pay off as many of the outstanding debts of the commune as possible. The Barberini edicts of 1658 explain in greater detail how the *depositario* should serve the village government, emphasizing his duty to keep good account books, avoid embezzlement, and pay papal taxes first, before all the communal funds ran out. Barberini edicts that discussed village officials in general emphasize the importance of putting people "good standing and reputation" in office and avoiding "debtors and vile, untrustworthy people of ill repute."[29]

The villagers were also concerned about the persons holding critical communal offices. Both the offices of the prior and the *depositario* received special scrutiny in the *consiglio*, where the debates about them had to do with perceived conflicts of interest. In 1678, for instance, one man picked to be prior was excluded because he worked for Maffeo Barberini, and two others were excluded at the same time because they were renters of communal property. Normally such conflicts of interest could be announced in the *consiglio* and alternates found. Some potential *depositari*, however, did not relinquish the office without an appeal to the noble family.[30]

In 1675, Simone Pellone's name was drawn from the sack of names of those eligible to be *depositario*, but he was already the renter of the communal general store or *pizzicheria*. Technically Simone should have been awarded the office, since his was the last name remaining in the *bussola*, but his rental compromised him as a candidate because no one was allowed to be both the payer and the recipient of communal income. While there was little disagreement about this in the *consiglio*, Simone himself took the matter to Maffeo Barberini. He related the *consiglio*'s reasons for excluding him and noted that the *auditore* had said that an existing edict prohibited him from being able to take the office. But Simone wanted Maffeo to confirm this local view, since, in Simone's opinion, renting the *pizzicheria* did not mean that he would be biased against the interests of the commune. The letter from the *auditore* that accompanied his letter suggested otherwise and noted that his nephew Giovanni Antonio Pellone, already in debt to the commune, probably would not be pressed by his uncle to pay up. (Not surprisingly, in the *consiglio* vote to exclude Simone, Giovanni Antonio did the village equivalent of abstaining, saying only that he would vote with the majority). The Barberini prince stood by the decision of the *consiglio*, probably because this was one area of communal practice where there was no dispute on the local level, although there is no mention of this aspect of the *depositario*'s office in the edicts of 1658.[31]

Appeals also went to the noble family if an individual who had assumed office refused to follow the rules associated with it. The *depositario* had to provide a security deposit before he could take office. In May 1671, the new *depositario*, Pietro Grifonetti, was late in putting up the deposit. When at the end of the month he had yet to offer this security, the priors convened the *consiglio* again, because "the majority of the people ran to his Excellency about the matter, and his Excellency said he should not be *depositario*." While the priors noted the need to pick new *sindici* who would make the list of potential *depositari*, they added the admonishment that on such a list should be only "suitable persons, so that no more disorders occur." But finding the "right people" evidently devolved into always finding the same people, as a comment made in the *consiglio* in 1679 makes clear. "Many lament that the office of *depositario* passes always among the same two or three people." A few months later the priors called for the *consiglio* to choose new *sindici* to select potential *depositari* for the *bussola*. Evidently, however, the process was less than successful, since the *consiglio* in August 1679 opened with the admonishment from the prince that he had heard "that among communal officials, there exist discords and rivalries, damaging and prejudicial to the public." Maffeo offered "paternal advice," which in this case amounted to telling the *consiglio* members to begin again the process of selecting those eligible to serve as *depositario*. While the *sindici* chosen at that *consiglio* meeting were the same ones that had been chosen in May, the list they drew up seems to have been more satisfactory to the "public" since, while other controversies continued in the 1680s, this one faded from debate in the *consiglio*.[32]

One issue that returned to the *consiglio* in the 1670s and 1680s was the debate about how the village government should rent the inn, a property that could generate between 30 and 50 scudi per year. First in 1674, and then again in 1680–1681, the issue inspired controversy in the *consiglio* and the writing of letters to the Barberini prince to intervene in the matter. *Consiglio* records and letters to the nobleman in the early 1670s and early 1680s reveal that some villagers thought Maffeo should play a more interventionist role in village politics. Despite his willingness to undermine the *consiglio* in Nerola, Maffeo, however, responded hesitantly and then negatively to such overtures from Monte Libretti, although his edicts reaffirmed the great discretion he should have in determining the law, and directing village government.

The first disagreement about the inn occurred in the early 1670s, during a particularly divisive phase of village politics. Typically throughout that decade about half of all the *consiglio* meetings ended in divided votes. Between 1671 and 1674, sixteen out of the twenty-four meetings ended that way. In 1674 alone, every meeting ended in a divided vote except one. That year many of the issues periodically faced by the *consiglio* in the late seventeenth century occurred in quick succession: The most important of which was the failure of the Orsini family to make interest payments on the money they borrowed from the commune.[33] A potential solution to the loss of one half the commune's revenue was to negotiate more lucrative contracts on communal property. At a *consiglio* meeting in October 1674, the priors unanimously passed a new rental contract for the inn. According to the priors, they had been approached by someone willing to rent the inn for 100 scudi for three years, but the potential renter wanted a total monopoly on the retail sale of wine in the village, meaning that no villager would be able to sell small quantities of wine (by the jug). While at that same meeting the selection of the new physician sparked acrimonious debate, the modification to the terms of the inn rental passed without discussion.[34]

Later in the month, however, some villagers presented what had happened in and after the *consiglio* in a more complex light in a letter to Maffeo Barberini. The protest letter from the "men and individuals" of Monte Libretti mentions the proposed rental of the inn for 100 scudi and the monopoly on the retail sale of wine. The protestors claimed, however, that the priors had added clauses beyond what the *consiglio* had sanctioned, specifically, an additional clause that the renter could charge as much as 8 quattrini per foglietta (about half a liter). After the meeting the priors raised the price by two quattrini "against the resolution of the *consiglio*." The letter protested this increase to the price as well as the clause that the renter of the inn was allowed to hold a monopoly on retail wine sales. "For this reason we run to Your Excellency in order to present the harm which will bring poverty; that chiefly many poor cannot help their families in need by selling a jug of wine in order to sustain their miserable families." The "men" claimed that this restriction on the sale of wine by inhabitants was the "first" time such a thing had happened and that the only thing gained from the contract was 10 more scudi per year in income for the commune. They implicate, in particular, the Chief Prior Valeriano Pasquale, who "has wanted to force this rental with great harm to the Public." The letter closed with the hope that "the supreme clemency of Your Excellency would address these and similar increases and damages done to the poor public." Maffeo's only intervention seems to have been writing to his *auditore* in Monte Libretti and ordering him to "hold off on any innovations" and to send the prince more information about the matter.[35] Each time Maffeo Barberini called upon the *consiglio* to debate or discuss an issue, his admonishment is recorded in the record. No such meeting appears to have been held.

The *auditore*'s letter defended the priors' action. He admitted that the *consiglio* vote had not included the clause about the price of the wine. The contract the priors drew up with the renter gave him the right to sell wine during the month of May for 8 quattrini and for 10 quattrini thereafter. Although the priors had added this detail in negotiating with the renter, they had followed the standard practices in order to find him, the practices described in the Barberini edicts of 1658. The *auditore* noted that the commune needed the inn rental— the Holy year was approaching, and the Orsini, after all, had not made good on their interest payments for two years. The village also had to raise the payment of the physician by 20 scudi per year in order to find someone willing to take the office. A letter from the priors reiterated many of the same points, admitting that "the people complained about the clauses" that fixed the price of the wine, but these were due to the poor grape harvest, which meant the renter would have to purchase wine at a high price himself to sell it at the inn. Without the clauses they would not be able to rent the inn for half the price, at a time when "for the maintenance of the community, it was necessary to increase rents: The Orsini would not pay them a quattrino and the physician now cost 80 scudi per year."[36]

The issues related to the inn rental were discussed again in 1677, when an outgoing renter complained about "the number of small wine sellers who provide drinks nonchalantly to villagers and to foreigners." The *consiglieri* were able to resolve the issue in favor of a monopoly on retail sales to foreigners, rather than to all the villagers. This created some difficulty in determining who was and who was not a foreigner, but it was eventually declared that anyone who worked and kept a house "open" in the village could be sold wine by someone other than the innkeeper.[37]

Even with this partial monopoly, subsequent renters still had difficulty making the rent payments on the inn. In May 1680, Francesco di Stefano was far enough behind in the rent that the priors proposed taking the keys back from him and finding a new renter, which they did. A month later di Stefano's successor also defaulted on the rent. By December 1680, Francesco di Stefano had returned as the renter. On March 4, 1681, the importance of forcing "foreigners" to drink at the inn was again raised in the *consiglio* and it generated new debate about who the foreigners were in Monte Libretti. The priors suggested identifying the "foreigners" as anyone who did not pay the *macinato* tax, but clearly this tighter definition proved to be too controversial in the *consiglio*, since the meeting concluded without a vote being taken, a very rare event in village politics.

A few days later Maffeo Barberini visited the village and was drawn into the decade-old question of whether the "public" was better served by individuals being able to sell wine retail to whomever they wanted, or whether the true "public good" was protected by raising communal income through more lucrative rental contracts that promised renters a monopoly on those sales. During his visit Maffeo Barberini ordered that a public *consiglio* be called regarding the inn's rental. A letter to him from two priors, Giuseppe Grifonetti and Petro Petetti, related their version of the events of this gathering on March 9.[38]

The issue at hand was whether Francesco di Stefano should be allowed to continue his rental of the inn in Monte Libretti, or whether the community should try to find a new renter. As far as the priors were concerned, and as His Excellency "was well informed," di Stefano was unqualified to be innkeeper. According to the letter from the priors to the prince, the "oldest and most judicious" men thought that the lease should be taken away from Francesco di Stefano and bids should be taken on a new contract. Yet a majority of those present thought di Stefano should continue. According to the priors they thought so because they did not consider the "obvious good of the public" or "the obedience owed to your Excellency."[39]

Against the wishes of the majority of the *consiglio*, the priors decided to dismiss di Stefano to find someone new. This was an extreme version of what their predecessors had done in 1674, when they modified the terms of the wine price in the contract. By taking new bids, the priors received an offer of 135 scudi for three years, and another of 150 scudi for three years. The priors communicated the disagreement within the *consiglio* to the prince because they wanted him to "have full information" about who voted against the measure so that "he can repress those who oppose the common benefit (*utile*) perhaps on account of private interest or passion." They therefore included a copy of the *consiglio* meeting, showing how each individual had voted. Despite the opposition of the majority of the *consiglieri*, the priors intended to draw up a contract the next day with the higher bidder, reckoning that "we will find favor with the will of Your Excellency, who, on account of his experience, has our benefit at heart."[40]

The priors' letter never specified the objections to the new renter, besides the reasons of "private interest" or "passion." They implied that the majority failed to show sufficient allegiance to the good of the commune, putting "private interest" (and the implication is money-making interest) before the public good. The priors call upon the prince to "repress the passions," as the historian Albert Hirschman would put it, a laudable, seventeenth-century goal.[41] The letter from the members of the *consiglio*, however, states the issues in different terms. The *consiglieri* objected to the new contract because it offered the controversial monopoly on the sale of wine to foreigners, in contrast to the terms offered to di Stefano, whose contract had allowed "each person to sell according to his will." As far as the *consiglieri* were concerned, the priors, in order to obtain 12 or 15 more scudi for the renting of the inn, did damage to the poor of the village. The villagers, they argued, could help the community on their own with the difference in the rental price. Most of these arguments echoed the protest letter of 1674, which had argued against the successful passage of the monopoly in the *consiglio* seven years before. In 1681, however, these arguments carried the day, with eighteen men voting for di Stefano's rental (no monopoly), eleven voting for a new rental (with a monopoly), and four men, sensing the divisiveness of the debate, hedging their bets by saying they would vote with the majority, making the vote twenty-two to eleven against the new contract.[42]

Apparently, the prince sided with the *consiglieri* in this matter, because a letter of March 21, 1681 to him from the priors indicates that because the provision against the villagers selling wine freely was taken out, no one wanted to rent the inn. As his "reverent vassals," they awaited his orders, letting it be known that as long as the villagers could sell freely it was difficult to rent the inn. They recommended, of course, that he sanction the price of 150 scudi and let them search for a new contract at that price, which would include a monopoly on retail wine sale for the renter. There is no evidence in the archives that Maffeo undid the majority's decision in this matter. This time, it seems, he did not even write for further information.[43]

The inn obviously cut into the village economy: What the innkeeper sold, the villagers also sold to neighbors, migrant workers, and passersby. Was the "public's" right to sell wine in these small quantities more important than the potential boost the monopoly offered to communal income? Communal income funded public goods, such as medical care, typically defined in the *consiglio* record as a "public" concern. But the protesters in 1674 claimed to speak for "the public" (especially the "poor Public"), while the priors characterize their position in terms of the economic realities of the commune; no interest payments from the Orsini combined with rising costs for the physician meant that rents from communal properties had to increase, "for the maintenance of the community." By the latter the priors meant the institution of the commune, and by extension the protection of the public that commune was supposed to serve. In the controversy in 1681, the priors equated their position with the "common good (or benefit)," (*utile Commune*) but since they capitalize the (misspelled word) *Commune*, it suggests that they are referring again to the commune as an institution. The priors dismissed the possibility that an opposing view might represent an alternate vision of the public good. Instead the opposition had to be motivated by their "private interest or passion." Those speaking for the majority in 1681 made no conceptual readjustments to the protest letter of 1674—except that in 1681 they noted the potential risk the priors posed to the institution of the *consiglio*—they declared the priors' actions "damaging to the consiglio and to the public ... and to the poor."[44]

The villagers had become enmeshed in a political situation in which neither their beloved *statuto*, nor their local customs, nor their lord could offer any definitive guidance. Deliberating the definition of the words the "public good" suggests the vitality of the village political community, but such debates are also potentially dangerous, since while they are raging they can tempt parties on either side to undermine the institutions that make the discussion of the public good possible in the first place. What did the villagers of Monte Libretti mean by the words the "public good"? In the *consiglio* record of Monte Libretti references to the "public" and to the "public good" are used in first lines of some *consiglio* meetings. Such prefatory statements explain why the priors called the village *consiglio*. The terms are invoked especially in reference to particular issues, suggesting that they were not merely part of a formula used for each *consiglio* meeting.[45] During the *consiglio* meetings the task of the participants was to offer their opinion on what constituted "the greatest benefit of the public." The *consiglieri* were asked to make choices that they "estimated useful and good for the public," especially in times "when the public [had] many urgent needs," usually due to a dearth of grain or oil.[46] The desire to provide the village with a physician or a surgeon is frequently cast in terms of "serving the public." The *consiglio* was called to ratify "in the name of all the public" the contracts made by the priors with renters of communal property, or with artisans who were doing work in the village. Within the institutional framework of village politics, the majority vote in the *consiglio* protected or served the public, thereby defining what constituted the public good.[47]

As we have seen, if there was a disjuncture between that majority's view and some vocal individuals in the community, the *consiglieri* often heard about it, either directly from the protestors, or via the Barberini prince who received complaints about political choices made by the *consiglio*. The purpose of the *consiglio* meetings was clearly to further village allegiance to the "Magnificent Commune of Monte Libretti," for whom decisions of the "greatest usefulness" had to be made.[48] Priors, *consiglio* participants, and anonymous individuals occasionally differed about whether what was "useful and good for the public" was the same thing as what was "good for the commune." These two constituencies were typically kept separate by the terms introducing the issues for the *consiglio* to consider. The absence of a physician, for instance, was a pressing matter because of the harm it could do the public, rather than because it posed an explicit threat to the commune as an institution.[49]

At the local level the public good was also defined as something only public institutions like the commune could accomplish. Even a number of individuals pooling together their financial resources were unable to bring a physician to the village. The solution was tried, briefly, in the late 1660s, but it did not seem to be a viable option, especially in an area where there was a shortage of physicians. If the village wanted access to a physician, only the commune seemed to have the institutional and financial resources to accomplish that. (Almost every vote cast in the *consiglio* was in favor of hiring a physician and surgeon; the disputes were primarily about whom to hire, and at what price). The protest on behalf of the poor defined a competing vision of the public good, one based primarily on the needs of villagers to have free access to the retail wine market, the part of the market sector where the smallest producers were likely to participate. Hence the appeal to the prince was couched in terms of defending the public and the poor, with the implication, in both letters on their behalf, that the condition of the poor would be of concern to the prince and of crucial importance to the *consiglio* as well.

Villagers evidently switched their position on these issues. Eleven of the men who voted for a limited monopoly for the innkeeper in 1677 returned to the *consiglio* to vote against it in 1681. (Five others did not change their position). In 1674 eight of the men who voted for the monopoly returned in 1681 to vote against it (four others who voted in both years supported it each time). One important variable seemed to be the status of village finances, especially in the face of the failure of the Orsini to pay their debts. The latter did not appear to be true in 1680–1681, leaving many villagers in what I suspect was the de facto position in the village, to leave the sale of wine without restriction, unless communal finances were in dire condition. Comments made in the *consiglio* in 1677 and 1680 suggest that the monopoly was very difficult to enforce, indicating that support for it in the village was weak.

The lord of the village, Maffeo Barberini, also had his own ideas about what constituted the public good. He was drawn into village politics both on his own initiative and at the urging of priors or individual villagers. In Maffeo Barberini's eyes, the public was best served when the "public tranquility" was maintained, or, conversely, whenever "disorders" were ended, or avoided altogether. The prince's contribution to the public, in this regard, was to offer "paternal advice" in order to end disagreements between communal officials or *consiglio* participants. The nobleman's concern for the public also encompassed basic local needs. He insisted, for instance, "that the People be served" by keeping the communal *pizzicheria* open. He was also petitioned by the *consiglio* for grain or oil in times of dearth, called upon to prove, by loans at least, his professed concern for the *popolo* of Monte Libretti.[50]

Both in the *consiglio* meeting and in the writing of the Barberini prince and his officials appear some familiar terms used in early modern political debates to describe the public. The public, in these two very different settings (aristocratic Rome and the village commune), was an entity in need of protection from dearth or from disease. In an anonymous letter to protest decisions made in the *consiglio* in 1674, the public is also described as the "poor public," to underscore its vulnerability to the misguided judgments of the *consiglio*. For Maffeo, the ideal public was a quiet one. Its fragility and its silence suggested feminine qualities, the extent to which it needed the protection of its wiser (and as far as we know) all male caregivers. Alas for the Barberini, the villagers found it easier to accept the vulnerability than the silence implied in noble ideals about the public. The politically motivated people in Monte Libretti complained a great deal. Priors or other villagers had the habit of dropping by the Barberini palace or sending letters when the politics of the village were not to their liking, or there was a question about whether the Prince's paternal concern for his vassals would be converted into a tangible good for the community.[51]

Maffeo hesitated to wade into this political quicksand. Frequently his entire intervention in such matters consisted of telling the *consiglio* members to follow the established practices and try again. Was it out of some profound respect for the institution of the *consiglio* on the part of the nobleman? Did he defend it better than the villagers who encouraged him to undermine it? In the neighboring village of Nerola, where Maffeo was in a decades' long controversy over hunting rights, he was certainly willing to force his will on the Nerolani, despite their insistence that his action ran counter to their *statuto*, to local practice, and to the majority in the *consiglio*. But in Nerola financial and jurisdictional interests were at stake for the nobleman. In Monte Libretti, Maffeo obvious disliked the disorderliness of village politics, but he was unwilling to tidy it if that meant usurping the role of the *consiglio*. Usurpation posed certain risks to the nobleman, and those were risks he would only run for very specific gains.[52]

Noble interference in village politics meant that the villagers were more likely to petition the lord for more such interference. But lords like the Barberini had what they considered to be sufficient contact with villagers. In a letter to the *auditore* in 1674, Maffeo Barberini complained that the priors of Monte Libretti had protested the posting of an edict prohibiting villagers from making "*pane casareccio*." While the Barberini prince awaited more information about the matter from his *auditore*, he had two pieces of advice for him. First, he was never to bother enforcing the edict, unless the renter of the Barberini oven in

Monte Libretti asked him to do so. Second, if the renter ever did complain, "He [the *auditore*] should drag his feet about enforcing it, and use every flattery [with the renter], in sum, we would like you to practice tolerance [and to] turn a blind eye, in such a way that in the future the priors will not come again before us with their complaints."[53] Maffeo simply wanted to be left alone unless a matter in the village impinged on his interests directly.

Maffeo's caution in Monte Libretti did strengthen the *consiglio* as an institution, an unintended consequence of the noble quest for solitude. Those who regretted the votes of the *consiglio* encouraged Maffeo to assume the role of the meddling "prince" implied by his own edicts. Despite the urging of the "poor" and later the priors, Maffeo did not undermine the *consiglio*, even when he was supplied with the requisite condemnatory adjectives that an evil prior persecuted the poor, or that the majority was moved by "passion" or "private interest" to undermine the public good. But in Monte Libretti, Maffeo left these difficult issues to the *consiglio*, a position that evidently shared wide support in the village, despite the attempts of some villagers to undermine it. His unwillingness to usurp the authority of the *consiglio* worked to the benefit of republican political culture in the village, but it may have infuriated the priors stuck with reconciling the villagers' desires for healthcare with the communal budget's deficits. Although absolutism appealed to the losing side as an occasional useful shortcut, the *consiglio* survived these attempted usurpations in the late seventeenth century. While far from achieving public tranquility, the majority succeeded in maintaining "the public and general *consiglio*," and ironically they did so with the assistance of the nobleman who was its worst enemy in the neighboring village.[54]

4

The Epistolary Ambush of Monte Libretti

How Nobles Met the Challenge of the Papacy in the Early Eighteenth Century

Crenellated tower of castello of Monte Libretti. Photograph by the author.

The Papal Congregation of the Buon Governo presented the greatest new institutional challenge to the Barberini governing of the *stato* of Monte Libretti. The noble family's old institutional rival, the village communes, remained by turns adversarial and compliant in the eighteenth century, with conflict dominating over deference as the century progressed. But the Buon Governo was a rival at the level of society where the Barberini thought they rightfully belonged as rulers of their fiefs, and this shaped how the noble family responded to its competition. The Buon Governo, charged with overseeing communal affairs, was over one hundred years old when Pope Clement XI (ruled 1700–1721), in the first decade of the eighteenth century, extended its authority in the countryside to the greatest extent it had hitherto achieved. He called special congregations to consider taxation on baronial lands and to extend the control of the papacy into the administration of baronial communes. He put the decisions of these congregations into action through the activities of the Buon Governo. The Congregation's purpose in the baronial communes was simple—to tax the wealth of the barons and to promote better accounting practices in the villages that would generate more revenue for Rome and prevent embezzlement of communal resources at the local level.[1]

The Barberini, by contrast, were at the nadir of their dynastic story. The family began to unravel in the late 1680s, after an astonishing seventy-year presence in Rome, including the remarkable papacy of Urban VIII and the purchase of prestigious territories that established them as one of the ruling baronial families. Following the death of Maffeo Barberini in 1685, the new heir to the family fortune, Urbano Barberini, tore his family apart by violent and spendthrift means. While Urbano was clearly the exception to the family's traditions of good management and interest in governing the countryside, as the primogenitor of the *casa*, he had considerable latitude. His mother claimed to be mystified by the disappearance of so much money; his brother, Cardinal Francesco Barberini, self-proclaimed savior of his *casa*, hypothesized nothing but disreputable destinations for the family patrimony squandered by Urbano. Family holdings in the countryside contracted as the family risked losing the very properties that secured their status as members of the baronial class. Not surprisingly, scant attention was paid to the governing of their fiefs in the countryside. The governing of the *stato* of Monte Libretti was particularly neglected as the Barberini struggled merely to secure their own financial survival.[2]

Cardinal Francesco Barberini's familial preoccupations contrasted sharply with the career of his contemporary, Cardinal Giuseppe Renato Imperiali, prefect of the Congregation of the Buon Governo from 1700 to 1737. While Francesco fought to save Barberini fiefs from alienation, Cardinal Imperiali, as head of an increasingly important bureaucracy, extended papal authority into baronial fiefs like those of Monte Libretti. Cardinal Francesco put his heart into protecting the estates bequeathed to his generation by his ancestors, and by the 1720s was able to return to the financial, judicial, and administrative details associated with such ownership. By then Cardinal Imperiali had spent twenty years building a bureaucracy free of papal nepotism that could take greater control of the administration and finances of communal governments, and extend papal taxation to baronial lands. Francesco had to work in a dynastic system in which the fate of a whole family could be placed in jeopardy by the misbehavior of a single son. Cardinal Imperiali's efforts helped solidify a bureaucracy that could better withstand the shortcomings of an irresponsible individual, a bureaucracy that could potentially challenge the seigneurial authority not only of Francesco, but of the entire baronial class of which he was a part.[3]

Francesco's brother Urbano's escapades and irresponsibility have been interpreted by most historians of the nobility as representative of the character of his class. By the time Urbano was tossing away family estates at the gaming table, the "inexorable gilded decadence" associated with Rome was more than a century old. Historians of the nobility and of the Congregation of the Buon Governo have argued that the advances of this congregation marked the decline of the barons' financial, administrative, and judicial control of their communes. In the face of a modernizing and centralizing bureaucracy, the absentee and erratic governing practices of the Roman nobles simply withered away. How could a floundering aristocratic family succeed against such an adversary? The chapter analyzes how the Barberini, having been immersed in a dynastic crisis during the decades of the Buon Governo's greatest expansion, finally addressed the threat it posed to their authority in the *stato* of Monte Libretti. In the 1720s, Cardinal Francesco proceeded haltingly, using methods from the seventeenth century, but by the 1740s, the family's new generation, Cornelia Costanza Barberini, and her husband, Giulio Cesare Barberini Colonna di Sciarra, undertook a letter-writing campaign to their officials in the countryside that was without precedent in the seventeenth century. As a result of the Barberini's "excessive" attention to village affairs, especially in the areas of interest to their bureaucratic rivals, the Buon Governo, the Barberini were able to retain their importance in many aspects of communal government, in contrast to what conventional interpretations of the nobility and the Buon Governo have hitherto asserted.[4]

While the Barberini and the Buon Governo competed to control rural tax collecting practices and financial accountability at the local level, villagers in Monte Libretti noticed their efforts, but remained skeptical of the relevance of either the taxes or the more carefully monitored means of collecting them. It was not due to lack of effort on the part of their "superiors" in Rome. Francesco cobbled together practices from the seventeenth century to meet the bureaucratic novelties of the Buon Governo. The next generation showed a whole new level of committed obsession to the matter of communal finances. Both illustrate the importance of such activities to the noble family, but it, like the bureaucrats of the Buon Governo had to contend, not only with each other, but also with the realities of rural life and competing notions in the villages about what it meant to govern fairly, not only tax successfully.

A Bureaucracy of Budgets

The bureaucracy Cardinal Imperiali commanded originated in a late sixteenth-century tax reform. In 1592 Pope Clement VIII eliminated the use of tax farm-ers (the *appaltatori*) to collect the numerous taxes and tariffs levied in the Papal States. He shifted this responsibility to the communes, and with the papal bull *Pro commissa* established a new Papal Congregation, the Buon Governo, to see that communes could adequately fulfill this function and that the "grave abuses" of communal governments came to an end. The Buon Governo, in name and in scope, was supposed to concern itself with "good government" and for the pa-pacy this meant that taxes both cameral (papal) and communal were properly and punctually collected, that communal expenses were kept within appropri-ate limits, and that communal resources were honestly managed and accounted for. Anything related to the commune was of interest, in some way to the Buon Governo, and from its numerous regulations it would appear that its authority extended into many aspects of rural life.[5]

During the seventeenth century, the Buon Governo had relatively little di-rect impact in the *stato* of Monte Libretti. The Barberini referred to its edicts in their attempts to regulate communal affairs, but the noble family played the more significant role in the village. It was not the case, however, that the Buon Governo had no contact with the communes of Monte Libretti. It received a letter from the commune of Monte Libretti in 1647, requesting a lowering on the *utensili soldati* tax and another in 1668 from the priors of several communes, including the six villages of Monte Libretti requesting debtors to the commune not be prosecuted. The baronial communes, like other communes, had always paid some papal taxes. The issue for the Buon Governo was increasing control of how those taxes were collected; forcing the barons to pay taxes on proper-ties in their communes; and regulating more carefully the accounts of com-munal governments. The Buon Governo's primary means of controlling these aspects of communal government was the yearly submission by each commune of a budget, but very few budgets from baronial communes were submitted to the papal congregation during the seventeenth century.[6]

Clement XI attempted to address these limitations on the powers of the Buon Governo by calling a special congregation in 1702 to investigate the baronial exemption from papal taxes. The special congregation concluded with a decree demanding that baronial properties be subject to the *sussidio triennale* as well as all other cameral taxes. The barons appealed their case to the Segnatura di Grazia but lost. In 1703, Clement XI called a second special congregation and placed Cardinal Imperiali, the prefect of the Buon Governo, at its head. From this congregation came the decree demanding visits to baronial communes by officials of the Buon Governo and new *catasti* (cadastral land surveys), which would include baronial properties. The edict of 1704 issued by Clement XI himself made it plainly clear that "baronial communes were under the jurisdiction of the Buon Governo in the same way as were the cameral communes."[7]

The able direction of the Buon Governo by Cardinal Imperiali helped turn the decrees of the congregations and the pope into action. Between 1704 and 1706 deputies of the Buon Governo visited 282 baronial communities (including those of Monte Libretti) where they described the state of local governments, noting discrepancies in their accounts and their tax collecting methods, and describing, more often than not, the poor state of communal record keeping. In Nerola the Apostolic Visitor Monsignore Pietro Paolo Testa (who was appointed to visit the Sabina) found that the communal accounting practices were "mediocre" and that the *catasto* on which taxation was based was "ancient," difficult to read, and the cause of disputes. He also noted some discrepancies in the way cameral taxes were collected, but since the commune's method was "always peacefully practiced, it was left in place, so as not to create a *novità* which would cause confusion."[8]

In Nerola Testa left behind twenty-two edicts that were to be posted in the place where the public *consiglio* was held. All the proposals and resolutions of the *consiglio* were to be recorded in writing. Record keeping—accurate, detailed, organized—this was the real goal of the Buon Governo and particularly of Testa's edicts. The centerpiece of the communal efforts, the umbilical cord that was supposed to tie the bureaucracy in Rome to the communal governments of the countryside was the *"tabella"* or yearly budget for which Testa left a model showing the required features and form (cameral income and expenses, *frutti di censi*, list of debtors, communal income and expenses, all balanced and legible). Once submitted to the Buon Governo it would be corrected, returned to the commune, and posted in the place where the councils met, along with Testa's edicts and other Buon Governo edicts. Any expenses beyond the agreed upon budget had to be approved by the Buon Governo.[9]

Testa's edicts also showed a concern with keeping better records for the rentals of communal properties, as well as of those individuals in debt to the commune, both of which were probably to help the commune pursue debtors more effectively. The other goal was greater accountability by communal officials, to be guaranteed in part by the tax collector (*esattore* or *camerlengo*) posting a security before assuming his office and by having his accounts reviewed by the auditor (*sindaco*) at the end of the year with the assistance of the governor and the chancellor.[10]

Apostolic visitors to communes were widely dismayed by what they observed in the villages of the Papal States. Testa found fault everywhere in the *stato* of Monte Libretti, and in each village he left a set of edicts on "good government," the core of which varied little from commune to commune. It is clear from his edicts and his commentaries, however, that he considered some communities worse off than others. In the village of Monte Libretti, for instance, he noted "the great negligence" in collecting from those in debt to the commune and "confusion in the books" on communal affairs. Testa left even more specific edicts about accounting procedures for the "capital" of the *stato* than he had for Nerola. In Monte Flavio, which must have seemed like the edge of civilization to Testa, he wrote

> the disorders I discovered there, are that they do not keep Books which are considered necessary for the administration of communal revenues [but rather] write confusedly: Income, *Consiglio*, Auditing, and other things without any Order, and all of this on account of a lack of individuals capable of such a business . . . [T]hey are negligent in collecting debts and for that reason there are many debtors of the community from whom it will be difficult to collect since the [debts] are so old; in extraordinary expenses, the Priors spend according to their own whim.

For Monte Flavio, Testa left edicts addressing these concerns, explicitly outlining the separate books to be kept for the different types of accounts, along with the rules and regulations similar to those of other communes.[11]

The Buon Governo's primary interest was in the expeditious collection of taxes, hence Testa's intense interest in deciphering the patchwork of tax-collecting methods in Monte Libretti. In the village of Monte Libretti, the salt tax was collected from individuals but the rest of the cameral taxes were paid from communal income. In Nerola, the situation was exactly reversed, with the salt tax being paid from communal income, and all the other cameral taxes paid by property-owners. In Montorio Romano all the cameral taxes were paid from the revenues of the commune, while in Ponticelli cameral taxes were divided among property-owners. In Corese the *macinato* was paid with communal revenues, and other cameral taxes were paid by property-owners, though "foreigners" and the Barberini claimed an exemption because they gave the *ius pascendi* on their lands to the commune. Such an exemption was under review by the Buon Governo in 1704. Finally, in Monte Flavio, the only tax was the *macinato* paid by individuals.[12]

Historians have located the tangible achievements of the Buon Governo not in its standardization of taxation practices, but in its breaking of baronial exemption of taxation. The Barberini's tax burdens in Monte Libretti during the seventeenth century were more complex than simple exemptions. Certainly where they had exemptions, the Barberini were determined to protect them. Urbano Barberini, for instance, argued in 1704 against drawing up a new *catasto* in the village of Monte Libretti, since "cameral taxes were not collected on the lands of those subjects," but rather paid from communal revenue. Urbano rightly characterized the nature of taxation in Monte Libretti, but local practices were a convenient protection for his interests, since he owned 50 percent of the land in the village. In Corese, the Barberini, along with the "foreigners," claimed to be exempt from paying taxes, so where they could, the Barberini hid behind other exemptions. In Nerola, however, the commune claimed in 1704 that the Barberini prince had always paid his share of the taxes. In that village Testa left orders that the noble family pay their taxes "into the hands of the Treasurer of the Province," probably to remove any possibility of the noble family dodging them in the future.[13]

The Buon Governo's attention to taxation made it a potential but problematic ally for the villagers, who were as little interested in paying taxes as the noble family was. But the Buon Governo's expansion in the countryside contained the possibilities for challenging unwelcome noble interference in village politics. The Barberini were able to intervene in the villages in part because they appointed and paid the governors in the *stato*. Governors were to be present at all the meetings of the *consiglio*. The Buon Governo edicts of the early eighteenth century reinforced this role, noting that the governor was required to be present at all public *consigli*, though as the Buon Governo edicts insist, "no one could be denied the liberty to advance matters useful to the public." But some Barberini governors present at the *consigli* did not so much guarantee liberty of speech as attempt to squelch it. In Montorio Romano the governor was said to have "impeded the liberty of the *consigli* when the interests of the Baron were involved." Some of his interference was probably related to the *macchie*, which the commune owned jointly with the baron and rented for 180 scudi per year. The *consiglieri* also reported to Testa that the prince used or rented the *macchie*, or woods "according to his whim." In Monte Flavio, where Testa had been exasperated by the lax accounting practices of village officials, he heard the protest that "[t]he current governor, in order to take away the liberty of the *consiglieri* has demanded the practice of taking votes in public whenever they relate to proposals which touch the interest of the Baron." If the Buon Governo could have turned such observations into effective reform of baronial behavior, and combined such reforms with the elimination of baronial demands to name those eligible to participate in the commune, then the Congregation could have been a powerful intermediary on the villagers' behalf. But these issues remained a peripheral rather than a central concern of the Buon Governo, whose main purpose, as revealed in the edicts of 1704, was to build a bridge of budgets between the villages and Rome, to ensure more organized and understandable communal accounts, and to pursue debtors to the communes more rigorously. During two decades in which familial and financial tangles curbed the activities of the Barberini in Monte Libretti, the Papal Congregation should have had an even greater opportunity to address the issues of communal finances, which were the real focus of the Congregation. By the 1720s the family was ready to tackle the challenges posed by the Buon Governo and village indebtedness.[14]

A Bureaucracy on Horseback

In the first years of eighteenth century, the Barberini seemed unlikely to meet the challenges posed by the expansion of the Buon Governo. After the death of Maffeo Barberini in 1685, his heir Urbano Barberini, his widow, Olimpia Giustiniani Barberini, and his other son, Cardinal Francesco Barberini Junior (1662–1738), sunk into a series of familial disputes over the dynastic and financial future of the family. Urbano Barberini was unreliable at best, dangerous on occasion, incapable of producing a legitimate heir after two marriages, and passionately unwilling to limit his love of spending long enough to rescue the Barberini properties his habits put into jeopardy. His mother, Olimpia, threw herself and her dowry into the mission of rescuing the Barberini from her financially destructive son, acting in consort with her brother-in-law, Cardinal Carlo Barberini, and her son, the Cardinal Francesco Barberini Junior. Olimpia had her own wishes as well, especially to tend to her daughters' marriages and to retain some financial autonomy from her sons. Cardinal Barberini accepted his mother's assistance, although he took a dim view of some of her actions and ideas, especially her belief that the family was a consortium of interests, rather than an absolutist regime. Francesco thought he as her son, knew best, and few Roman nobles ever preached that gospel as eloquently as Francesco.[15]

From the late 1680s through the 1710s, these dynamic personalities clashed over money and familial matters, with a number of years constituting significant blows to the family's seventeenth-century achievements. In 1699, the family was forced to sell Monte Rotondo, one of the first fiefs they had purchased during the reign of Urban VIII. In 1704 Urbano mortgaged the woods of the *stato* of Monte Libretti, about 50 percent of the entire territory of the *stato*. In 1708 the Barberini were nearly forced to sell the territory attached to the villa of Palestrina, the most prestigious fief of the noble family. Cardinal Francesco wrangled to save the territory by assuming the entire debt associated with it. Urbano's spending continued to threaten other fiefs in the 1710s. His unfailing commitment to draining the family dry during that decade must have infuriated the cardinal, since Urbano had, at last, with his third wife, produced a legitimate heir, Cornelia Costanza Barberini, born in 1716. But a legitimate heir was insufficient motivation for Urbano to reform his spendthrift ways. Francesco barely outmaneuvered him from the sale of Ponticelli, one of the fiefs of Monte Libretti, in 1720.[16]

Finally, in 1722, death assisted the determined cardinal. Urbano passed away that year, and with him gone to collect his divine reward, Francesco could at last definitively settle his brother's worldly debts. With dynastic troubles now under greater control, Francesco could turn his attention to the governing of the territories under Barberini jurisdiction, especially the communes of Monte Libretti. Their problems were diagnosed in terms already familiar to the cardinal: They were sunk in debt and at risk of "extermination." Francesco, who had worked so long to solve similar problems in his noble family, found a new outlet for his passion for balancing the world, one account at a time.[17]

Francesco had held the family's jurisdiction over Monte Libretti since the early eighteenth century. In 1700 Pope Innocent XII (ruled 1691–1700) gave Francesco the right to exercise criminal jurisdiction in the fiefs belonging to the Barberini family. With the help of his uncle Carlo, Francesco had himself named "economo" or "universalem administratorem" of the entire stato Monte Libretti in 1703, with authority in both civil and criminal jurisdictions. It was only the anarchy within his own family that kept the good cardinal from returning to the governing of the familial fiefs. Documents from the 1720s after the death of his brother demonstrate a Roman baron's keen interest in the good governing of his territories. Letters from the villagers and his officials, as well as narratives written in defense of Francesco's activities in Monte Libretti provide a clear picture of the way the cardinal hoped to govern Monte Libretti, as well as how such governing tactics were received by the villagers.[18]

Francesco's preoccupation during that decade was with the level of communal indebtedness in Monte Libretti. He claimed altruistic motives for his intervention: A "great clamor" drew his attention to this serious fault in communal governing, but the cardinal was doubtless aware of the importance such issues were given by his peers like Cardinal Imperiali, and while he was chasing the dilatory villagers, Francesco was also chasing the Papal Congregation that had expanded into his territory. But could one Roman baron, twenty years behind the work of his peers, hope to match the achievements of the Buon Governo? Initially he confined his efforts to directing the governor of the stato to find out why the communes were "reduced to such a deplorable state and subject to debts so considerable." The governor discovered that there were as many and in some villages more outstanding debts to a particular commune than the commune owed to the Apostolic Camera. Individual debtors had a variety of explanations for the presence of their names on the list of debtors. Some claimed:

> a payment on their debt was missing and demanded to see the *conto lungo*, others that they had put the money into the hands of the *Depositorio* and that he had never given them a receipt, still others that their debt was compensated by another account [of theirs with the commune] and others denied their debts completely.

The governor believed it would be necessary either to take judicial action or to take "some other extraordinary expedient" in order to sift through the complexities of the excuses offered in villages where everyone, and yet simultaneously no one, owed money to the commune. Francesco advised him to continue and if his troubles went beyond carnival, then the cardinal himself would go to the *stato* and take the "appropriate expedients to ward off the total extermination of his poor subject communes."[19]

The governor then prepared a more precise report on the matter by confronting each debtor who contested the record of his debts, and then approaching each depositor whom the debtor claimed to have paid. He also reviewed the notarized contracts on rentals and "made a *conto lungo* for each debtor to convince them that they owed the remaining sum and then by having them sign it, they would not have any more room to quibble." The governor also noted however (as letter writers to the Buon Governo on behalf of the villagers also admitted) that every debtor who requested postponement from the *consiglio* received it, and so were made "innumerable accounts, the majority of which were today uncollectible." After twenty years of "interference" on the part of the Buon Governo, the collecting of taxes in Monte Libretti had scarcely moved beyond practices utilized in the seventeenth century. Individual villagers and collectively the communes were willing to mortgage a future in which such debts might never come due. That was, after all, how nobles "paid" many of their debts. A change of papal regimes might also lead to the suspensions of the tax, or so they might have hoped in the countryside.[20]

All the great efforts of the governor, however, had produced little results, since he had to attend to both "the civil and criminal administration (*governo*) of the whole *stato* and every other ordinary and extraordinary need [of the *stato*]." Francesco turned instead to a method used by his "ancestors" and used by him in "the other communes subject to him." He chose another official, competent in both legal and communal affairs, and charged him with visiting the villages frequently, and writing weekly reports on his auditing activities in the communes. Francesco's primitive officialdom would achieve his goal of securing "the total relief of the communes" from their debt.[21]

Francesco hoped, in other words, to restore the communes to financial health by improving the system employed by his ancestors. His father, Maffeo Barberini, used such a system in order to audit the accounts of the communal governments and settle disputes among communal officials over finances. Even the wayward Urbano sent a special official to review communal accounts in 1699. However, in the intervening two decades, the Barberini presence in the fiefs had been much more limited, distracted as they were by their own financial and dynastic upheaval. Maffeo Barberini, after all, had more contact with the villagers than simply sending the occasional auditor. Francesco's generation had little interaction with the villagers of Monte Libretti up until the 1720s, and as a result, the villagers were particularly resentful of noble interventions in the collections of taxes. Since no agents of the Buon Governo had come to the village since 1704, villagers had been able to enjoy the neglect of both noble and clerical superiors in Rome. Playing one Roman authority against the other was a prudent strategy on the part of the villagers in the 1720s, and at a minimum could allow them to stall in paying their debts. Could the potentially powerful but generally remote Congregation of the Buon Governo be used to drive off the newly mended Barberini dynasty? Francesco himself acknowledged in his defense that, while three years of account auditing by his new official had scarcely caused a stir in the villages, his official's most recent efforts to collect probably prompted the protest in 1725, when, "on occasion of the recent fertile harvest, he gave the order that the debtors be harassed with a little greater vigor." This new effort probably provoked the appeal to the Buon Governo. Counting debts was fine, but collecting them was another matter entirely.[22]

In his new official, Domenico Camilli, Francesco had found an efficient and diligent protégé, who moved methodically through the village paper trails in search of debtors. Camilli had much in common with his employer patron, Francesco. He, like the cardinal, understood the world in terms of the trinity of God, casa, and good account books. He appreciated devotion to record keeping in literary and philosophical terms, as did Francesco. Francesco's governor had looked everywhere for someone of this caliber, "but, in truth, they are scarce every place outside of Rome." Since Camilli had practiced law for a few years in the *stato* of Monte Libretti, by temperament and trade seemed to be a perfect choice for Francesco's dream of "rescuing" the communes from their debt.[23]

According to the narrative in Francesco's defense written for the Buon Governo, the debtors began to pay, due to the labors and the travels of Camilli, Camilli's weekly communication with Francesco's official in Rome, and the watchful eye of the governor on his efforts. Unfortunately for Camilli, the villagers had a rather different view of his activities in Monte Libretti, especially his "pressing" of the debtors in a year of good harvests. An anonymous letter to the Buon Governo in September 1725, written in the name of the *"Popolo"* of the *stato* of Monte Libretti, complained about the encroachments of the Barberini official Domenico Camilli into the affairs of the communes.[24]

The successful collection of outstanding debts would have been viewed as a triumph by the prelates of the congregation, so the villagers were stuck with the dilemma of finding a legitimate fault with Camilli. The *Popolo* of Monte Libretti claimed that the "poor communes of the *stato*" were being overcharged by his review of their accounts and questioned his right to exercise the office of auditor. They complained that Camilli, along with the governor, wanted to charge 3 scudi per commune as recompense for their accounting labors. They also maintained that Camilli himself had no right to any such office, since he was in debt to one of the communes. He was accused of protecting his relatives, whom he did not prosecute for debt. The anonymous protestors argued that there was no reason for Camilli to pursue any debtors, since the village chancellor was responsible for collecting their debts. Amounts owed to the commune were also handled during the meeting of the *consiglio*, at which the *comunisti* called on the debtors to fulfill their obligations, and then issued those individuals a postponement if they could not pay at that time. This practice was probably common in the countryside, but disturbing to the officials of the Buon Governo, who hoped that more rigorous accounting practices would result in less dilatory payments, or at a minimum, eventual payment.[25]

To underscore the illegitimacy of Camilli's practices, the advocates for the *"Popolo"* emphasized both the poverty of the communes (*"le povere comunità"*) and the poverty of those he was prosecuting for debt. According to the letter, Camilli demanded a *caposoldo* or an extra fee from the poor, a charge which would allow them to escape paying their debts. This extorted fee was supposed to be earning him "hundreds" of scudi while doing nothing to decrease the debts of the community, since Camilli merely collected his fees and dropped his case against the debtors once he had his money. Aside from the obvious damage such practices would do to communal finances, the letter emphasized that there were no *caposoldi* which Camilli could legally charge, and the individual debtors of the community could not appeal to the Buon Governo "because they were afraid of being jailed." The anonymous authors of the letter appealed to the Papal Congregation to have Camilli removed and to have the money he had collected returned to the "poor."[26]

Was Camilli really an extortionist, a persecutor of the poor, a dishonest deputy of the Barberini family? The letter he wrote to Francesco Barberini in his own defense offered a rather different version of his activities in the *stato*. "That some people, for their own pleasure," his letter began, "want to send a petition to the Sacred Congregation of the Buon Governo, that [action] I am powerless to stop, but, as you have taught me, every person has the liberty to act in his own way, though he is always subject to justice for the approval or the correction of [those actions]." Camilli claimed that he found no other way to understand the accusations of those who said they were wrongly charged fees by his auditing of their accounts. The Barberini deputy argued that because "of the great negligence of the chancellors" in keeping track of communal affairs, he "had to find fault with everything," though he had tried to show, "kindly indulgence" with everyone. He reminded Francesco (in the same sentence) that for three straight years they had been auditing the communes "to put them in good order."[27]

"I confess before God," Camilli proclaimed, "that if I did not make a mistake in a calculation, then for offense or for malice, I did not seek to overcharge anyone, and may God use the same attention in the interests of my own Casa." As for his father's debt with the commune of Corese from the time he was prior in 1708–1709, Camilli claimed to have wanted to pay the debt to Salvatore Papi, whom Francesco had chosen as *Depositorio*, but according to Camilli, Papi did not want to be bothered by such a "trifle," since he had never pursued such a "scant sum" from any other debtor of the commune. Camilli had since forced his payment on the present priors, from whom Camilli had requested a receipt, which he included with his letter to Francesco.

In the report defending Francesco's actions in the *stato*, Camilli's activities could be justified as both right and necessary to the successful collection of taxes in the *stato*. The report admitted that the official (obviously Camilli) was to charge 3 scudi per commune, or a "scant recompense . . . that would not even cover the cost of his horse, besides the paper which would be consumed, the loss of many, many days, and the food at his own expense when he was away from his own house." A bureaucrat on horseback was not cheap, especially if he had to travel many times to each village in order to collect.[28]

Francesco's defense called into question whether the appeal itself came from the "*Popolo*" of the whole *stato*. According to the report, "In every commune there is a priest, or someone fearful of God, who knows the benefit that His Excellency wants to bring there and on account of this they bless God and concede gratitude toward the *Padrone*." Not so in Ponticelli, according to the report, from where, it hypothesized, the letter of protest must have come, being in name only from the *Popolo* of the whole *stato*. The lack of a seal on the letter was cited as another reason why the origins of the document were questioned.[29]

As regards the financial improprieties of the official, the report claimed that the *caposoldi* requested from individuals did not seem "unjust" considering that the governor and the chancellor did not labor "without their required recompense" and that it only had to be paid by the debtors in arrears. The defense also admitted that Camilli had owed a small debt to one of the communes, but used the debt to highlight the "negligence of the *comunisti*" on account of which "everyone more or less was a debtor" to the commune, adding that if such a fact was used to exclude someone from being an official of the noble family, then no one in the entire *stato* could have been found to exercise the office. Camilli, the report noted, had satisfied the small debt. As for the debts of his relatives, the anonymous author could neither "deny nor concede it," since he could not find them, but assured the officials of the Buon Governo that Francesco intended to "squeeze equally" all the debtors of the *stato*. That only the poor were being pursued was also refuted, since all debtors were being pressed to settle. In fact, Francesco, "seeing the obstinacy of the Debtors, has recently ordered that an Edict be posted with the names and debts of each Debtor, and the time allotted to pay the debt, otherwise they were to be threatened with prosecution." As for the claim that the Chancellor was able to maintain "the good order" of communal finances, the report called him a *paesano* "tainted with the same errors as the others."[30]

The officials of the Buon Governo could side with the communes, but "experience," the report claimed, "has shown us the contrary." "Despite the many cares taken by His Excellency with such rigor," went the rhetoric of the report, "it wasn't possible to achieve his purpose, though he hopes to do so in a little time, provided the [Buon Governo] will not impede what he arranged and he plans to continue subsequently." If Francesco's officials were allowed to proceed, the author of his letter promised no less than the end of all the debts of the communes of Monte Libretti to the Camera Apostolica.[31]

The records of the debts owed in 1725 were included in Francesco's report to illustrate the "depravity" of the situation. It is impossible to tell the origins of the debts from the list: Some individuals may have owed money at the end of their tenure as officials of the commune (as Camilli's father evidently had), others may have been unable to pay taxes, while some might have been carrying a debt from the rental of communal property. The levels of indebtedness for each commune varied from as much as over 1,016 scudi in Corese to as low as 156 scudi in Ponticelli (the village in which Francesco's official claimed to have found no God-fearing individuals). Except for Ponticelli, most villages had one or two very large debtors. In Corese, for instance, one person owed over 568 scudi, more than half the total amount of debts to the commune. In Montorio Romano the debt was over 640 scudi, but one person owed more than 420 scudi of it. If we exclude the largest amount owed in each village, the average amount owed by debtors ranged from 4 to 13 scudi everywhere in the *stato* except Monte Flavio, where the average was about 18.5 scudi.[32]

As for the notion that "everyone" was in debt to the commune, the list of debtors suggest that in some villages owing money to the commune was a common experience. In Nerola, which at the turn of the century had 108 households, 76 people were listed as debtors. In Corese there were 42 households and

69 debtors, in the village of Monte Libretti, 56 debtors and 90 households, and in Ponticelli, 20 debtors and 45 households. Montorio Romano and Monte Flavio were somewhat different.

In their letter to the Buon Governo, the advocates for the *popolo* had made no pretense of pursuing the debtors with the vigor that supposedly characterized Francesco's efforts. That the communes were facing "extermination," as was claimed in the Barberini report, seemed to be unknown in the villages, at least as far as the protest letter characterized local concerns. The system of bookkeeping described in that letter consisted largely of paying when one could pay, and receiving an "extension" for payment when one could not. Whatever the origin of the debt, it seems that the *comunisti* were inclined to look the other way regarding individual debt. The Buon Governo attributed this to bad bookkeeping and negligence, an interpretation confirmed by Francesco's report, stressing also the element of complicity and corruption so widespread that the debts were likely to remain indefinitely.

The reasons for the lengthy list of debtors may be less ominous than either Francesco or the officials of the Buon Governo believed. In villages where, by the Buon Governo's own reports in 1704, it could be difficult to find officials able to handle the books according to the congregation's specifications, some of the accounts may have been paid off and never marked paid (as the villagers claimed). Verbal agreements may have been sufficient in these small rural settings. Perhaps the *depositario* of Corese was justified in writing off a small debt like that of Camilli's father; it might have cost him more in paper just to write a receipt for the sum than the outstanding debt was actually worth.[33]

In the agro-pastoralism of this region, resources of rural people were often stretched to their limits, and survival required a creative juggling of assets, including land, family and immigrant labor, and livestock. Falling into or remaining in debt to the commune may have been a safety net used especially when the harvests were not particularly good (a situation implied in Francesco's comment that debtors should be pressed "with more vigor" when the harvest was a good one). Communal officials chosen by the Barberini (who could be considered a kind of "elite" on the local level) may have had more possibilities to abuse the system, given the nature of local record keeping. As we have seen, however, in Monte Libretti, Nerola, and Corese, the large number of debtors indicates that the potential benefits to such a system were rather widespread in those villages. In local terms, the supposed "extermination" of the communes due to their debts was perceived as less important than the financial difficulties of individual families.[34]

In contrast to the suspicious nature of local affairs, Francesco's defense portrays the cardinal as a responsible *padrone*, a landowner concerned, like the Buon Governo, with the good government of his fiefs. Its opening draws attention to this commitment: "despite his infinite cares related to the *cardinalate*, the Protectorate of religious, his Bishopric, and Abbacy ... [he] does not neglect to exercise every attention for the precise jurisdictional and economic adminis-tration of his fiefs, as is well known to everyone, and is not ignored by this con-gregation." Motivated by the "outcries" over the debt of the communes (which must have come from the Buon Governo, and not the communes themselves), the image of Francesco emphasizes the common opinions shared by both the cardinal and the papal administrators. Those values included the belief that knowledgeable individuals were difficult to find outside of Rome, that village chancellors were mere "*paesani,*" and that locals were united in a web of deceit to maintain the practice of permanent indebtedness to the communes. By contrast Francesco's officialdom offered careful monitoring from Rome, an emphasis on the importance of good bookkeeping, and a vigorous pursuit of debtors.[35]

Other features of Francesco's defense, however, assert the independence of his administration from that of the Buon Governo. In his account, the decision to select a special official to audit communal accounts is attributed to the prac-tices of "his ancestors" and his own administration of other fiefs. The report also concludes confidently that "experience" was the only sufficient guide to de-cision making in the villages, and that experience, the report implied, belonged to Francesco and his officials.

In comparison to that of the Buon Governo, Francesco's bureaucracy (though not without its own limitations) showed a clearer understanding of what was required to have an impact on village government. Debtors would be pursued, even if it meant pushing the costs of doing so on local communities. During the first two decades of the eighteenth century the Buon Governo did expand its reach into baronial fiefs, but it made insufficient provisions for ful-filling its own aims. While Testa's edicts outlined a detailed papal agenda for "good government" in 1704, few papal officials were available to repeat his trav-els to the villages, and evaluate what, if anything, had changed because of them. According to Armando Lodolini, in the early eighteenth century the idea of having "two perpetual visitors" crossing the countryside in an established itin-erary was proposed but never put into effect, and almost sixty years passed be-fore another papal visitor reached the fiefs of Monte Libretti.[36]

Although the expansion of the Buon Governo in 1704 has been inter-preted as a crucial turning point in the century-long decline of noble auton-omy in the countryside, a close look at Monte Libretti reveals, however, both the limitations of the Buon Governo and some of the less obvious adminis-trative assets of families like the Barberini. Family traditions of lordship pro-foundly shaped and inspired Francesco's actions. Rural properties were closely tied to the past and the future existence of the family. They inspired an intensity of interest on the part of Francesco, which papal visitors and bureaucrats would never be able to match considering the large number of fiefs under their administration. While obviously an "absentee" landlord, Francesco managed fiefs through an inherited bureaucratic structure that he further developed and improved. As the report defending his actions makes clear, being a good *signore* meant being a good administrator, the manager of an effective bureaucracy, which, in Monte Libretti, was more extensive and more permanent than that of the Buon Governo.[37]

But the officials of the Buon Governo were evidently aware of the strength of the administrations of noble families like the Barberini. At least one noble official was on the road in the fiefs, evidently loyal to Francesco, his patron and benefactor. In the case of the controversy regarding Domenico Camilli's work as auditor, the Buon Governo sided with Francesco. A letter from the *Popolo* of Monte Libretti dated 19 October 1725 restates many of the charges of the previous letter, and notes that in response to that first letter the Buon Governo had requested information from the *auditore [generale]* of the Baron, "who, being in favor of ... Camilli and the governor, did not provide any information at all." So the letter requested again the "suitable remedy," that is, "removing the ... deputy and the unjust burdens and expenses from this poor people who have no need of this so-called deputy, having their chancellor who has to keep the accounts of the interests of these communes." Three decades after the village controversies regarding his initial work in the 1720s, Camilli was still working for the Barberini as the auditor of communal accounts and occasionally facing some serious dilemmas in that role.[38]

The Buon Governo preferred the efforts of Francesco's deputy over the casual treatment of debt by the villagers. The administrative structures of Francesco's "ancestors" and of the old cardinal himself had proved to be a powerful match for the expanding papal bureaucracy. As a cleric and responsible *padrone* of Monte Libretti, Francesco's worldview was, not surprisingly, remarkably close to that of the Buon Governo. His letters to the Congregation stressed their common aims, and the overlap in those areas was real, not simply feigned by the cardinal. He was, after all, both a Barberini and a cardinal, and an individual who shared the ideals of good management that were an integral part of Roman culture. But would the secular members of the next generation of the family adhere more to his values or to those of the spendthrift Urbano? The tax burden demanded of the countryside by the papal government increased dramatically during the mid-eighteenth century, while the peasants continued to be recalcitrant in making tax payments, and, as it turns out, the next generation of the noble family was more determined than ever before to see that such payments were met.[39]

*Administrative Vagabonds
and Unreliable* Paesani: *Officials
in Service to the Barberini*

The generation following Francesco rivaled the cardinal in dedication and in-
novation in the task of governing the *stato* of Monte Libretti. Cardinal Francesco had a significant impact on who would succeed him in the Barberini dynasty. He disinherited his brother's legitimated bastard, Maffeo Callisto, and
named Cornelia Costanza the only heir, making the choice of marriage partner for her extremely critical to the family's future. During a childhood marred
by bitter custody battles between Francesco and her mother, she was married
to Giulio Cesare Colonna di Sciarra in 1728. He agreed to assume the Barberini family name after their marriage, along with all of the "honors, rank, titles,
privileges, pre-eminences and distinctions, dignities, and prerogatives," which
the Barberini family had ever enjoyed, "as though the said Don Giulio Cesare
were born of the true blood ... [of] the Barberini Family." The couple was to
hold all of the property jointly "to maintain their Family splendidly according to their rank." Giulio Cesare was 20, his bride Cornelia, 12. According to
the agreement between the two families, the oldest son would become the
"Prince of Carbognano" and inherit the patrimony of the Colonna di Sciarra
family, while the second son would take the title "Prince of Palestrina" and the
patrimony of the Barberini family.[40]

During the 1730s, Cornelia was obviously busy with childbearing (she bore
seven children in the first nine years of marriage). She was, however, officially
co-ruler of the Barberini properties, a status that created confusion among
some of the family's officials. Giovanni Francesco Ramirez, administrator of
the family fiefs in the Regno, wrote to Francesco in 1731 to express his confusion about how to address the new couple: Was he to write only to the *Signore
Principe* as the administrator for the Princess, or was he to write to the two of
them separately, or only to the prince?[41]

While the protocol of letter writing was easy to explain to his former officials, Francesco found it difficult to relinquish control of the fiefs to the young
Barberini heirs. Although the couple took formal possession of the *stato* in
1729, it took until 1732 for Francesco to relinquish control of the territory of
Monte Libretti. The accord stipulated that the revenue of various parts of the
stato was to belong to Cornelia Costanza Barberini: the *tenuta* of Monte Maggiore and Monte Calvo, the inns and "*passi*" of Nerola, Corese, and Monte Libretti, as well as the *sesta* on wine collected in the village of Monte Libretti.
Such revenues (only part of those of the whole *stato*) were estimated to be
worth 60,000 scudi per year. Although they might travel freely to all of the Barberini estates, the Princess (together with her *consorte*) retained the right to the

jurisdiction only of Monte Libretti's villages and lands. Everywhere else Cardinal Francesco remained the "administrator of the jurisdiction . . . of all the other effects of the patrimony." The *stato* was thus the first territory in which Cornelia Costanza and Giulio Cesare were the official governors. The outpouring of letters from Rome to the officials in Monte Libretti that began in 1733 does not merely reflect the enthusiasm of "new" owners without many other properties to manage; their interest remained intense and nearly continuous from the early 1730s to the early 1760s.[42]

Although Giulio Cesare and Cornelia Costanza were keenly interested in the governing of the *stato*, they were unable to control larger issues of taxation that shifted dramatically in the Papal States during the 1740s. During the first half of the eighteenth century the passage of foreign troops to and from the kingdom of Naples created enormous financial burdens for the cities and villages of the Papal States, which not only had to quarter the soldiers, but also had to pay the costs of their passage for decades. The wars of succession, especially the War of Austrian Succession (1742–1746), left behind staggering debts, which were barely eliminated before the arrival of Napoleon's troops at the century's end. Such expenditures gave new urgency to the activities of the Buon Governo in the countryside, where the burden of new taxes was finally fully extended to the barons. The expenses of war were to be met not only by the villagers, but also by the "most privileged" in Roman society, "barons and feudatories" who were required to contribute 12 percent and 4.92 percent, respectively of the revenues from their lands to the debt burdens of their communes.[43]

In the countryside the Buon Governo challenged the political position of the barons by continuing to interfere in the governing of the communes. The only mention of the Barberini in these edicts is the assessment of their tax burden and the way in which they were to pay it (either along with the commune or separately). They are perhaps indirectly suggested in the description of the secretary's responsibilities to be "diligent" in registering the letters of "superiors," but otherwise the edicts of 1762, like those of 1704, are based on the presupposition that the communal government answered directly to the officials of the Buon Governo. New taxes were levied, to be sure, but the ideas about their implementation in the countryside of Rome were sixty years old. In light of the pressing tax situation in the Papal States, the Papal Congregation was at last compelled to put them into action.[44]

In this respect the Buon Governo posed an even greater challenge to the Barberini family than it had in the generation of Francesco, when papal taxes were comparatively low. Once again, however, the Barberini were able to outmatch the efforts of the Papal Congregation. Like their uncle Francesco, Giulio Cesare and Cornelia Costanza were able to govern in consort with the Buon

Governo. Testy, of course, about their own tax burdens, they nonetheless shared many of the aims of the Congregation regarding the villagers and showed themselves far more thorough and knowledgeable about the villagers than the bureaucrats of the Congregation, who were forced to rely upon the Barberini family for the implementation of their policies.

How were the Barberini able to do this? Although they remained absentee landlords as their ancestors had been in the seventeenth century, Giulio Cesare and Cornelia Costanza threw themselves into the role in an obsessive way, without precedent in any generation of the Barberini family. From the 1740s through the 1760s, the co-rulers of the *stato* carried out a continuous literary assault on the *stato* of Monte Libretti. Between 1738 and 1761 they sent thousands of letters to their officials in the territory. To enforce the noble vision of the governing of the countryside, they could never really stop writing.

The recipients of this correspondence simply outnumbered and outdid the agents of the Buon Governo. Cornelia Costanza and Giulio Cesare relied on a network of functionaries, just as their uncle Francesco and their other ancestors had done before them. In the eighteenth century, however, Cornelia Costanza and Giulio Cesare expected their officials to respond to their demands with near religious zeal. The officialdom necessary for the Barberini's meticulous absentee lordship included many people, but the most important figures in their primitive bureaucracy were still the local governors (who were also nominally officials of the Buon Governo) and the *soprintendente generale* (who managed the revenues of the noble family). The governors were appointed by the Barberini for six-month terms. They insisted on picking the governors themselves, and they had many opinions about who the best person for the job would be, especially when they were facing difficulties in a village. Governors were thus closer to the family's administration than they were to the bureaucracy of the Buon Governo. They were considered by the Barberini to be more reliable than their assistants, the vice-governors. The vice-governors, as Giulio Cesare noted, were mere *"paesani,"* or natives of the villages they served, while typically the governors came from outside the *stato*. Vice-governors were supposed to be in attendance at every *consiglio* meeting, while the governor was allowed to skip when matters under discussion were not too serious. The two governors and the *soprintendente* were the main figures on whom the Barberini relied, although priests were also an important source of information for the noble family.[45]

The "general governor" of Monte Libretti was the clear judicial descendent of the *"auditore generale,"* who, during the rule of the Orsini family, had issued edicts pertaining to the whole *stato*. In eighteenth-century edicts the general governor's title also appropriately included the older term, *"auditore generale,"* since he had similar responsibilities to his seventeenth-century predecessor.

Given the increasing number of the noble family's demands during the eighteenth century, however, the responsibilities of the general governor tended to be divided between two people. In the 1750s, for instance, Antonio Pasqualoni issued edicts for all of Monte Libretti as *auditore generale*, but only exercised the office of governor of the villages of Monte Libretti, Nerola, and Corese. Assisting him in the eastern half of the *stato* was a governor with the responsibility for the villages of Montorio Romano (where the eastern governor usually resided), Monte Flavio (where the commune had to pay for his lodgings when he came to the village), and Ponticelli.[46]

As judges, governors served as preliminary arbiters of disputes in the villages and they derived their income from the exercise of justice. As they had done in the seventeenth century, governors also convened public councils and were in charge of keeping order during those meetings. The Buon Governo's edicts of 1704 reconfirmed this power and charged the governors in baronial communes with the review of communal records and communal budgets. The governors were also beholden to the noble family and received frequent correspondence and requests from them. Giantomaso Martelli, the governor residing in the village of Monte Libretti, was sent by Giulio Cesare in 1757 to gather information about individuals involved in a lawsuit with the Barberini. Such demands were not unusual, though by and large governors were supposed to remain in the *stato*, requesting permission from the Barberini before leaving their "*Tribunale*." When traveling to Rome, they could be requested to present themselves at the Barberini palace and speak with the family's officials and legal advisors. Such visits were essentially required, as Giulio Cesare hinted to a *soprintendente* reluctant to show himself at the Barberini palace, "One would think that you do not like to see the face of your *Padrone*, in fact you seem to flee it." The official in question was being thrown into the seemingly endless struggle between the Barberini and the villagers of Monte Flavio. He probably had good reason to avoid his *Padrone*'s face. There seemed to be no way around his frequent letters.[47]

The *soprintendente* was more exclusively a "Barberini" official, since he reported to them alone and was the ultimate authority of the noble family in the fiefs. His responsibilities were vast, and his income reflected his importance in the affairs of Monte Libretti. When necessary he oversaw the activities of the governors. Although his responsibilities were distinct from those of the governors, their powers and duties overlapped somewhat, especially during the absence of a governor, when the *soprintendente* assumed his obligations. The *soprintendente*'s primary responsibility was the maintenance and improvement of all Barberini properties in the *stato*, including their rights to pasturage, hunting, and certain seigneurial dues paid in cash and in kind. He was responsible for finding suitable renters for the Barberini mills, ovens, and inns, as well as agricultural and pasture lands. He informed the renters about the terms of their contracts and monitored their activities to see that they lived up to those terms. He also had to oversee the "renting" of individual villages, that is the renting of the rights to collect dues owed to the Barberini there. It was to the *soprintendente* that Cornelia Costanza wrote to complain about the quality of olive oil she had received, or his lateness in sending the bounty of her trout reserve during Lent, or the supposed stupidity of his choice for renter of the oven in Monte Libretti. He was to ensure that the best products of the *stato* reached the noble family's table, and that the rents owed to them by the *mercanti di campagna* who leased their lands were also punctually paid and fairly collected.[48]

Besides adhering to the basic Christian virtues, an official was supposed to demonstrate "diligence" and "officiousness" or courtesy in exercising his office. A Barberini official was asked to be ever vigilant in all matters related to the Barberini's interest. The Barberini expected their officials to do this by scrupulously following the noble family's instructions and avoiding the introduction of any kind of *novità* (innovations). Giulio Cesare expressed surprise that the governor of Monte Libretti had seriously considered the requests of the priors and other "grumblers" who wanted to change certain milling practices. A good official should be intimately aware of the issues involved in the business of the fiefs, but he was supposed to remain above the disputes that were a nearly constant part of rural life.[49]

Officials had to wade through a steady stream of requests and complaints pouring from Rome. In response to the official who had written to explain the pitiful quantity of game for Cornelia Costanza's table, she replied that the hunter's claim that the woodcock (*beccaccie*) would have been more numerous "if the gunpowder had been better" was the "usual excuse of hunters, who want to hide all of their own defects with the supposed defects of the powder." Giulio Cesare fretted over the low rent offered for one of the Barberini olive presses, and once sarcastically described a *soprintendente* as taking an eternity to comply with the prince's request. And so it went throughout the eighteenth century as the letters steeped in skepticism and complaints flowed from Rome to the officials and through them (or so the Barberini hoped) to the various corners of the *stato* where the family's interests demanded careful monitoring.[50]

The dilemma for the Barberini officials was more complicated than simply meeting the noble family's demands, endless as they must have seemed to the beleaguered officials. Both the governors and the *soprintendenti* were forced to deal with the contradictions of Barberini lordship in Monte Libretti. Barberini edicts referred to the "fatherly affection" of Giulio Cesare, while their letters reminded officials that harvest time was not the moment to "be charitable with the property of others" (meaning that of the Barberini). Officials were supposed to "maintain Baronial rights," while not "burdening the vassals any more than necessary."[51]

Ambiguity permeated the relations between villagers and the Barberini in Monte Libretti; inconsistencies punctuated the dialogue between noble ideals and village resistance. As the primary negotiators between these two worlds, officials were required to do the will of the noble family while living among the "vassals." Officials were often casualties in the contentious old regime, administrative vagabonds in search of a more agreeable village and a less demanding noble family. But wherever they wandered, it seems, they found the familiar preoccupations of an ever vigilant absentee landlord and the same uneasy relations between villagers and nobles. Rising papal taxes intensified the everyday political struggles in the countryside.[52]

Controlling Politics in a Land "Where Everyone Is a Debtor"

In a territory where everyone seemed to be in hock to the commune, the Barberini could be the biggest deadbeats in the land. They were easiest to squeeze for a one-time payment. In 1744, for instance, the Barberini had to pay 10 percent of the yearly income of Monte Libretti, valued at 13,160 scudi. But even in pursuit of the yearly taxes the Barberini owed in the villages of Monte Libretti, the Buon Governo could be a successful if plodding village ally. In 1704 the commune of Corese was in dispute with the Barberini family and with the "foreigners" in the village who claimed that they owed no taxes because they gave pasturage rights to the commune on their lands. Officials of the Buon Governo reached a decision in the case in 1758, requiring the Barberini to pay 766 scudi in taxes owed since 1704, and outlining the family's tax burden for the new taxes raised to pay for the passage of troops. This particular case shows the way in which the Buon Governo had become an important tribunal for the communes; through it, village governments were able to challenge the noble family and win, though in this case it did require over a half a century of effort, as causes like this were handed down in the village from one politically active generation of the villagers to the next.[53]

In the village of Monte Libretti the precise value of the Barberini's holdings were difficult to assess because the family had granted pasturage and gathering rights on its lands to the community in 1654. A public *consiglio* was called in August of 1761 to determine how to value the baron's tax obligation. From the *consiglio* emerged a "unanimous sentiment" that "they had to come to an honest tax, in a friendly way, so as to avoid any possibility of a dispute with their Baron Prince." The *consiglio* agreed to abide by the decisions of two deputies chosen to assess the tax burden: the archpriest Don Paolo Mazzetti and another villager, Nicola Cornacchia. They assessed the Barberini's yearly contribution at 35 scudi per year, which the family agreed to pay.[54]

Papal contributions to the wars of mid-century could scarcely be financed from the wealth of the barons (unless the popes were willing to push them to the point of rebellion). The labor of the common people of the Papal States sustained those distant (and to the villagers) largely unimportant conflicts. So the villagers' "ally" in the scramble against the noble family also forced them to a financial debacle in which they had no interest. Ample evidence to this effect was gathered by the agents of the Buon Governo when they returned to the villages in 1762, when apostolic visitors to the *stato* had to reissue essentially the same decrees their predecessors had issued almost sixty years before. Toward this end, another apostolic visitor, Monsignore Dentice, came to the *stato* in 1762 to survey the state of village affairs and to leave behind a set of decrees designed to rectify the most serious "disorders." As his predecessor had decreed in 1704, the edicts were to be posted in the hall where the *consigli* met, and "every year were to be read aloud in the public *consiglio*, so that the *comunisti* and the priors would not be able to claim ignorance of them." The regulations of the Buon Governo further elaborated some of the same features of good government described in the edicts of 1704. The apostolic visitor in 1762 reiterated that no expenditures of any kind were allowed, beyond those approved by the Buon Governo, without the explicit license of the papal institution. His budgets indicated the limits of communal expenditures, assigned tax obligations, and were intended as a model for the commune's future budget submissions to the Buon Governo. He carefully stipulated the duties and salary of each paid communal official (including the secretary, the debt collector, and the auditor) and described the trail of paper for which each official was responsible.[55]

While the edicts ignored the noble family's presence in the villages, the day-to-day functioning of village communal government was largely monitored by the officialdom of the noble family. The village budgets, for instance, which were supposed to go from the village to the Buon Governo and back to the village again, were passed from the Buon Governo back to the noble family. The approved communal budget of Nerola, for instance, passed from the Buon Governo to Cornelia Costanza, who then forwarded it to the governor, informing him to record it in the public records and to see that it was followed.[56]

Even after the expansion of the Buon Governo into the fiefs of the barons, communal budgets seem to have arrived in its offices in Rome only rarely. In the *stato* of Monte Libretti, the beleaguered Domenico Camilli triumphed over the initial opposition to his work and ended up securing many of the budgets and accounts of the villagers for the Barberini family. As *revisore*, or auditor of the communal accounts, he forwarded the budgets of the community to them.

Employees like Camilli provided continuity to the Barberini interference in village affairs. He was still working for the family as late as 1755, when it was acknowledged by Giulio Cesare that he was getting too old and would have to be replaced. The determined Camilli seems to have succeeded in mastering the details of the communal finances of the six villages, thereby helping the Barberini supersede the Buon Governo in this area. Half a century after his spirited defense of his own efforts, bureaucrats in the papal government admitted that no budget from the village of Monte Libretti had reached the Buon Governo since 1707.[57]

Camilli's loyalty to the Barberini and his success in securing the documents related to communal finances was doubtless difficult and probably dangerous work, since the amount of debt imposed on the villages by the papal government in the eighteenth century was staggering. The budgets of the village of Monte Libretti (for which there are still records for both the seventeenth and the eighteenth centuries) suggest the scale of the burden imposed. In the seventeenth century the village owed the papal government about 111 scudi, a sum basically paid from the revenues of the commune itself, that is, from the rental of communal properties, or from the interest the commune earned from loans it had made earlier in the century. By the eighteenth century papal taxes had now risen to over four times that amount, or about 468 scudi by the year 1762, 111 scudi of which was to pay off a portion of back taxes, and interest on loans secured from the papacy to pay some of the back taxes. The village of Monte Libretti, for instance, had a levy of almost 800 scudi imposed upon it in 1748, payable immediately, or payable by papal loan at 3 percent interest. The papacy attempted to mortgage the future of the villagers to the demands of war, especially the war of Austrian succession. Villagers remained skeptical about the value of such an exchange.[58]

By whatever inadequate means the villagers kept records, the shift in demands could not fail to be noticed by anyone involved in communal affairs. Many of the other older communal expenses had scarcely budged in value since the seventeenth century. Village revenues from communal assets largely remained stationary. But the papacy quadrupled its demands and left as few loopholes as possible when the new taxes were imposed. In Monte Libretti those taxes would have to come out of the pockets of the villagers, rather than from resources of its communal government. Accounting sleights of hand were apparently easily found, although it was the noble family, rather than the papal government officials, who noticed them. Giulio Cesare expressed astonishment that Camilli's village communal accounts for the year 1745 all balanced (expenses equaled revenues) and yet there were still large numbers of people in debt to the commune. In contrast to his stance a few decades before, Camilli evidently conceded that the communal governments followed the practice of granting "an honest deferment" to all the villagers who still owed back taxes to the commune. The villagers freely showed Camilli the list of their debtors, but they had no intention of collecting from them, and evidently even Camilli pressed them no further by the 1740s. In the fall of 1746, even Giulio Cesare admitted a partial defeat by conceding that anyone in debt to the communes should receive an automatic deferment of seven years. The villagers had failed to have Camilli ousted from his post, but their vision of handling debtors to the commune seems to have triumphed. The debts remained. The commune remained. The former, in contrast to Francesco's rhetoric, did not succeed in "exterminating" the latter.[59]

While throughout the mid-eighteenth century the villagers would try by a variety of means to dodge both the taxes and the positions in the communal government related to their collection, the Barberini expended considerable effort in seeing that the villagers fulfilled such obligations. They were diligent collaborators with the papal government in this quest, even if they, too, were defeated by the wily counter-strategies of the villagers. How did the Barberini think they could have an influence on communal finances, beyond the oversight of communal budgets? They attempted, where possible, to enforce the Buon Governo's edicts against allowing communal governments to spend beyond their budgets and they did this largely without the assistance of the papal government. Giulio Cesare issued his own edict in 1752 stipulating that any commune that wanted to spend beyond its approved budget had to request permission from him. Surviving copies of letters to the Barberini as late as the 1770s include requests from the priors of the villages of Corese, Nerola, Monte Libretti, and Montorio Romano to approve additional expenses. Such requests suggest that in the late eighteenth century the Barberini were playing a role in local communal finances which the Buon Governo was supposed to have assumed many decades before.[60]

The noble family and its officials were an important conduit of information between the papal government and the communal governments. Toward that end Giulio Cesare facilitated the publicity of papal edicts related to tax collection in his territory. The noble family charged their officials with publicizing the decisions of the Congregation. The officials of the Buon Governo relied on the noble family to provide it with information about a variety of issues in the countryside. The Buon Governo wrote to the Barberini in 1746 to secure a copy of a *consiglio* resolution from Corese regarding taxation in that village. In the case of a controversy over tax collection in Monte Flavio, papal officials turned to the Barberini for information. The particular communal official involved in that case seemed beyond prosecution by the papal bureaucrats until the noble family became involved. Almost any village controversy generating more than a couple of letters to or from the papal bureaucrats inevitably required the participation of the Barberini to bring the matter to resolution. This included the thorny problem of controversies between villages over their respective tax burdens. The village of Monte Flavio and Monte Libretti were involved in a number of such disputes, because of the frequency with which villagers of Monte Flavio migrated to work in Monte Libretti, sometimes residing there a considerable portion of the year.[61]

The Barberini did not shy away from interfering in the rough daily details of tax collection in the countryside, including the behavior of tax-collecting employees of the commune. The noble family believed that such employees did not generally work with sufficient diligence, but they also insisted that those employees not use violence against the debtors to the commune. Individuals who believed they were wrongly assessed by the commune petitioned the noble family to have their tax situation reconsidered and the Barberini charged the governors to devote themselves to that task. Debtors also petitioned the family when they believed they were being wrongly prosecuted. The problems in collecting papal taxes seemed as numerous as the taxes themselves, but the Barberini urged the communal officials to use the full extent of their authority. In some cases the noble family even encouraged imprisonment of the debtors, although this was an unpopular strategy in the village, and aligning oneself with it was bound to create friction for the noble family in the countryside.[62]

The Barberini occasionally offered their own suggestions to help the Buon Governo achieve its aims. In 1761 no one could be found in Monte Flavio who would take the office of *esattore degli Arretrati* (collector of outstanding debts). Given the daunting nature of the task in Monte Flavio (twenty-five individuals owed a total of about 1,212 scudi, compared to Monte Libretti's total debts of about 68 scudi at that time), Giulio Cesare suggested that the Monsignore Visitore increase the pay of the office in order to attract the "*Benestanti* to apply for the job," noting, however, that the person chosen should be "qualified." Cornelia Costanza wrote the governor in Montorio Romano in 1774 to ask him to carry out the commands of papal administrators, who had been trying to remove the paid employees of Ponticelli since 1765. She also responded to a request from the Buon Governo asking for more information about Giuseppe Petricca, who wanted to be exempt from serving as *montista* because he could not read or write and had already been prior the year before, "a great inconvenience and a great disadvantage to his own interests." In two weeks she had gathered the information from the vice-governor in Nerola, forwarded it to the Buon Governo, and communicated to Giuseppe that his request had been denied.[63]

Cornelia Costanza also willingly turned her fierce demands on her officials to the critical matter of pursuing debtors to the commune. In 1774 she expressed disgust with the way a governor had handled Giocchino Papi, secretary of the community of Nerola. Papi had refused to write up the list of debtors to the commune, an action that initially the governor had condemned harshly. But subsequently, according to Cornelia Costanza, the governor had refused to take adequate measures, "showing himself to be a good-for-nothing, who did not know how to avail himself either of his own authority or the superior authority assigned to him by the Buon Governo." She later discovered that the governor had written one letter to her criticizing various actions of the same secretary, while writing another letter shortly thereafter to the Buon Governo praising the way Papi exercised his office. "Which of these two reports is true?" she wondered to her official, advising him to be more "cautious and circumspect in his future communications."[64]

The Buon Governo relied on the Barberini and their officials for assistance in implementing papal financial policies in village government. The Congregation also benefited from the information the noble family supplied about various individuals and events in the villages. The Barberini also used the Buon Governo's information to perform similar checks on their own knowledge. Both bureaucrats and nobles shared a suspicion of villagers and both were heavily dependent on the help of local officials like the governors. However, by virtue of their extensive correspondence and relentlessness in dealing with their own functionaries, the Barberini were the strongest link in a (rather weak) chain that bound the villages to the "outsiders" in Rome.[65]

Thus despite its efforts to solidify its authority in baronial fiefs, the Buon Governo never developed a bureaucratic structure independent of the noble officialdom that the Barberini had already put in place in the territory. The Buon Governo also never challenged the right of the barons to determine who would be eligible to participate in the *consiglio*, or to serve in the priorate or in other communal offices. This privilege, along with the Barberini's knowledge of their villages and their ability to achieve results through their officials, indicate that they were more than capable of maintaining their right to rule alongside the Buon Governo. In the day-to-day governing of the *stato* of Monte Libretti, it was the Barberini who remained more involved in village affairs. Baronial authority continued to be a powerful presence in Monte Libretti, where the Barberini did not hesitate to exercise their right to shape communal governments or to intervene in village affairs when they considered it necessary. Their behavior undermines the interpretation that the aristocrats were indifferent to, or inactive in, the governing of the countryside. But while the Barberini's actions in support of their jurisdiction or of papal policies were essential components of their governing strategies, allying themselves so closely with the taxing ambitions of the Buon Governo was bound to have an impact on the dynamic between nobles and villagers in the countryside.

5

*P*aternalism and Politics

Benevolent Adversaries, Antagonistic Patrons

View of the countryside from Monte Libretti. Photograph by the author.

The Barberini's activities in service of the Buon Governo's agenda provided an essential conduit of information between the villagers and the Papal Congregation. The other notable shift in the countryside was the ever-increasing activity on the part of the Barberini family in other aspects of village life. Such interference was promoted by the Barberini as an example of their paternal concern for their vassals. The enormous literary output of the family maps this noble worldview and its policies during the eighteenth-century, when lordship, as defined by the Barberini, became a near obsessive concern for the family. The dimensions of this lordship will be explored here not only in terms of how the Barberini imagined them, but also in terms of how they were received in the villages of the *stato*. The wide-ranging letters of the family allow us to gauge village response to the Barberini throughout the territory, a response that it is usually easiest to see for well-documented villages like Monte Libretti. The Barberini letters are an invaluable repository of information about the villages whose communal archives are now vanished, but which during the eighteenth century still existed, although they were not always accessible to the noble family.

During the early eighteenth century, the Barberini had been too concerned with dynastic troubles to pay much attention to the particulars of governing the territory. The villagers had been relatively shielded too, from papal taxes. By mid-century, taxes hit villagers and the Barberini at unprecedented levels, and the Barberini were more organized than they ever had been in intervening in village affairs. For the Barberini, the problems of governing Monte Libretti could be resolved easily if the villagers were willing to accept noble tutelage. By and large the Barberini had the same dream for all the villages, regardless of their particular circumstances. However, as the second half of the chapter will show, the reception of Barberini ideas about governing was far from positive. Even the village of Monte Libretti, which in the seventeenth-century had attempted to involve the noble family in the resolution of its disputes, became instead routinely more adversarial toward the noble family. The commune resorted to threats of lawsuits, even when its dwindling assets (burdened with new tax payments) left the villagers unable to continue their disputes with the Barberini in papal courts.

Populations were also rising in the countryside, and thus the agrarian and pastoral economies were facing new strains, at a time when the Barberini and the villagers were becoming more meticulous about exploiting the *stato*'s resources in order to pay those taxes. The two communal governments that made the most trouble for the noble family, Monte Libretti and Monte Flavio, also faced the greatest population increase during the first half of the eighteenth century. This exacerbated the increasingly tense relations between the noble family and its vassals.

The Barberini promoted a consistent body of ideals about governing the countryside between the 1740s and early 1760s. Those ideals reiterated the noble benevolence that motivated the Barberini lord, but Giulio Cesare became a ruler who complicated and antagonized, rather than one who clarified and harmonized conflicts in the villages. Giulio Cesare's edicts idealized order and public peace. But increasingly in the eighteenth-century his vassals turned to minor political skirmishes, threats of judicial ones, the creation of new sources, and the everyday tactics of stalling to thwart the plans of the nobleman. The villagers never managed to rewrite the language of his edicts, but it is clear from his practice of lordship, that he had to take into account their demands, if he wished to rule effectively in Monte Libretti.

The Lord's Catechism

To assure himself that he was not merely the noble representative of the papal bureaucracy, Giulio Cesare expanded his ancestor's interests in the well-being of Barberini vassals. Such benevolent interest underscored the grandiose claims of the family as the pinnacle of rural politics. In tending to public order, the Barberini asserted roles and goals for their governing beyond their attention to the account books of the communes. Giulio Cesare had aligned himself with unpopular papal taxation policies and offered his services and those of his officials toward their collection. The repetitive declaration of his paternal tenderness seems to have been a compensatory rhetorical strategy during decades characterized by unwelcome interventions in village politics by the nobleman on behalf of the Buon Governo. Giulio Cesare emphasized that most rural problems were caused by the villagers and thus could be resolved if the villagers followed the Barberini's wise lead. Strict adherence to his edicts would allow the topsy-turvy power relations in the countryside to right themselves and remain in that good order ordained by God and dutifully maintained by the noble family.

In the eyes of the Barberini and their officials, disorder in the villages sprang from the same everyday evils that had plagued the countryside at least since the seventeenth century: gambling, wandering about aimlessly in the wee hours of the morning, singing at night, or indeed, singing in general. These were still a concern for Giulio Cesare and Cornelia Costanza much as they had been for her grandfather Maffeo Barberini. "With great displeasure," the Barberini prince heard that the "infamous vice" of card-playing was (despite all of the edicts of his ancestors) evidently still being played in "taverns and other local haunts . . . for money or for drink . . . for recreation or for conversation."

Damaging to "families and households," this dangerous entertainment was the source from which "most disturbances and homicides emanated," according to the Barberini edicts.[1]

Also still badly viewed by the Barberini and their ministers were the late night songfests whose participants wandered noisily in and around the villages. Such gatherings

> resulted in a great disturbance to the public tranquility not only because of the secret meetings, riots, and revelries that on these occasions commonly result from the wildness of some young ruffians, but also because of the evil quality and terrible content of these songs which frequently damage the reputation of honest youth.

More organized musical performances were nonetheless still a potential site for disorder, and Giulio Cesare insisted on their supervision by the governors. A group in Monte Libretti wanted to perform a *burletta* (comedy) in the fall of 1745. The nobleman charged the governor with prohibiting "even the minimum Disorder," thereby doubtless dooming the performance in the name of saving village decorum. Undaunted, the musical talent in Monte Libretti was back with the same request the following year, prompting Giulio Cesare to look for more information about the quality of the individuals involved—whether they were "peaceful" or not, scarcely the essential quality in a performer of *Comediole*, as they were called in the countryside.[2]

The Barberini, however, did not limit their proscriptions for rural society to controversial entertainments. They and their officials issued hundreds of edicts in the eighteenth century on matters related to noble revenues, proper agricultural practices, hunting, mills, and other noble monopolies, communal government, and public order. Many of the edicts issued by the ministers of the Barberini refer to specific letters and desires of the noble family: "as we have been strictly commissioned by the Most Excellent Princess" or "[i]n obedience with the orders given us by the Illustrious . . . Prince in his letter of the 29th of the last month." The Barberini stoically reissued edicts previously issued (sometimes stretching back decades), as though the willingness of Barberini predecessors to issue similar edicts and the refusal of the villagers' ancestors to comply would make anyone more likely to do so subsequently.[3]

Although the laws repeated earlier concerns, many edicts, especially those concerned with public well-being or cleanliness (as they were perceived by the Barberini), cast the intervention of the family in terms of "paternal tenderness." Seventeenth-century edicts had stressed the importance of maintaining peace and avoiding scandal, but they had few explicit references to this aspect of the relationship between nobles and villagers. Eighteenth-century edicts prohibiting the export of grain during bad harvests noted that the Prince "greatly desires to provide for the needs . . . of his subjects" or they referred to the "paternal care and vigilance of His Excellency . . . always attentive to the good supervision of his most delightful vassals." The vassals of Monte Libretti were charged in 1766 with keeping their streets free of garbage and human excrement, an edict inspired by the Barberini's "fatherly love for their subjects." Rooting out the "evils" of gambling and singing was cast in terms of the Barberini's "paternal zeal which is inclined primarily to procure the tranquility of [their] Vassals."[4]

Living and dead vassals came under the Barberini prince's paternal scrutiny. In the village of Monte Libretti he worried about the state of the sepulcher and wrote the archpriest to complain about the dead being removed too early from the graves, "producing an insufferable stench." Giulio Cesare also concerned himself with the state of the *pizzicherie* and slaughterhouses. The "miserable families of Monte Flavio" wrote to ask the prince to investigate the condition of those entities in the village, and such requests rarely went unaddressed by Giulio Cesare. Similarly the good functioning of communal ovens were a concern about which he frequently questioned his officials.[5]

Beyond hygiene Giulio Cesare was also generally concerned with how justice was administered in his fiefs. Governors collected their pay from the imposition of fines for judicial offenses, and the prince insisted on careful record keeping in their collection. Not surprisingly, Giulio Cesare paid the greatest attention to particular cases when such prosecutions involved villagers he believed had damaged his interests. He also followed some exceptional cases in the villages, such as the fate of a man jailed for rape. The nobleman was especially interested in how plans for his impending marriage to the victim were proceeding. He kept track of the case through his governor, and through the parish priest of Montorio Romano, where the victim resided. No surviving records prior to 1770 document how often the nobleman may have been petitioned by ordinary villagers for his intervention in their particular cases. Giulio Cesare's letters contain a few references to the lowering of penalties for grazing violations, and he occasionally released the prisoners (who must have been very few) in honor of Easter, or because they were being held for debt, usually to the commune.[6]

Relative to their total income from Monte Libretti in this period, the exercise of justice generated little profit for the Barberini. Elsewhere in Latium the situation was similar for other noble families. However, it is probably more accurate to think of the administration of justice in the fiefs not as a declining and insignificant noble revenue (and by extension, an unimportant concern for the nobility), but rather as an important signifier of their lordship in a time they were being challenged by the papacy, and as a means of inculcating noble values in the villagers. Edicts were the equivalent of letters to villagers, and villagers were supposed to register all the edicts from the nobleman in the *libro del consiglio*. No reply except obedience was required. Order in the villages was important in part because it made them more attractive to potential renters and to potential inhabitants alike. These practical advantages, along with what I would call the religious dimension of Barberini lordship, explain why (relative to its revenue) the Barberini still expended effort in the administration of justice in the *stato* of Monte Libretti.[7]

The "decline" of noble administration of justice in the countryside has also been substantiated by the transformation of the fortified castle from the center of noble power, with rooms for prisons and quartering troops, into a building used primarily for agricultural production during the eighteenth century. The two "*palazzi*" belonging to the Barberini in Corese were devoted to agricultural production and included granaries, rooms for chickens, stables, storage cellars, a store for selling flour, and an oven. In Ponticelli the "old" and the "new" *palazzi* both included storage for agricultural products. However, an inventory of the jail in the Barberini fortified castle of Nerola in 1756 described a structure of four rooms, one for the constable, a cell for prisoners, another tiny room, and a last chamber referred to as the "so-called secret room." Iron locks, wooden bars to block doors, leg and neck irons, chains, handcuffs, and the iron pillory in the courtyard indicate that the local jail was a functioning one. A description from 1770 also refers to prison cells in the village of Monte Libretti, where the *sbirri* had two rooms for their use.[8]

In the 1770s, Cornelia Costanza investigated the possibility of building another jail for the *stato* in Montorio Romano. Montorio Romano's "Palazzo Baronale" was evidently a simple two-story structure of a few rooms, with an attached courtyard and orchard. Here she evidently hoped to adapt some rooms for use as a jail, though it was probably intended as much for lodging the constables who traveled to the villages in the eastern half of the *stato* as it was for punishment. In the *stato* jails played an important but relatively minor part in maintaining law and order. This may explain why rooms in noble *palazzi* were often converted to agricultural purposes. Individuals were usually only detained there for grievous offenses before being shipped to the papal jails or the galleys or because they could not pay the fines or a deposit on the fine for the minor offense they had committed. Although imprisonment was called for in many of the edicts (especially the edicts that had been issued multiple times to no effect), monetary fines and banishment were more frequently used as punishments.[9]

The Barberini's "fatherly" rule of their (potentially) "delightful" subjects had a religious aspect recognized by the noble family and the inhabitants themselves. Requests for charity and the Barberini response to those requests were an important marker of the family's religious paternalism and another area in which they could extend their reach in the villages beyond the monitoring of communal finances. As was the case in the Barberini reduction of fines and penalties, noble charity in the villages was usually (though not always) given in response to the written requests of specific individuals. The noble family scrutinized requests for charity carefully, and they often responded to these petitions by sending ministers on fact-finding missions or by asking for more information from someone else they trusted in the *stato*. When Marcello Giorgi of the village of Monte Libretti wrote asking the Barberini for some oil to treat his painful gall stones, the Barberini asked the *soprintendente* to check and see whether or not the oil would be the appropriate remedy before they sent it. In 1746, the Barberini ordered their superintendent to tend to a man wounded while hunting in Monte Flavio.[10]

Requests from the villagers mimicked the interaction between the noble family and its officials, who exchanged goods and pleasantries of various kinds on a more frequent basis. Giulio Cesare was the godfather of the child of the governor in Montorio Romano. At the death of his *soprintendente*, Giulio Cesare had thirty masses said for the repose of his soul. With the daughter of his deceased vice-governor he exchanged a number of letters (death seemed to bring out the best in the nobleman). She asked him for advice about which of two suitors she should marry. She sent him wild plums and other agricultural products and wrote him to announce the birth of her son.[11]

Most other inhabitants had less frequent and less personal experience of the generous side of Barberini lordship, but charity extended to anyone was clearly intended to create a positive perception of the Barberini in the *stato*. Widows were the most likely individuals to receive some charitable donation from the Barberini prince. His letters contain lists of widows from a number of villages who petitioned him for grain at Christmas time. The noble family also responded to the requests of other villagers for food, especially during bad harvests. Communal governments wrote to request bread from the noble family, but even without such petitions, the Barberini carefully monitored the supply of grain and the production of bread in the fiefs, a responsibility with which, as we have seen, they had been charged by papal edict in the late seventeenth century. In June 1746, Giulio Cesare contacted the archpriest of Monte Libretti to enlist his support in distributing bread to the poor. In that same village, the Barberini prince suggested placing one villager in charge of all such efforts and approved the *consiglio*'s choice of the archpriest Paolo Mazzetti for the job. In Monte Flavio the nobleman's "charity" amounted to hounding the *consiglio* to see that it provided grain in times of dearth. Most communal governments were supposed to keep a small supply of grain to distribute to the poor in such moments. He also issued edicts to prevent the export of foodstuffs during times of famine, and he supervised closely the activities of bakers in the *stato*. Giulio Cesare ordered the baker to keep 10 rubbia of grain on hand at all times "per lo sfamo del Popolo." He added that in case "some family has need and otherwise would not have the means to have bread, I give you permission to credit half a quarto [of grain] per family, so they do not perish." The baker was required to obtain the grain from the office of the Annona for the "usual" price of 7 scudi per rubbio.[12]

Villagers and parish priests thought the nobleman should assist them in maintaining churches, and he frequently saw that he could further his own interests in doing so. In the case of Ponticelli, the church was in need of such profound restoration that it had to be completely reconstructed. A preacher who traveled to the village in the early 1750s called together the heads of households and urged them to restore the "wretched church." Those gathered pledged a small amount of money, and, as they put it, "our women and children to carry water and other materials for its construction, as well as our animals for the transport of materials." To their efforts Giulio Cesare donated a small structure of three rooms near the noble "palace" for the construction of a new church in 1753. The previous year the Barberini prince had also pledged a cut of wood from his lands at the request of the archpriest of Ponticelli, provided that the archpriest and the bishop could settle on the church's design. He took a personal interest in the restoration of some church interiors. He followed carefully the renovations of the parish church of Nerola, insisting to the archpriest that he was positioning the pew designated for the priors too far from the altar. Giulio Cesare was not concerned about the priors craning their necks to see (although he conceded that they symbolized "all the people"). He was worried that the governor, who "represented the Person of the Prince," was also to sit in that pew, and he needed to be seated at the front of the church where he could be seen by the entire congregation, rather than hidden in the back behind two pilasters.[13]

The Barberini also saw the provisioning of the villages with schoolteachers as a central aspect of their lordship. The presence of a schoolteacher in the village had long been important to the residents of the *stato*. Even in the mid-eighteenth century, with the demands of the papal government pressing harder upon communal resources, village records show that the villagers were able to meet this expense. So here, the Barberini usually could escape fiscal responsibility, but the noble family sometimes insisted on naming the schoolteacher, or they wanted at least to approve him. Giulio Cesare followed with interest a controversy in Monte Flavio over whom to select as the village schoolteacher. The schoolteacher was important to the nobleman because he was to work on the "edification of the people." The goal of education, as far as the nobleman was concerned, was to teach boys "their letters, basic instruction on our Holy Faith, and good manners." The right priest would keep the potentially dangerous skill of reading out of the archives and in the catechism books where it belonged.

Giulio Cesare recognized the potential benefits of such education for girls and offered a widow in Monte Libretti free lodging if she would run a school for the girls of that village. He insisted, however, that "she teach them all without making any distinctions between who was miserably poor, and who was well off."[14]

Giulio Cesare's insistence that the poor girls be educated alongside the well-to-do was part of a larger pattern of protecting the poor, especially poor women. When meddling in the collection of taxes, Giulio Cesare insisted that rich villagers should always pay more than the poor, and that men should always pay more than women. This was largely the way villagers saw the world as well, since the *consiglio* of the village of Monte Libretti typically embedded the same priorities in its resolutions. Giulio Cesare (like the politically active men in the countryside) derived part of his political identity from occupying this superior position vis-à-vis his vassals, especially his female vassals.[15]

The Barberini's attention to their obligations to the villagers was a reminder to the vassals of the gulf between their lords and their lowly selves. The Barberini prince thought that religious paternalism was a useful tool to bend stubborn *comunisti* to his will or to legitimate the demands he made in the edicts. The extent to which this was successful in the villages depended in large part on how cleverly the rhetoric was combined with other methods including negotiation, flattery, and dogged persistence on the part of Barberini officials. For the first time in the eighteenth century the Barberini consistently linked their lordship to "fatherly affection." This clearly left the villagers in the position of "children" and "social inferiors," but it also created greater ambiguities about the nature of their power in the countryside. Eighteenth-century lordship was more than the symbolic sum of its parts; it was certainly more important than the income derived from it might lead us to believe.[16] The Barberini clung to its responsibilities and the surveillance of communal governments, activities from which they derived little economic benefit. The religious paternalism of the Barberini surfaces again and again in various contexts in the eighteenth century. It was not an inherited role played occasionally by the family, but rather an interest more vital to them than it had been in any previous generation. In that lordship, boldness, deceit, Catholic charity, subterfuge, and good manners would all have a place.

Dreaming of the Well-Ordered
Consiglio: *Barberini Efforts*
to Limit Political Participation

The ideal view of an orderly village world expressed in the Barberini edicts extended to the village *consiglio*, where the noble family also hoped to build an assembly of vassals receptive to noble wishes. Any bureaucrat really interested in breaking the power of the nobility should have destroyed its right to control the village *consiglio*, when the reach of the Buon Governo was extended to baronial fiefs in 1704. But the Buon Governo left that power untouched. Hence the Barberini became more and more involved in attempts to control the membership of that assembly. They hoped for tranquil *consigli* compliant to their will. Whereas in the seventeenth century, Maffeo Barberini had paid sporadic attention to monitoring who was eligible for village offices, in the eighteenth century, the Barberini scrutinized such choices regularly and rigorously, rejecting candidates they considered ill-suited to the office.[17] In monitoring this part of village government from Rome, the Barberini relied on the knowledge of the local governor to help them select eligible office-holders, but the noble family often had its own strong opinions on these matters, suggesting that they were not merely fabricating their opinions about village politics, but were especially attentive readers of the political situation and the political actors in the villages. The diligence of Giulio Cesare and Cornelia Costanza in village affairs was not always enough, however, to produce the desired results in the *consiglio*.

The priors were especially important in local affairs, and the Barberini replaced the lists of eligible individuals about every three to six years, depending on the commune. In the village, selection of priors from the eligible lists was either by lot or by vote of the *consiglio*. In November 1761, Giulio Cesare wrote to commend his governor for "suspending the endorsement of the *consiglio* held by the commune of Nerola, by which was elected prior Angeloni, whom we regard as not well suited to participate in public affairs." The Barberini requested that the official merely suggest to the members of the *consiglio* that it would be to the noble family's "greater satisfaction and for the commune's greater favor, if instead of Angeloni, they elected Calloni, whom we heard had also been proposed." The insight that the villagers should be coaxed, rather than coerced into the noble's choice was by the early 1760s a familiar refrain in his dynamic with his vassals.[18]

The size of the village *consiglio* varied considerably throughout the *stato*, from as few as sixteen in Corese to as many as forty in Monte Flavio. Membership in the *consiglio* was usually for life, and the evidence suggests that such a responsibility could stretch across many decades. One important issue for the Barberini in controlling the membership of the *consiglio* was ensuring that no one lacking the noble family's approval participated in its deliberations. Drawing on the precedent set by "our uncle Cardinal Francesco" in 1724, the Barberini reminded local officials that approved lists of *consiglieri* were to be posted in the room where public councils were held and recorded in the book of public councils. Cornelia Costanza showed particular concern for controlling participation through these lists, which would mean that it "would be known to everyone who the *consiglieri* were, [and] others [especially those who are not of a certain rank (*ceto*)] would not intrude in the public *consigli*, so that disturbances do not happen, as have happened some time in the past." Later that same year she wrote: "we do not want others to be admitted in the *ceto* of the *consiglieri*, if they are not approved by us." What Cornelia Costanza may have meant by controlling the *ceto* is not entirely clear. The Barberini in various edicts and letters certainly placed emphasis on the importance of ownership of property as an indication of trustworthiness, defined more broadly as being "*benestante*" or "comfortably well off." *Ceto* for Cornelia Costanza seems to have had this meaning of social class as well as a more archaic meaning of assembly, or meeting, hence her second sentence: the *ceto* or meeting of the *consiglieri*.[19]

The impetus to limit the number in the public *consigli* seems to have originated in the communities themselves (in the case of Monte Flavio, as early as 1687), but Francesco also played a role in furthering this change in the 1720s. During the eighteenth century the village of Montorio Romano was the first in which Francesco attempted to limit the number of *consiglieri*. The wording of the edict claims that since the *consiglio* was not "fixed," it caused confusion, prompting the "public" to request that the Barberini limit the number who could participate in it. After consulting the general governor of the *stato*, Francesco called a general *consiglio* of all the heads of household, which voted to reduce the number of *consiglieri* to thirty. Francesco's decree stipulated that any decisions made by the *consiglio* had to carry two-thirds majority, and any replacements to the list would be made by Francesco and his successors. After Francesco's edict for Montorio Romano in the fall of 1724, the priors of Monte Libretti made a similar request for limiting the *consiglio*, and there too a general *consiglio* reached this same agreement. In an edict of October 1725, Francesco limited their *consiglio* to thirty fixed members. Nerola followed the lead of the other two villages, and its *consiglio* was limited by Francesco in May 1726.[20]

In this matter Cornelia Costanza and Giulio Cesare supported the policies of Francesco and continued to limit the *consiglio* to a fixed number of families. The results of this policy can be seen in the 1770s, a decade for which good records of who was eligible for local offices still exist. The majority of the men who participated or who had the possibility for participation in the local communal government shared the privilege with another person with the same last name. If we consider all the lists of the 1770s, including the lists of those who were recently eligible for the priorship but were now excluded (the *spicciolati*), it is clear that while no one family appears to dominate, there was a "core" of ruling clans in each village. In Monte Flavio fifty people were eligible for various offices, and forty-one of them shared a last name with someone else in the *consiglio* or on a list of other potential village officials. Among the forty-one who shared a last name, only sixteen different last names were represented. In Corese fourteen of the twenty-six individuals eligible for office had one of six last names; in Ponticelli it was fourteen out of twenty-five people who shared a last name. This pattern is most obvious in Nerola, where of the thirty people named for office, twenty-two shared a last name with another eligible person in the village and three others with another person also eligible for participation in another village in the *stato*. While a group of clans seemed to dominate local government in most villages of the *stato*, only in Nerola did one family seem to predominate over the others. Seven out of the forty-two people named as eligible or as recently eligible for office were members of the Papi family. A clique of about six to eight families (none of which predominated) characterized the communal governments of Montorio Romano, Nerola, Corese, and Ponticelli.[21]

The simple analysis of last names only suggests part of the story. As Renata Ago has shown for other areas of Latium, newcomers to villages often intermarried with local women, and ties between families tended to be created and maintained through women.[22] So in part the strong correlation of patrilineal names only suggests the surface of the interconnectedness of local "governing" families; extending beyond it are probably other matrilineal ties, perhaps stronger than the potentially loose kin associations suggested by a common last name.

The Barberini's insistence that tight restrictions be maintained in the *consiglio* might have fulfilled the noble agenda to maintain order in the countryside and to support the *"persone commode"* of the village whom nobles had considered the most reliable inhabitants at least since the seventeenth-century. Ironically it also reinforced a network of families, giving them greater control of the villages and a greater ability to challenge the noble family that had named them to their positions of power in the first place. Whenever the Barberini disliked the determination of a village to fight them on a particular issue, they continued to pronounce it (as Maffeo had done in the seventeenth century) the work of "a few." It was the noble family's attempts to control village politics that could have significantly narrowed its political base. As we will see in the village of Monte Libretti, however, participants in the *consiglio* behaved responsibly in their struggles against the Barberini, and when a matter of broad concern for the village was discussed, the attendance at the *consiglio* could easily rise to double the allotted number, without anyone bothering to note whether it was a general or restricted *consiglio*.

While clearly the nobleman hoped to exclude certain people from participation in the *consiglio*, desperate measures were becoming necessary to find villagers willing to hold the posts of treasurer, tax collector, and in some villages, collector of back taxes, an even more heinous job. Typically, the individuals who assumed the posts were chosen by lot from those deemed eligible by the *consiglio*, subject to the approval of the noble family. These jobs were particularly difficult in the eighteenth century, when papal taxes rose dramatically and the papal bureaucracy was becoming more insistent about their collection. In his efforts to get the villagers to fulfill the most problematic of village positions, Giulio Cesare faced many obstacles, and he was forced to make concessions in order to get the villagers to assume the unpopular positions in communal government that were related to taxes.

Beyond Tax Trouble in the Village:
Clerics, Shirkers, and Vanishing Archives

While noble edicts and control of village political participation was asserted in the name of public order, it no more adequately addressed the needs of villagers than did the Buon Governo's quixotic observation that better record keeping was all that stood in the way of village payment of taxes. The latter was to remain a recurrent problem for village *consigli* in the *stato* of Monte Libretti, as the evidence from the village of Monte Libretti clearly shows. Issues related to papal taxes were discussed at almost half the meetings between the late 1740s and early 1750s, rivaling the still controversial problem of providing the village with a surgeon and a physician. While in the seventeenth century the village had enjoyed relatively tranquil relations with Maffeo Barberini, their political descendants joined those villagers in the rest of the *stato* who had protested Camilli's work. In the village of Monte Libretti differences with the noble family proliferated and became more complex as noble interference intensified and as the demands for papal taxes grew.

However, some continuity with the politics of seventeenth-century Monte Libretti remained. The *consiglio* of Monte Libretti still sought the approval, if not the assistance, of the noble family in dealing with some issues. In the face of rising papal taxes, the *consiglio* contemplated selling one of its vineyards, and *consiglieri* recommended that priors write to get the nobleman's opinion on the matter. In a *consiglio* discussion about how to raise the money to repair the campanile, speakers acknowledged that they would have to get permission from the Barberini prince before liquidating one of the commune's loans whose principal could be used to pay for the repairs. Giulio Cesare was asked to approve additional expenditures for the same problem a few years later. The noble family was still asked to approve the renewal of the contracts of the village physician and surgeon. Before breaking the contract with the renter of the *pizzicheria*, the *consiglio* wrote to the nobleman to ask his permission to do so. Much of the time in *consiglio* meetings continued to be spent on solving everyday dilemmas in the village, in this case, including resolving whether the renter of the *pizzicheria* should have a monopoly on *salume* sales and be required to sell cod and pickled tuna.[23]

Other issues required more direct input from the nobleman, and he intervened more frequently than his seventeenth-century predecessors, with or without the request of the villagers. As taxes continued to rise, communal offices like that of the *depositario* became more difficult to fill. As had been the case with his seventeenth-century predecessors, Giulio Cesare was occasionally petitioned by an individual who took issue with the villagers' choice of *depositario*. One individual, for instance, complained that Francesco Grifonetti was chosen *depositario*, but he was already vice-governor. Giulio Cesare concurred that this was an unacceptable choice and demanded that the priors draw another name from their list of potential *depositari*. But willing candidates for the office were evidently getting difficult to find. Giulio Cesare recommended in 1751 that the communal government take bids on the office, and if that did not work they should make a new list of the "capable and well off" in the village and offer them 20 scudi to do the job, "as was usually done" (although I can find no evidence that *depositari* had ever been paid). The filling of positions related to the finances of the commune became a personal cause for Giulio Cesare. Concessions had to be made. Whereas he hoped to limit the total number of participants in the *consiglio*, he advised his governors to coax villagers into accepting the truly demanding offices of the village communal government. Noble coaxing was cheaper at the local level than having the *consiglio* cough up 20 scudi for the *depositario*'s salary at a time when communal finances were already strained. Even in the face of such monetary and well-mannered enticements, villagers hesitated to accept such offices. One musically talented individual offered to play the organ for free if he could be excused from all communal duties. Other villagers contrived different ways to dodge service. Financial positions in the communal government potentially placed the individual villager's own property in peril, since a failure in those accounts could fall personally on the office-holder. A villager could be stuck with the entire indebtedness of the village if he was not careful. The Barberini insisted that the governors address the evasive strategies and recalcitrance of the villagers, as an example from the early 1740s illustrates.[24]

Salvatore Barbetta resisted being appointed treasurer of the village of Monte Libretti. Giulio Cesare told the governor to "order him absolutely in our name to accept the responsibility of treasurer." Later Giulio Cesare wrote a letter to the governor's assistant, instructing him to tell Salvatore that taking the office was "an act of obedience" that he was obliged to do. When the resistant Salvatore refused again the nobleman wrote the governor to "force" him and to push the priors to get involved by impressing upon them the harm that would occur if this office was not filled. The Barberini clearly tried to rely on their superior position as lords to get the hesitant Salvatore to comply.[25]

Salvatore relented under Barberini pressure, although it had to be applied many times, and by the nobleman's own admission, such pressure might not be enough to keep Salvatore at his post. Writing in March of 1741, Giulio Cesare discussed the disrespect that one Nicola Venastra had shown the governor, "mistreating him with words," as the nobleman put it. Giulio Cesare cautioned his official that such an act was terrible for the official's "image" in the village and merited immediate "humiliation of this reckless person." The nobleman's governor "represented the Person of the Prince," as the nobleman expressed it a few years later. Hence an insult to the governor was indirectly an insult to the prince. The nobleman's official was compelled to address this affront to his honor. But, in this case, Giulio Cesare added, Nicola was the nephew of Salvatore Barbetta, who had at last agreed to be the treasurer of Monte Libretti, so perhaps the official could "let things go" this time and ignore the threat to his authority in the village.[26]

In order to persuade the villagers to accept his point of view and to assist him in securing social harmony, Giulio Cesare also relied on local priests. Some were apparently willing to work on the nobleman's behalf. The archpriest of Monte Libretti evidently promoted the nobleman's position in the *consiglio*. There the archpriest was involved in several controversial incidents in the late 1740s and 1750s, including the appointment of the village physician, still a source of tension in the eighteenth century. The rejection by the *consiglio* of a candidate for physician in December 1754 prompted Giulio Cesare (perhaps petitioned by some unhappy villagers?) to propose that the villagers reconsider the rejected physician's candidacy at a later meeting. The archpriest Mazzetti urged the *consiglio* to confirm the physician, as the nobleman evidently wished. The candidate did get more votes the second time around, but not enough to elect him. The requirement that the *consiglio* repeat the vote inspired a lengthy speech by Nicola Venastra, a clearly outspoken individual, who had insulted the governor earlier in the decade. Nicola critiqued the candidate's suitability, describing him as "my enemy, and the friend of my enemies" — certainly an undesirable quality in one's physician. (Luigi Palozzi dismissed Venastra's dramatic declaration as "nothing.") Villagers were finally able to agree upon a different physician at a later meeting, illustrating that even with the archpriest on the Barberini side, the villagers pursued their own choices.

The following year the controversy was over the hiring of the surgeon. The outgoing surgeon had been unsatisfactory because he had refused to cut the men's beards. In this debate, too, the archpriest took a leading role in the discussion, suggesting that the surgeon be decided upon before the *consiglieri* addressed what his duties should be. The archpriest's suggestion won the day, and rather than have the surgeon cut the beards, they agreed to pay him less and assign the job of cutting beards once a week to one of the *consiglieri*, Federico Pergentile. Federico was either rewarded for his skill with razors or he managed to stay far enough above village political controversies that they could let him cut their beards without fear that he might cut their throats. Later that same month, the archpriest again urged the *consiglieri*, at the prince's request, to reconsider the candidacy of a physician whose election was narrowly lost a few meetings before. Although Nicola Cornacchi opposed the reconsideration of the candidate since they had already voted against him in a previous meeting, and because Nicola had a long list of grievances against him, the second vote produced the results the Barberini prince had hoped for, and the physician was confirmed by the *consiglio*.[27]

Having had a taste of success with the politics of village healthcare, the archpriest continued to speak up at subsequent meetings that year, offering advice about how to elect the *perito* to estimate the tax debt of individual villagers and urging villagers to accept the prince's offer to rent his hunting rights in the land of the village, as the commune had done since the seventeenth century. *Consiglio* records identify the priest's statements as *"consultando"* or advising as opposed to *"arringando"* or delivering a speech or *"pleading"* a particular case before the *consiglio*. Still for one only *"consultando"* the priest was doing a considerable amount of politicking on behalf of the lord's interest in the village.

This would seem to support the interpretation that secular and religious hierarchies tended to reinforce each other, but elsewhere in the *stato* the priests' relationship to the *consiglio* seemed much more dangerous, according to clear evidence in Giulio Cesare's own letters. While he found some reliable allies among the village priests, he seemed suspicious of them in general and had rather deep animosities toward a few in particular. When his governor in Nerola was attempting to put together a new list of approved *consiglieri* for the village, Giulio Cesare suggested that he avoid "grumblers, clerics, and debtors to the commune," his triad of trouble in many villages. In the village of Ponticelli, Giulio Cesare was convinced that the archpriest absolutely had to be excluded from the village archive because he would change the content of its documents. A month after the first letter expressing this suspicion, Giulio Cesare again wrote to the governor, insisting that the priest be barred access to the archive. Finally, after pressuring the priors, the Barberini prince was satisfied that the priest would not be allowed to see communal records. The events of the 1750s made Giulio Cesare especially skeptical of priests, since in the village of Monte Flavio several priests were active in formulating justifications for the villagers' strike against the payment of seigneurial dues. Village testimony, the *statuto*, and other notarized contracts in the archive were especially important in rural resistance to the payment of some seigneurial dues. The Barberini were dependent on the content of village archives, since as Giulio Cesare himself noted "foreign notaries and chancellors" working in the *stato* "carried away their documents without leaving copies." Village archives were thus precious resources, especially in times of controversy, which, by the mid-eighteenth century, appeared to be most of the time in the nobleman's eyes.[28]

In a conflict over grazing rights between the Barberini and the commune of Corese, Giulio Cesare was never able to access the village records that might have facilitated his cause. The noble family wanted to pasture their horses in the lands of the village. Shepherds renting the pasture lands in the territory of Corese also became involved when they (along with the priors) removed the Barberini's horses from the area. The letters Giulio Cesare wrote to the *soprintendente* of Monte Libretti on this subject offer some intriguing ruminations by a nobleman on what it took to maintain noble rights in the countryside.[29]

At first Giulio Cesare appeared self-confident in the rightfulness of his claim. The *soprintendente* should have returned his horses to the territory, and presented the priors with the summons from the Camera Baronale, which had supported the baron's grazing rights in the entire territory of Corese. His rights were secure not only by his *Dominio* or lordship "over the pastures" but also "on account of *Jus Civico*, which," as he wrote, "without a doubt belongs to me as first Citizen." The Barberini prince ordered that his horses be returned to pasture and that anyone who might try to remove them be "jailed immediately, since it is not right that these priors administer justice on their own, against the Tribunals of Rome." The guards and the *sbirri* should be notified of the situation to "prevent any violence" that might occur.[30]

Giulio Cesare's insistence that his rights be honored by the villagers echoes the confident language of eighteenth-century edicts that refer to the "obedience owed from vassals." Such obligations were described at greater length in an edict of 1754:

> Every one of the vassals of the most Excellent and Illustrious Signori Principi Padroni ought to, in gratitude not only for the paternal tenderness that these [princes] have displayed toward them but also in fulfillment of their duty . . . to maintain with a certain exactness the rights belonging to the Most Excellent Camera [of the princes] in compliance with every law, human and divine.

Other edicts stressed the importance of "reminding everyone of the duty of the Faithful Vassal, who . . . must have at heart the preservation of the rights justly belonging to the Most Illustrious . . . Princes."[31]

In his disagreement in Corese, however, Giulio Cesare did not rely solely on the fanfare of his rights—especially since his horses had already been removed once (if not more times). He also sent the local governor digging for legal precedents that would support what were supposedly his rights in Corese. He maintained that "formerly, and up to 1683, the Community did not and could not sell pasture without the express permission of the Baron; this permission was asked and conceded only to pay for the *Pesi Camerali*" (papal taxes).

Giulio Cesare was convinced that the granting of baronial permission had continued after 1683, and the governor would surely find these permissions inserted into the *consiglio* books or with the records of the proceeds from the renting of the communal pasture lands. The governor was supposed to exercise some caution in examining the records in the communal chancellery of Corese. He should arrange his visit "kindly" requesting (*di buona maniera*) to see the books in question "under some pretext, in such a way that the priors have no knowledge of what he really wants." Once the governor found the necessary documents he was to note the date and "to think later about how to formally extract the information."[32]

The governor was apparently an unwilling accomplice. He suggested that the Barberini get an order from a magistrate to procure the records. The baron explained that they first needed proof of the existence and the relevance of the documents, and pressed the governor again to "use diligence" and "to do it without fear of any suspicion, relying especially on the authority given to him by Monsignore Dentice [the recent apostolic visitor to the *stato*], to oversee the interests of this community." Under this title he could easily ask to see the communal records to "describe in general the quality of these books." Why the governor hesitated to carry out the Barberini's wishes is not clear. The historian Armando Lodolini has argued that the governors were weak officials, too afraid of alienating local families to be able to challenge how they were running the communal government. Was he afraid of reprisals from the priors? Or was he stalling so the Barberini would offer some additional perks?[33]

Whatever his motivations, in the end the governor claimed that it was impossible to carry out the mission entrusted to him by Giulio Cesare. The priors were not keeping the books in the communal chancellery anymore, but rather in their own homes; they were unwilling to allow the governor to have a look at the communal records, whether he was authorized by the Buon Governo or not. Giulio Cesare claimed to be "astonished" by this revelation and ordered the priors to return the books to the communal chancellery immediately. It was "a monstrous thing" he wrote, "that books pass into the hands of individuals . . . without the permission of superiors." The governor in Corese evidently found that the political actors from whom he had the most to fear were "only" a few villagers, priors at that time of the commune.[34]

Limiting the Barberini official's access to village records also happened in Monte Libretti, where in 1754 the priors of that village Libretti denied the governor the right to see the records of their *consiglio*. Monte Libretti's extensive *consiglio* records make the conflict that produced such a refusal easier to analyze at the village level, where Giulio Cesare's paternalism would be invoked, but not always in the terms he defined it.

Induce Them with Kindness
to Comply with the Law

As early as 1746 the commune of Monte Libretti and the noble family clashed over the commune's rights to rent its pasture. From such rentals of grazing rights in villages where pasture superseded local needs, the commune could generate a little extra income with which to meet rising papal taxes. The Barberini prince denied the commune the right to rent it, and ordered the governor to "confiscate and incarcerate the animals in the village present under these conditions and to send [the nobleman] notice of the same." The priors did not bend under the Barberini threat, but rather pressed on, determined to rent it anyway. How did the nobleman explain this type of behavior on the part of the villagers, especially the villagers of Monte Libretti, who had once been so enamored of their lord?

> The *consiglio* meetings of that commune are ruled by four or five demagogues [*capopopoli*] who spread their propaganda, and so communal affairs are resolved tumultuously, and not by secret vote, in such a way that many *consiglieri*, conquered by human considerations, most of the time are constrained to take sides they would rather avoid.

To address the abuse, the Barberini suggested the return to secret voting and the implementation of the rules they and their predecessors had already decreed for the affairs of the commune. Two years later the Barberini were still attempting to bend the villagers to the Barberini's view of their grazing rights in Monte Libretti. They issued additional edicts calling for the confiscation of "foreign" animals in the village. The *consiglieri* would have none of it. They reaffirmed the laws of the *statuto*, prohibiting animals of any origin to roam in vineyards, cultivated fields, or olive groves, but they otherwise reaffirmed that the commune had the right to rent pasture on the *macchie*, meadow, and the harvested fields.[35]

The nobleman's problems in the village were bigger than the voting practices of the *consiglio* (especially since in contrast to what Giulio Cesare had affirmed, the *consiglieri* mostly voted by secret ballot during the 1740s and the 1750s, as opposed to the public voting of the seventeenth century). What was lacking in the village was the cash to meet papal taxes and village patience with what had come to be seen as "excessive" Barberini demands. Between the late 1740s and the mid-1750s, the daily politics of Monte Libretti were punctuated by adversarial exchanges between the villagers and the Barberini over a number of issues. The issues were summarized in a meeting of August 16, 1750. The governor had clearly expected trouble at that meeting, since he refused to give permission to the priors to call the *consiglio*. In the notes of the meeting, it was recorded that a "common cry" of all those present had enumerated the grievances of the villagers against the noble family. Whereas typical *consiglio* meeting notes suggest that the priors listed the issues to be addressed, at this particular meeting the priors apparently only announced one issue before those in the assembly began yelling. The priors stated that the Barberini officials had posted an edict requiring the villagers to pay one-sixth of the corn (*granturco*) harvest to the noble family, despite the fact that "the *statuto* never stipulated any payment at all for corn." (This omission is not surprising, since corn had yet to enter European agriculture at the time the *statuto* was written.) The announcement prompted "everyone to cry together" against the illegal charge on their corn harvest; the Barberini demand to take one-sixth of what the villagers regarded as their gathering rights from various trees, including chestnut trees; the Barberini denial of the right to take wood from oak trees; the noble family's insistence that the commune could not sell pasturage; and the noble family's issuance of edicts that imposed penalties on animals pastured due to those rentals. The *consiglio* participants also lamented the Barberini edict that made it illegal to call the *consiglio* unless the governor gave permission. (Evidently the *consiglieri* had no difficulty coming together for this particular meeting, even without the permission of the governor.) The stated objection to this rule was that the priors had to pay the cost of travel to Nerola, where he resided, just to see whether he would approve of the meeting, which they intended to hold whether he approved of it or not.[36]

The record of this meeting resembles a petition of the kind usually sent by anonymous "individuals" from the village, or petitions from the priors sent in the name of the people of Monte Libretti. Here, however, the *consiglieri*, in effect, signed the petition, by the enclosure of their names at the end of the meeting. The notes conclude with the statement that despite the commune's inability to pursue their causes judicially (due to the commune's financial trouble), the villagers would, if necessary, throw themselves at the feet of "His Holiness." The *consiglio* meeting constituted the draft of a petition to the pope. It could be copied (and may very well have been copied) and sent to the noble family. The combination of this threat, combined with the admission that the commune was too broke to sue was intended to be a preamble to negotiations with the noble family.[37]

Charges and counter-charges between nobles and villagers continued for five years over the issues outlined in the tense meeting of August 1750. In the months immediately following it, the "Poor Faithful Vassal Community," as it was called at the meeting, was relatively tranquil, or at least its *consiglio* meetings were free of discussion about the controversies. The following summer the issue resurfaced when the villagers were required to donate a day's labor to building a road between Monte Libretti and Monte Maggiore. Of the sixty-one individuals present, all refused to do the labor and "stated that they were resolved to go to Rome and to talk to whomever necessary . . . and to remind them that village pasture and gathering rights were still in dispute," the implication being that those issues should be addressed before the villagers could be asked to provide any labor.

Opinions about how to deal with the Barberini varied in the *consiglio*. Some *consiglieri* advised more antagonistic approaches and others more conciliatory strategies with the noble family. The response in the village *consiglio* to an edict issued by the Barberini in the summer of 1750 reflects the variety of opinions among the villagers. Some villagers described the edict on the contested issues as "prejudicial to [village] rights." Luigi Palozzi counseled consulting the historical record. He claimed that the community and a former Barberini prince had signed a *concordia* about these issues on May 4, 1654. A copy of that document, Palozzi reminded the assembly, had been sent to the Barberini two years earlier and should have settled the matter. More conciliatory voices, however, were heard at a subsequent meeting to decide whether the commune should rent the hunting rights belonging to the noble family, Nicola Venastra suggested that a failure to rent the rights could be damaging to the villagers' interests, meaning that it could cost them something in their negotiations with the noble family. Other villagers strategized about how to put more pressure on the noble family, rather than cultivate their good will. Speakers argued that representatives of the village should be sent to Rome, to present "our rights in the *statuto*," and if that did not work, "to take it right to the pope's house." The archpriest Mazzetti was chosen to present the villagers' case to the powers-that-be in Rome.[38] In all these strategies the villagers relied on the methods of adversarial literacy practiced since the seventeenth century, publicizing the sources that would best support their causes and pushing the threat of judicial avenues, the statement that they would pursue the matter to the pope's domicile reinforcing their determination—they knew where he lived, a declaration bordering on a threat to noble and clerical authorities in Rome.

A month later, the *consiglio* met to discuss the letter Mazzetti brought from the Barberini. The letter attempted to reverse the village perspective on who had offended whom. It urged the priest to try to make the villagers understand that the Barberini prince "had never intended to impose new burdens, but only to conserve the rights that belonged to him." Since the villagers were beginning to introduce the cultivation of *granturco* into the territory, Giulio Cesare was obliged to charge one-sixth on it, or his "Right to one-sixth of the harvest would be useless." The Barberini prince felt that villagers had no right to complain, but rather "he was justified in feeling bad about what the villagers were doing," since they wrote to him in this manner. After all, "he had a just title and therefore had to require the payment." So in order to make them understand "the tenderness that [he] had for them" he was waiving the collection of the one-sixth payment on *granturco* for that year "as a favor, and not because it was the right thing to do," and villagers should be prepared to pay it in the following year.[39]

This one-year reprieve from paying the disputed dues and tender account of the prince's hurt feelings failed to persuade the *consiglio*. All but one of the forty-six villagers present agreed with Luigi Palozzi's assessment of the Barberini offer: "If [the prince] wanted to show how loving he was toward this people, in light of the damages suffered by this commune on account of his Excellency, and given that this commune is unable to continue any legal battles, he would come to a compromise with us next month." Giulio Cesare's response to this specific and demanding overture was to issue another proclamation declaring his intention to extract the sixth "on all the yields, manufactured as well as natural, but he was willing to come to a compromise and had selected a lawyer to negotiate it." The villagers decided to send their lawyer, accompanied by the chancellor and two villagers, one of them the cleric, Salvatore Barbetta.

Although no budgets survive for the commune that year, it was evidently in financial difficulty, since at a later meeting it was resolved that the surgeon's pay would have to come from each household, rather than from communal funds. Households "without men," that is of "of poor widows and other houses of women," would pay half the rate. The physician was also working without pay during the spring of 1752, and the *comunisti* were under orders by the governor to see that they compensated him. At that same time the news of a new papal tax, the "Gabella delli due Milioni," was reaching the villagers, with the repetition of the demand that it was time to pay up on the back taxes. So in the middle of the conflict with the Barberini, villagers were forced to choose new assessors of individual property to impose new burdens on the villagers to pay the papacy at least something on its newest demands.[40]

The commune's negotiations with the Barberini in this period proceeded with little success. A new edict about corn cultivation issued in June 1752 was the nobleman's response to village overtures, re-emphasizing that the year of "grace" granted to the villagers the previous fall would indeed come to an end. Not surprisingly, the Barberini issued an edict for the entire *stato* later that summer, reemphasizing that no commune was allowed to exceed the expenses outlined in the budget approved by the Barberini. The cost of lawsuits would have been one of the "extraordinary" expenses targeted by such an edict. Even if the Barberini edict was couched in concern for the public good and echoed a similar set of concerns expressed in the edicts of the Buon Governo, it was also a convenient expedient to intimidate the villagers from pursuing their differences with the prince in the law courts. It seemed unlikely that the prince would approve additional expenditures for litigation against his own interests.[41]

The commune's financial troubles continued throughout the winter of 1753. Things were no better when the commune's lawyer wrote in April of that year that he needed more money if he was to take the various conflicts with the Barberini to the court of the Segnatura. Such demands created a thorny technical problem that residents in the neighboring village of Monte Flavio chose to ignore. According to noble edict, the villagers would have to ask the Barberini for permission to allot communal funds to pay for the lawyer to battle the noble family in court. Appealing instead to the Buon Governo for approval of this expenditure was briefly discussed in the *consiglio*, but abandoned, probably since the commune's indebtedness to the papacy would have made the bureaucrats as unlikely as the nobleman to approve the expenditure. Rather than petition either party, the *comunisti* elected to issue their own edict, making the owners of animals in the village responsible for the cost of the lawsuits, especially since one of the conflicts was over pasturage rights, where animal owners had the most interests. Simultaneously, some attempt was apparently also made to secure the permission of the noble family, but even without a reply either way from the Barberini, a month later the *consiglio* began to raise the funds for the lawsuit. The villagers' causes were defeated in the court of the Segnatura in June, leaving the villagers with the familiar problem of deciding whether to abandon the case altogether, or to raise the funds to continue the case on appeal. In the *consiglio* debates, the lawyer was described as having "too little zeal for the interests of the commune," and he was to be fired in favor of a more aggressive advocate, if the case were to continue.

How could the case continue as long as the commune was strapped for cash? Nicola Cornacchia noted that among the disputed issues, the case over the payment of one sixth of the corn harvest fell mostly upon the poor, since they were the ones who tended to grow it. But under no circumstances did he believe that any money to pursue the case should be raised from "widows or women who were truly poor and without men in the household." Fighting the Barberini had to come out of the pockets of those with more resources, and every individual who attended the *consiglio* that day agreed with him. This was the same strategy chosen to raise the money for the next new imposition of taxes in November 1753. To raise the new taxes the *consiglio* decided that the commune should secure a loan using the communal lands as collateral, with the payments on the loans to be met by peasants and artisans, those "who were really capable of earning a living," and not the "real poor and those unable to work." In a later discussion of what to do about the debtors to the commune it was acknowledged in the *consiglio* that it was pointless to imprison those "powerless and impoverished," and leave them to rot in the jail. In raising money to fight the legal suit the villagers followed a similarly practical route of sparing the poorest, from whom it was clearly impossible to ask anything.[42]

Immersed in the burden of raising the tax money for the papacy and the ordinary details of everyday politics, the *consiglieri* put aside the discussion of appealing the lawsuit until June of the following year, 1754. At that time, the lawyer again demanded additional funds to appeal the case. Giacomo Grifonetti offered a combination of aggressive and conciliatory strategies, by suggesting that they should attempt to raise the money in the village, and to follow the procedure of at least asking the Barberini prince for permission. Should the prince decline to approve it, they should appeal to the Buon Governo. The *consiglio* agreed with his strategy.

Although the community succeeded in hiring the lawyer, they lost the appeal on the dispute over pasturage and wood-gathering rights. In the *consiglio* meeting it was announced that they lost the case because the Barberini were able to secure the testimony of three individuals who substantiated some of the Barberini assertions, especially that the village use rights (*jus lignandi*) never gave them the right to take oak trees, only "softer woods." Mattia Pellone gave an impassioned speech clearly intended to counterbalance the testimony offered in favor of the noble family and to rally the villagers to continue the fight. He gave his age (86 years) and said that he knew that custom had always allowed them to take the oak trees without requesting a license and that he had done so himself to make storage vats. Mattia encouraged the priors to submit whatever documents were necessary to the Buon Governo, "including the copy of this *consiglio*" in order to get permission to raise money for the case. Mattia's speech to a packed *consiglio* of seventy-five villagers was a success. They voted unanimously to support him.[43]

Without waiting for permission from the Buon Governo the commune continued to fight the case. They requested permission from the Papal Congregation, but continued to spend money without it. The community lost yet again on appeal in the fall of 1755, but villagers pronounced themselves ready to appeal again, even if they had to borrow against the assets of the village to do so. They also decided to send two or three more representatives of the village to confer with their lawyer about other evidence they might be able to gather. The *comunisti* also followed up with the Buon Governo with yet another request to raise money to continue the case using money from the owners of animals in the village.[44]

As the daily politics in Monte Libretti became more adversarial toward the Barberini lord, the *consiglio* itself became a site for generating testimony to substantiate village use rights. As a result the typically schematic content of the seventeenth-century *consiglio* record was turned toward other genres, especially the genre of the *fede*, or sworn testimony written usually by a notary in the presence of two or more witnesses. Matteo's speech reads as though he were offering sworn testimony to a notary in preparation for a legal trial, since he provided his age, a rare declaration in a *consiglio* meeting. In the earlier *consiglio* meeting regarding the same case such testimony was presented as the "common cry" of the entire assembly who offered a degree of details one would expect in sworn testimony, rather than in the usually abbreviated notes of the *consiglio* meeting.[45]

In the European legal system this was the role allotted the villagers: they were charged with the task of remembering, and their testimony carried more weight when it was given by old villagers, or in their absence, by villagers who had heard the "facts" from "ancestors of decrepit age." Since the Middle Ages villagers had fulfilled such a role in the legal system, although written sources were long-standing competitors to villagers' possibilities for defining customary practice, especially for trimming it of burdens unfavorable to their cause. Without a notary, the *consiglio* record would not carry the same legal legitimacy of sworn testimony, but because the noble's official was present at the *consiglio*, and because the text of the *consiglio* could be copied and forwarded to the noble family and papal officials, it served as "notice" to those authorities as to the content of the notarized testimony that could be gathered. It announced the details of the official sources the villagers would make should their adversaries wish to push it into the judicial arena.[46]

Giulio Cesare clearly understood the political importance of the *consiglio*, hence his attempt to control its membership and its meetings. Meetings in which a "common cry" of the villagers produced a lengthy and detailed list of local grievances against the Barberini were considered "tumultuous" by the nobleman. For the Barberini an "excessive number" of participants was supposed to lead to "disorder." Villagers who could measure up to the nobleman's ideal *consiglio* participant were rare in the *stato*. He maligned the "crass ignorance" of the *consiglio* of Monte Flavio, which was, however, sufficiently intelligent to defy him for over sixteen years. To counter these problems he insisted one of his minor officials (the vice-governor) attend the village meetings, and he required that the villagers secure the consent of the governor before convening the *consiglio*. Although as we have seen, the *consiglio* met in Monte Libretti, even without the governor's consent, and Giulio Cesare's frequent complaint about "irregular" meetings of the *consiglio* in various villages suggest this was an ideal rather than a reality in the *stato*. On rare occasions, Giulio Cesare attempted to annul the outcomes of some *consigli*, although this practice did not always produce the results the nobleman desired. Giulio Cesare grudgingly acknowledged the *consiglio*'s political power when he urged his official in the summer of 1750 to personally carry the nobleman's edict on grazing to each village *consiglio* of the territory: "We do not have a hope that the specific clauses [of the edict] can possibly work with success, without your personal assistance [in the *consiglio*]."[47]

In the years following the pasturage and use rights controversy, Giulio Cesare had clear support in the constitution for the legitimacy of the demands he wished to make upon the villagers of Monte Libretti, but he counseled his official to negotiate rather than dictate this right in 1761. In the fall of that year, he began making plans to build a new lime kiln in the village of Monte Libretti. According to Giulio Cesare the lord and the community had the right to make a lime kiln, and when the lord chose to do so, the inhabitants owed to him a certain amount of labor. The community, he believed, should agree to the project, because in the end "the baron has his precedent in the *statuto* to require the rendering of these few works." The nobleman acknowledged, however, that the right to collect wood for the kiln belonged to the community and would have to be respected—his rights, in other words, were entangled in the villagers' rights. The prince also cautiously advised his official in the village that he "was to handle the priors in a friendly way, to induce them with *buona maniera* (tactfully, with good manners) to comply with what the *statuto* prescribed in favor of the baron (i.e. Giulio Cesare)." Only by nudging the villagers with politeness toward what in principle was his by law, could Cesare successfully extract from the villagers their cooperation and their wood.[48]

To encourage an official to accept insult, to counsel another in using good manners, and to negotiate rather than dictate noble rights was to grant to villagers better treatment than their status in the social hierarchy would suggest they deserved. Giulio Cesare, for instance, reminded one of his officials in charge of his financial interests in the *stato* to be careful about how he treated his lowly steward. He counseled him to treat him "with all propriety and *buona Maniera*, [do not] treat him like a farm boy." "*Con buona maniera*" as a way of handling the villagers suggests treating them too with a dignity beyond their station. Allowing oneself to be insulted by a social inferior required the official to go beyond good manners to descend to the level of accepting damage to his honor, thereby lowering his status beneath those of the villagers he was supposed to "command" in the name of the Barberini lord.[49]

What drove the Barberini to promote this view and to resort to negotiating with the villagers, even when they had clear written precedents in the *statuto* to support their claims upon the villagers? As this brief summary of the situation in Monte Libretti suggests, the villagers lost many of their cases against the Barberini. Nonetheless, the Barberini had to take villagers into greater account because of their adversarial tactics in the village and their proven ability to create texts from the *consiglio* record to serve their cause. But the noble family also had to coax the villagers to carry out their wishes because the villagers remained rather ambivalent in their allegiance to papal views of governing, in contrast to the noble family. To compete with the challenge of the expanding papal bureaucracy, the Barberini put their efforts into meticulously monitoring the communal governments, especially (but not exclusively) how well the villages delivered their taxes. But it was an impossible task, squeezing more money out of the villagers, and of little interest to the villagers, who did not judge how good their local government was by how well it could pay papal taxes. Their loyalty to the local was rooted primarily in the commune's ability to deliver more of what villagers' wanted (doctors, schoolteachers, and resistance to the noble family, when required). The noble family threw itself into the papacy's impossible task, and, as everyone knows, when an impossible job is divided among more individuals, it helps further the delusion that it might be done. To entice the villagers to join in the hopeless scheme (or to get them to comply with controversial parts of the *statuto*), the Barberini sometimes had to accept the villagers' point of view. Since the seventeenth century, the people of Monte Libretti believed that their labor was offered only in exchange for goods or services from the noble family; that noble rights were entangled with, rather than greater than village rights; and that to get villagers to do the most unpleasant tasks, which were a priority to the Barberini, would cost the nobleman or his officialdom something (in the case of the village governor, a loss of his honor).

Boldness, deceit, cajoling: these were some of the tools of eighteenth-century lordship as practiced by Giulio Cesare. His maneuvering suggests that behind baronial "control" of local governments and the grand pretensions of baronial rights, landowners recognized the limits of both on the village level. Rights could be turned into realities only if they met with some measure of public consent on the part of communal officials and villagers in general. The villagers of Monte Libretti retained their standard tactics of using the *statuto*, attempting to bend it to their needs. Did the *statuto* ever use the word *granturco*? Villagers could be even more constructionist in their interpretation of the *statuto* than even the clerics who typically read only a handful of words in the *statuto* in order to rule in a particular case. But in the sources the villagers created for themselves in the *consiglio*, the villagers showed themselves to more creative, making porous the normally clear boundary between *consiglio* records and notarized testimony, using the *consiglio* as a site for questioning what that quality of the Barberini's "love" for their vassals really was, and hypothesizing that the best response to such paternal affection was to continue with the threat of a lawsuit.

E. P. Thompson analyzed the structure of such exchanges in England, where he argues, they amounted to little more than "gestures and postures rather than actual responsibilities" and likened paternalism more to a backward-looking "myth," or to theater rather than to a lived reality. Elsewhere he refers to the dynamic between "rulers" and the "crowd" as "theater and countertheater," an analogy that applies well to Monte Libretti, where the villagers were not in open rebellion but resisting through the testimonial possibilities of the *consiglio*.[50]

The century's old version of such theater in the Roman countryside suggested the endless intertwining of benevolent lordship and peasant obligation, the latter owed to the lord because of his benevolent lordship, the benevolent lordship extended to the villagers because peasants met their obligations. Was this the potential constant in a territory where *novità* were evidently commonplace, and a scramble over resources now a constant part of daily politics? Inequality cloaked by the gift cycle is a web of lies that holds out some benefits to even the lowliest members of society. The noble performance of paternalism suggests that there were benefits valuable enough to entice some villagers to join the refrain. Paternalism was cast in terms that made sense in the language of local politics, where the men of the village *consiglio* of Monte Libretti also saw themselves as the protectors of the poor, especially the female poor and their children. In that regard Giulio Cesare told them a story of his motivations that resonated with their own.

But in every village there were at least a few individuals who could see the absurdity of the claim that a *jus civico* could belong to an aristocrat who had never set foot in the village, or that a lifetime, and an ancestor's lifetime of protecting village records was done in order to serve his interests. The villagers' empty archives speak more eloquently than any petition to the Barberini framed in the language of noble beneficence. The notion that the religious paternalism of the Barberini could be a fair compensation for noble demands was clearly, for some, a strange refrain to sing in the countryside.[51]

The same words from the refrain of paternalism, combined with the recalcitrant villagers' view of the world, could become instead the deus ex machina that allowed the play to end differently. What if the implications of that idealized near-religious relationship were applied to sources to which no one in Rome would have thought them connected? Could paternalism's emphasis on protecting the poor be viewed through the lens of justice, instead of the lens of charity? No one in Monte Flavio could meet the standards of literacy required by the elites who ruled them in Rome. But they could use their adversarial literacy to unpack the terms defining their subjugation. To their success belongs the rest of this book.

6

Writing Resistance

Village Attacks on Textual Monopolies in Eighteenth-Century Italy

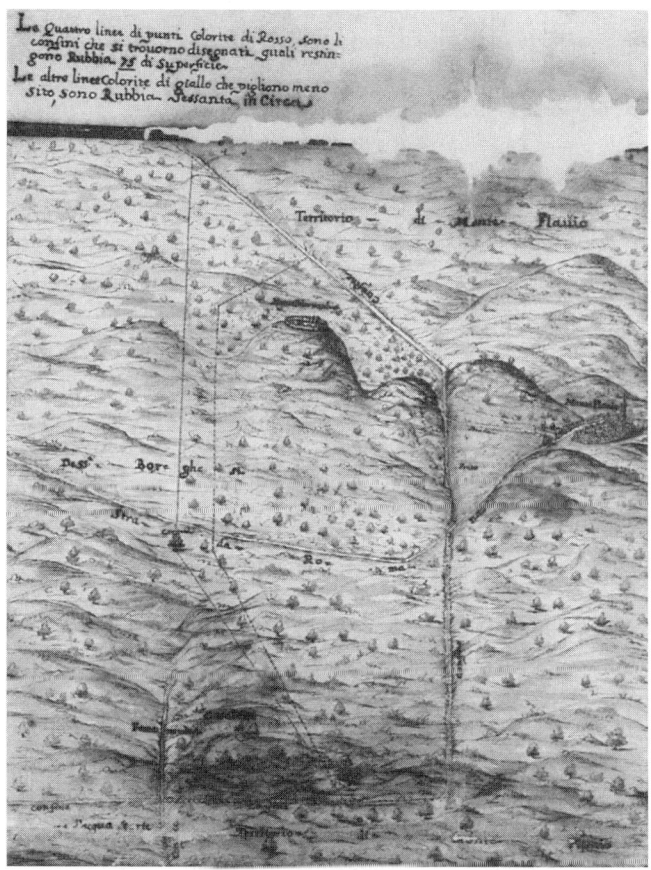

*Map showing the village of Monte Flavio (far right) with the lands of Monte Falco
demarcated. Monte Falco is near the center of the image, and its lands belonged to the
Borghese family and were rented by the commune of Monte Flavio to supplement
village pasture. Photo copyright Vatican Library, Barb. Lat. 9903, f. 65.*

In the winter of 1761–1762, Monsignor Dentice, emissary of the Papal Congregation of the Buon Governo, swept through the *stato* of Monte Libretti. For over half a century the Buon Governo had been trying to bring the communes subject to baronial jurisdiction under tighter fiscal control by the Congregation. Dentice hoped to audit the accounts of the six communal governments in the territory, but bookkeeping irregularities still abounded in the *stato*, nowhere more so than in the village of Monte Flavio. Dentice's disillusioned report is strikingly similar to the one written by his predecessor in 1704, who had also noted the haphazard bookkeeping practices of the Monte Flavisti: "they do not keep books which are considered necessary for the administration of communal revenues [but rather] write confusedly: Income, *Consiglio*, Auditing, and other things without any order, and all of this on account of a lack of individuals capable of such a business." The later eighteenth-century lord of the village agreed with all these bleak bureaucratic assessments. Giulio Cesare Barberini complained that the priors (the executive officers of the village) were "ignorant" and that there was a "universal incompetence" among all those eligible for public office in Monte Flavio. On really bad days he maligned the "crass ignorance" of the entire *consiglio*, whose membership he hoped to narrow to a more controllable group. Perhaps he hoped for a *consiglio* of the merely ignorant, rather than those crassly so? The nobleman's exasperation is clearer than his plans for addressing the issue.[1]

It is not surprising that Romans who had enjoyed the early modern luxury of advanced education disparaged the bookkeeping skills of the villagers of Monte Flavio. Perched at the highest elevation in the *stato* (800 meters), its relatively poor lands made the inhabitants peripatetic laborers: They pastured their animals in the nearby lands of Stazzano, they wandered down to Monte Libretti to grow grapes and raise grain, they trekked up to Mount Pellecchia to haul snow down to Rome. A seventeenth-century observer had optimistically noted that in Monte Flavio's "cold perfect air" residents lived to an extremely old age. To reach old age in Monte Flavio, however, required a lifetime of descending from its salubrious atmosphere to wherever the work was. Keeping proper account books for papal taxes must have been a low priority for the migratory villagers. There were better things to do when one got home.[2]

In the *stato* of Monte Libretti villagers could and did pay close attention to the sources that supported their cause. In the neighboring village of Nerola, for instance, seventeenth-century villagers had pursued the defense of their rights against the lord in papal court. Political leaders in the village assembly, or *consiglio* of Nerola, like their peers elsewhere in Europe, showed themselves to be highly skilled in adversarial literacy, employing such documents to defend their rights through the judicial system of the papal monarchy.[3]

What were the possibilities for resistance to seigneurial demands when the written sources, especially the constitution, failed to support the villagers' point of view? As Walter Ong has suggested, the written word was "inherently contumacious," stating in perpetuity the same claims forever, sometimes inspiring its destruction by implicated parties. Steven Justice called this choice "insurgent literacy," or the application of practical literacy skills to the selective destruction of documents during times of rebellion. In the German peasant war of the early sixteenth century, peasants faced a similar blockage to the furthering of their interests and resorted to "Godly" or "divine law" as an antidote to the limitations placed upon their rights by the written sources. Between the late seventeenth and late eighteenth century, European villagers like those in the *stato* tended toward nonviolent protest, sparing their adversaries and the "contumacious" documents, attempting instead to advance their cause through the preservation of sources and through litigation, the latter strategy hopefully leading to negotiations with their adversaries.[4]

What could villagers do when the sources failed to support their cause? The villagers in Monte Flavio found themselves in such awkward circumstances—they contested the legitimacy of paying some seigneurial dues, even though those dues were outlined in the village constitution. Through their political participation in the commune, the villagers in Monte Flavio waged a legal battle over dues that stretched from the 1740s to the early 1760s. In letters to his officials, Giulio Cesare rarely mentioned the villagers without a qualifying adjective: "the insolent men of Monte Flavio" or "the most rebellious people of the *stato*." I leave to the reader's imagination the names he must have muttered under his breath before he delivered these relatively gentile choices to his secretary. Their repetition suggests his outrage.[5]

Giulio Cesare was familiar with resistance on the part of other villagers in the *stato* and wrote frequently to his officials to coach them in the arts of persuading, flattering, and threatening the villagers into doing what the nobleman wanted. But the controversy in Monte Flavio was a *"rivoluzione,"* although villagers committed little or no violence and destroyed no documents. The villagers did defiantly reject the conventional reading of their *statuto*, the centerpiece of village politics since at least the seventeenth century. Some villagers in Monte Flavio took the *statuto* in new directions, calling for the reinterpretation of the document according to the historical context in which it was created, and according to the standards of Christian charity. Such analyses emphasized the failure of the noble family to fulfill its promises to the villagers and equated subsequent noble demands for the disputed dues with the oppression of the poor. In the early 1750s, some villagers wrote their own tally sheet of the debits and credits between noble and peasant. While most villagers may have ignored the details of tax accounting, some of them were doing some fairly so-phisticated political accounting, and not surprisingly, it was the elites in Rome who came up short, especially the Barberini.

This conflict between the villagers of Monte Flavio and the Barberini can tell us a great deal about the evolution of adversarial literacy, especially the de-velopment of reading strategies that encouraged villagers to reinterpret, rather than to destroy old "contumacious" sources. In some parts of Europe, such as France, villagers took up this new interpretive task with the assistance of high-ranking royal officials like the intendant. But the same process occurred in areas of Europe like the Roman countryside, where papal authorities did not dem-onstrate comparable activism on the part of the peasants.

This was the most widespread form of resistance in eighteenth-century Europe, but it was by no means a form limited to Europe or to the eighteenth century. As its most inspired investigators have already noted, it was a powerful feature of ordinary people's lives, but we know relatively little about it, since it was so often kept from view, or expressed obliquely in order to avoid persecu-tion. E. P. Thompson demonstrated the ingenuity of this off the beaten track resistance, found in the forest, the tavern, or the home. It expressed itself in anonymous letters, sabotage, theft, or, as villagers might term the latter, the ap-propriation of what was theirs by customary right, if not by contemporary law. The willful political determination of the villagers of Monte Flavio is not his-torically unique, but it does take place in the context of a highly developed ju-dicial system in which villagers could petition magistrates and seek legal redress for their grievances, in a world, in other words, where villagers could challenge nobles in law courts that became the political arena in which what the anthro-pologist James Scott called the "private transcript" could be aired. In that arena the villagers of Monte Flavio were able to leave record of their resistance in texts that were more complex than brief petitions; their declarations for the court could provide the explanatory justification for the villagers' refusal to pay the disputed dues, or for the occasional threat issued to their enemies.[6]

What drove political individuals in rural communities to the level of protest demonstrated in Monte Flavio? Peasants gazed across a vast landscape of injus-tice in the eighteenth century—what made them seize upon a particular feature and commit themselves to its removal, especially when they lacked documentary support for their claims? This chapter examines the motivations of the villagers of Monte Flavio in order to see the context that created such protest and the tac-tics of adversarial literacy that were employed to support it. One year, 1750, was a fertile moment for such experiments in Monte Flavio. Although the villagers were insufficiently literate for the lord, and for the Buon Governo, they clearly drew upon a highly developed form of literacy to challenge elites in Rome. Vil-lagers stymied them, in fact, for a decade, with what they created in 1750.

The tense relations between the villagers and the noble family during the 1750s were probably unforeseen in the 1740s, when there were only the ubiquitous minor skirmishes between the villagers and their superiors in Rome. The simultaneity of several controversies exacerbated them, as did the Barberini's alignment with the papacy in the collection of taxes. Increasing cash demands from one set of rulers tended to send villagers looking for ways to lower other payments, including payments to their lords.

From 1739 to 1746, the communal government had engaged in a legal fight over the payment of tithes on the lands of Monte Falco (Stazzano), which the commune rented from the Borghese family. Villagers argued that the lands of Monte Falco, which had been rented for over a quarter century, were agriculturally quite poor, but they could be used to supplement the even more meager pasture of Monte Flavio. In Monte Falco, the villagers were able to have some impact on the harsh environment. "By their industry and their fatiguing labors," they turned part of the mountainous territory into cultivated land, another useful asset for the villagers, since their own lands could grow so little. The abbot of San Giovanni noted the improvements and demanded the tithe on the harvests, since those lands were under his ecclesiastical jurisdiction. Despite village protests and legal agitation that led all the way to the court of the Rota in Rome, the abbot, the "pastor" of Monte Falco (where no one resided), prevailed in 1745, and the villagers had to set aside one-tenth of their yields for the prelate. In Monte Flavio this decision was difficult to accept, and the commune hoped by petitioning the Congregation of the Buon Governo to win a new audience for their case in the summer of 1746. This appeal led nowhere, and the villagers continued to protest by dragging their feet on the payment of the tithes, prompting Giulio Cesare to take up the issue with his governor in Nerola, whom he sent to Monte Flavio's priors to remind them not to keep the abbot waiting for his tithes. This could not have improved Giulio Cesare's standing with the villagers, who had found an ally in the Borghese family when they fought their legal battle against the imposition of the new tithe.[7]

New tax demands also arrived from Rome in the 1740s, when the papacy, merely a passive participant in the War of Austrian succession, had to come up with three million scudi to cover the costs of moving troops from the Kingdom of Naples to the Holy Roman Empire. Baronial communes like those of the *stato*, formerly excluded from some papal taxes, were to be subject to all the eighteenth-century taxes created to cover the costs of papal contributions. Taxes were annoying enough, but the troops themselves were also physically present in the *stato* and meant new mouths to feed, always a strain on village society, especially when they were armed mouths. The bureaucrats arrived in

Monte Flavio in the summer of 1744, asking to see the village archive in order to review village taxes and village assets.[8]

New taxes were always unwelcome, of course, but they contributed to an already strained financial situation in Monte Flavio during the 1740s, where as was typical throughout the stato, no one could be found to assume the office of tax collector. In the mid-1740s the tax collector was a priest, Sante Sciarra, who found it impossible to collect the debts owed to the commune from almost fifty out of approximately two hundred households in the village. By papal law as well as Barberini edict, Sciarra was ineligible to serve in the communal office because he was a cleric. Other priests in Monte Flavio sent a letter to the Barberini prince to register their dismay. By Sciarra's own admission, it was an awful undertaking, and he found himself accused by the Barberini officials of a number of mutually contradictory faults in his failure to make the villagers pay up, since the debtors in some cases simply closed themselves in their houses. The Barberini governor of 1746 maligned him for breaking down the doors, while the governor of 1748 condemned him for lacking diligence in his debt collection and suggested to the bureaucrats of the Buon Governo that he be held financially responsible for the outstanding debts. For his part Sciarra thought that the copious documentation he provided to the Congregation should suffice, noting that if it did not, the situation required nothing less than one of the four Evangelists to testify on his behalf. Sciarra eventually found himself without any allies, frequently the fate of the village tax collector. It is not surprising that by the 1770s the villagers who participated in the *consiglio*, or village assembly, were accused of electing "incapable, illiterate, miserable people" to the office of tax collector. As the taxes imposed by the papacy proved to be increasingly impossible to raise in the village, anyone with their wits and a little money about them wanted nothing to do with their collection.[9]

Despite the unpopularity of new papal taxes, sometimes the arrival of a papal bureaucrat scrounging the countryside for new taxes could have unexpected benefits. It could, at least, for those who were willing to listen carefully to the literacy experts when they rode into town. In 1744, emissaries from the Buon Governo attempting to find new tax possibilities began by visiting with the priors, reviewing their accounts, as well as any other written records in the village archive, especially, although not exclusively, the village constitution. During their visit to Monte Flavio in August of that year, they noted that the "*minuti*" of Monte Flavio, annual dues that inhabitants paid to the noble family, were being improperly collected. These dues, along with the other incomes the noble family derived from the village, were paid to Felice Antonio Petrucci, who "rented" their collection from the noble family. The dues in question were described in the text of the constitution this way:

All the animals of the inhabitants can remain within the lands [of Monte Flavio] without paying *"erbatici"* [tribute for grazing] and in recognition of these animals [being allowed to graze] the inhabitants are required to pay to the Illustrious Lord [the following payments]: whoever has thirty sheep, a lamb at Easter, and whoever has other kinds of animals a ham at Easter, a hen at the feast of Santa Maria in August, a pair of chickens per household per year.

The sentence contained a number of ambiguities. Did the phrase "per household per year" apply only to the payment of chickens, or did it apply to all the items that preceded it (except for the lamb, which seems to belong pretty clearly with the sheep)? Did only those with "other animals" have to provide the Easter ham, or did all the households need to do so? What if a villager had no animals at all? And what of the Santa Maria hen floating in mid-sentence? Did the papal bureaucrats who visited the village in August actually see some of that poultry collected? Did only the villagers who owned animals owe the hen, or were the hens expected from every household? Some interpretations were clearly more favorable to the renter's interest, some to the villagers'. The *statuto*, which papal law and papal courts typically sustained as the document that established fixed dues villagers owed their lords, was supposed to clarify those obligations. Such payments were not to be changed against the peasants' interests by the lord. But the wording of the *statuto* in this case seemed to muddle, rather than clarify the situation. The papal visitors may also have noted the obvious, that the constitution described payments in kind, and that it was more common in the 1740s for villagers to pay the *minuti* in cash. Housing two hundred hens would require considerable organization, to say nothing of a high tolerance for clucking.[10]

Discrepancies uncovered between the *statuto* and local practices were usually the inspiration for villagers to approach the noble family (and other Roman elites) for redress. In the fall and winter of 1744 and 1745, at least some villagers evidently started their protest by refusing to pay the *minuti*. In February 1745, Felice Antonio Petrucci, the renter of the *minuti*, wrote the noble family to complain that he could not collect the dues. Recalcitrant villagers behaved much as they did when they could not pay their taxes. They closed their doors and kept them closed when Petrucci (who had been the renter for over thirty years) came knocking. Giulio Cesare put his local allies into action, instructing the governor "to force the doors open . . . but without unbridled violence," meaning perhaps to rough up only the building, rather than its occupants as well. He was already in touch with the archpriest of Monte Libretti, from whom he had gleaned information about terms of various rentals in the *stato*, and he made plans to write to Petrucci in Monte Flavio for more details.

Unfortunately for the Barberini, Petrucci himself was ailing, and the dual roles in which he had served the noble family, as both the renter of the noble income in Monte Flavio, and the "vice-governor," or assistant, to the Barberini's general governor of the whole *stato*, were coming to an end. He resigned the latter position in the summer of 1745 and died the following year, leaving his only child, Silvia Petrucci, to assume the collection of the controversial revenues of Monte Flavio.[11]

From 1745 through the summer of 1746, the controversy over the *minuti* was only one of a variety of difficulties in the village, including the new taxes and the problems of the beleaguered tax collectors. Other disputes involving the Barberini included a controversy over the "illegal planting" of hemp in various places in the village. The tactics used by the villagers in the *minuti* controversy were exploratory at this point—by petition-writing and withholding payments, they were attempting to address the issue of who should pay and how much. During December 1745, "the People and the Poor of Monte Flavio" petitioned the noble family to resolve these problems and to stop the violence used in the collection of the "*Regaglie,*" implying that the governor had used, if not unbridled violence, then at least some violence against individuals in order to get them to pay up. Although the petition does not survive, its language was doubtless couched in the terms of humble subjugation of vassals toward their lord. But as the anthropologist James Scott has argued, we can most accurately consider this a threat to the family, rather than merely a friendly invitation to the nobles to solve the problem and practice some Christian charity at Christmas time. The communal government was taking other steps simultaneously, including filing a petition with the Sacra Consulta. Giulio Cesare could certainly see the potential lawsuit coming and asked to have a copy of the *statuto* forwarded to him in early 1746, so that he could see the text that villagers said substantiated the claims that "some individuals" did not have to pay the *minuti.*[12]

Between 1746 and 1749 the controversy remained at a stalemate, much to the consternation of the nobleman. He spent those three years trying to shore up allies in the village, and to ferret out and punish, if possible, those hostile to the payment of the *minuti*. He showed special interest in the daughter of the deceased renter, Silvia Petrucci. Silvia initially tried to finish her father's contract for the rental, which terminated at the end of 1747. She assumed the rental in September 1746, but found that her attempts to collect the *minuti* netted her only citations from magistrates in Rome. Such citations demanded that the collection of *minuti* be halted, until the controversy over the terms of their payment could be settled. In the fall of 1746, some villagers evidently stepped up pressure tactics against her, damaging her crops. She appealed to Giulio Cesare for protection, sending him a basket of fruit, and asking him to post guards on her land. In the spring of 1747, she wrote him for advice about choosing a husband. She was considering two suitors, one a young man from Monte Flavio named Petricca, who was also her third cousin, and the other an older man named Mei from Monte Rotondo. Giulio Cesare favored the latter, believing him to be "more mature, more cultured, more well-to-do, and more expert in business" than the younger cousin. The nobleman sent a priest from Nerola to Silvia Petrucci to express his opinion, although he stressed that Silvia had to follow her own "inclination" and not consider herself "forced" into the nobleman's opinion, since it was "up to her." Silvia decided against the nobleman's advice and married her cousin, which did not seem to disturb Giulio Cesare at all.[13]

More distressing to the nobleman was the potential loss of cash, since la Petrucci was unable to collect the *minuti* and was behind on both what she and her father owed. In August 1747, he had the governor of the *stato* post a list of the names of all those who owed the *minuti*. But the posting did not bring any villagers forward with payments. Giulio Cesare exchanged letters about Silvia with other officials, since she hesitated to renounce the rental. For Silvia, there were risks in both scenarios, since renunciation freed her from the problem of dealing with the recalcitrant villagers, but it left her more vulnerable to debt prosecution by the Barberini. She vacillated about continuing the rental and finally renounced it in the spring of 1748, offering a small vineyard as payment for what she and her father still owed the noble family. Giulio Cesare declined the vineyard, saying that he could wait for the debt payment until after the controversy was over (although he never quite forgot about it, and the two families were still in dispute over the payments in the 1770s). Giulio Cesare needed to stay on good terms with Silvia in the 1740s. She held her father's account books on his collection of the *minuti*, and he needed those records to invalidate the villagers' claims that the *minuti* payments were wrongly collected. The villagers hoped that by protesting the *minuti* payments, they would lower their costs, especially for those who owned fewer than thirty animals, that is, for most of the villagers. Giulio Cesare's correspondence with the governor makes it clear that as far as he was concerned the yearly hams, hens, and chickens were required of each household, whether they owned animals or not. He tried in 1747 to collect written evidence favoring his interpretation from the inhabitants themselves, but few came forward. He hoped that Silvia's husband could be useful in the cause of collecting the testimony, and that her father's records would help substantiate his claims. They remained on cordial terms throughout the increasingly tense years of 1749–1751. She wrote him to announce the birth of her son in 1750, to which he responded that she should raise him with the "attention and fidelity of a good vassal."[14]

Good vassals were clearly in short supply in Monte Flavio. Giulio Cesare tried to regain the support of the commune by making common cause with it against its declared "enemy," in this case, the hapless Sante Sciarra, whom the commune wanted to make the sacrificial lamb of village debts. From the village point of view, this was a way to avoid the prosecution of his predecessors, Saturnino Petrucci and Basilio Cagnoli. From the perspective of the Barberini, the contestation of the *minuti* was the conspiracy of a few individuals, including the archpriest of the village, Amico Mancini, the brothers Antonio and Saturnino Petrucci, Sante Sciarra, and Antonio Petricca. To complicate the charges in the Buon Governo against Sciarra for not successfully collecting all the outstanding debts, the Barberini governor wrote a vituperative and unconvincing letter claiming that Sciarra had fomented public opinion against the payment of the *minuti*, because of the "hatred he had of the renter, and that he would pursue the case from the Sacra Consulta, to the Buon Governo, right to Our Lord himself, to cause desperation in the renter, and to make him die angry, angry as his own father had died." While avenging a father's bitter death seems plausible on an emotional level, it is unlikely that Sciarra, even if he was opposed to the *minuti*, single-handedly engineered the strike against their payment. Threats in the *consiglio* to confiscate Sciarra's property as payment for his debts received the backing of the Barberini prince. It is hard to imagine that Sciarra was left with much sympathy for the cause of the villagers, who had a tendency to devour their allies along with their adversaries. Sciarra's name, in fact, does not appear in any of the testimony given against the *minuti* payment in the lawsuit records of the 1750s.[15]

But there was anger in the village, and it did not simply vanish with the death of the old renter. The Barberini had high hopes for Signor Antonio Petricca, the new renter of the income from Monte Flavio. Antonio Petricca did not press the villagers for the *minuti* in 1748, and an exasperated Giulio Cesare told the governor to push the new renter in that direction, noting that the prohibition against collecting the *minuti* was without "substance," and calling the renter to Rome so that he could give the nobleman "an account of his administration" and doubtless so Giulio Cesare could give him a piece of his mind. But by summer of the following year, Petricca had yet to collect anything except a few undisputed payments, avoiding the collection of the rest "in order to avoid the hatred of his fellow citizens," as he explained in his letter to the Barberini. Petricca fished for more specific excuses, noting that after the bad practices of the previous renter, it was difficult to collect anything. Giulio Cesare concurred that the previous renter had been "negligent," and the nobleman fretted about how to "save this right." He suggested to the governor that he post a list of debtors and prosecute them for what they owed in the *minuti* payment. By the summer of 1749, unfortunately, this meant listing the name of every head of household in the village. He further cautioned the renter that they should be pressed to pay, but not so hard that they returned to the Buon Governo to file a petition against the collection of the dues. Again, the nobleman's complex designs were difficult to understand even for his officials and his renters, who must have noticed the practical challenges to implementing them.[16]

The hatred of the dues had increased rather than lessened with the lapse in their payments. The "strike" against the *minuti* seemed to be extending to other seigneurial dues as well, as the villagers were also refusing to haul snow for the renter of this income. Finally grasping the level of animosity toward the payments in the village, Giulio Cesare wrote to advise the renter of the snow collection to use "a more easygoing manner with the villagers, employ-ing the sweetest tactic the renter could use to get them to do what he wanted." Meanwhile the communal government prosecuted Antonio Petricca for debts that he owed while he was the tax collector in 1741. Clearly, while the prince hoped to turn his tactics toward *buona maniera*, the villagers were using the worst weapons they had left against the Barberini renter.[17]

Finally, at the end of the summer of 1749, the Barberini received a break in their struggle that must have seemed like a sign from God: The archpriest of Monte Flavio died. If the archpriest was, as the governor and the nobleman claimed, one of those arguing against the payment of the *minuti*, then his death would leave the protestors less one leader. The Barberini showed considerable interest in naming his successor, removing the one chosen by the *consiglio* of Monte Flavio and substituting instead the schoolmaster from Monte Libretti, Salvatore Rosati. If Rosati worked diligently to edify the villagers, he might be able to persuade them to end their dispute with the noble family. Of course, Giulio Cesare still pressed the renter for the collection of the *minuti*, but now counseled him to practice "all sweetness" with the villagers when the renter was to meet with them in November 1749. The Barberini's "right" to the *minuti* had been in jeopardy for five years—but with a new archpriest and kinder forms of coercion, perhaps the villagers could be coaxed back into accepting it. Giulio Cesare wrote warmly to the new priest in February 1750, lamenting that a near accord with the community over the payment of the dues had been ru-ined by four new petitions filed on the part of villagers. These seem to have been related to other disputes, but they underscored the tension among the vil-lagers, the renter, and the noble family. The Barberini counseled caution and moderation in dealing with their officials and renters. With the archpriest as an ally, the villagers might yet come around.[18]

While negotiating their way to village compliance was the best long-term strategy for the Barberini, it probably did not look very attractive to the renter, Antonio Petricca. He was left in the unenviable position of owing the Barbe-rini money, but not being able to collect the dues from the villagers to pay it back and make a profit. Negotiations resulting in better terms for the villagers might not cover his debts to the noble family. Petricca's meeting with the villagers in November 1749 might have been amicable enough, but the dues were evidently not forthcoming. He was stuck with the recommended Barberini strategy of pressing the renters, but not so hard that they appealed again to Roman magistrates. Evidently Petricca never achieved proficiency in walking this interpersonal tightrope, because the villagers took the dispute to the next legal level, approaching the magistrates at the court of the Segnatura in May with a petition that forced Petricca to cease collecting the dues until the controversy was settled. The court obliged with two orders to this effect in May and June 1750. It was time for Petricca to back down.[19]

The court orders, however, inspired Petricca to take his harassment of the villagers further, apparently against the wishes of the noble family. How might the situation in the village have looked to the renter? Even without the recently deceased archpriest to lead them (if indeed he ever did), and despite the absence of a surely disillusioned Sante Sciarra, there were evidently enough villagers committed to the cause of the *minuti* to pursue it legally in Rome. Once a lawsuit began, its trajectory could be long, possibly as long as his nine-year rental. Negotiating outside the law courts probably appeared equally hopeless. How was the new archpriest Rosati supposed to work the miracle of Monte Flavio and turn the stubborn hearts of the villagers into two hundred hams, two hundred hens, and twice as many chickens? Petricca evidently thought that he and the governor could devise a better strategy. Despite the new orders from the court of the Segnatura, Petricca continued to try to collect the *minuti*, pursuing some debtors to their homes, and ordering the governor of the *stato* to post notices with the names of the others. Finally, in the last week of August 1750, he took his pressure on the villagers to a new level by ordering the governor to confiscate 120 animals (mostly pigs, it seems) belonging to the villagers. What followed, according to three witnesses, was the "revolution of all the people of Monte Flavio."[20]

Antonio Petricca, who doubtless considered himself in the right, since he was the long-suffering renter, broke one of the most important unwritten rules in the countryside—one should refrain from harming (or potentially harming) the livestock of other villagers. As petitions to the noble family in the 1770s make clear, merely threatening the confiscation of the livestock of another villager could lead to blows, even if the livestock in question had damaged another person's crops or vineyards. Livestock was the living capital of the villagers, sometimes their only capital. It was a fragile investment, as even Giulio Cesare recognized when he wrote to his official to complain about the death of one of his cows, an animal whose demise the official had chalked up to "influenza, and a punishment from God." While Giulio Cesare agreed, he noted that the care one gave livestock could also be a factor in their longevity. Confiscation was a potential death sentence if the animal was neglected.

Petrucci had the one hundred twenty animals moved to the inn at Montorio Romano. Would they be fed? Would they be watered? It was rumored in the village that he was planning to auction them off, intensifying the threat to the animals for the villagers. The innkeeper eventually let the pigs go, under pressure from a magistrate in Rome who mandated their liberation.[21]

Writing to an official in Nerola a month later, Giulio Cesare expressed satisfaction over the pigs' return. Going against the magistrates in Rome would not help the Barberini cause in the law courts, and it would only make the villagers more determined. But the damage was already done. Bold claims against the payment of the *minuti* that had been at the margins of village debate in the mid-1740s moved to the center of village politics. Six years earlier the textual experts of the Buon Governo had made a passing observation about the ambiguities of the payment of the dues in the constitution. The villagers would take this seemingly small observation and in 1750 turn it into a critique of the constitution and of the noble family's lordship.[22]

Making History in Monte Flavio, 1750

The liberation of the livestock scarcely alleviated the tension between the villagers and Petricca. In September he was seen debating in public with four villagers about the collection of the *minuti*. While the *minuti* were still a contentious topic of discussion in the village, they had yet to be paid. In the last days of November, Petricca convinced the Barberini governor to issue a warrant for the arrest of Giovanni Domenico Pettinella and Saturnino Petrucci, (the village surgeon) men who, along with everyone else, owed Petricca the *minuti*. Pettinella evidently eluded capture, but on Saturday, December 5, Saturnino was taken into custody. "With great prejudice and inconvenience to the ill of the village," Saturnino was confined to the jail of Nerola, about six miles away, cut off from the residents of Monte Flavio first by a torrential rain, and then by a heavy snow storm, which made impassable the poor mountain road between their village and his jail cell. As they had done for the pigs, the Roman magistrates demanded the release of the surgeon.[23]

Why imprison Saturnino, when there were so many debtors to choose from? A letter by Giulio Cesare in June 1747 identified Saturnino Petrucci as part of the same conspiracy, a group that included the archpriest Don Amico Mancini, Saturnino's brother Antonio, Sante Sciarra, Antonio Petricca, and "others." If Saturnino was one of the leaders, capturing him might discourage the rest of the villagers from continuing their strike against the *minuti*. Despite his imprisonment, other villagers stepped forward to provide testimony against the collection of the disputed dues. Those villagers probably also knew that, since the summer of 1747, Barberini officials had been trying to collect oral testimony from villagers asserting that the *minuti* had been paid in Monte Flavio. Giulio Cesare sent his governor clear directions about the details such testimony should contain. His explicit directions contained an error, however. He instructed the witnesses to say "two hens" when the language of the constitution clearly stated "one hen." (In leading the witness, one should at least be true to the written sources that support one's side.) Witnesses corroborating the Barberini's claim were very few and had to be coaxed into testifying in the winter and spring of 1751. Village testimony recorded in the fall of 1750 was all in favor of the villagers' position and was intended to challenge the obviously literal interpretation of the *statuto*, as well as the evidence in ledgers and receipts that suggested that the *minuti* had always been paid.[24]

Village testimony was still important evidence in the legal system in Rome during the eighteenth century, hence Giulio Cesare's effort to collect persuasive testimony that would support his case. Sworn testimonies (*fedi*) were assembled even before a controversy devolved into a lawsuit, often in the hopes that the impressive testimony in one's favor would be enough to make a potential adversary back down. Noble archives, like those of the Barberini, bulge with such *fedi*, and an incident from 1741 suggests how they could be used outside of court. That year a Barberini official was trying to settle a boundary dispute with priests from the neighboring abbey and agreed to meet them at the contested border. Both sides arrived armed with sworn testimony that they whipped from their pockets at the appropriate moment to compare the quantity and the quality of the testimony. During this "dueling *fedi* at twenty paces" the Barberini minister scanned his rivals' documents to see if they were "convincing," meaning to see whether they had the right combination of aged witnesses, local experience, and specific details to support the claims of the testimony. In the Roman legal system the role of the villagers was carefully delineated: They were charged with the task of remembering, and their testimony carried more weight when it was given by old villagers, or in their absence, by villagers who had heard the "facts" from "ancestors of decrepit age." Since the Middle Ages villagers had fulfilled such a role in the legal system, although written sources were long-standing competitors to villagers' possibilities for defining customary practice, especially for trimming it of burdens and practices unfavorable to their cause.[25]

During the fall of 1750, the villagers offered such testimony and employed a number of strategies to challenge the straightforward interpretation of the constitution. To undermine the Barberini's claims, villagers insisted that the historical context and Christian charity for the poor undermined a literal interpretation of the *statuto*. These two features of the villagers' position can be seen in testimony provided by two witnesses on the first of December 1750:

Monte Flavio . . . is located in the middle of mountains of rock where there have never been and there could never be planted either olive trees, or vineyards or fruit trees of any kind. It is a miserable and impoverished territory, only three miles in circumference. . . . The people have no means to cultivate or to pasture their animals, so these miserable inhabitants are constrained to go begging for land in the villages of Palombara, Stazzano and other foreign territories . . . .Whoever has a mule or a horse . . . is constrained to buy hay to feed it . . . the poor keep inside each house an *animale nero* at their own expense for three years before slaughtering it. On account of the lack of agricultural and pasture lands the individuals of the village never paid the *minuti*, and if someone did pay them, it was because they were forced to or they were ignorant or sometimes [the *minuti*] were extorted from some poor inhabitant. . . . The mountain in the territory of Monte Flavio is covered with snow for most of the year, and it is useless for any productive purpose . . . the inhabitants are constrained to search for wood in the Montagna di Stazzano . . . we have heard that in the past a Governor resided in Monte Flavio as judge to administer civil and criminal justice, but now for any need the villagers have to go to the Governor who resides in Nerola, six miles from the village on terrible mountain roads, requiring these poor people to walk twelve miles round trip . . . usually repeating the trip because they could not find the Governor, or the involved parties did not appear, and if the litigation takes a long time then they have to make the trip in the rainy season, and then in the snow with great damage and inconvenience to themselves because they lose their daily wages and leave their work behind at home . . . we heard all these things from our ancestors and they from their forebears and that is what they practiced and what they saw, and what they heard was practiced.[26]

This was the longest and most elaborate testimony offered by villagers in 1750, although it echoes themes in other village testimony, suggesting a convergence of opinion was forming among politically active villagers. Both witnesses, Filippo Jazzoni and Giuseppe Pettinelli, could sign their names, and they shared family names with others who testified against the validity of the payment of the *minuti*. Jazzoni and Pettinelli may have been the ideological ringleaders of the movement. They were priests, and several priests had already been identified by the Barberini and one of their officials as inciting the villagers to resist the payment of the *minuti*. However, these two priests in particular were never named by the Barberini.

The poverty of the inhabitants and the interpretation of the *minuti* as an extortion of the poor appears in other village testimony. The priests' emphasis on the poverty of the village has precedent in earlier testimony given by six inhabitants of Monte Flavio in September 1750, regarding the impropriety of demanding certain payments from the poorest villagers of Monte Flavio. Contemporaneous to the struggle over the *minuti*, a controversy had erupted over whether Petricca could collect one-sixth of the hemp harvest in the village. Such a payment was also specified in the constitution, as were the *minuti*. The villagers explained the unfairness of the hemp payments in this way: "We have seen and we heard our ancestors say that a few families and miserable widows who did not have opportunities or lands elsewhere were constrained to sow a couple of rows of hemp among the rocks of Monte Flavio just out of necessity to cover their very miserable nudity." These elderly villages noted that poor families and widows were never charged one-sixth of the hemp harvest, but rather "the renter, arbitrary oppressor of poverty, wants to introduce these and other evil abuses out of spite."[27]

Then in the last days of December 1750, some villagers took the historical and moral framework sketched by the two priests and teased out its implications for reinterpreting the constitution. On December 27, 1750, twenty-one villagers of Monte Flavio either signed or made the sign of the cross to a *fede* that connected their refusal to pay the *minuti* to the failure of the lord to provide adequate land for cultivation and for pasture: "We even heard it from our ancestors, and they from their forebears, that they did not pay, and they had never paid [the *minuti*] because the terms [of the *statuto*] stipulating that sufficient land and pasture be given . . . were never upheld."

The villagers' interpretation demands a broader reading of the *statuto* than would have been the convention in the Roman legal system. The typical legal use of the *statuto* focused only on a very few sentences and ignored the larger implications of the text in which those sentences were situated. The very first sentence of the *statuto* states that the villagers were not required to pay any dues for use of pasture (*erbatici*) but were instead (in the second sentence) required to pay yearly, in recognition of the lords allowing their animals pasture, one sheep (for each thirty they owned), one ham, one hen, and one pair of chickens per household. By contrast the villagers make it clear in their sworn testimony that they were interpreting the *statuto* more broadly. They suggested that there were promises made to villagers beyond the simple equivalence of *minuti* payments representing the substitute for *erbatici* payments. The implicit hope expressed in the *statuto*'s opening paragraphs is that Monte Flavio would become a fertile site for agriculture, especially vineyards, since the payments that the villagers would owe on these developed lands is also specified (although no such vineyards existed at the founding of Monte Flavio). The lands of the village were rocky and generally poor in the eighteenth-century (as they had been in the sixteenth century, and as they were described by the priests). So the villagers made their living by "begging" for land in other villages, as the priests had also asserted. Although the *statuto* mentioned that "often the inhabitants would not have enough animals to use all of the pasture lands of the village," the situation in Monte Flavio was clearly quite different—the communal government had to rent pasture lands from the Borghese family to accommodate all the animals owned (or kept) by the villagers. In that regard, too, the Orsini and their successors (the Barberini) failed to fulfill one of the "promises" of the *statuto*.[28]

Most villagers either stuck with their story or they refused to participate in the Barberini's effort to undermine it. However, a few witnesses for the Barberini provide some insight into how the villagers' new history of Monte Flavio may have come into being. Signor Antonio Petrucci and Nicola Ranieri charged that the village chancellor, Felice Antonio Iazzoni, was not, in fact, a notary, but rather a shoemaker, an occupational incapacity that called into question the "legality of the *fedi*" that he took down. Ranieri might have been a notary, although he does not make that claim in his testimony. He was Iazzone's predecessor as chancellor of the village communal government. Since Ranieri sided with the Barberini, he probably was not trusted to take down the villagers' testimony, notary or not.[29]

Another witness, Belardino Paleotti, claimed that the authors of the late December testimony and its signatories were involved in an elaborate ruse. Belardino said that he was called by Andrea Petrucci, then prior of the commune, to the house of the village chancellor, Felice Antonio Iazzone. The latter had already written out the *fede*, which, Belardino was told, stated that "after the controversy started between the commune and His Excellency, the *minuti* were no longer paid." But Belardino claimed to have "seen through the document," and grasped that its message was that he and his ancestors had never paid the *minuti*, "something that was untrue, most untrue, since I know that the *minuti* were paid by my ancestors, and even by myself and my brother Giovanni, and that we kept a small book recording such payments." It is hard to know which of Belardino's signed statements to believe, since, to accept the second one (the retraction) forces one to conclude that he signed the first knowing he was signing a lie, and that "clearing his conscience" was not a matter pressing enough to bring him forward before two months had elapsed.[30]

Another villager's retraction suggests some of the ways the history writers attempted to negotiate with the signatories. Giovanni Rosati claimed that he was invited by the prior Andrea Petrucci to come to the house of Felice Antonio Iazzone in December 1750 and sign a *fede* saying that he had never paid the *minuti*. Giovanni claimed in his March 1751 retraction that, even though he signed the petition, during the encounter he had stuck to the moral high ground, proclaiming that "his father had paid, and that the receipts were in the hands of Bernardina, his sister, and that since he was a worker for various bosses outside of Monte Flavio ... he had not paid the *minuti* himself," to which the calculating Andrea and Felice Antonio were supposed to have replied, "Sign it a bit, as you can." The problem with Rosati's retraction is that his name does not appear on the list of those who signed the petition, calling into question which of his stories is true. Two villagers who did sign (and who later did not disavow their testimony) added the qualification in their own hand, "I affirm that I have never paid the *minuti*." These were Antonio Gasparri and Bernardino Fedele, who were perhaps "signing it a bit, as [they] could," showing their unwillingness to go as far as the claims of the petition about the ancestors, something twenty-one other villagers (minus Belardino Paleotti, who later retracted) were willing to do.[31]

Village resistance to the *minuti* payments was certainly fueled by tax increases and the mishandling of the controversy by Barberini officials and renters. But what was the inspiration for the particular historical and moral critique of the *minuti* that was formulated to justify that resistance? Like their peers in France, the villagers would fail in their repeated attempts to address their grievance by judicial means. Unlike French peasants, however, they challenged the seigneurial system without substantive help from anyone at the level of the intendants of France, royal officials who were supposed to have been the critical actors in the lawsuits against seigneurial dues in the eighteenth century. Village culture provided alternate frameworks with which the inhabitants of Monte Flavio could question the legitimacy of the *minuti*, even without the aid of papal officials. Aspects of oral culture, an intimate familiarity with written documents, and the skills among the villagers to write new ones, as well as the unconventional application of Christian morality, constituted an adversarial literacy that facilitated the creation of resistance ideology during the mid-eighteenth century.[32]

Oral culture, although severely constrained by the legal preeminence of written sources, offered the villagers valuable alternative readings to challenge the strict literal interpretation of the constitution. The accusation that the terms of the *statuto* had not been fulfilled by the noble family was evidently an old one, although it was rarely captured in writing. An anonymous folio in the Barberini archive noted that the villagers of Monte Flavio claimed that the terms of the *statuto* had never been fulfilled, specifically, that sufficient pasture and sufficient agricultural land had been promised in the *statuto*, but never delivered. This incidental observation, recorded by a seventeenth-century hand, in an Italian heavily influenced by the dialect, suggests that the animosity against the nobility's failure to fulfill the *statuto* in Monte Flavio was as much as a century old when the papal bureaucrats noted the discrepancy in the collection of the *minuti* in 1744. The bureaucrats' observation ignited a longstanding grievance, turning it into a strike against paying the dues, and then eventually into a lawsuit to test their legal legitimacy.[33]

This more comprehensive reading of the *statuto* put forward by the villagers in December 1750 was probably inspired by the everyday economy of Monte Flavio. Villagers were long familiar with fairly complex contracts stipulating the terms of the leasing of animals or land. The communal government made contracts with the Borghese family; local shepherds made contracts with other villages to pasture their flocks during the winter; villagers leased vineyards from the Barberini family in the more hospitable lands of Monte Libretti. Contracts were the stuff of everyday life, and they implicated both sides in a number of obligations. The villagers were reading the *statuto* not in the piecemeal way of the lawyers and the magistrates, but in a broader interpretive way, as a contract with a multiplicity of clauses, all of which had to be fulfilled for any of them to be binding.

Oral culture helped reinforce the legitimacy of such a reading in the village. Unlike highly literate culture, oral culture stresses the context of written sources, rather than their literal meaning. Village testimony introduced larger social and historical frameworks with which to evaluate the contract-constitution of Monte Flavio. With their peripatetic lifestyle, villagers were probably prone to see Monte Flavio in its comparative contemporary context, as the two priests did when they compared Monte Flavio to the villages to which its inhabitants traveled in search of pastoral and agricultural land. Oral culture also tends to situate such observations in narratives in order to better record and remember this adversarial history told from the village point of view, as the priests attempted to do in the most comprehensive testimony. If, as Walter Benjamin suggested, wandering is conducive to storytelling, the residents of Monte Flavio should have been the best storytellers in the region, with their priests and their shoemaker serving as the conduit of this local literary output.[34]

The villagers' reading of the constitution made it clear that there was no reason for the villagers to pay the *minuti* at all, since some of the *statuto*'s "terms" had never been upheld by the lords. In their account of the situation in Monte Flavio, the evidence of a "broken contract" is clear: The *statuto* had promised land that could be cultivated, but for the most part the land of Monte Flavio was too poor for growing crops; the *statuto* refers to abundant pasture land, but the commune was forced to rent pasture outside the village. The lawsuit's duration of more than a decade suggests that this view enjoyed wide support in the village, since the village *consiglio* continued to approve the necessary expenditures to sustain the lawsuit, and it continued to do so, despite the pressure by the Barberini lord against such expenditure.[35]

To think politically in the village was to demand a different reading of a document long recognized in the legal system as the primary determinant of legitimate local practice. Such a comprehensive rereading required the villagers to reinterpret the significance of the founding of the village as it was described in those first documents. The villagers and the Barberini returned to the *statuto* as the document that was supposed to clarify rights and obligations in the rural world. For the Barberini and their lawyers, the *statuto* clearly stated what the noble family deserved as income from the village. For some villagers, however, considering the specific terms of the payment of the *minuti* required a reconsideration of all the issues raised within it—the *statuto* provided evidence that the promises made at the founding of the village had been broken, and that on that basis the villagers and their ancestors had refused to make the payments described in the *statuto*.

The presence of the shoemaker-chancellor in the dispute suggests that the villagers could find individuals among themselves capable of creating the sources to support their cause. While many generations of illiterate and semi-literate people relied on notaries for such purposes, in Monte Flavio this writing capability extended even to the local shoemaker. Shoemakers have a history of radicalism and literacy, beginning in the late eighteenth century, and Monte Flavio's shoemaker was an early example of one of these "intellectual artisans." He evidently navigated a number of difficulties in recording the villagers' testimony, including the problem that the *minuti*, while perhaps unjust, had been paid, at least by some individuals. In wrestling with these issues, the chancellor, the prior, and the willing signatories, were creating what the anthropologist Liisa Malkki called a "mythico-history," that is a history written with more focus on "a deeply moral scheme of good and evil" than on a strict evaluation of what was true and what was false in the telling. To authenticate Monte Flavio's mythico-history, the ancestors, too, had to have shared their descendants' dilemma over the *minuti*. The ancestors are summoned in the testimony to establish that the immorality of the system was old, recognized by generations of villagers, and rightfully resisted by them whenever possible. If some villagers told a lie about whether or not the *minuti* were paid, they might well have been telling it in the service of this (in their eyes) "greater" truth. Those villagers who were squeamish about the breadth of the claims were urged to "Sign it a bit, as [they could]," a move reminiscent of the way individual voters voted in *consiglio*, agreeing with a proposal, but modifying it slightly while casting their vote. The night of December 27, 1750 marked an attempt to negotiate a new history of Monte Flavio in these terms.[36]

The villagers' stories about Monte Flavio also drew upon what was one of the more important local commonplaces, as *consiglio* deliberations in the neighboring village of Monte Libretti clearly show: The poor in society were to be protected, not persecuted. In Monte Flavio this concept appears in the village complaint about the collection of the sixth of the hemp production from "a few families and miserable widows," whose poverty was exacerbated, in effect,

by the "renter, arbitrary oppressor of poverty." The priests' testimony general-
izes the poverty of widows and the poorest families (the most vulnerable in village society) to the village as a whole. In light of the physical shortcomings of
the village lands, the villagers were all poor in the sense that the struggle for
their livelihood was a daunting undertaking, especially relative to other villages,
where they went searching for land. The priests noted the additional burden
imposed by the lack of access to the lord's justice. Seigneurial dues, if collected, were to be considered an unjustifiable burden on an already burdened
village. Since justice was the business of the noble family, the remoteness of
this judge was an indictment of the noble family, whose members, in addition
to extorting money in the form of the *minuti*, were remiss in providing one of
the services in the village integral to their lordship. Such a criticism would provide the magistrates reviewing the case with a sense of the broad failure of the
Barberini's whole seigneurial enterprise in Monte Flavio.[37]

Was this the gospel preached in Monte Flavio? Or did the priests derive
their inspiration from the political culture of the villagers? In early sixteenth-
century Germany, peasant rebellion had been similarly blocked by the weight
of the written record in favor of hated seigneurial dues, and there peasants also
turned to "godly law" to rupture such barriers and to change their status vis-
à-vis their lords. Peter Blickle has captured the synergy between the communal
rebellion and the Reformation, a regretted synergy, in the eyes of the former
priest Martin Luther, but a revolutionary synergy by which all later early modern peasant rebellions are judged. In the absence of records from village *consiglio* meetings, it is impossible to say whether the priests were the instigators of
this particular critique of disputed dues. Giulio Cesare Barberini evidently
thought that the parish priest could have great influence with the faithful,
hence his interest in naming the deceased archpriest's successor. The Barberini's
hope that the right priest would lend his support to the noble cause parallels
his reliance on the archpriest Mazzetti, in the village of Monte Libretti. In
Monte Flavio (as in other villages of the *stato*) Giulio Cesare found mixed support from the priests. Barberini edicts and letters expressed high hopes for the
symbiotic intertwining of ecclesiastical and governing hierarchies. An edict issued (reissued multiple times) in the 1750s stressed this catechism: "every
human and divine law demanded that [Barberini] vassals faithfully maintain
the rights of the noble family." Another edict from that same decade enjoined
the "faithful vassals . . . that they should have at heart the maintenance of the
rights rightfully belonging to the Barberini Princes." The Barberini hoped to
make the parish priest a useful ally in their struggle to teach the lord's catechism and in so doing create more disciplined and compliant vassals out of the
apparently unruly inhabitants of Monte Flavio.[38]

The villagers of Monte Flavio evidently strayed far from this catechism. While in many ways, they identify themselves as the most subjugated members of society, their self-identification served the intention of exploiting the paradoxes of their "lowly" position. They reversed the notion that various kinds of hierarchies reinforced each other, suggesting instead that if God had anything to do with poultry dues he would not be on the side of those doing the collecting, but rather on the side of those who had to pay. Penny Lernoux summarized this alternative Catholicism simply, but accurately, twenty years ago: "Although frequently in the past Christianity has appeared in ideological guises, it is essentially a critical discipline, a constant call for justice." The villagers made explicit this message, latent in early modern Catholicism, and thereby made a damning critique of the noble family on several levels.[39]

In their letters and their edicts the Barberini represented themselves as the defenders of their poor vassals, especially women and widows, who wrote the Barberini prince for his protection or his charity and to whom such charity was usually extended. So to connect the Barberini to their persecution undercut the noble family's religious paternalism, a centerpiece of the noble family's image of itself in the eighteenth century. Clerics in Rome inside the papal government, as well as private elite individuals, devoted considerable effort to public assistance. The charge that the Barberini failed to support the poor in their own territories, made in the semi-public forum of the courts, was intended to get the attention of clerics in Rome, who were steeped in the centrality of charity to the practice of Catholicism.[40]

The critique of the dues as a persecution of the poor was a challenge to papal magistrates as well as the noble family. Since the villagers had only a limited possibility for making the law in their village assembly, or *consiglio*, and no possibility for officially interpreting it in the capacity enjoyed by the magistrates, they could only suggest that the conventional reading of the *statuto* be evaluated according to Catholic theology. This was a superficially innocent request, considering they resided in a theocratic state; however, this form of village resistance forced papal magistrates to decide whether they were judges first and priests second, or vice versa. Did the magistrates enforce manmade law or did they live the gospel? Resistance is often built from this type of wily maneuvering on the part of the powerless, who juxtapose two discourses that contain contrary elements. By making the contradictions plain, marginalized individuals hope to force those who govern to prioritize them, hopefully in their favor, or at a minimum to create a level of discomfort with the contradiction that would facilitate reform or compromise of one sort or another. This level of interpretive cleverness was common in the Old Regime, where adversarial literacy, and tactics of this sort, were developed instead of violent rebellion as a means of settling conflict.[41]

Clerical Response to
Adversarial Literacy

The villagers of Monte Flavio were unable to convince elites in Rome that their reading of the constitution and their critique of Barberini lordship undermined the legitimacy of the *minuti*. Although the village case had a moral core that the nobleman's position clearly lacked, the villagers lost their case, which was referred by the Segnatura to the court of appeal, the Rota, in 1753. Villagers lost every appeal thereafter, in 1755, 1758, and 1759. To some extent, the magistrates reviewed a version of the same evidence each time (with a slight variation in 1759) so in the summary of the villagers' judicial losses that follows, the reasoning of the judge who made his case most clearly will be cited, and their decisions will not be reviewed in chronological order. Close attention will also be given to the way in which individual magistrates responded to the villagers' interpretation of the constitution and the dues.[42]

The judgment against the villagers was facilitated by the Barberini's attempt to create confusion in the minds of the magistrates about the identity and the integrity of those testifying on behalf of the villagers. The Barberini were assisted in this to some extent by the sheer repetitiveness of the family names in the village. One can imagine a Roman magistrate, sinking into his chair after a heavy midday meal, feeling his eyes close as he pored over the repetitive village roll call in the written documents and the oral testimony. The Petrucci–Petricca axis alone would certainly befuddle any but the most attentive reader (one wishes, for instance, that Silvia Petrucci had married the Mei rather than the Petricca, just to add some clarity to the entanglements of the 1740s). Then whether lapsing into a light sleep or merely struggling to stay awake, who could avoid being at least momentarily mesmerized by the contrary reincarnation of Giovanni Iezzone—who swore in 1750 that he and his ancestors had never paid the *minuti*, from the Giovanni Iezzone of 1675, who evidently had collected them?[43]

The testimony that convinced the magistrates of the Rota was not from the contemporary villagers, but from the villagers of the seventeenth century. A *fede* from 1694 was eventually uncovered by the Barberini that was particularly damaging to the villagers' case. Only three villagers testified at that time, but they were the priors of the village, and they offered testimony asserting that the *minuti* were being collected. They offered the testimony not at the noble family's request, but in the context of another lawsuit, an important detail for the magistrates. A similar paper trail from 1700 clinched it for the magistrate of the Rota who wrote the decision against the villagers in 1758. It was difficult to accept the testimony of the contemporary villagers as more credible than the older testimony, since the former was all given by inhabitants on behalf of their own cause. Although the judges also emphasized the retractions, they ignored the fact that much time had elapsed since 1694/1700 and that most villagers who testified against the *minuti* never retracted their statement, and were never discredited as witnesses.[44]

The villagers' lawyer had clearly done some of his own digging in the seventeenth century to try to substantiate the villagers claims and he had produced a few interesting finds from the previous century. Some villagers were so poor that they had to do labor for the renter, since they had neither cash nor goods with which to pay the *minuti*. The situation had occurred periodically even until the 1720s, under the renter Felice Antonio Petrucci. Such evidence suggested the hardship the *minuti* imposed on the villagers, but Roman judges found it difficult to conceptualize the *minuti* as a hardship. The magistrate of 1755 discounted the claim that the *minuti* imposed a particularly heavy burden, referring to them as "paucis praestationibus." Indeed, they must have seemed like relatively light feudal dues: two scrawny country chickens, a ham, and a hen—they would fit on the magistrate's table. How could they be much of a burden for a country household?[45]

The answer, of course, depends on the household. In 1746, when Sante Sciarra labored to collect the last of the debts to the commune, he entered forty of the forty-seven households so indebted. Of those forty households, sixteen of them contained nothing at all which could be offered to pay the delinquent taxes, and most of the rest offered not the cash they owed, but regular household effects: pots, basins, shovels, iron chains, bed warmers, and even a gun. Sciarra's report to the Buon Governo indicates that for some villagers even meeting a small tax payment was hard, and in the 1740s payments owed by villagers only seemed to be rising, with new tithes on the lands the villagers had to rent from the Borghese because their own noble family had not provided them enough pasture land, new taxes for foreign wars, the imposition of "old" burdens that the previous renter may have ignored (such as collecting one-sixth of the hemp production). It is in this larger context that even the "small" burden of the *minuti* seems to have become intolerable.[46]

The magistrates, however, saw no legal way around the clear evidence for the *minuti* in the constitution. As the magistrate in 1755 noted, at the founding of the village, the villagers had accepted for themselves and the future inhabitants that the constitution was the law. The villagers' ancestors locked themselves and their descendants into the terms of their obligations. Who else lived under the rigidity of such bargains? The noble family was also constrained by the particulars of the *statuto*, but they were terms that favored the noble family, regardless of how well the Barberini delivered the "services" of their lordship. The popes were able to strip off their historical straitjackets, imposing new taxes (in effect, rewriting the terms of their subjects' lives) when it suited their purposes, including the purpose of the Habsburg ascendancy to the throne of the Holy Roman Empire, an event of little or no significance in the Roman countryside. The villagers' persistence in reinterpreting the *statuto* was an attempt to find an exit from the texts that would allow them to shed some old payments at a time when the papacy imposed new burdens, and the Barberini insisted upon their collection. During the controversy over the *minuti* villagers resisted the notion that only those in power can create the texts that shape the world, and that those same monopolists should have the final say in what they mean.[47]

After losing on appeal again in 1758 (the magistrate's decision of that year at least acknowledged that the land was inhospitable, but noted that the dues had always been collected), the villagers tried one last time in 1759, asking the court to consider that the terms of the payments in the *statuto* were still not clear. The magistrate (who concurred with the reasoning of his predecessor) settled the issue of the ambiguity of the language, especially to what payments the expression "per household per year" referred. He asserted that every household was required to pay, regardless of whether they owned animals or not, one ham, one hen, and two chickens, per year. Thus ended the village protest by means of the papal courts. Villagers then turned to negotiations with the noble family two years later, by which time the *minuti* had still yet to be paid, suggesting that the strike continued, even if the lawsuit did not.[48]

CONCLUSION

During the seventeenth and eighteenth centuries, the aristocratic Barberini family traced its political genealogy to God. Once the monarchical family of the Papal States during the papacy of Maffeo Barberini (Pope Urban VIII, 1623–1644), upon his death his nephews and their descendants had to "settle" for merely ruling the country territories where they had bought their way to lordship during his reign. Seventeenth-century edicts issued for the semi-independent *stato* of Monte Libretti made grand claims for the sovereignty of the noble family in the territory, including the right not only to issue the laws, but also to interpret them in the case of any ambiguity. Seventeenth-century edicts also asserted that rural officials stood in place of the noble family and deserved all the reverence that would ordinarily be shown to the aristocratic lord. One should, in their presence, "take off one's cap, and speak with every reverence, calmly, and in a way which does not cause public or private scandal." For an "intentional" violation of this law that included ridiculing or laughing at the official, the penalty was the *strappado* and exile from the *stato*. Throughout the eighteenth century, Barberini edicts continued to assert the importance of village reverence for Barberini rule. As an edict issued (and reissued) in the 1750s put it: "every human and divine law demanded that [Barberini] vassals faithfully maintain the rights of the noble family." A village assembly that produced decisions that contravened the noble family's opinions had clearly made an error due to having been swayed by "human considerations," rather than the venerable orders of the noble family. In the proclamations and letters of the noble family, obedience to noble laws remained intertwined with the divine order of the universe, a political theology that suggested there were links between eternal life and edicts on pig grazing.[1]

The family's territorial goals during the papacy of Urban VIII had been higher than the *stato* of Monte Libretti. Ambitiously and disastrously, the Barberini coveted the Duchy of Castro during the early 1640s. Yet the *stato* of Monte Libretti was still an impressive consolation prize, chosen, like the Duchy before it, for what it offered the Barberini in terms of governing: an extensive semi-independent territory indirectly subject to the pope. Losing the papacy and acquiring such a territory showed the Barberini the drawbacks of their still lofty but lowered status in Roman society. Their peers in Rome punished them for their formerly grandiose ambitions, and their newly acquired vassals did not hesitate to question the limits of their seigneurial demands through the papal courts. Monte Libretti's economic shortcomings became evident early in Barberini ownership. With net incomes lower than what the sellers had promised, the family of Urban VIII also found itself embroiled in a labor controversy with the villagers, which the villagers ultimately won. It was the first of many rural controversies for the noble family.

Maffeo Barberini rebounded from these initial difficulties and became a Roman baron engaged in the ruling of his territory between the 1660s and the 1680s. His strategy was inconsistent, willfully so. In Nerola, he issued edicts on his hunting monopoly that contravened the terms of the *statuto* of the village, and a Roman court upheld his right to do so. His legal success was tough to enforce in the village, where the *statuto*, rather than noble laws or papal decrees held more sway. In the neighboring village of Monte Libretti, villagers asked him to settle political disputes between villagers over how to allocate scarce communal resources. Some priors and villagers hoped he would weigh in on their side and in some cases that he would overturn legitimate majorities in the consiglio. Maffeo hesitated in the village of Monte Libretti, in part to avoid settling disputes where any decision was bound to make some enemies, and in part to limit how much the villagers could ask of him. With their propensity to travel to Rome, or petition the Barberini prince, the concerns of the villagers of Monte Libretti arrived too frequently at the Barberini palace for the nobleman's tastes.

During the first decades of the eighteenth century the Barberini family endured the repeated disasters inflicted by an irresponsible heir (Urbano Barberini, 1664–1722). Simultaneously early eighteenth-century popes turned their attention to the baronial fiefs yet outside their direct jurisdiction. Through occasional visits to such villages by the bureaucrats of the Papal Congregation of the Buon Governo and the imposition of new taxes on the wealth of the nobility, the papal government challenged baronial power and privilege. Rather than supplant the connection between the aristocratic family and their vassals, however, the papacy's interest only piqued the Barberini's interest in governing. Urbano's brother Francesco did his best simply to hold on to control of the Barberini territories, and in the *stato* of Monte Libretti he advanced the interests of Buon Governo itself in eliminating the indebtedness of the communes. His niece and nephew-in-law, Cornelia Costanza and Giulio Cesare Barberini Colonna di Sciarra, expanded their presence in the villages beyond his or any previous generation. They scrupulously monitored communal affairs; became essential conduits of information between the Buon Governo and the villages; insisted on the villagers' prompt payment of taxes; exercised their noble right to control participation in village communal politics; and monitored justice and maintained jails. They continually advanced the idea that there was a connection between their meticulous administration and the divine order of the universe. They claimed that it was their paternal love for the villagers that prompted their tender intervention into issues ranging from the education of the children to the burial of the village dead. By the mid-eighteenth-century, attention to the fate of the vassals in the countryside consumed noble literary efforts and shaped noble identity to a greater extent than ever before. Nobles like the Barberini had remained a ruling class in the territories that were under their jurisdiction. A clerical regime had proved no barrier to this transformation; on the contrary, its expansion had partially inspired it.

The Barberini's letters and edicts increasingly celebrated the sacred legitimacy of their rule, but such a theological perspective was evidently easier to see in Rome than it was to recognize in the countryside. Many villagers in the territory of Monte Libretti thought that you could shake the lofty aristocratic perch a bit and not risk divine wrath. Hierarchical systems like those of early modern Europe frequently oscillated due to such shoves. E. P. Thompson and a number of persuasive successors have analyzed the political content of these everyday nudges, insisting on the politics embedded in grumbling, foot dragging, anonymous petition-writing, and practicing "rights piecemeal ... [that] were denied in law." Villagers in central Italy, however, shifted from dragging their feet to dragging their lords into the judicial avenues offered by the papal government for addressing their grievances. The willingness and skill with which villagers around Rome availed themselves of these possibilities underscores the political vitality of the early modern period, especially the extent to which its civic culture thrived from Castile to Württemberg, from central Italy to eastern France. Clearly the state itself had a role in shaping the development of this political culture. In a recent and provocative analysis of political culture in late eighteenth-century Germany, the historian Ian McNeely has allotted it most of the credit for the emergence of modern civil society. However, the willingness of ordinary people to avail themselves of its possibilities and to push it in directions beyond its adherents' intended scope suggests that early modern civil society flourished in part not because of the state, but in spite of it. The early modern state did indeed act as a broker between competing social groups, but villagers in central Italy showed themselves remarkably determined to recast its deal-making in terms more favorable to them. Several aspects of village culture contributed to this type of political activism on the part of the villagers. Village political activities shaped the ruling practices of the Barberini, who continued to make extensive claims in the eighteenth century about their right to rule and who remained the most consistent governing presence in the *stato*.[2]

Between the mid-seventeenth and the mid-eighteenth century, villagers in the *stato* of Monte Libretti were able to sustain their struggle against the Barberini through the use of adversarial literacy, a type of early modern literacy still relatively understudied. Yet it was critical to village resistance and, while not called by that name, it was recognized by the Barberini family as key source of the troublemaking in the village, hence the noble family's promotion of other forms of literacy. Despite the noble family's opposition, adversarial literacy reached its target. Although, in the course of one hundred years, little changed in the rhetorical claims to power on the part of the family, and many of the family's rights to intervene in village politics remained formally in place, the Barberini were forced to concede in practice that the villagers were an important political force in the countryside.

How were peasants with little education and minimal political power beyond the village able to accomplish this? Villagers in the Barberini territory availed themselves of all the possibilities offered by the papacy to challenge the terms of noble rule. In the mid-seventeenth century, they used the avenues offered by the papal law courts, and in the eighteenth century, the possibilities offered by the expansion of the Papal Congregation of the Buon Governo, which was devoted to auditing communal accounts and collecting taxes. Gradually, over several generations, the villagers' tactics increased in sophistication and in frequency. By the mid-eighteenth century the new ruler of the territory of Monte Libretti had to take this level of adversarial literacy into account in order to govern, if he wished to accomplish his goals. The Barberini accepted that the noble right to rule had to be negotiated with villagers, especially with the villagers who participated in the politics of their local communal governments. Surviving noble letters illustrate that this reality was recognized by the Barberini lord by the mid-eighteenth century, even if it was not always acted upon—imposing his will remained too attractive to abandon altogether, despite its inefficiency.

Thus the story of the Roman countryside can no longer be told as the story of the struggle between the papal monarch and the great aristocratic families, since the villagers constituted such an effective threat to the noble family through their participation in village communal government. This reality of local politics had to be shown to the Barberini repeatedly during the seventeenth century by the citizens of the *stato*. The first rulers of the territory tried to rule simply by issuing decrees through their officials, typically through their chief judicial magistrate, the *auditore*, or through governors who assisted the *auditore* in publicizing and enforcing Barberini law. In the seventeenth century, the skills required to oppose such tactics were learned in the oral give and take of discussion in the *consiglio*. Even if technical skills of writing were quite poor in the village, they were made to be sufficient to the struggle, or the aid of notaries and more trained individuals was enlisted.

Seventeenth-century *consiglio* records are occasionally written in a language so rough that its transcription has stunned some scholarly readers. Such orthographic and grammatical failings, combined with the villagers' tendency to focus not so much on getting a text "right," but rather on getting their rights with it, widen the gulf between past village writers and contemporary academic readers. The villagers would, I suspect, be equally mystified by how our subtle abilities to decipher and create texts exists alongside our anemic advocacy for our own labor in an environment where the same work receives remarkably varied compensation. If you are not writing to get your rights, what are you writing for? This is the basic premise of the villagers' adversarial literacy, especially as it reached its full development during the eighteenth century.

European peasants developed the skills of adversarial literacy rather than resort to violence to address their grievances. Although during the eighteenth century they continued to use the *statuto* to defend their rights, they further refined their use of the document, insisting on alternate readings of it and other texts. They applied paradigms, including religious ones, to sources like constitutions, where they were typically not applied. To reinterpret those texts, they employed strategies more common to the oral tradition, in which the context in which texts were created was as important as the literal reading of them. Finally, villagers reached a level of autonomy in the writing of sources, rather than merely reading them. They turned more of their village records, like the notes of the *consiglio* meeting, into tools to use during their legal skirmishes with the noble family. In the village of Monte Flavio, the shoemaker helped villagers stitch resistance together from the threads of long-standing dissatisfaction with the payments they owed the lord on their poor lands. The alternative readings of old sources and the increasing frequency with which villagers made new ones differentiates the adversarial literacy of the eighteenth-century villagers from the literate practices of their ancestors several generations before.

The mid-eighteenth-century ruler of the territory, Giulio Cesare Barberini Colonna di Sciarra, considered most of these developments a real liability to his governing of the *stato* of Monte Libretti. Yet it was the nobleman and his predecessors who had inadvertently brought about such a transformation in village politics. Simply by insisting on primary education for the boys appears to have had an impact. The historian R. A. Houston has argued in his recent survey of early modern literacy that schooling at the basic level offered in the villages of Monte Libretti was unlikely to encourage either the skills of composition or the capacity for "critical understanding," as he put it. But the basic skills combined with the discussion in and out of the *consiglio* about political matters of interest to the villagers could in some individuals facilitate the skills both to create and to critique. One important beneficiary of noble educational concern in Monte Flavio was the shoemaker, Felice Antonio Iezzone, who was also the chancellor of the village. Ironically neither the Buon Governo nor the Barberini could achieve the goal of financially solvent tax-paying communities without the reading and writing skills like those of the shoemaker-chancellor. Visitors from the Buon Governo lamented the lack of such skills among the villages of the *stato* of Monte Libretti, including and especially Monte Flavio. Giulio Cesare insisted on the presence of a schoolteacher in the village, someone who would teach its boys "their letters, basic instruction in our Holy Faith, and good manners." But in Monte Flavio even Roman Catholicism, ostensibly the theological glue of the society, cut to the antagonisms in the social order about as powerfully as it mended them. Giulio Cesare feared priests who favored the former rather than the latter potential of Roman Catholicism, especially from priests willing to participate in politics. He maligned the presence of troublemakers, that is, "clerics and grumblers" among the participants in the *consiglio* and the officials of the communes. Evidently reliable allies in teaching the lord's catechism were everywhere difficult to find.[3]

Even in "crassly ignorant" Monte Flavio, Felice Antonio Iezzone had learned more than the Barberini catechism. As a boy he bowed his head over the rudiments of learning alongside his brother, Filippo. Later in life, one brother turned to shoemaking, and the other to school teaching as a trade. Felice Antonio's writing efforts on the part of the villagers were not at all what Giulio Cesare had in mind when he promoted primary education. Although he admitted to Filippo that he would prefer someone besides his brother to serve as village chancellor, after three intense years of legal battle with the villagers, the nobleman was willing to accept Felice's place in the village government. Indeed, he wrote of the "loving regard" in which he held the shoemaker-chancellor. Having tried tactics as varied as gifts of white damask *baldacchini*, annulled *consigli*, "offers to purge the souls of the false witnesses" (who testified for Felice), and exhortations to submit to his divinely ordained seigneurial rights, Giulio Cesare turned to the good manners he recommended his officials employ with the villagers. How this last Trojan horse of Giulio Cesare's was seen in the village is not known, but the villagers battled on in the law courts.[4]

Iezzone turned the skills that ruling elites probably helped to provide him to contentious purposes. He put to paper a complaint at least as old as the oldest villager and gave written form to the grumbling the villagers must have done as they walked home to Monte Flavio from the borrowed lands in the valleys below. He would no doubt be surprised, to see the testimony of Monte Flavio's disgruntled wanderers come to rest here on the pages of this book. Michael Ignatieff is right about individuals like Iezzone—they owe us nothing; they wrote for their times, not for ours. It is we, he insists, who "owe . . . them the fidelity to the truth of the lives they had led." For me, Iezzone provides a lesson, however unintentional: that we would do well to facilitate the reading and writing of texts from the powerless who constitute most of the world's people, and to consider the possibilities for meaningful change they offer, rather than read them defensively or exclusively as threats to our rights and privileges, or merely as a side road taking us away from our grander and more telegenic ideologies.[5]

From a single observation left casually by the agents of the Buon Governo when they came looking for taxes in 1744, the villagers of Monte Flavio proceeded to create new texts and to rethink old ones in a way that would have facilitated the gradual reform of the seigneurial system of which they were a part. Although the magistrates were not convinced, their repeated willingness to reconsider the case at least acknowledges that the villagers had gotten their attention, if not their support, for the critique of the disputed dues. Later in the century, villagers fatigued by just this kind of judicial dodging would force change by returning to the burning of texts, orchestrating the demise of the seigneurial regime in France in the summer of 1789. The revolutionaries, stuck with the same tax dilemmas that plagued the eighteenth century, combined with the novelty of an improvised political world at Versailles, had no choice but to grant the villagers what they wanted. The abolition of the feudal regime did not, of course, inaugurate democracy or overturn the paternalistic order at the level of the village, in which there was no place for women's participation or for the participation of the poor, except as recipients of protection from tax-paying participants in local government. Yet male villagers were among the most politically organized people in Europe, and it is perhaps not surprising that they emerged everywhere in the west from the chaos of the French Revolution with this success in their hands. Although it scarcely solved all the dilemmas of rural society, it effectively undid the seigneurial regime. It would find few defenders, even in central Italy after the Restoration of the popes to their theocratic state in the early nineteenth century. As historians of modern Italy have noted, Roman (and other Italian) elites accepted the values of the

French Revolution more readily than most of their contemporaries elsewhere in Europe. The role of villagers in Italy in this shift has scarcely been explored, indeed many contemporary observers and historians have assumed that since villagers lacked "any political right," they could not have contributed to this transformation. The challenge of the seigneurial regime in the law courts of Rome, sustained by villagers working through their communal institutions, was quite old by the time the French Revolution came to Italy via Napoleon. The shortcomings of the seigneurial regime had been protested in the remotest corners of the Roman countryside, by the practices of adversarial literacy, which held the potential for reshaping the seemingly unquestionable fixtures that sustained the Old Regime. Villagers like those of the *stato* of Monte Libretti were leading the way in the mid-eighteenth century, but found no elites yet ready to follow.[6]

The Barberini Family Tree

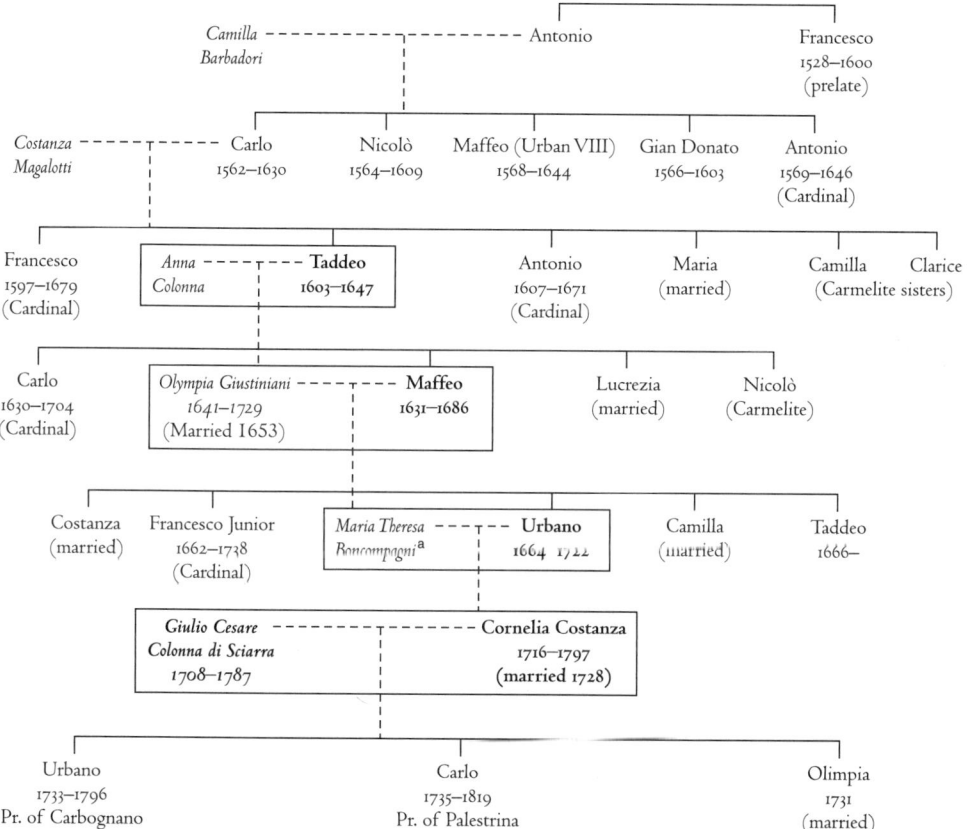

Note: Italicized names are of individuals who married into the Barberini family. Readers will find a more complete tree in Waddy, *Seventeenth-Century Palaces*, figure 50.

[a] Maria Theresa Boncompagni was the third wife of Urbano Barberini. Urbano also had an illegitimate son, Maffeo Callisto (1688–?), who was given the title Marchese of Corese, but was later disinherited from all property by his uncle Francesco.

APPENDIX 2:

Money, Weights, and Measures

Land measurements[a]
rubbio = 4.5 acres = 1.84 hectares = 4 quarte
pezzo = .65 acre (7 pezze = 1 rubbio)
rubbiatella = 2 quarte = 2.5 acres

Weight and volumetric measurements
rubbio = 294.46 liters = 8.36 bushels
rubbio = 203.45 kg = 600 libre romane = 447.59 American pounds

Money
Scudo = 100 baiocchi
Giulio = 10 baiocchi
Quattrino = 1/5 of a baiocco[b]

Note: In sorting out the sytem of measures in Rome, I benefited greatly from the knowledge and expertise of Mirka Beneš.

[a]Alfio Cortonesi has consulted a great many sources to compile a very thorough table of measures for Rome. See his *Terre e signori nel Lazio medioevale: Un'economia rurale nei secoli XIII–XIV* (Naples, 1988), 25–26.

[b]Laurie Nussdorfer, *Civic Politics in the Rome of Urban VIII* (Princeton, 1922), xvii.

APPENDIX 3:

Population of the Stato
of Monte Libretti

Village	1656	1701	1708	1742
Monte Libretti	339	417	430	553
Nerola	420	430	450	383
Corese	119	206	174	174
Ponticelli	158	250	227	254
Montorio Romano	407	487	495	535
Monte Flavio	700	685	740	849
TOTAL	2,143	2,505	2,516	2,748

Note: All population figures are from Francesco Corridore, *La populazione dello Stato Romano (1656–1901)* (Rome, 1906). Corridore based his figures on manuscripts of individual census scattered throughout Rome. Corridore, 90, 94–95, 142, and 218. For 1656, only individuals more than 3 years of age were counted.

NOTES

INTRODUCTION

1. Campanelli's survey was divided into two parts, the first sent to Maffeo in November 1811, the second or "Supplemento" in the first days of 1812. Page references here are my own and refer to the copy of the two parts entitled "Dettaglio dell'Antichità, e preggi di Nerola, Terra Principale dello Stato di Monte Libretti ... d'Innocenzo Campanelli a 20 Novembre 1811." See especially pp. 3 and 10 on the virtues of Nerola and Sabina; pp. 15–22 on the excellence of the Nerolani; p. 9 on the conditions of agriculture and agricultural labor; p. 28 on the appeal to the prince. Archivio Barberini Colonna di Sciarra, Biblioteca Apostolica Vaticana (hereinafter ABCS) 271, fasc. 1. On the proliferation and significance of commemorative inscriptions in Italian during the eighteenth century, see Raymond Grew, "Finding Social Capital: The French Revolution in Italy," 417–418.

2. Archivio Barberini Computisteria, Vatican Library (hereinafter ABC) 997, 527r–528; ABC 990, 453r. On the fire in Monte Flavio that destroyed most of its archive, see Angela Barberi and Maria Teresa De Nigris, *Comune di Monte Flavio: Inventario dell'Archivio Storico Comunale.*

3. Eavan Boland, *Object Lessons: The Life of the Woman and the Poet in Our Time,* 16.

4. "Inexorable gilded decadence" summarizes their problems for Pio Pecchiai, *I Barberini,* 227. The interpretation that the villagers accepted the burdens of the papacy without protest is Jean Delumeau, *Vie économique et sociale de Rome dans la seconde moitié du XVIe siècle,* esp. vol. 2, 842–843.

5. William Beik, *Absolutism and Society in Seventeenth-Century France: State Power and Provincial Aristocracy in Languedoc.*

6. My examination of noble jurisdiction has benefited greatly from Laurie Nuss-dorfer's work on overlapping jurisdictions in the city of Rome. See *Civic Politics in the Rome of Urban VIII.* Many authors have commented on the preponderance of baronial jurisdiction around Rome. See the recent summary in Roberto Volpi, *Le Regioni introva-bili: Centralizzazione e regionalizzazione dello Stato Pontificio,* 66–68. On the notion of "direct" and "indirect" subjugation to the pope, see Lando Scotoni, *I Territori Autonomi dello Stato Ecclesiastico nel Cinquecento: Cartografia e aspetti amministrativi, economici e sociali,* 59–60.

7. On Nerola and Ponticelli, see ABCS 271, fasc. 27; on Monte Libretti, see ABCS 244, fasc. 2. All of these *possessi* took place in 1729. There is also a record of the *possesso* in 1732 of Monte Maggiore, which records the Barberini properties in the *tenuta* (ABCS 247, fasc. 47). The priors and *consiglieri* of Nerola promised that they would be "true and faithful vassals" of the Barberini and "to never participate in any *consiglio* with assis-tance, words or actions against the person, life, honor, status and goods of the said . . . Prince and Princess." They also promised to thwart any plots they knew of against the ruling couple or to inform someone if they could not do so. ABCS 271, fasc. 27.

8. On the persistence of such language despite its apparent obsolescence, see Guido Pescosolido, *Terra e nobiltà: I Borghese, secoli XVIII e XIX,* 49–50.

9. Of the vast literature on the countryside around Rome, see especially, the early nineteenth-century author, Nicola Maria Nicolaj, who attempted the first broad compendium historical and geographical examination of the *campagna romana.* See an overview of it in Alberto Canaletti Guadenti, *La Politica agraria ed annonaria dello Stato Pontificio da Benedetto XIV a Pio VII,* 65–96. Philippe De Tournon provided one of the most revealing analyses of Rome and its countryside, in *Études statistiques sur Rome et la partie occidentale des États Romains.* Cesare De Cupis in his *Le vicende dell'agricoltura e della pastorizia nella campagna romana* offered a chronological summary of changes in the countryside. Giovanni Curis, *Usi civici, proprietà collettive e latifondi nell'Italia centrale e nell'Emilia,* focused on legal issues. Werner Sombart, *La Campagna Romana: studio economico-sociale,* attempted to summarize the inquest literature of the nineteenth century. The Tomassetti (father and son) working at the beginning of the twentieth century created an enduring work on the Roman countryside. See especially the new edition of it, which also contains extensive bibliographic notes. Giuseppe Tomassetti, *La Campagna Romana: antica mediovale e moderna,* 2nd ed., 7 vols. Jean Coste issued the call for a more accurate methodology in his article, "La Topographie médiévale de la Campagne romaine et l'histoire socio-économique: pistes de recherche." Pecchiai, *I Barberini,* 214; Curis, *Usi civici,* 424, 703–704.

10. Giovanni Curis and Cesare De Cupis praised the valiant efforts of the popes to limit the power of the barons, protect rights of inhabitants, and promote cultivation. Writing in the 1950s, Jean Delumeau criticized the absentee nobles (whose financial difficulties he rightly emphasized) and shifted the blame more to the failures of the popes themselves to encourage industry and successfully expand grain cultivation with policies, which, had the popes actually followed them, would have been unique in Europe. See his *Vie économique.* The tragic interpretation of the Roman countryside has

proved amazingly resilient, even in the face of evidence that suggests that it needs to be reevaluated and modified. See the recent summary of literature on the *agro romano* by Hanns Gross in his *Rome in the Age of Enlightenment*, 152–174.

11. In his study of the economic administration of the Roman noble family, (the Borghese), Pescosolido dismissed noble jurisdiction in a few paragraphs, arguing that the expansion of the papal congregation of the Buon Governo in 1704 superseded the nobility's role in the fiefs. See Pescosolido, 48–50. Other authors also mention jurisdiction briefly—see for instance Hurtubise, *Une famille-témoin, Les Salviati*, 389–390. Recent scholarship on the Roman nobility complicates this view. See the general survey of this scholarship offered by Maria Antonietta Visceglia, "La Nobiltà romana: dibattito storiografico e ricerche in corso," in *La Nobiltà romana in età moderna: Profili istituzionali e pratiche sociali*, ed. Maria Antonietta Visceglia, xiii–xli. Other important acticles in the anthology related to the history of the Roman nobility in the countryside include the essay by Bertrand Forclaz, who argues that the Borghese's attention to the administraion of justice in their territories was much more important than its low economic worth indicates. See her article, "Le Relazioni complesse tra signore e vassalli: La famiglia Borghese e i suoi feudi nel Seicento," 165–201. David Armando and Adriano Ruggeri underscore the continuing importance of noble jurisdiction during the eighteenth century in their essay, "La Geografia feudale del Lazio alla fine del Settecento," 401–445. Noble administration of justice in the sixteenth century is analyzed in Marina D'Amelia, *Orgoglio Baronale e Giustizia: Castel Viscardo alla fine del Cinquecento*. A monograph rich in the primary sources (some of which are reproduced in facsimile) is Nicola La Marca, *La Nobiltà romana e i suoi strumenti di perpetuazione del potere*, 3 vols. Volume 1 focuses on the early modern period.

12. ABC 999, 285v [March 18, 1775].

13. The German peasant wars of 1525 were the most radical in their demands, but they also were exceptional in that regard. Peasant rebellion in a variety of European contexts is available in Tom Scott, ed., *Peasantries of Europe: From the Fourteenth to the Eighteenth Centuries*. The participation of rural people in early modern rebellions is analyzed in Yves-Marie Bercé, *Revolt and Revolution in Early Modern Europe: An Essay on the History of Political Violence*. Wayne Te Brake links peasant revolts and the political practices of ordinary people to European state development in his *Shaping History: Ordinary People in European Politics, 1500–1700*.

14. For "an ongoing," see Te Brake, *Shaping History*, 6. On the connections between griping, stealing, and other forms of peasant political behavior, see E. P. Thompson, *Whigs and Hunters* and James C. Scott, *Domination and the Arts of Resistance: Hidden Transcripts*. For "better opportunities," see Stephan R. Epstein, "The Peasantries of Italy, 1350–1750," 85. Epstein's article provides an overview of what is known about rural people in Italy. His treatment of their political history (82–87) is very brief, reflecting how little attention village political culture has received. For the works in Italian historiography that examine the politics of what was once called the "periphery," see Elena Fasano Guarini, "Center and Periphery," in *The Origins of the State in Italy, 1300–1600*, ed. Julius Kirshner, 74–96. Other recent works in English that examine the politics of the "periphery," whether geographical or social, include: Tommaso Astarita, *Village Justice*; Gio-

vanna Benadusi, *A Provincial Elite in Early Modern Tuscany: Family and Power in the Creation of the State*; Samuel Kline Cohn, *Creating the Florentine State: Peasants and Rebellion, 1348–1434*; Edward Muir, *Mad Blood Stirring: Vendetta and Factions in Friuli during the Renaissance*. For additional bibliography, see Epstein or the synthesis offered by Muir. In his theoretical reappraisal of Italian state development, Pierangelo Schiera underscored the centrality of the state's role as mediator, noting that on the part of citizens or subjects, it meant exercising "collective discipline" or voluntary acquiescence to state power in exchange for public order. See his article, "Legitimacy, Discipline, and Institutions: Three Necessary Conditions for the Birth of the Modern State," especially 13–14.

15. Kirshner, ed., *Origins of the State in Italy*, especially his introduction, "The State is 'Back In,'" 1–10; also relevant here are: Schiera, "Legitimacy, Discipline, and Institutions," 11–33; Giorgio Chittolini, "The 'Private,' the 'Public,' the State," 34–61; and Aldo Mazzacane, "Law and Jurists in the Formation of the Modern State in Italy," 61–73. Robert Putnam, with Robert Leonardi and Raffaella Y. Nanetti, "Tracing the Roots of the Civic Community," in *Making Democracy Work: Civic Traditions in Modern Italy*, 121–162. Edward Muir, "The Sources of Civil Society in Italy," 379–406. In that same issue, see also Gene Brucker, "Civic Traditions in Premodern Italy," 357–378, which formulates a radically different view of Italian civic culture after the Renaissance from that offered by Raymond Grew in the same issue. Grew argues that Italy's "cultural capital" was very similar to that of France, which made Italy highly receptive to both the Enlightenment and the French Revolution. See his "Finding Social Capital," 407–433. A compelling critique of Putnam for understanding contemporary Italian politics is Filippo Sabetti, *The Search for Good Government: Understanding the Paradox of Italian Democracy*.

16. Laurie Nussdorfer has persuasively traced the survival of civic institutions and political participation in seventeenth-century Rome. See her *Civic Politics in the Rome of Urban VIII*. Through interviews, Sydel Silverman was able to piece together broader definitions of *civiltà*. These included qualities that can be glimpsed in early modern communal sources, even if they are impossible to elaborate to the same degree Silverman could with her informants: "showing generosity, fulfilling obligations appropriate to one's rank, and displaying a combination of authority and concern for those over whom one has authority. . . self-presentation . . . identifying with the community and expressing commitment to it; assuming responsibility for public projects . . . showing civic feeling and pride." *Three Bells of Civilization: The Life of an Italian Hill Town*, 4.

17. Peter Blickle, *The Revolution of 1525: The German Peasants' War from a New Perspective* and *Communal Reformation*. The villagers of central Italy, like their German sixteenth-century predecessors before them, were engaged in a struggle against seigneurialism, a jurisdictional battle as well as an economic one. See Blickle, *Communal Reformation*, 155, 168–171, 184. On the commune in rural Italy, see Edward Muir, "The Idea of Community in Renaissance Italy."

A comprehensive overview of scholarship on village communes is analyzed by Giovanni Tocci, in the introduction to his *Le Comunità negli stati italiani d'Antico Regime*, 9–58. On family and faction in Italian villages, see Osvaldo Raggio, *Faide e parentele: lo stato Genovese visto dalla Fontanabuona*. Dabid Sabean analyzes "cousin politics" as it emerged in the German village of Neckarhausen. This is the primary political discourse explored in depth for Neckarhausen, and it fits neatly with the valuable analysis of village records from the point of view of family history. Of the rest of their political discourse not much is known, including whether or how they resisted ducal policies. Sabean cautions against generalizing from his findings to villages quite close to his Neckarhausen. Clearly in village politics, authors may successfully go in a variety of directions, and the emphasis here on village resistance to seigneurial demands could be complemented in future studies by a closer reading of genealogy or demography than was possible in the scope of this study. David Sabean, *Kinship in Neckarhausen, 1700–1870*, especially 37–89. For other treatments of political struggles in rural Germany, see the microhistories in his *Power in the Blood*.

18. David Sabean reflects on the difficulty of comparisons even with relatively close villages in the first volume of his study of Neckarhausen, *Property, Production, and Family in Neckarhausen, 1700–1870*, 8. On the control of the administration of justice by villagers in Germany, see Blickle, *Communal Reformation*, 156; 161, 163. Blickle argued that village control of justice distinguished Germany from Italy and France. Roman lords, however, could also issue edicts, in contrast to their counterparts in France. I thank Donald Sutherland for reminding me of the importance of this difference between Roman and French lordship in the early modern period.

19. Scott, *Domination and the Arts of Resistance*. The records of the village *consiglio* meetings present historians with a number of dilemmas. In the six villages that are the focus of my research, only two have records from their village *consiglio*. Of those two villages, gaps in the records as long as ninety-three years exist. One gets a glimpse of the seventeenth-century political culture of Nerola, for instance, through fifteen years of *consiglio* records, but after that the *consiglio* records vanish until the mid-eighteenth century.

20. R. A. Houston's recent survey offers a wonderful overview of literacy, with some attention to states and literacy and a comprehensive survey of literacy in a variety of other aspects. His skepticism about the potential impact of literacy is expressed throughout, but he acknowledges that what people do with literacy is ultimately unpredictable (8–9). *Literacy in Early Modern Europe*, 106–112; 8–9. On the centrality of the state to the development of civil society, see Ian F. McNeely, *The Emancipation of Writing: German Civil Society in the Making, 1790s–1820s*. On the state as a broker or mediator between social groups, see John A. Marino, *Pastoral Economics in the Kingdom of Naples*; Antonio Calabria and John A. Marino, eds., *Good Government in Spanish Naples*; Julius Kirshner, ed., *The Origins of the State in Italy, 1300–1600*. On early modern politics outside of Italy, see especially Helen Nader, *Liberty in Absolutist Spain*; David Rollison, *The Local Origins of Modern Society: Gloucestershire 1500–1800*; Hilton Root, *Peasants and King in Burgundy: Agrarian Foundations of French Absolutism*; Sabean, *Power in the Blood*. On the truly radical demands of German-speaking villagers during the rebellion of 1525 and the intertwining of writing and their rebellion, see Blickle, *The Revolution of 1525*, especially p. 12, and *Communal Reformation*. Blickle pursued the fate of communal government after the Reformation in *Obedient Germans? A Rebuttal: A New View of German History*.

21. Sharpe suggests that Derrida's rejection of "binary opposition" in the interpretation of sources has been especially helpful in understanding the early modern period,

which shared many of the predilections of postmodernism. See *Reading Revolutions: The Politics of Reading in Early Modern England*, 16–17. Renata Ago has categorized peasant language in the Roman countryside according to whether or not it had a communal government. She points to the vitality of village language in *Un Feudo esemplare*. Sabean, *Power in the Blood*, for the importance of repetition in village language.

22. Chapters 2 and 6 are microhistories, but I employ the techniques of microhistory, as described by Edward Muir throughout the book. See his "Observing Trifles," in Muir and Ruggiero, *Microhistory and the Lost Peoples of Europe*, vii–xxvii.

CHAPTER I

1. ABCS 243, fasc. 13; ABCS 243, fasc. 14.

2. Giulio Silvestrelli, *Città, castelli, e terre della regione romana*, 295; Ludwig Von Pastor, *The History of the Popes*, 30: 14–15.

3. Tomassetti, *La Campagna Romana* (1910), 1: 129. On the three rings of property around Rome and the social significance of such a division, see Mirka Beneš, "Villa Pamphilj (1630–1670): Family, Gardens and Land in Papal Rome."

4. ABCS 243, fasc. 14, pp. 49; 45–46. Fernand Braudel, *The Mediterranean and Mediterranean World in the Age of Philip II*, 1: 28–29; Delumeau, *Vie économique*, 1: 398; Lando Scotoni, "Raccolta e commercio della neve nel circondario delle 60 miglia (Lazio)," 60–70.

5. Pescosolido, *Terra e nobiltà*, 16, 24. On the position of the Borghese and the Barberini in relation to other landlords in Latium during the eighteenth-century, see Gross, *Rome in the Age of Enlightenment*, 162; Pecchiai, *I Barberini*, 165; Richard Ferraro, personal communication, May 14, 1990. The Borghese acquired property throughout the Borghese papacy and distributed their acquisitions throughout the region, including lands in Sabina. In 1637 the Borghese bought Poggio Moiono and Poggio Nativo for 105,000 scudi. Palombara and Stazzano, important fiefs also in Sabina, cost them 385,000 scudi. Estates in Sabina, as was the case elsewhere in Latium, could cost a great deal, especially in the frenzied land market of the seventeenth century. See Pescosolido, *Terra e nobiltà*, 16, 24.

6. "Patchwork City," from Michel de Montaigne (trans. and ed. E. J. Trechmann), *The Diary of Montaigne's Journey to Italy in 1580 and 1581*, 163. Pastor, *The History of the Popes*, 28: 25, on the significance of Urban's name. For a detailed history of the Barberini family, see Pecchiai, *I Barberini*, esp. 145. His treatment of Maffeo Barberini and the subsequent generations in Rome is fairly critical of the family. My account draws on Pecchiai, as well as the fundamental study of the papacy by Pastor, *The History of the Popes*, vols. 28–30. My interpretation of the Barberini in Roman society has been influenced by the more recent and more sympathetic scholarship on the family: John Beldon Scott, *Images of Nepotism: The Painted Ceilings of Palazzo Barberini*; Patricia Waddy, *Seventeenth-Century Roman Palaces: Use and the Art of the Plan*.

7. Pastor, *The History of the Popes*, 28: 15–25; Judith Hook, "Urban VIII: The Paradox of a Spiritual Monarchy," 221.

8. Paolo Prodi, *The Papal Prince: One Body and Two Souls: The Papal Monarchy in Early Modern Europe*, 20–22. Pecchiai, in contrast to more favorable treatments of Urban VIII,

claims that his ascension to the papacy signaled "the beginning of his moral decline." Pecchiai, *I Barberini*, 148. For an overview of the artistic patronage of Urban VIII and his relatives, see Francis Haskell, "Pope Urban VIII and his Entourage," in *Patrons and Painters: A Study in the Relations between Italian Art and Society in the Age of the Baroque*, 24–62. See also Hook's sketch of Urban's circle, "Urban VIII," 220; and Pastor's chapter, "The States of the Church and the War of Castro," in *The History of the Popes*, vol. 29. According to Pastor, Urban took great pride in his improvements. He claimed in 1628 to have spent 800,000 scudi on the fortifications of Castel S. Angelo alone (ibid., 29: 365). On Bernini and Urban VIII, see Howard Hibbard, *Bernini*, 68–115. On Urban VIII and the medieval papacy, see Pastor, *The History of the Popes*, 29: 400; and Hibbard, *Bernini*, 101. On the fortresses at Valtellina, see Pastor, *The History of the Popes*, 28: 67–99; 196–259.

9. On papal control of benefices, see Barbara McClung Hallman, *Italian Cardinals, Reform, and the Church as Property, 1492–1563*, 164–168. Delumeau discusses the Italianization of Rome, *Vie économique*, 1: 219; and Hallman offers insightful analysis of how many Italian families sought the cardinalate, *Italian Cardinals*, 158–161. Peter Partner has argued that the primary achievement of the papacy after the fourteenth century was the establishment of temporal rule in Italy and that its influence here took on more significance as the papacy's power declined outside of Italy. See his *Renaissance Rome 1500–1559: A Portrait of a Society*, 10–11. Prodi and Delumeau see increasing centralization of the Papal States in the sixteenth and seventeenth centuries. See Prodi, *The Papal Prince*; and Delumeau, *Vie économique*, as well as Delumeau's article, "Rome: Political and Administrative Centralization in the Papal State in the Sixteenth Century," in *The Late Italian Renaissance: 1525–1630*, ed. Eric Cochrane, 287–304. For an opposing view, see Mario Caravale and Alberto Caracciolo, *Lo Stato Pontificio da Martino V a Pio IX*. For a summary of the literature on this subject and an overview on the nature of papal government, see Gross, *Rome in the Age of Enlightenment*, 40–54.

10. Scott, *Images of Nepotism*, 4–5; 198–199. On the changes in Rome during the sixteenth century, see Delumeau, *Vie économique*, 1: 435; 2: 779, 781, 817, and 821. On the nationalized elite, see Hallman, *Italian Cardinals*, 159, 162, and 167. Renata Ago continues this analysis of the interconnection between cardinals in her monograph on the seventeenth and eighteenth centuries, *Carriere e clientele nella Roma barocca*.

11. On the cost of palaces, see Delumeau, *Vie économique*, 2: 931; 1: 359. See also David R. Coffin, *The Villa in the Life of Renaissance Rome*, 21–22, 64, for the importance of palace building. On the minimum number of attendants and new status symbols, see Waddy, *Seventeenth-Century Roman Palaces*, 32–33; 54–66; and Delumeau, *Vie économique*, 1: 443.

12. On the system of papal loans to the aristocracy, see Delumeau, *Vie économique*, 1: 471, 475; Teodor Amayden, *A New Relation of Rome as to the Government of the City*, 17. On the debt problems of the Farnese, see Delumeau, *Vie économique*, 2: 817 and 1: 484. There are historians who differ with this picture, most notably, Richard Ferraro, who argues that these old families sold estates because it was a good economic choice in a time of inflated land prices in Rome (personal communication, May 14, 1990). On the rapidity of the sales of estates, see Delumeau, *Vie économique*, 1: 479.

13. On the northern origins of the cardinals, see Hallman, *Italian Cardinals*, 5. On the

financiers, see Peter Partner, "Papal Financial Policy in the Renaissance and Counter-Reformation," 20.

14. Charles L. Stinger in *The Renaissance in Rome*, 334, uses these terms by humanists. On the Borghese, see Wolfgang Reinhard, "Papal Power and Family Strategy in the Sixteenth and Seventeenth Centuries," in *Princes, Patrons, and the Nobility*, ed. Ronald Asch and Adolf M. Birke, 329–356. See Beneš, "Villa Pamphilj" for the Pamphilj family's path to "romanizing" itself.

15. On the insecurity of the Barberini, see Scott, *Images of Nepotism*, 4–5; 198–199.

16. "Making Appear," Domenico Bernini, *Vita del Cavalier Gio. Lorenzo Bernino*, 57; quoted in Frederick Hammond, "Bernini and the 'Fiera di Farfa,'" 119. Pastor chronicles Maffeo Barberini's favors for his own family, see *The History of the Popes*, 28: 40–43. As Pecchiai points out, Urban was not the only pope to name more than one nephew to the cardinalate: Julius II made four nephews cardinals; Gregory XIII did the same for two of his nephews, as did Clement VIII. See Pecchiai, *I Barberini*, 149.

17. On the Barberini purchases from 1624 and 1625, see Pastor, *The History of the Popes*, 28: 44. On the purchase of Palestrina, see Waddy, *Seventeenth-Century Roman Palaces*, 272; 402, n. 1. On the new title for Carbognano, see S. Andretta, "Francesco Colonna," in *Dizionario degli Italiani*, 6: 303–304. On the movement of the bones from Palestrina, see Prospero Colonna, *I Colonna*, 266–267.

18. On Taddeo's management of the estates, see Waddy, *Seventeenth-Century Roman Palaces*, 272. Taddeo continued to add to the family patrimony in the 1630s by purchasing Valmontone from the Sforza family in 1634. On his marriage to Anna Colonna, see ibid., 277. On the building of the new palace, Pastor, *The History of the Popes*, 29: 498; and Waddy, *Seventeenth-Century Roman Palaces*, xi–xii; 173–271.

19. Scott, *Images of Nepotism*, 108.

20. Ibid., 108–109.

21. On Farfa, see Delumeau, *Vie économique*, 1: 94; and Silvestrelli, *Città, castelli*, 306–308. Hallman, *Italian Cardinals*, 166, explains who controlled the benefice. After Cardinal Francesco held the benefice, it passed to Cardinal Carlo Barberini in 1666 until his death in 1704. The last Barberini holder of the benefice was Cardinal Francesco in 1728. Farfa's seventeenth-century castles were: Bocchignano, Castelnuovo di Farfa, Fara, Montopoli, Monte S. Maria, Poggio Mirteto, Poggio S. Lorenzo, Rocca Baldesca, Salisano, and Toffia. Its eighteenth-century castles were limited to the following: Poggio Mirteto, Toffia, Montopoli, Salsisano, Rocca Baldesca, Castelnuovo di Farfa, Monte S. Maria, and Fara. Silvestrelli, *Città, castelli*, 306–308; Waddy, *Seventeenth-Century Roman Palaces*, 246–247; 57–58, discusses the Barberini theater.

22. Waddy outlines the patronage of the three nephews, *Seventeenth-Century Roman Palaces*, 57–58. The letter is cited in Alessandro Ademollo, *I Teatri di Roma nel secolo decimosettimo*, 28–31.

23. On the libretto, see Torgil Magnuson, *Rome in the Age of Bernini*, 1: 250. See Ademollo, *I Teatri di Roma* and Frederick Hammond, "Bernini and the 'Fiera di Farfa.'" Two descriptions of the production are in the *Avvisi di Roma* and are translated in Hammond, 115–116. Domenico Bernini, *Vita del Cavalier Gio. Lorenzo Bernino*, 57; quoted in Hammond, 119. For a description of the Fair of Farfa, see ibid., 116.

24. Margaret Murata describes the audience for the operas in *Operas for the Papal Court, 1631–1668*, 3. Hammond discusses the circulation of the libretti, "Bernini and the 'Fiera di Farfa,'" 119. "Linear logic" and the other terms are used by Murata, who provides a good discussion of the weaknesses of plot and the aims of the baroque opera, though she does not link the themes with the experience of the nobility. Murata, *Operas for the Papal Court*, 80, 81. The story is from the Decameron, the Fifth Day, Ninth story. See also ibid., 81, 258–259, for a longer summary of the plot than is presented here.

25. On the fair, see Hammond, "Bernini and the 'Fiera di Farfa,'" 119, 121–124, for the libretto of the intermezzo.

26. See Hammond on the battle, "Bernini and the 'Fiera di Farfa,'" 120. Montecuccoli describes the battle as "furious and very realistic." G. Briganti, L. Trezzani, and L. Laureati, *The Bamboccianti: The Painters of Everyday Life in Seventeenth Century Rome*. See also Haskell, *Patrons and Painters*, 132–141, on the success of these painters in Rome, especially the discussion in chapter 5 on the *Bamboccianti*. Briganti, Trezzani, and Laureati, *The Bamboccianti*, "arouses," 13; "Visibly contented," 14. Ibid., 16, on the motivation of noble patrons in buying the *Bamboccianti* paintings. Briganti argues that this sanitized version of the poor allowed wealthy patrons to view the poor more with delight than with admonishment.

27. On the Barberini–Farnese rivalry, see Scott, *Images of Nepotism*, 6, 11, 18; on the Barberini movement of the funeral monument, see Hibbard, *Bernini*, 105.

28. Nussdorfer, *Civic Politics*, 206–208. Scott provides a brief but useful overview of the War of Castro (see *Images of Nepotism*, 6). He argues that the Farnese saw the Barberini as members of the "vulgar classes," but Pastor points out that some of the animosity of the Farnese against the Barberini goes back to the thwarted plans of Odoardo to capture the Duchy of Milan through the help of Richelieu. The Barberini had also opposed his plan. See Pastor, *The History of the Popes*, 29: 383; 384–385.

29. Two authors are superb on the conflict and its disastrous management by the Barberini. See Nussdorfer, *Civic Politics*, 208–209, for the escalation leading to war and on its reception in Rome, 217–227. Pastor is a good guide to the war's escalation and on the international response, *The History of the Popes*, 29: 386–388; 390, 392.

30. Nussdorfer, *Civic Politics*, 222; Pastor, *The History of the Popes*, 29: 398.

31. Scott, *Images of Nepotism*, 6.

32. Hallman, *Italian Cardinals*, 161; Scotoni, *I Territori Autonomi dello Stato Ecclesiastico nel Cinquecento*, 7; 69; 99. Scotoni also argues that there was a real "flowering of autonomous territories" in the second half of the sixteenth century (5). He contrasts the differences between the *terrae immediate subiectae* and *terrae mediate subiectae*, arguing that the Papal States were a patchwork of administrations and jurisdictions, lacking "cohesion" and centralization (60). Silvio Zotta studies a similar kind of territory in southern Italy. See his article, "The Agrarian Crisis and Feudal Politics in the Kingdom of Naples: The Doria at Melfi (1585–1615)," 127–203.

33. On the creation of the duchy, see Nussdorfer, *Civic Politics*, 205. Pecchiai argues that the potential marriage alliance was the Barberini's first strategy for acquiring the duchy (*I Barberini*, 150). For the sale, see ABCS 243, fasc. 13; Silvestrelli, *Città, castelli,*

294–296; on the consolidation of the villages, see Archivio Barberini, Indici I–IV, Vatican Library (hereinafter AB), Ind. II, 2637; on the *auditore generale*, see ABCS 248, fasc. 7. Not enough is really known about the "centralizing" efforts of the Roman nobles in this period, though Silvestrelli argues that what happened in Monte Libretti was part of a common pattern. See Silvestrelli, *Città, castelli*, 294–295. For a discussion of other autonomous territories in the sixteenth century, see Scotoni, *I Territori Autonomi dello Stato Ecclesiastico nel Cinquecento*. Scotoni claims there was an increase in these territories in the sixteenth century.

On the *stato* of Monte Libretti, Gavello was the *General'Auditor*, or the chief judicial magistrate for the Orsini, although there were other officials in each village who had to answer to the noble family, see chapter 3.

34. ABCS 243, fasc. 14, pp. 3, 35, 41.

35. ABCS 248, fasc. 7. Decree 95. The terms of the sale to the Barberini stipulated that they acquired civil, criminal, and mixed jurisdiction of the *stato*. Scotoni, *I Territori Autonomi dello Stato Ecclesiastico nel Cinquecento*, discusses the terms of the sale on p. 69 and notes that the term *merum et mixtum imperium* was the highest kind of jurisdiction. Ibid., 60, note 112; ABCS 248, fasc. 7. The decrees date from the ownership of the *stato* by Giovanni Antonio Orsini, Duke of S. Gemini and Ferdinando Orsini, his grandson, also Duke of S. Gemini.

36. See Pastor, *The History of the Popes*, 30: 18–19, 51; Waddy, *Seventeenth-Century Roman Palaces*, 170; Scott, *Images of Nepotism*, 198–199.

37. Pastor recounts the various machinations by which the Barberini were finally convinced to support Pamphilj, who was strongly opposed by France (*The History of the Popes*, 30: 19–23). Beneš analyzes the marriage negotiations pending between the Barberini and the Pamphilj family at the time of the conclave ("Villa Pamphilj," 249–258). On the Barberini difficulties after the election of Innocent X, see Pastor, *The History of the Popes*, 30: 48–49, 21–22; 55.

38. Ibid., 30: 57–58; 52–53. See also Emete Rossi, "La fuga del Cardinale Antonio Barberini," 303–327. On the investigation of the Barberini and their flight to France, see Pastor, *The History of the Popes*, 30: 54–55; Scott, *Images of Nepotism*, 198.

39. The text of the intermezzo is in Hammond, "Bernini and the 'Fiera di Farfa,'" 124.

40. Pastor, *The History of the Popes*, 30: 55–56, chronicles the sequestration. Pecchiai cites Anna's letter (*I Barberini*, 184).

41. Pastor, *The History of the Popes*, 30: 56, argues that this sale of confiscated properties was proposed on February 20, 1646, so about a month after Taddeo Barberini had fled Rome. On the dates for Anna's trip, see Waddy, *Seventeenth-Century Roman Palaces*, 170.

42. On the machinations of Mazarin, see Pastor, *The History of the Popes*, 30: 58–63. The inventory is in the Barberini Collection, Historical Collections, Baker Library, Harvard University (hereinafter BC), vol. 5, 99v–118r. A good summary of the loans arranged for these final payments is in the Orsini Family Archive, Special Collections Department, Collection 902, University of California at Los Angeles (hereinafter OFA), Box 112. It shows that in April 1647 the Barberini still owed 434,560 scudi on the originally agreed upon price of 1,160,000 scudi.

43. On the possession of Monti Libretti, ABCS 244, fasc. 3. For the records of

Anna's *congregazioni* and her specific directions to ministers in various fiefs from 1647 to 1651, see AB, Ind. II, 2467, especially 93r and the entry of August 15, 1648. Several residents of Corese addressed a letter to the Prefectessa Anna Colonna on July 10, 1648, requesting that the case against them for hunting violations be dropped. Anna Colonna, signing herself "Madre e Curatrice" accepted their version of events and complied with their wishes (ABCS 249, fasc. 6).

44. On Francesco's return to Rome, see Pastor, *The History of the Popes*, 30: 64. Pio Pecchiai argues that Francesco had always been "secretly" in control of the secular fortune of the family, and after the death of his brother was left free to do so openly. See *I Barberini*, 214–215.

For a more sympathetic and generous view of Taddeo as an independent administrator, see Waddy's chapter on Taddeo, *Seventeenth-Century Roman Palace*, 283–290 and appendix 3, in which she reproduces a biography of Taddeo by his brother Francesco, which shows Taddeo in a similar light. On Antonio, see A. Merola, "Antonio Barberini." On the change in Barberini heirs, see Pastor, *The History of the Popes*, 30: 92. According to Mirka Beneš, Donna Olimpia Pamphilj, sister-in-law of Innocent X, organized the marriage of her niece to Maffeo Barberini. See her "Villa Pamphilj," 236.

Pietro Ercole Visconti notes that the couple went initially to live in the Pamphilj palace in Piazza Navona, so hesitant was Donna Olimpia to separate herself from her young ward. *Città e famiglie nobili e celebri dello Stato pontificio: Dizionario storico*, 4: 762. The libretto was by Giulio Rospigliosi, the future Clement IX. See Margaret Murata, *Operas for the Papal Court, 1631–1668*, 4. Murata valiantly chronicles the plot on pp. 348–349.

45. OWNERSHIP OF ARABLE LAND IN MONTE LIBRETTI (IN RUBBIA)

	Barberini	Others	Total	B.%[a]
Corese	222	0	222	100
Monte Flavio	0	122.75	122.75	0
Monte Libretti	276	305	581	48
Monte Maggiore	1,190.5	0	1,190.5	100
Montorio	3	305	308	1
Nerola	73	288	361	20
Ponticelli	130	477.75	607.75	21
TOTAL	1,894.5	1,498.5	3,393	56

[a]Indicates the percentage of arable land owned by the Barberini.

Source: Figures are based on ABCS 243, fasc. 14

Other manuscripts offer some variations on the measurements. Please note that these figures do not represent the total amount of land in the *stato*, only the arable half of it. Giovanni Curis saw the origins of these two categories of landownership in the fifteenth century, when lords granted lands to villagers who then possessed them *libere et absolute* (*Usi civici*, 436). Payments on these lands, according to Curis, were fixed by the village *statuti*. For more on the *statuti*, see chapter 2. The history of papal intervention in agriculture is too long to recount here, though two positive perspectives on it are provided by Curis in *Usi civici* and Cesare De Cupis in his *Le vicende dell'agricultura*. See the brief summary provided by Canaletti Guadenti, *La Politica agraria ed annonaria*, 7–23. For more recent work on papal intervention in the Roman countryside, see the recent work by Renata Ago, cited in note 2 of chapter 2.

Canaletti Guadenti rightly pointed also to the importance of the *annona* or the papal bureaucracy charged with provisioning the city of Rome. The *annona* has also inspired several scholarly treatments. See Jacques Revel, "Le Grain de Rome et la crise de l'Annone dans la seconde moitié du XVIIIe siècle"; "Les Privilèges d'une capitale: l'approvisionnement de Rome à l'époque moderne"; Ago, "Popolo e papi"; Volker Reinhardt, *Uberleben in der frühneuzeitlichen Stadt: Annona und Getreideversorgung in Rom, 1563–1797*; Curis, *Usi civici*, 548, 686.

46. Closer to Rome, the popes did set limits on what could be charged as rents. De Cupis, *Le vicende dell'agricultura*, 110. The part of the harvest that could be taken by the proprietor was established by papal law in the early sixteenth century during the pontificate of Leo X: "*quinta parte del raccolto*, nelle tenute nel raggio di sette miglia da Roma; alla *ottava e nona parte del raccolto*, per i luoghi non vicini al Tevere, e che erano posti nel raggio da sette a dieci miglia da Roma: per i luoghi prossimi al Tevere, compresi nel raggio sopradetto, attesa la comodità del trasporto per mezzo del fiume, si doveva pagare per corrisposta la *sesta parte del raccolto*." Modernizing agrarian practices would have required the introduction of artificial rather than natural pasture. It would have necessitated the close integration of animal husbandry (which would have supplied valuable fertilizer) and the cultivation of grain. Due to the use of artificial pasture, the total amount of grazing lands can actually be decreased, which allows for more grain cultivation. ABCS 247, fasc. 49, describes cultivation practices. ABCS 243, fasc. 14, p. 25, shows the payment for use as pasture falling from 2 scudi per rubbio to 1.6 scudi per rubbio in the *tenuta* of Monte Maggiore, a relatively fertile area. In the territory of the village of Monte Libretti, in a *quarto* called Nati and Tinta Rossa, which had a total area of about 100 rubbia, the rental price for pasture fell from 100 to 65 scudi during the second year of use as pasture; ibid., 8.

47. According to master ledgers in the Vatican Library, initially at least, the income from Monte Libretti was more in keeping with the estimates made at the time of the sale. In 1648 income was 29,376.99 2/3 scudi. It was in the decades after the 1640s that the income apparently began to fall. See AB, Ind. II, 2642, for a copy of the estimate made by Pietro Vanninni in 1646, using such a percentage figure; AB, Ind. II, 2640, on revenue of 1662; ABCS 246, fasc. 3, on revenue of 1685.

48. ABCS 243, fasc. 14, p. 59.

49. Ibid., 533–552.

50. OFA, Box 95, [Monte Libretti] Instrum[entum] Venditionij Status Montis Libretti : "Vassalli teneantur d. frum[entum] deferre ad flumen Tiberij . . ." Several of the disputes between the villagers and their noble lords traced their origin to the terms of the bill of sale between the Orsini and the Barberini. The phrase asserting that the villagers had to perform the labor appeared in the same sentence that estimated how much grain from the *stato* was actually worth. For the letter from Monte Flavio, see ABCS 291, fasc. 31.

John Bossy emphasized the disciplinary nature of Catholicism during the early modern period, noting its tendency to "[reduce] Christianity to whatever could be taught and learnt. . . . Catechism was well designed to instill obedience and mark out boundaries. . . . It was less well adapted to inspiring a sense of the Church as a *comunitas*, a feeling for the sacraments as social institutions, or simply the love of one's neighbor" (*Christianity in the West*, 120). On the conflation of political and religious authority, see Wolfgang Reinhard, who summarized the evidence supporting the mutual support of state and church after the reformation in his "Reformation, Counter-Reformation, and the Early Modern State—A Reassessment," 383–404. William V. Hudon provides some reasons for using the "social disciplining" thesis with caution, "Religion and Society in Early Modern Italy—Old Questions, New Insights," 784–804. See also John W. O'Malley, *Trent and all That: Renaming Catholicism in the Early Modern Era*, especially his reservations about the social disciplining thesis, 101–117.

51. For Securantia's testimony, see OFA, box 96 [Monte Libretti] Depositio Pietro Securantia, November 6, 1646. For a picture of legal trajectory of the case in the papal law courts, see ABCS 251 (chronicles the case as it moved from the court of the Segnatura to the Sacra Rota); 252 (Decisions of the Rota, regarding the case); 253 (the manuscript collection of documents and oral testimonies).

52. OFA, box 96 [Monte Libretti] Fede of October 21, 1645, by the "massari" of Monte Libretti, Raimondo Eugenio, Giocchino Petetti, and Angelo Pasquale di Tiburzio. Testimony from all six villages of Monte Libretti has not survived, but a summary from 1647 in the Barberini archive attempts to list all the protests lodged against the Barberini by the villagers after the purchase of the *stato* in 1644. It contains the note that "Tutte le Communità dello Stato hanno fatto dichiarat[io]ne di non esser tenute condurre il grano, e biade spettanti al S Prencipe ad alcun Luogo," a protest that suggests that each village lodged a similar complaint.

Archivio Storico del Comune di Nerola, Serie I, Registro I, Registro dei Consigli di Comunità (hereinafter, Consigli di Nerola), [October 15, 1645], 47v. A literal transcription without corrections of grammar or spelling reads as follows: "circa la trasportat.e delli grani che noi non havemo obligo nesuno a favor delli Sri Padroni ma che (e se?) vero che li grani raccolti et altri lavori ancora in terr.o di Nerola p cortesia nra e p molte gratie che giornalm.te ricevamo da essi Ssri e p li suoi (?) Trattam.ti che ci facevamo la portarture dal grannaro di Nerola à Montelibretti, o al porto e loro ci davano la collazione ò con tanto a testa p collazione,"

The full testimony of the villagers of Monte Libretti reads as follows: "che essi nela Com[uni]ta ò popolo tanto uniti quanto come singoli no[n] sono nel fiume mai obligati di condurre ne far condurre a spese p[ro]prie grano biade et altra robba spettante all'Eccmi. SS.ri Proni. Di d.a terra o raccolti o non raccolti nel sud.o terreno di essa Terro in luogo alcuno especialm.e al porto del Tevere" (sworn testimony of Joacchino Petetta and Raimondo Eugenij, priors of Monte Libretti, April 14, 1646, ABCS 245, fasc. 40). Despite the variety in the spelling of their names, these two priors are probably two of the three who gave testimony in the previous fall.

53. See the final decision of the court of the Sacra Rota, June 12, 1662 in ABCS 252.

54. Marcel Mauss (trans. Ian Cunnison), *The Gift: Forms and Functions of Exchange in*

Archaic Societies, on the variety of forms of gifts, see p. 27. Mary Douglas wrote a thought-provoking analysis of Mauss that sheds light on the attitudes of the villagers in this controversy. See her forward, "No Free Gifts," in Marcel Mauss (trans. W. D. Halls), *The Gift,* especially her comments, "Mauss's fertile idea was to present the gift cycle as a theoretical counterpart to the invisible hand" (xiv). On the eighteenth-century *possesso,* see ABCS 271, fasc. 27. For a lengthier description of a *possesso,* see Caroline Castiglione, "Political Culture in Italian Villages," 532. On the centrality of oaths to early modern Italian political culture, see Paolo Prodi, *Il sacramento del potere.* In Germany, Peter Blickle believed that, in contrast to what Martin Luther thought, the oath of peasants to their lords gave them the right of resistance: "There are many instances in the pre-reformation period where the allegiance was denied or given as a conditional promise. Authority in the tradition of the Middle Ages was not absolute authority" (*Communal Reformation,* 143).

55. ABCS 271, fasc. 5, 29v. "Quod Granum pro Vita D[omi]ni portetura Vassallis: Item quod Vassalli teneantur granum D[omi]ni per usu[m] su[a]e Curi[a]e, et hopitij portare, ac etiam Annonam ipsius equis, etiam quando vellet Granu[m] vendere in foro ad pena[m] solidorum decem, et in Curia tenatur dare pro quolibet Rubro portantibus dictum Granum solidos quinque." Of the six villages that are the focus of my research, five of them had a *statuto* in the eighteenth century.

CHAPTER 2

1. Consigli di Nerola, May 1, 1645, 38r.

2. Renata Ago's scholarship offers many interesting insights on the politics of the village commune in the area around Rome, especially during the eighteenth century. See "Braccianti, contadini e grandi proprietari in un villaggio laziale nel primo Settecento," 60–89; "Conflitti e politica nel feudo: le campagne romane del Settecento," 847–874. For the late eighteenth century and the nineteenth century, see Andreina De Clementi, *Vivere nel latifondo: le comunità della campagna laziale fra '700 e '800.* Ago notes that after the sixteenth-century papal tribunals (the Congregazione Camerale, the Sacra Rota, and the Buon Governo) were increasingly involved in judging disputes between village communal governments and large landowners. See "Popolo e papi," 18. The debate about whether the papacy successfully centralized its administration during the early modern period is explored in two fundamental works: Prodi, *The Papal Prince* and Caravale and Caracciolo, *Lo Stato Pontificio da Martino V a Pio IX.* Many authors have commented on the preponderance of baronial jurisdiction around Rome. See the summary in Volpi, *Le Regioni introvabili,* 66–68.

3. ABCS 249, fasc. 18, testimony of the guard (August 4, 1685).

4. Ibid., the letter is from the *auditore* Giacomo Pensa (August 19, 1685).

5. Ibid., "tocca troppo sul vivo questi Nerolani."

6. Comments on March 29, 1654 and April 19, 1654 suggest that timing prompted the calling of the smaller *consiglio* "p[er] n[on] esser potuto radunare il Conseglio *Generale*" (Consigli di Nerola, 137v–138r; 138v–139v). The meetings from 1645 (Consigli di Nerola, 32v–48v) are particularly complete and carefully recorded. Of the 114 individu-

als who attended either the meetings of the general *consiglio* (8) or the meetings of the *consiglio delli dodici* (3), twenty-three attended more than five times that year; twenty-one others attended four times; thirty-seven two or three times; thirty-three only once. There do not appear to be any designated meeting days for the *consiglio*. The *consiglio* was convened only when necessary: "to address some needs of the *comunità*" (134v–135r [November 30, 1653]). A comment from 1654 suggests that the number of meetings was intentionally kept to a minimum: the *consiglieri* hoped to settle matters quickly, in order "to avoid calling these *consigli* everyday" (32v [January 1, 1645]), "with the majority" (40r [June 15, 1645]). Sometimes votes had to be taken several times to sort out the issue to the satisfaction of all present. See 31r–32r (December 18, 1644). The *consiglio* almost always ended in a vote that resolved the matter (at least for that day). Some of the most politically inclined individuals in the village came from the following families: Angelonio, Campanelli, Chico, Ferrazzoli, Gallonio, Granci, Marianelli, Orfeo, Palmeri, Pancratio, Pandolfi, Papi, Portasacco, Raimondi, Retale, Rubini, del Signore, Saviola, and Teofilo.

7. Scotoni, *I Territori Autonomi dello Stato Ecclesiastico nel Cinquecento*, 7.

8. ABCS 271, fasc. 27.

9. Ibid. "in mnibus dicti Illmi dni. Abbatis de Paulinis ... sendentis et nom.e praelaudatorum dominorum Principum ut supra acceptantis, statutaque dictae Terrae."

10. E. Celani described the *statuto* of Montelibretti that he found in the communal archive in 1892. It has since vanished. He argued that Francesco Orsini, mentioned at the beginning of the *statuto* of Monte Libretti (who is also mentioned at the beginning of that of Nerola), commissioned a compendium of already existing laws and local practices, which were probably scattered in a number of different documents. The *statuto* of Nerola probably had similar origins. See E. Celani, "Lo Statuto del Comune di Montelibretti," 401–417. Giovanni Curis claims that the rural *statuti* were written as early as the thirteenth century, although most much later (see *Usi civici*, 508). On the development of the *statuto* in an Orsini fief during the early sixteenth century, see Piero Ugolini, *Un paese della campagna romana: Formello. Storia ed economia agraria*, 32–35. On the relationship between *statuti*, the rise of the commune, and seigneurial power in the countryside, see Alfio Cortonesi, *Terre e signori nel Lazio medioevale: Un'economia rurale nei secoli XIII–XIV*, 175. Consigli di Nerola, 53v (March 18, 1646). On the political and agricultural significance of statutes in the Republic of Genoa, see Osvaldo Raggio, "Norme e pratiche. Gli statute campestri come fonti per una storia locale." No copy of the *statuto* of Nerola exists in the village archive today, but there are two copies (one sixteenth century and one eighteenth century) in the Barberini archive of the Vatican Library. See ABCS 271, fasc. 5.

11. See Cortonesi, *Terre e signori nel Lazio medioevale*, 175; on the *statuto* in Ponticelli, ABCS 278, fasc. 13.

12. Caravale and Caracciolo, *Lo Stato Pontificio da Martino V a Pio IX*. On this phenomenon in the city, see Nussdorfer, *Civic Politics in the Rome of Urban VIII*.

13. Consigli di Nerola, 29r–30r (October 28, 1644).

14. Ibid.

15. Ibid.

16. Ibid., 32v–34r (January 1, 1645). Villagers in sixteenth-century Germany had made the exact same claims about the process necessary to change their village constitutions. See Blickle, *Communal Reformation*, 178.

17. Consigli di Nerola, 53v (March 18, 1646).

18. Ibid.

19. ABCS 271, fasc. 5. The first reference to hunting specifies three animals (*cervo, capreolo, et porco*). The following excerpts are transcribed from a comparison of the sixteenth- and eighteenth-century copies in the Vatican Library. In the passages related to hunting, the text was essentially the same in the two copies. The spelling and grammar are from these two copies.

> De Venatio habenda: De Venatione capta p Societates ultra Curia habere debeat de Cervo, Capreolo, et Porco in signum Dni caput cum collo, et de ceto Piscium habeat quartam partem salvo quando fit pro Nuptiis Curia nihil habeat. De Exemptione Venientum ad habitandum: Venientes ad habitandum in Terris Nris ab omni reali factione sint immunes, et etiam personali pro primo anno, praeter quam de Oste, et Guardia.
>
> De Venatione, aucupatione, et Piscatione portanda: Item quod quilibit teneatur intus Castrum deferre Venationem, et aucupationem, et etiam piscationem, et vendat ipsam in Castro, et non alibi ad poenam vice qualibet solidorum decem.
>
> De non vendendo Forensibus Victualia: Nulla persona vendat alicui causa portandi extra Castrum Venationes aucupationes vel piscationes, aut Ova, Pullos, et his similia ad poenam solidorum quinque, et portans extra Castrum sine licentia perdat quod portaverit, salvo si tenuerit dicta animalia silvestria per diem unam in macello ordinato, et ipsa vendere non potuerit justo pretio quod tunc possit portare alibi, et vendere cui voluerit sine poena.

The testimony taken at the *consiglio delli dodici* is in Consigli di Nerola, 46v–48r (October 15, 1645). Both of the documents prohibiting hunting are in ABCS 275, fasc. 8. ("Posizione della causa *Sabinen iuris prohibendi venationem* contro la Comunità di Nerola"). For the testimony of the priors, see "Cong.ne Sign.re Just.ae... Summarium (Nº 5º) Pro Communitate, et Hominibus Terrae Nerulae"; "despite the fact," Consigli di Nerola, 71r (February 26, 1648).

20. Ibid., 188v (June 23, 1652).

21. A copy of the edict is in ABCS 278, fasc. 8. The original bando was issued on September 23, 1613. Consigli di Nerola, 128r–128v (February 23, 1653). All of the notes for this chapter preserve the spelling and the grammar of the original source, in part to show the level of literacy in the village. In this case, however, though the actual notes from the meeting refer to the speaker as Pietro Cranzio, not Pietro Granci. The speaker must have been Pietro Granci for several reasons. First, none of the *consiglio* records of the 1640s and 1650s contain a single participant with the family name Cranzio. Second, in the meeting subsequent to this one (April 27, 1653), the note taker records the name as Pietro Granzio. Pietro Granci appears in the notes for the subsequent meeting (July

20, 1653), written by this same hand, which is particularly rough and prone to many spelling errors. The note taker probably made an error in recording the speaker's name. The only other alternative is that the note taker meant to record the name of a member of the Pancrazio family. However, given Granci's frequent participation at the *consiglio* meetings, he was most likely the speaker at the February 1653 meeting. Pietro Granci's speech refers to Cardinal Barberini, probably meaning Francesco Barberini, the uncle of Maffeo Barberini, the young *"padrone"* in training.

22. Ibid., 134v–135r (November 30, 1653). "Io sono di parere che ... p l'Interesse della com.ta con S.E. li Sri massari vadino da S.E. gli mostrino il statu. e preghino S.E. che veglia cose Pre (paterne?), e Prone (padrone?) e remettesi alla sua benignita."

23. Ibid., 107r (March 25, 1651). The language of this meeting is confusing. The priors refer to a "commissario dell'archivio," which seems to be a garbled reference to a papal bureaucrat, though such an office is never mentioned either in the village or the noble family's records. See Santoncini, *Il Buon Governo*, 122–123.

24. See Laurie Nussdorfer's discussion of a similar situation faced by the *popolo romano*, who held several fiefs as titled lords in the countryside. Besieged by requests and visitors from the villagers, they promulgated decrees limiting the days that the villagers could appear. Nussdorfer, *Civic Politics*, 136–144. On the Barberini edict, ABCS 248, fasc. 21.

25. ABCS 248, fasc. 7, Edict 95.

26. Ibid., Edict 21; Edict 16; Edict 22.

27. Norbert Elias (trans. Edmund Jephcott), *The Civilizing Process*. Muir argues for the importance of the spread of manners in cultivating allegiance to the state in "The Sources of Civil Society in Italy" and *Mad Blood Stirring*.

28. Alessandro Manzoni (trans. Bruce Penman), *The Betrothed*, 268. ABCS 275, fasc. 8. Edicts of October 29, 1660; March 9 and 12, 1672; July 19, 1678; letter of October 8, 1682. Another edict reminded all the villagers of the *stato* to comply with previous edicts related to hunting and fishing (May 8, 1677), ABCS 248, fasc. 7. The trial of Gattani is in ABCS 249, fasc. 11.

29. Ibid.

30. Ibid.

31. Ibid.

32. For Minichella's trials, see ABCS 249, fasc. 10, testimony of November 28, 1672. The first time he was prosecuted, according to the prince's letter was in November 1672, and the second time in October 1673. The Barberini archive contains an account of the second of these two accusations; it seems that the discrepancies among the witnesses at that time resulted in a pardon for Minichella. There is a sketchy account of the conclusions of this second case in ABCS 249, fasc. 12, which contains documents related to the third case in 1677.

33. Ibid., letter signed by Maffeo Barberini in Rome on February 28, 1678.

34. In 1663, 1667, 1673, 1677, 1678, 1680, 1682, and 1685, all those prosecuted were from outside the boundaries of the *stato* of Monte Libretti. See ABCS 249, fasc. 7, 8, 10, 1–14, 16, 17.

35. ABCS 275, fasc. 8, Edicts of October 29, 1660; March 9 and 12, 1672; July 19,

1678; letter of October 8, 1682. Another edict reminded all the villagers of the *stato* to comply with previous edicts related to hunting and fishing (May 8, 1677), ABCS 248, fasc. 7. On the administration of justice in the territory, ABCS 249, fasc. 15, letter and decree of August 29, 1681. Maffeo wanted very specific information about the cases: the type of crime and all of its circumstances; the evidence for the crime; if a violent crime, whether it was life threatening; whether a peaceful settlement had been reached between warring parties; whether weapons were involved; a list of all imprisoned parties, and an account of how their cases were progressing month to month; a list of those declared in contempt of court.

36. ABCS 247, fasc. 68.

37. ABCS 247, fasc. 72 and 74.

38. Since the pope did not have a fleet of ships, convicts were imprisoned at Civitavecchia, where they did odd jobs and labor for which they were paid. See Gross, *Rome in the Age of Enlightenment*, 230. See Scott, *Domination and the Arts of Resistance*, 193, for a similar observation about the subversive aspect of petitions. According to the edicts, the penalties for hunting were the *strappado* and 25 scudi, and for violating the fishing bans, five years' imprisonment (Edict of July 19, 1678 in ABCS 275, fasc. 8). The torture of the *strappado* (called the *corda* [the rope] in Italian) consisted of pulling people in the air by their wrists, which were tied behind their back. In ibid., the letter was dated October 8, 1682. The deferential language to the Barberini read, "Intendo ... d.º Popolo essere fedeliss.mo all'E.V., e caminare con la debita riverenza che si conviene sperando al'Incontro, che la somma benign. e retta conscienza [*sic*] dell'E.V. non permetterrà si facci pregiudizio alcuno à d.º Publico nelle loro Jus."

39. ABCS 275, fasc. 8. The testimony supporting the Barberini case was taken down in April 1683 and March 1684. The originals or copies of the originals are in this fascicolo. The testimony in favor of the villagers can be read in ibid., "Cong.ne Sign.re Just.ae ... Summarium (Nº 4º) Pro Communitate, et Hominibus Terrae Nerulae." The judgment of the magistrate of the Apostolic Chamber is in "Cong:ne Sig.re Justitiae ... Summarium (Nº Pº) Pro Communitate, et Hominibus Terrae Nerulae."

40. A good summary of the Barberini position is in ABCS 275, fasc. 8, "Cong.ne Sign.re Just.ae ... Sabinen Juris prohibendi venationem Pro ... Dno ... Pnpe: Facti," especially, "Possessio autem per annos septuaginta ad evidentiam iustificata remanet, mediantibus supradictis, et aliis pluribus Bandimentis." On Salciccia's torture, see the testimony of Polidaro Rosato Ferro, resident of Ginestra, April 24, 1683, ibid.

41. ABCS 275, fasc. 8, "Cong.ne Sign.re Just.ae ... Sabinen. Juris prohibendi venationem Pro ... Dno ... Pnpe: Facti," especially, "prout in casu nostro multiplex non deficit consensus subditorum, qui prohibitioni à Pnpe facta acquiescant, longo praeterlabente tempore ... quod nemo reclamavit, Bandimenta dicantur effectum fortita." The Barberini lawyers words were "fuisse pro graviori delicto ... quam homicidium."

42. Ibid. The clearest statement of the villagers' position is in: "Cong.ne Sig.re Just.ae ... Pro Communitate, et Hominibus Terrae Nerulae ... Facti 19 July 1685." The relevant testimony appears in "Summarium ... Pro Communitate, et Hominibus Terrae Nerulae," especially Nº 5º, testimony of the priors of Nerola taken on April 13, 1646. The "free right" language (in Facti pro communitate) was "Jus venandi sit liberum

Populi, quod Barones non habentes Jus alti Dominij," and the ancient right (in ibid.). "Aliud est quod Populus non obstantibus . . . bandis conservaverit suam antiquam possessionem venandi."

43. Ibid. "Sententia . . . June 22, 1685."

44. ABCS 249, fasc. 18. This is the same letter from the *auditore*, Giacomo Pensa, August 19, 1685 cited in note 4.

45. *Ibid.* Vincenzo claimed to be fishing for the guardians of the Barberini properties, whose pay was partly in kind in the *auditore*'s letter of August 19, 1685.

46. ABCS 248, fasc. 7, Edicts of Giovanni Antonio Orsini, Edict 43.

47. See ABCS 279, fasc. 66. As opposed to a *consiglio generale*, this meeting was a "pieno consiglio," of "la Maggiore, e più sana parte del Popolo, nulla di meno per l'Infanti, infermi, assenti."

48. On the financial crisis of the Barberini and its impact on the dynamics between family members, see Caroline Castiglione, "Accounting for Affection: Battles between Aristocratic Mothers and Sons in Early Modern Rome," 405–431.

49. ABCS 279, fasc. 66.

50. For the draft of the hunting *concordia*, see ABCS 279, fasc. 65.

51. The three best-attended meetings of the general *consiglio* dealt with papal taxes in 1645 (forty-eight attended); the posting of the Barberini edicts on hunting in 1653 (forty-seven attended); locating and copying the village *statuto* (forty-six attended). Consigli di Nerola, 43r–44r, 128r–128v, 53r–54v. Consigli di Nerola, 49r–51v (February 12, 1646) treats the approval of the expenditures. The *auditore*'s assessment of the situation in the village is in the letter of August 1685, cited in note 4.

52. Muir makes the observation about notaries in "The Sources of Civil Society in Italy," 396–400. On notarial culture in the urban setting of early modern France, see Julie Hardwick, *The Practice of Patriarchy: Gender and the Politics of Household Authority in Early Modern France*. On the importance of notaries in Rome for financial transactions, see Ago, "Enforcing Agreements: Notaries and Courts in Early Modern Rome," 191–206. My point about the relationship between political culture and notarial culture is inspired, in part, by François Furet and Jacques Ozouf's analysis of the "demand" for reading and writing skills in France. See *Lire et écrire*, esp. chapter 4.

53. ABCS 279, fasc. 8.

54. Ibid.

55. See Nussdorfer, *Civic Politics in the Rome of Urban VIII*, 8–10, 218–253.

56. Schiera, "Legitimacy, Discipline, and Institutions," 13–14. Thomas Cohen analyzed a conflict in a nearby village, commenting on the relations between the villagers and the representatives of papal authority. See his "Long Day in Monte Rotondo: The Politics of Jeopardy in a Village Uprising (1558)," 639–668. A very thorough study of how well an early modern Italian state could operate as mediator between different social groups is Marino's *Pastoral Economics*.

57. Zora Neale Hurston, *Their Eyes Were Watching God*, 1–2. In the sixteenth-century German peasants' rebellion, villagers actually uttered the words, rather than only enacting them, as the villagers of Nerola did: "We want to be lords and liberate ourselves." See Blickle, *Communal Reformation*, 172.

CHAPTER 3

1. The quote is from a description of the *stato* of Monte Libretti, circa 1688, ABCS 243, fasc. 14.

2. Pietro Grifonetti described the Commune of Monte Libretti in these terms in Archivio del Comune di Monte Libretti, Libro del Consiglio, Registro 2, hereinafter ML, Consiglio, R.2, 3r–4r (November 23, 1670). Giovanni Curis describes the basic functions of the commune in *Usi civici*, 408. The "Magnificent Community" was an expression used periodically in the *consiglio* records, see ML Consiglio, R.2, November 28, 1677. One debate about a grazing controversy in the village occurred on July 25, 1675. ML, Consiglio, R.2, 31r–31v. Peter Blickle's definition of community also works here, village community meant "an association capable of taking political action" (*Communal Reformation*, 159).

3. The "publico e general Conseglio di un homo à fuoco" and the definition of citizenship were first raised in the *consiglio* of Monte Libretti on November 23, 1670 (3r–4r). On the restriction of the *consiglio* elsewhere in Latium, see Ago, "Braccianti, contadini e grandi proprietari," 73. Maffeo Barberini issued thirty-four edicts on communal government in 1658, admonishing the governors to see that they were closely followed, see ABCS 245, fasc. 5. On the restriction of the *consiglio* in Monte Flavio, see ABCS 291, fasc. 25. The development of a more restricted *consiglio* in the *stato* is discussed further in chapter 4.

4. Two meetings during which the formation of the *bussola* for the office of *depositario* are in ML, Consiglio, R.2, 6v–7r (May 31, 1671) and 29v–30v (April 21, 1675), when the *bussola* had to be assembled by the *sindici* for the "maggior utile del pubblico."

5. There are only four surviving seventeenth-century budgets for Monte Libretti, for the years 1662, 1665, 1672, and 1682. In comparison with the *consiglio* meeting notes, the existing budgets seem to be incomplete and fanciful overviews of village finances. Lawyer fees are mentioned in the budget of 1682. ABCS 246, fasc. 1. See the *consiglio* meeting of June 24, 1675, for another reference to the village lawyer. ML, Consiglio, R.2, 30v–31r.

6. On distributing surplus grain, see ML, Consiglio, R.2, 20r–20v (May 21, 1674); shortages of grain or oil are discussed in ibid., 41r–42r (April 6, 1677); 45r–46r (January 6, 1678); 46r–47r (January 23, 1678). It is clear from a comparison of the *consiglio* record with the letters from the villagers of Monte Libretti to Maffeo Barberini that neither source tells the complete story of contact between the prince and the villagers. Maffeo was petitioned more often than the *consiglio* record suggests in Monte Libretti. Comparatively speaking the Barberini were the subject of discussion about the same number of times in the village of Monte Libretti in the 1670s and Nerola between the mid-1640s and mid-1650s (twenty and nineteen times, respectively). In Nerola, too, the Barberini were petitioned as patrons, but about two-thirds of the time the family was discussed in order to protest their activities in the village.

7. On the Lenten preacher, see ML, Consiglio, R.2, 18r–19v (March 11, 1674) and 52v–53r (December 11, 1678). Bartolomeo Simeoni's two requests are in ibid., 4r–5r (March 19, 1671) and 11v–12r (February 21, 1672). For the schoolteacher as dance instructor, see ibid., 34v–35r (February 6, 1676).

8. The letters are in ABCS 245, fasc. 37.

9. Ibid. the letter of November 7, 1669 discusses Maffeo's concerns about the location of the school. On the church bell, see ibid., letter of March 11, 1674. Maffeo's request that the communal government do more for the church was discussed in the *consiglio*, see ML, Consiglio, R.2, 49r–50r (March 19, 1678).

10. On the *consiglieri's* skepticism about the parish priest's request, see ibid., 49r–50r (March 19, 1678). The parish priest's request to the *consiglieri* is in ibid., 53r–54r (January 24, 1679).

11. Bartolomeo Simeoni's contribution to the music of church services is cited in note 7. The expenses for the confraternity of San Nicola were raised in ML, Consiglio, R.2, 29v–30v (April 21, 1675). The debate about raising the money for the Lenten preacher is in ibid., 18r–19v (March 11, 1674).

12. On the church bell, see ibid., 1r–1v (June 16, 1670); 2r–3r (July 9, 1670); 4r–5r (March 19, 1671); 12v–13r (June 23, 1672); 14r–14v (September 16, 1673); 15v–17r (December 18, 1673); 17v–18r (December 31, 1673); ABCS 245, fasc. 37, letter of March 11, 1674.

13. The expenses for the church bell is discussed in ML, Consiglio, R.2, 26v–27v (November 25, 1674); 28r–28v (January 20, 1675). Its fall and the aftermath is in ibid., 54r–55v (March 5, 1679, March 29, 1679).

14. "per quiete di questo Popolo l'habbiamo licentiato," ABCS 245, fasc. 37, letter of December 5, 1672; ibid., January 26, 1670; "Subbito partito V. E. da Monte Libretti il Canonico D. Gioseppe Ricci abbandonò la scola e mai più l'ha voluto aprire" ibid., June 16, 1674; "per non vedere spersi i figliuoli hanno cercato et scrito in più luoghi, finalmente hanno trovato questo Giovine di età, ma vecchio di giuditio e di dottrina, et se n'è havuta bonissima relatione." The response of the prince was "Deputar il Maestro di Scuola a beneplacito di S.E."; ibid., June 16, 1674.

15. See ML, Consiglio, R.2, 37v–38r (May 10, 1676); on Ricci's replacement, see ABCS 245, fasc. 37, letter of December 28, 1676.

16. Ibid., letter of June 16, 1674, see note 14 above. To replace the wayward Maioli, the priors proposed to the *consiglio* that they write the prince to see whether he could recommend a good candidate for the post. ML, Consiglio, R.2, May 10, 1676; "Figliuoli," is the expression used in the letter, probably meaning boys only, ABCS 245, fasc. 37, September 17, 1669; on the unavailability of housing, see, ibid., letter of November 7, 1669.

17. On the importance of the Orsini funds, see ibid., July 9, 1663. This continued to be an issue in the 1680s. In 1685 problems with the schoolteacher's salary again threatened the position of the *maestro di scuola*, Andrea Pellone. The priors wrote three times to the prince requesting that they be allowed to cash in more of their loan shares in order to pay the schoolmaster more. Ibid., letters of November 16, 1685 and November 21, 1685. The prince's reply is written on the later letter: "The *comunità* can give the supplement for the lack of funds caused by the fall of the *monti*."

18. Nerola, Libro dei Consigli, meeting and license of the surgeon are on 41r–42v (July 23, 1645).

19. ABCS 245, fasc. 37, letters of May 16, 1665; June 25, 1665; July 31, 1665.

20. Ibid., letter of July 31, 1665.

21. Ibid., letters of November 23, 1665, July 9, 1668, and undated letter written "for the community of Monte Libretti."

22. Ibid., letter of July 9, 1668.

23. ML, Consiglio, R.2, 39v–40r (September 20, 1676); 41r–42r (April 6, 1677); 43r–44r (October 17, 1677); 54r–55r (March 5, 1679); 56v–57v (July 16, 1679).

24. On quinine, see William H. McNeill, *Plagues and Peoples*, 247. For a description of the physician's duties compared to the surgeon, see ML, Consiglio, R.2, 79v–80r (March 8, 1682).

25. Nerola, Libro dei Consigli, 89r–90r (April 23, 1649); 112v–113v (November 18, 1651).

26. Ibid., 66v–68r (August 21, 1680); 68r–68v (October 20, 1680); 73v–74r (August 15, 1681); 79v–80r (March 8, 1682).

27. ABCS 245, fasc. 37, letter of July 31, 1665. The edicts are in ABCS 245, fasc. 5. See especially Edict 32 and Edict 28 (where Maffeo is described as "primo cittadino").

28. Edicts, ABCS 245, fasc. 5. The budgets for Monte Libretti are in ABCS 245, fasc. 1 (1662, 1665, 1672, and 1682). In 1684 it seems they only went to Nerola, perhaps a way to harass the communal officials during the dispute over hunting. For Callisto's visit, see ABCS 245, fasc. 13.

29. For the village budgets, see ABCS 246, fasc. 1. On the *depositario* and other communal officials in the Barberini edicts, see ABCS 245, fasc. 5, especially Edicts 7–12, 19, 23, 25–26.

30. ML, Consiglio, R.2, 51r–51v (May 1, 1678).

31. ABCS 245, fasc. 37, letters of April 25 (from Simone Pellone) and April 28, 1675 (from the *auditore* to the Barberini prince). ML, Consiglio, R.2, 29v–30v (April 21, 1675).

32. Ibid., 5r–5v (May 10, 1671); 6v–7r (May 31, 1671); 55r–55v (March 29, 1679); 56r (May 20, 1679); 58r–58v (August 6, 1679).

33. Ibid., *consiglio* meetings of 1674, 18r–27v. On the schoolteacher, see ABCS 245, fasc. 37, letter of June 16, 1674.

34. ML, Consiglio, R.2, 18r–19v (March 11, 1674); 24r–25r (October 7, 1674).

35. ABCS 245, fasc. 37, letter of November 2, 1674.

36. Ibid., letter from priors and the *auditore* with a reply from the prince dated November 10, 1674.

37. ML, Consiglio, R.2, 43r–44r (October 17, 1677).

38. Ibid., 61r–61v (May 1, 1680); 65v–66v (June 2, 1680); 70r–70v (March 4, 1681); 71r–71v (March 9, 1681); ABCS 245, fasc. 37, letter of March 9, 1681.

39. Ibid.

40. Ibid., "Per tanto se ne fà parte all'Eccellenza Vostra acciò habbia piena informatione per potere reprimere quelli, che si oppongono al utile Commune forse per privato interesse, o passione"; "non mancheremo perciò domatina d'istromentare all'ultimo, è più offerente, stimando incontrare il volere di V. E. a cui per esperienza e molto à cuore il nostro utile."

41. Albert O. Hirschman, *The Passions and the Interests: Political Arguments for Capitalism before Its Triumph*, 9, 15–16.

42. ABCS 245, fasc. 37, undated letter, with internal evidence suggesting March 1681: "nel'Istrom.to fatto stava che ogn'uno vendesse à Suo arbitrio." The priors evidently sent the prince a copy of the *consiglio* record (dated March 9, 1681), including the names of all the *consiglieri* and how they voted.

43. Ibid., letter of March 21, 1681.

44. Peter Blickle notes a similar problem in trying to define the "common man" for Germany: "above the common man were the lords, lay and clerical, and below him were the lower social classes and those groups entirely outside the hierarchy of social estates" (*Communal Reformation*, 4).

45. This might reflect the peculiarities of note takers, many of whom are not identified. It is occasionally clear that the governor, a Barberini official, did some of the writing (frequently, their writing was terrible). The governor was usually identified as "doctor of two laws," and his education might account for the presence of these terms in the record. His professional peers, however, in the neighboring village of Nerola did not make use of these terms. [Perhaps explained by difference in chronology, Nerola's records are from the 1640s and 1650s.] I contend that such references crop up in Monte Libretti for specific local reasons related to its communal politics, rather than merely to the presence of the governor. Monte Libretti had many more communal revenues, and therefore more ambitious expenditures than Nerola. *Consiglio* votes in Nerola tended to be unanimous.

46. ML, Consiglio, R.2, 29v–30v (April 21, 1675); 41r–42r (April 6, 1677); 45r–46r, (January 6, 1678); on the physician and the surgeons, see especially, 42r–43r (September 26, 1677); 68r–68v (October 20, 1680); 79v–80r (March 8, 1682).

47. Ibid., 55r–55v (March 29, 1679). The word "public" was also used when the *consiglio* needed to select the best possible candidates for *depositario*. See 29v–30v (April 21, 1675).

48. Ibid., 6v–7r (May 31, 1671) "La maggior parte del Popolo"; 88v–89r (March 18, 1684): "on the greatest usefulness of the Magnificent Commune." Papal officials, for instance, worried about good investments of village funds in years when communal finances were in the black.

49. Ibid., these languages were conflated in the meeting of October 17, 1677 (43r–44r).

50. Ibid., 9v–10r (December 6, 1671); 6v–7r (May 31, 1671); 9v–10r (December 6, 1671); 70r–70v (March 4, 1681).

51. ABCS 243, fasc. 14.

52. On the *depositario* controversy, see ML, Consiglio, R.2, 58r–58v (August 6, 1679); on the bell maker, ibid., 14r–14v (September 16, 1673).

53. ABCS 245, fasc. 37, letter of January 17, 1674.

54. See Laurie Nussdorfer's discussion of a similar situation faced by the *popolo romano*, who in the countryside held several fiefs as titled lords. They were also besieged by requests and visitors from the villagers and promulgated decrees limiting the days the villagers could appear. See her chapter entitled, "Vassals," in *Civic Politics in the Rome of Urban VIII*.

The Barberini had issued a similar decree in 1648, not allowing any prior to come to

Rome at the expense of the commune without the permission of the prince or his auditor. The number of letters from Monte Libretti drafted by the Barberini secretary in Rome indicate that the priors were still coming in person during Maffeo's rule.

CHAPTER 4

1. Lodolini, *L'Archivio della S. Congregazione del Buon Governo*, xxxiv–xxxvi. For a recent perspective on the Buon Governo in the Papal States see Santoncini, *Il Buon Governo*.

2. For a more detailed examination of the family politics during this period of the Barberini's decline, see Castiglione, "Accounting for Affection," 405–431.

3. Lodolini, *L'Archivio della S. Congregazione del Buon Governo*, xx–xxii; xxxiv–xxxvi.

4. Patricia Waddy, for instance, considered Taddeo Barberini a good administrator of the family's patrimony during the seventeenth century. See her *Seventeenth-Century Roman Palaces*, 276–278; 283–290. For negative views of the Barberini's (and Rome's) gilded decadency, see Pecchiai, *I Barberini*, 277. Hanns Gross calls 1704 the "death blow" of the barons' "jurisdictional prerogatives" in their communes, see his *Rome in the Age of Enlightenment*, 161. Mario Tosi argued that this rendered the nobility nothing more than a "corpo sociale, che può definirsi nobiltà di corte" (*La società romana dalla feudalità al patriziato* [1816–1853], 127–128). See also Pescosolido, *Terra e nobiltà*, 48–50; and Carlo Mistruzzi, "La nobiltà nello Stato Pontificio," 208–209, 215, 219. It is also important to note that the Buon Governo was concerned with communal affairs; it would, for instance, only become involved in public disturbances or legal suits if they were related to communal finances or affairs.

5. The already existing S. Consulta had regulated local governments, though many of its functions would eventually be taken over by the Buon Governo. The responsibilities for taxation belonging to the Congregazione degli Sgravi (which had been established by Sixtus V in 1588) were also gradually absorbed by the Buon Governo. See Lodolini, *L'Archivio della S. Congregazione del Buon Governo*, xiii–xv. On the goal of ending abuses in communal government, see Armando Lodolini, "L'Amministrazione pontificia del 'Buon Governo,'" 199–200. The Buon Governo had some judicial authority in the countryside, but only as it related to properties or interests of the commune. See Lodolini, *L'Archivio della S. Congregazione del Buon Governo*, cl–cliv.

6. Archivio del Buon Governo, Archivio di Stato di Roma (hereinafter ABG), Serie II, b. 2622. A smattering of seventeenth-century letters indicates that the Buon Governo was already making at least preliminary efforts to audit communal finances. As I also noted in chapter 3, Maffeo Barberini referred to the edicts of the Buon Governo when he issued edicts regarding the regulation of communal affairs. Lando Scotoni argued that the autonomous *stati* like Monte Libretti paid fewer taxes to the papacy than other areas of the Papal States. He also maintained that additional seigneurial dues owed to the baronial families in the autonomous states more than made up for this difference, though he does not have much evidence for this assertion. See his *I Territori Autonomi dello Stato Ecclesiastico nel Cinquecento*, pp. 91, 93. Elio Lodolini notes that the budgets of baronial communes occur in greater numbers beginning in the eighteenth century (*L'Archivio della S. Congregazione del Buon Governo*, xxxvi). He also

notes, however, that many communities, both baronial and cameral often did not submit budgets for decades (ibid., xxxviii).

7. Ibid., xxxvi.

8. According to Elio Lodolini, during Imperiali's tenure as prefect the "Buon Governo acquisitò un'importanza sempre maggiore." Lodolini, *L'Archivio della S. Congregazione del Buon Governo*, xxii. A. Lodolini gives Imperiali the credit for reducing baronial control of communes and for forcing them to pay taxes in their lands. Lodolini, "L'Amministrazione pontificia del 'Buon Governo,'" 221.

9. ABCS 271, fasc. 24, Edict 22. For a general summary of the edicts and procedures for local governments created by the Buon Governo, see Lodolini, *L'Archivio della S. Congregazione del Buon Governo*, xxxvi–xlvii. On the budget, see ABCS 271, fasc. 25. On posting the budget, see ABCS 271, fasc. 24, Edict 3. On the edicts of the Buon Governo, see ibid., Edict 10, Edict 13 also contained the provision that all of the edicts of the Buon Governo also be registered in a book in the commune, along with the edicts of "altri Signori Superiori," meaning, I would assume, the Barberini. On the necessity of the Buon Governo, see ibid., Edict 12.

10. On the records of rentals, see ibid., Edict 9. On debtors, see Edict 16. On the pursuit of debtors, see Edict 18. In the edicts Testa wrote for the fief of Monte Libretti, the *esattore* was to be elected by the consiglio. Edict 17 in ABCS 245, fasc. 29. See ABCS 271, fasc. 24, Edict 17, for the role of the governor and chancellor.

11. A. Lodolini cites some phrases representative of their despair that resemble what visitors said about the record keeping in Monte Libretti ("L'Amministrazione pontificia del 'Buon Governo,'" 212n.). For "the disorders I discovered there," see ABCS 291, fasc. 27. On technicalities of bookkeeping, see ibid., Edicts 9–13.

12. See Scotoni, *I Territori Autonomi dello Stato Ecclesiastico*, 60. For the focus on tax collecting, see Lodolini, *L'Archivio della S. Congregazione del Buon Governo*, xlviii; and ABCS 245, fasc. 30, on the varieties of taxation in the *stato*.

13. A. Lodolini ("L'Amministrazione pontificia del 'Buon Governo,'" 221): According to Armando Lodolini, breaking the baronial exemption on taxation was the primary accomplishment of the Buon Governo because it relieved the tax burdens on the inhabitants of their territories. For "cameral taxes," see ABG, Serie II, b. 2622; and ABCS 271, fasc. 24, on Nerola. The Barberini controlled the lists of villagers eligible to serve as priors and as tax collectors.

14. Sometimes he received a small payment from villages when he visited them. See ABCS 271, fasc. 24, Edict 15, for the liberty to speak freely in the *consiglio*. For "impeded the liberty of the *consigli*" and "according to his whim," ABCS 245, fasc. 30; and ABCS 291, fasc. 27, for "the current Governor."

15. Castiglione, "Accounting for Affection," 405–431. On Olimpia, see Castiglione, "Honor and the Female Self: Olimpia Giustiniani Barberini (1641–1729)."

16. AB, Ind. II, 2278. The fiefs considered for sale were Coll'Alto, Marcitelli, San Giovanni in Campo Oratio, Castello di San Vittorino, Castel Vecchio. On the near sale of Ponticelli, see AB, Ind. II, 2280.

17. During the 1720s Francesco was in conflict with his sister-in-law Maria Teresa Boncompagni over the custody of Cornelia Costanza Barberini, whom Francesco had

named the sole heir to all the Barberini properties. See Castiglione, "Extravagant Pretensions," for more on this familial dispute.

18. For Francesco's right to exercise criminal jurisdiction, see AB, Ind. I, 882. For Francesco's nomination to "*economo*," see AB, Ind. II, 2256.

19. ABCS 245, fasc. 33, is an undated manuscript that includes a list of debtors to the various communes. See that manuscript, folios 2r–2v, for "a payment on their debt," and for the governor's assessment and Francesco's response to the situation.

20. For "made a *conto lungo*," see ibid., 2r–2v, and "innumerable accounts."

21. Ibid., 3v., is the source for all direct quotes.

22. Ibid., 4r–4v. After the third folio of this document, the author ceased to number the pages. My numbering noted here and below continues the folio numbers as the author began them.

23. Ibid., 4v–5r.

24. ABCS 245, fasc. 33, letter dated 22 September 1725.

25. Ibid., "facendo tra loro il Conseglio, conforme si è stilato l'altre volte, si vede chi è debitore, se gli fà fare l'oblighi alli debitori, che non possono pagare, e darle la sua dilatione, e non procedere solamente a fine indiretta."

26. Ibid.

27. Ibid., letter dated October 10, 1725.

28. Ibid., undated manuscript, which includes a list of debtors to the various communes.

29. Ibid., 5r. "In ogn'una delle Communità vi è qualche Sacerdote, e Persona timorato di Dio, che conosce il beneficio, che dall'Eccelenza Sua vuole apportarglivi, e perciò da tutti se ne benedice il Signore e ne consenta gratitudine verso il Padrone."

30. Ibid., 5v–6r. "astringe ugualmente tutti alla Sodisfattione [*sic*] del loro debito." (6r)

31. For "experience," see ibid., 6r–6v. For "Despite the many cares," see ibid., 3r.

32. The following figures show the total amount of debt in the other villages followed by the amount owed by the largest debtor. Here I have rounded off to the nearest scudo: Monte Flavio: 476 scudi [291 scudi]; Nerola: 456 scudi [143 scudi]; Monte Libretti: 645 scudi [138 scudi]; Ponticelli: 156 scudi [30 scudi].

33. Armando Lodolini claims that the government of cities in the Papal States was much more corrupt than it was in the *ville* or the *castelli*. He hypothesizes that this was because their "finanze erano più fortemente temuta e sentita; or forse gli amministratori locali più ingenui." The comments made by Testa about the fiefs of Monte Libretti did not suggest he had the same faith in the government of the villages. See Lodolini's article, "L'Amministrazione pontificia del 'Buon Governo,'" 211. An edict issued by the Barberini in 1750 allowed the Barberini officials to charge 6 baiocchi for a sheet of paper.

34. Renata Ago has analyzed the economic strategies pursued by individual villagers in her *Un Feudo esemplare*, 51–89. She also found widespread indebtedness in the communal governments she studied, though she argued it was limited to those eligible to participate in the village *consiglio*. See her "Braccianti, contadini e grandi proprietari," 75–76.

35. This was argued to be the case in Monte Flavio by Monsignore Testa in 1704.

36. Lodolini, "L'Amministrazione pontificia del 'Buon Governo,'" attributes this failure to either a lack of funds or to a preference by the monsignori for the old system (p. 215). On the visit of Monsignor Dentice to the *stato* of Monte Libretti in 1762, see chapter 6. On the failure of the Buon Governo to develop a sufficient bureaucratic structure to meet its stated agenda, see also Lodolini, "L'Amministrazione pontificia del 'Buon Governo,'" 211, 214, 215, which should be compared with his grudging (and somewhat contradictory) praise for the papal institution on pp. 187 and 221.

37. Pescosolido, *Terra e nobiltà,* 48–50; Mistruzzi, "La nobiltà nello Stato Pontificio," 208–209, 215, 219.

38. In 1729 Giovanni Tosta, the General Governor received a letter from the Apostolic Commissioner Monsignor Fabretti instructing Fabretti to post the enclosed bans in Nerola and Monte Libretti. Tosta considered it "his duty" to inform Francesco and receive the cardinal's opinion on the matter before carrying out the *Commissario's* orders. ABCS 273, fasc. 14; letter from Fabretti, dated August 24, 1729, actually addressed to the *auditore* of Nerola. Although the edicts themselves are not included in the fascicolo (and may have been forwarded to the community), the letter contains information about the posting and recording of the edicts in the chancellery. For "who, being in favor of," see ABCS 245, fasc. 33.

39. An edict issued in 1731 by the priors of Montorio Romano also suggests that Francesco, rather than the Buon Governo, remained an important player in pursuing local debtors to the communes. The edict allowed debtors to pay the amounts they owed in grain at a fixed price, and it was issued with the sanction of the Barberini prince and the public *consiglio,* with no mention of the Buon Governo. A letter of December 1734 from the priors of Nerola was addressed to Cardinal Imperiali himself. They had evidently been assigned the responsibility to collect the *pesi camerali* in areas where they claimed to have no jurisdiction. They requested "le facoltà di poter procedere contro i morosi di dd luoghi con la mano reggia e more cammerali come procedono i Commissarij Cavalcanti che si spediscono dalli Banchi contro le Comunità," ABCS 387, fasc. 7, letter dated December 26, 1734. On the *commissari cavalcanti,* see Santoncini, *Il Buon Governo,* 72.

40. AB, Ind. II, 1246, "Dote e Capitoli Matrimoniali," dated May 14, 1728.

41. Pecchiai, *I Barberini,* 226. Pecchiai finds it strange that the first son, who would inherit the Colonna di Sciarra properties would receive the name Urbano, the "typical" Barberini name, but actually, Carlo was a name as frequently used in the family (though perhaps without the fame of Urban VIII). On the protocol of letter writing, see AB, Ind. II, 1311.

42. In official documents both Giulio Cesare and Cornelia Costanza are named as the "princes of Palestrina," the owners and lords of Monte Libretti (including the various titles associated with the individual villages of the *stato*). Edicts often bear both of their names, though as I explain below, from the 1730s to the 1760s Giulio Cesare took a more active role in the management of the *stato,* and in the 1770s such responsibility shifted to Cornelia Costanza and then to their son Carlo. See AB, Ind. II, 2308, for more on the agreement with Francesco including the other types of income such as the

rents of the Abbey of S. Maria di Grottaferrata and some *censi*. The years 1762–1769 are missing from the Vatican Library. Other correspondence from 1733 to1775 is found in ABC 545, 546, and 989–999.

43. Elio Lodolini chronicles the conflicts and the related tax burdens for this period in his *L'Archivio della S. Congregazione del Buon Governo*, lxix–lxxiv. On the duration of the debts, see lxix. He estimates that the war of Austrian succession alone cost the communities of the Papal States 3,000,000 scudi and that the total amount of new taxes that had to be raised to finance the papacy's role in all the conflicts combined was 4,900,000 scudi; see especially lxxiii–lxiv; lxxiv.

44. ABCS 245, fasc. 26, Edict 6.

45. Thousands of letters from the noble family to their officials are in the Barberini archives. In Renata Ago's work on Latium she separates the *ministri* (in the Barberini documents, the *soprintendenti*) from the governors. See her *Un Feudo esemplare*. On similiar features in the Borghese administration, see Forclaz, "Le relazioni complesse," 171–176.

I use the words officials and functionaries to refer to both *soprintendenti* and governors. As I explain below, despite their conflicting allegiances, the governors were very closely monitored by the noble family. On the Barberini appointment of the governors and their monitoring by the Barberini, see ABC 992, 70v [July 1, 1747], 415v [March 22, 1749], 438r [April 26, 1749]; ABC 995, 23r [February 9, 1754]; ABC 991, 547v [July 30, 1746]. The governors were aided by "vice-governors" who also occasionally received letters from the Barberini (ABC 999, 282r). Giulio Cesare also rejected some of the suggestions by the governors for the selection of vice-governors. See ABC 992, 465r [June 16, 1749]. On the *paesani* as vice-governors, see ABC 994, 45r [March 4, 1752]. On who should attend the *consiglio*, see ABC 992, 246v–247r [April 13, 1748], 341r [September 28, 1748].

As a check on the activities of the *soprintendente*, the Barberini also relied on their correspondence with the accountant. Through the accountant they monitored income from various fiefs and settled with renters at the end of their leases. After the arrival of a new *soprintendente*, the accountant was expected to instruct him in all of the matters related to the *stato*, especially those pending at the time he took office; ABC, 997, 531r; ABC, 999, 42r, 43r, 44r, 282v. Renata Ago has argued that archpriests should be considered noble officials, and the evidence from Monte Libretti suggests that connections between the Barberini and a number of local prelates were an important part of the noble family's regime, although as chapter 6 will show, they were not easily controlled by the noble family. For Ago's argument, see *Un Feudo esemplare*, 134.

46. See the edicts, ABCS 248, fasc. 96 and 103; and ABCS 291, fasc. 27, on the jurisdiction of the governors.

47. The governor had a six-month term and was paid from the penalties owed by guilty parties. ABC 999, 145r; ABC 1007, p. 247. Curis notes that he had both civil and criminal jurisdiction in the villages where he worked. See Curis, *Usi civici*, 424.

The governor was assisted by the chancellor, another important figure in the local court of the Barberini, who also derived his income from the legal proceedings of their tribunal; ABC 1007, Libro Mastro, 1770–1771, p. 9.

Ago claims that unsettled cases proceeded from the governors to the Buon Governo.

She also argues that the Buon Governo relied on the governors for information about those cases, but had a difficult time getting impartial information from them. See her article, "Conflitti e politica nel feudo," 853–858. As officials in capacity to review budgets, Armando Lodolini found them lacking the necessary skills to review communal finances or the personal will to challenge the "arrogant communal officials," whose accounts they were supposed to be reviewing; Armando Lodolini, "L'Amministrazione pontificia del 'Buon Governo,'" 216. Ago's analysis of the village of Anguillara, reveals, however, that the governor could also be in conflict with local elites, though as an "outsider" he was rarely successful in outwitting local families; "Braccianti, contadini e grandi proprietari," 74–76. A few letters from the officials have survived, including those of Giantomaso Martelli regarding this case; ABCS 280, fasc. 2, letters of January 16, 1757 and October 10, 1757. On presenting themselves in Rome, see ABC 999, 237v–238r. On fleeing the *Padrone*'s face, see ABC 994, 383r [June 2, 1753].

48. In 1739 the *soprintendente* earned 180 scudi in cash in addition to his allowances in bread and "*guardarobba*" or other supplies necessary to his life in the *stato*; BC, vol. 17, f. 306. The *soprintendente* was also in charge of seeing that the governors left the palaces where they had resided in good order, and for providing new governors with at least the minimal items necessary for their comfort; ABC 999, 278r, 287v.

49. Tommaso Pagani, general governor of Monte Libretti in 1732 referred to "diligence" and "officiousness" to describe himself during a difficult conflict with the *soprintendente* of the *stato*; ABCS 277, fasc. 8. The command "*invigilare*" or "*vigilare*" is everywhere in the letters from the Barberini. Correspondence with an official often refers to an earlier letter, or to the "precise words used in [an earlier] letter;" ABC 999, 261v. "Non venga mai ad innovar cosa alcuna," or similar statements against "novità" are common in the letterbooks and related to a variety of issues; ABC, 999, 249r; 282v.

Ago maintains that feudal functionaries were prized for their moderation and that "[t]he peace of the fief, the absence of scandal or disorder" was the ultimate goal for which a baron would sacrifice an employee if necessary ("Conflitti e politica nel feudo," 861, 865). In the letters of the noble family it is clear that their agenda was more involved than simply securing tranquility in the fiefs. On the trouble with grumblers, see ABC 994, 188v [September 1752].

50. ABC 998, 270r; ABC 997, 516v; ABC 994, 196v.

51. The edict (from 1759) is in ABCS 283, fasc. 13. The letter is from 1774: ABC 999, 206r–206v: "Questi sono i tempi, ne quali si distingue la diligenza di un buon Ministro, ne saremo a veder gli effetti. . . . Ella invigili su questo punto [*sic*], e non faccia il caritatevole sulla Roba degli Altri, ma astringa i Medesimi prima, che voli via il Grano da Loro raccolto"; ABC 999, 291v.

52. In *Un Feudo esemplare* (18, 45), Ago calls "feudal functionaries" the "unique interlocutors of the feudatory and the unique mouthpiece of the peasantry," while claiming also that these functionaries reinforced negative stereotypes of the peasantry held by ruling elites, which would hardly make them a useful "mouthpiece" for the peasantry. Such contradictions suggest the ambiguous position of the officials between lords and vassals, which I believe caused the functionaries to have shifting, rather than clear-cut loyalties to either side. She also notes the short terms of the feudal functionaries in

Un Feudo esemplare (137–138) attributing their frequent departures to the false accusations of sexual improprieties made against them by the peasantry in Monteromano. I have found no such accusations in Monte Libretti, whose conflicts more closely resemble those of Anguillara and Bassano documented by Ago in "Conflitti e politica nel feudo" (869–871).

The rapid turnover of governors in Latium is not merely the result of accusations by the inhabitants, but also has to do with their short appointment of only six months.

53. On the taxes owed by the Barberini, see BC, vol. 17, 524 (*debit*). On these percentage taxes on elite landowners, see Lodolini, *L'Archivio della S. Congregazione del Buon Governo*, lxxiv.

The so-called *Tassa del milione*, which levied 1,000,000 scudi on the Papal States amounted to a much lower payment for the Barberini, BC, vol. 17, 494 (*debit*). The taxes assessed in 1739 for the passage of troops were much higher, ranging from 15 to 66 scudi per fief; BC, vol. 17, 254 (*debit*).

On the dispute in Corese, see ABCS 245, fasc. 30; ABCS 280, fasc. 3. The decree was issued by the Secretary of Buon Governo in the case called Sabiniensis Onorum Cameralium. In 1770 the Barberini paid these papal taxes as well as taxes in Ponticelli, another village where the taxes owed by the baron were at last successfully collected; ABC, 1007, pp. 114–115.

54. See ABCS 245, fasc. 24 [August 6, 1761], for the settlement of the Barberini taxes in the village of Monte Libretti.

55. Nerola, ABCS 271, fasc. 36; Monte Flavio, ABCS 291, fasc. 29; Ponticelli, ABCS 287, fasc. 15; Monte Libretti, ABCS 245, fasc. 26. The visitation of the villages of Sabina was done by Monsignore Dentice, the deputy of Cardinal Lante, Prefect of the Buon Governo and Bishop of Palestrina; "every year" is from the edicts of Nerola and Monte Flavio.

56. ABC 999, 290v.

57. On Camilli and the budgets, see ABC 991, 583v [October 1, 1746]. On his aging, and his successor, see ABC 995, 174v [August 31, 1746]. For the admission of the papal bureaucrat, see ABG, Serie II, b. 2622, village of Monte Libretti, 1773.

58. On the seventeenth-century budgets of the village of Monte Libretti, see ABCS 246, fasc. 1. On the eighteenth-century budgets of that same village, see ABCS 245, fasc. 26.

59. Camilli's activities in the *stato* can be surveyed in ABC 991, 417v–418r [October 23, 1745]; 557r [August 6, 1746]; 581r [September 24, 1746]; 583v [October 1746]. Camilli was imprisoned by the governor in 1748, for an unspecified offense, the same year in which the greatest burdens imposed by the papal government were beginning to be felt in the village, ABC 992, 202r [January 20, 1748].

60. Up to 1760, I can only find one such request, from the village of Monte Libretti, for the Buon Governo to approve an additional extraordinary expenditure. See ABG, Serie II, b. 2622, years, 1755–1756. I found no examples for Monte Flavio. See ABG, Serie II, b. 2528. Requests to the noble family from the village of Monte Libretti, ABCS 245, fasc. 26, Edict 6; ABC 708, 5v; 8v; 18v; 28v; 30r; 47v; 50v; 62v; 90r–90v. These requests are often related to repairing a local church. Copies of records from the

community of Monte Flavio indicate that a similar request was made to the Barberini for church expenses in 1725, 1726, 1736, and 1751; ABCS 273, fasc. 27.

61. On edicts, see ABC 991, 398r [September 18, 1745]. See the battle between Monte Flavio and Monte Libretti over the *macinato*, ABC 991, 438v [November 20, 1745]. On the publicity of papal decisions, see ABC 991, 585r [October 8, 1746]. On the *consiglio* in Corese, see ABC 991 [December 31, 1746]. On the inevitability of the Barberini getting drawn into the fray, see the case of Sante Sciarra discussed at length in chapter 6. He petitioned the Barberini from prison, and the Barberini followed the case with interest. See especially ABC 992, 219r [February 17, 1748]; 233v [March 16, 1748]; 245v [April 6, 1748]; 252r [April 27, 1748]; 267v [June 8, 1748]; 321r [September 7, 1748]. On the symbiotic and therefore friction-prone relations between Monte Libretti and Monte Flavio, see ABC 991, 408r [October 9, 1745]; 528r [May 28, 1746]; 538r [June 25, 1746]; ABC 992, 92r [August 12, 1747].

62. On watching the collection of the *macinato*, see the letters of ABC 992, 70v [July 1, 1747]; 101r [August 26, 1747]; 101v [August 26, 1747, a letter specifically to Camilli]; on improprieties in their collection, ABC 991, 422r [October 30, 1745]; 425r [November 6, 1745]; ABC 992, 86r [August 5, 1747]; 187r [December 9, 1747]; on unfair assessments, ABC 991, 539v [July 2, 1746]; 562r [August 20, 1746]; 617r [December 10, 1746]. For a petition to the noble family for past debts, see ABC 992, 524r [August 16, 1749] and ABC 994, 199r [September 9, 1752].

63. For "Benestanti," see ABC 997, 510v. The Barberini also monitored the collection of taxes in Monte Flavio. See ABC 992, 86r [August 5, 1747]; on the employees in Ponticelli, see ABC 999, 149r–149v. On Giuseppe Petricca, see ABC 999, 279v; 287r–287v.

64. For "showing himself," see ABC 999, 144v. And for "which of these reports," see ABC 999, 176v.

65. Some of the other cases in which the assistance of the Barberini was requested include helping to guarantee the proper renting of communal property; the settling of debts of the renter of communal ovens; the conveying of various decisions by the Buon Governo; see ABC 999, 263v; 267v; 268r; ABC 994, 188v–189r. Ago has also noted the difficulty for the Buon Governo in relying on the information it received from the governors; see "Conflitti e politica nel feudo," 858.

CHAPTER 5

1. These descriptions come from the edicts ABCS 248, fasc. 93 [November 14, 1754], issued in regards to Nerola and Corese, and ABCS 248, fasc. 102 [October 2, 1756], issued specifically for the village of Monte Libretti. See also ABCS 291, fasc. 36 [January 10, 1748], issued for Monte Flavio. This edict of 1748 also referred to the papal "*bandi generali*" of 1740, which had set the punishment at three *tratti di corda* and loss of money or goods involved in the game. The edict of 1754 also added the high monetary penalty of 40 scudi. A letter of May 4, 1754 to the governors in the territory stresses that the papacy was issuing similar edicts against card-playing in this period, another indication of how engaged the Barberini were with the papal government's agenda for the countryside.

2. ABCS 248, fasc. 124 [May 15, 1769]. Ibid., Edict of January 17, 1772, which

added the possibility of incarceration to the penalty. A similar edict was issued for Monte Flavio, ABCS 291, fasc. 37 [May 31, 1756], which prohibited singing without a license. The penalty was 20 giuli. On the performances, see ABC 991, 404r [October 2, 1745]; ibid., 576r [September 10, 1746].

3. "as we have," ABCS 248, fasc. 123 [February 1, 1770]; "in obedience," ABCS 248, fasc. 97 [December 2, 1755].

4. "paternal tenderness," ABCS 248, fasc. 98 [August 10, 1754]; "greatly desires," ABCS 243, fasc. 13 [September 5, 1758]. This expression of fatherly concern varied from edict to edict. See also ABCS 243, fasc. 14 [August 9, 1759]; "paternal care," ABCS 248, fasc. 110 [August 8, 1763]; "fatherly love," ABCS 248, fasc. 112 [April 21, 1766]; "paternal zeal," ABCS 248, fasc. 124 [May 15, 1769].

5. On the graves, see ABC 991, 612r [December 3, 1746]; ABC 995, 123v [May 25, 1754]; ABC 994, 25v [January 29, 1752], for how the official was to address the issue in Monte Flavio.

6. On keeping track of the penalties, see ABC 991, 407v–408r [October 9, 1745] and ABC 994, 263r [November 25, 1752]; on controlling access to the books, ABC 994, 218r [September 26, 1752]. On cases involving disputed use rights, see ABC 992, 381r [November 16, 1748] and ABC 994, 340v (bis) [August 18, 1753]. The rape case is discussed in ABC 991, 403r–403v [September 25, 1745]. For the lowering of penalties, see ABC 991, 539r [June 25, 1746]. On the release of prisoners, see ABC 991, 510r [April 2, 1746] and ABC 992, 37r [March 25, 1747].

7. Between May 1 and December 31, 1770, the *soprintendente* paid the constable and sheriffs 139:50 or almost 20 scudi per month, which did not include 68:03 scudi for the same period in costs for the transportation and feeding of the occasional prisoner in the *stato*. ABC 1007, p. 247. See Pescosolido, *Terra e nobiltà* (51), which describes the very limited income the Borghese family derived from the exercise of justice and seigneurial rights. Most of their income (90 percent) came from rents on their lands. Pescosolido also notes that the income from the administration of justice generated much more for nobles in the kingdom of Naples (50). On registering the edicts, see ABC 991, 427v [November 6, 1745]. While other expenses for the *stato* could be considerably greater (restoration work to buildings or the costs for storing grain, for instance), many of the costs of keeping order in Monte Libretti were paid indirectly, in the wages of the *soprintendente* or in the perks and extra benefits offered to the governor to investigate disturbances in the fiefs. Not all of the Barberini efforts in this area can be calculated in terms of monetary costs.

8. ABC 1007, pp. 50–51. In Monte Flavio the Barberini owned no structures except the oven. Ibid., pp. 72, 77. For a description of the jail, see ABCS 387, fasc. 17. ABC 1007, p. 14. The same source also mentions the prison cells and the rooms for the constable and the *birri* in the castle of Nerola and notes that they had been restored in 1740 (p. 35).

9. ABC 999, 255v. Not surprisingly, she did not like the cost estimate of 129.50 scudi for the building of the jail. She wrote her minister that she knew of someone who would build a jail in Coll'alto, another Barberini fief, for much less. On the jail in Montorio Romano, see ABC 1007, p. 63.

10. ABC 997, 527r [September 28, 1761]. Officials also had frequent requests for the Barberini. In February 1775, Cornelia Costanza agreed to pay the physician's bill of the governor at Montorio Romano, though she let the physician know that he had to be satisfied with 10 scudi (ABC 999, 270v). The governor Giantomaso Martelli enjoyed the coffee the Barberini sent him so much that he asked the family for two more pounds, devoutly adding that he drank it on fasting days the way the local people used wine (ABC 280, fasc. 2 [letter of January 20, 1758]). On the wounded man in Monte Flavio, see ABC 991, 511r [April 9, 1746].

11. For Giulio Cesare as godfather, see ABC 994, 28r–28v [February 12, 1752]. On masses for the superintendent, see ABC 992, 383r [November 16, 1748]. ABC 992, 32r [March 18, 1747]; ABC 992, 414r [March 22, 1749]; ABC 993, 69r–69v [April 18, 1750].

12. ABC 999, 252r. Letter from Cornelia Costanza noting that the inhabitants of the village of Monte Libretti had written asking for a donation of bread from the Barberini "as they had done the year before." The papal edict of 1680 charged the owners of ovens with maintaining the same quality of bread demanded in Rome. The penalties were enormous—10,000 scudi for the owner who violated the decree. ABCS 244, fasc. 89. The Barberini evidently took this obligation very seriously. One of Cornelia Costanza's angriest exchanges with any minister, for instance, had to do with that minister making a new contract with a baker whom Cornelia Costanza had repeatedly reprimanded for the poor quality of his bread. ABC 998, ff. 270r–272v. On the distribution of the bread to the poor, ABC 991, 535v [June 18, 1746]; ABC 992, 112r [September 23, 1747]. Mazzetti's election and approval by the Barberini is recorded in Archivio del Comune di Monte Libretti, Libro del Consiglio, Registro 6, hereinafter ML, Consiglio, R.6, 41v–42r [June 11, 1752] and ibid., 42. For the command from Giulio Cesare to Monte Flavio, see ABC 992, 230r [March 9, 1748] and ABC 995, 63r [March 23, 1754]; "per lo sfamo" and the "usual price," ABC 989, 302r–302v.

13. ABCS 287, fasc. 14 [May 6, 1753]; cut of wood, ABC 994 [September 2, 1752]; on the placement of the pew, ABC 992, 223v [February 24, 1748] to the governor and ibid., 226r [March 2, 1748] to the archpriest. On the solicitation of his patronage of the restoration of the organ in Monte Libretti, see ABC 991, 628v [December 24, 1746]; ABC 992, 19r [February 18, 1747].

14. See the example of the schoolteacher in Corese, ABC 991, 594r [October 22, 1746]. On the controversy in Monte Flavio, see ABC 995, 156v [August 10, 1754] and ibid., 167r [August 24, 1754]. On the edification of the people, see ABC 992, 544r [September 6, 1749]. On Giulio Cesare's version of education, see ABC 995, 196v [September 14, 1754]. Regarding the school for the girls, Giulio Cesare wrote to the archpriest to say that the widow could charge the families of the well-to-do students, but if she did that he would withdraw his offer of free lodgings for her. See ABC 994, 18v [January 22, 1752]. Giulio Cesare's views on education were shared by other elites in Europe. See the survey of such attitudes in Houston, *Literacy in Early Modern Europe*, 15–20.

15. On Giulio Cesare's thoughts on taxes, see, ABC 991, 517r [April 23, 1746] and ABC 992, 92r [August 12, 1747]. On the priorities of the Consiglio of Monte Libretti, ML, Consiglio, R.6, 65v–66v [September 15, 1754], for the recognition that the poor

given their "impotence and their misery" would probably never be able to meet the tax demands of the papacy, and it was pointless, therefore, to "make them rot in the jails."

16. For two recent and exemplary examinations of the nature of the relationship between lords and vassals in Italy, see Astarita, *The Continuity of Feudal Power*, 108–157, and Forclaz, "Le relazioni complesse tra signore e vassalli," 165–201.

17. The other offices included the office of *depositario, esattore, stimatore,* and *grasciere.*

18. In Corese, Monte Libretti, and Nerola, the list of priors were good for six years, in Ponticelli for three years, and in Montorio Romano for four years. ABC 708, 16v; 19v; 22r; 69v; 7 1r; on Angeloni, ABC 997, 523v.

19. In Montorio Romano the *consiglieri* numbered 30, in Nerola, 24, and in Ponticelli, 17. These figures are from the most complete list of members I could find in the Barberini archive. They date from the 1770s. See ABC 708, 8v; 13r; 19v–20r; 79r; 11r. Among the records of Monte Libretti are a few requests by individuals who wished to be excused from service to the *comunità*, on account of age or infirmity. See ABC 999, 264r, letter to the governor in Monte Libretti, January 21, 1775. ABC 708, 8v, preamble to the list of *consiglieri* of Corese. See also Cornelia Costanza's comments on this matter in ABC 999, 145v; 167v; "would be known," ABC 999, 145v [January 15, 1774]; "we do not want," ABC 999, 167v; on property, see ABC 999, 264v; "benestante," ABCS 271, fasc. 34, on description of those most suited to be *montisti* of the *monte detto frumentario* in Nerola, 1761.

20. The request to limit the number of *consiglieri* in Monte Flavio to fify came from the "the *comunità* and the priors of Monte Flavio" who complained that because there were no limits on who could participate, the *consigli* tended to be dominated by one person who caused great confusion; fathers tended to send sons to represent the family's interests and this kept matters from being decided. A public *consiglio* in Monte Flavio had already approved the measure and allowed the priors to pick the fifty men; the *comunità* was only requesting the prince's confirmation of these "fifty good men." ABCS 291, fasc. 25. Meetings of the general *consiglio* in villages throughout Latium were becoming less common during the eighteenth century, according to Renata Ago, who interprets the local *comunità* as representing only the interests of local elites. "Braccianti, contadini e grandi proprietari," 73–74; Francesco's edict, ABCS 283, fasc. 37, Edict of November 8, 1724; on *consiglio* of thirty, ABCS 245, fasc. 28; on *consiglio* of Nerola, ABCS 271, fasc. 26.

21. The analysis of Monte Flavio also includes a list of *esattori,* or village tax collectors, because no list of priors was available. See ABC 708, 13r, 20v. On Corese, see ABC 708, 8v, 69v; on Ponticelli, see ABC 708, 11r, 71r; on Nerola, ABC 708, 16v, 79r. The two villages that seem to represent a somewhat different pattern are Monte Flavio and Monte Libretti. Monte Flavio with its much larger *consiglio* (fifty members) had as many as sixteen family names, shared by forty-one of those eligible for office. ABC 708, 13r; 20v. Unfortunately, I do not have *consiglio* lists for Monte Libretti in this period, though I do have lists of those eligible for the offices of prior, *depositario, stimatore,* and *grasciere* in December 1770. They also demonstrate the Barberini's interest in limiting participation in local government. Excluding the *spicciolati* of that year, there were fifty possible places in the various *bussoli* of the *comunità*. Only twenty-three men were listed as eligible for

these offices, which meant that most were eligible for at least two offices, a few were eligible for three offices, and two men were eligible for all four offices. While one person could not simultaneously hold all of these offices, the restriction of eligibility for office-holding is clear. Ibid., 22r.

22. Ago, *Un Feudo esemplare*, 102.

23. On the *campanile*, see ML, Consiglio, R.6, 1r–2r [April 21, 1748]; on new expenditures for the project, see 58r–59r [November 29, 1753]; on the surgeon and physician, see ibid., 9v–10r [June 19, 1749]; on the *pizzicheria*, see 80r–80v [January 11, 1756].

24. On Grifonetti, see ibid., 61v [January 20, 1754]; on paying the *depositario*, see ibid., 20r [February 24, 1751]. I cannot find any evidence in the surviving budgets that pay was offered to the *depositario*. See the eighteenth-century budgets of Monte Libretti in ABCS 245, fasc. 29 (1704) and ABCS 245, fasc. 26 (1762).

25. By the 1770s the villagers in Monte Flavio had resorted to the strategy of appointing the poorest and least qualified person to the job (perhaps even without his knowledge). Presumably, such an individual had the least to lose. See ABG, Serie II, 2528, Monte Flavio, 1704–1775 [letter of January 30, 1776]; on the case of Salvatore Barbetta, see ABC 990, 455v [January 28, 1741], 458v [February 4, 1741] , 468r [February 25, 1741]. The case of Anastasio Stefani is also interesting. He resisted becoming the collector of back taxes because he claimed to have served in that office the previous year. Mysteriously, his was the only name in the hat when it came time to draw from the *bussola* for the office. See ABC 990, 468r [February 25, 1741]; 469v–470r [March 4, 1741].

26. ABC 990, 469r [March 4, 1741]; on the governor representing the person of the prince, see ABC 992, 226r [March 2, 1748].

27. The archpriest's activities in the *consiglio* are in 67v–68v [December 29, 1754]; 72v–74r [April 6, 1755]; on the confirmation of the physician, see 74r–74v [April 27, 1755]. Pergentile as village barber is in 83r–83v [April 4, 1756]. The successful second vote for the same previously rejected physician is on 83v–86r [April 20, 1756].

28. On whom to exclude from the *consiglio*, see ABC 995, 207r [September 28, 1754]; on barring the priest in Ponticelli, see ABC 992, 288v [July 13, 1748]; 303v [August 17, 1748]; 330v [September 2, 1748]; 338v [September 28, 1748]. On foreign notaries, see ABC 994, 42r [March 4, 1752].

29. On village records, ABC 997, 511r [October 29, 1761]; removal of Barberini horses, ibid., 513v [November 7, 1761].

30. On the Camera Baronale, see ABC 997, 511r; 512r; "over the pastures," ibid., 512r; "jailed" and "prevent any violence," ibid., 512v.

31. ABCS 248, fasc. 89; elsewhere in the same edict, the stated aims of the Barberini were to "compel the disobedient vassals to remember their duty," "Everyone of the vassals," ABCS 248, fasc. 98. The language comes from edicts prohibiting inhabitants of the *stato* from extracting the sap of the flowering ash trees without a license or the payment of the proper dues to the Barberini. Reissues of the same edict in this fascicolo: 1750, 1751, 1753, 1756; "reminding everyone," ABCS 248, fasc. 107. An edict of 1752 prohibiting the priors from spending anything beyond the commune's approved expenses without the approval of the prince, mixed the language of the "public interest," with that of the "required obedience" of the vassals. See ABCS 248, fasc. 89.

32. ABC 997, 514r–514v. Giulio Cesare is apparently reasoning that if the community had to get permission to rent its communal lands, then the Barberini had rights to pasture there, a legal leap of faith that the priors probably would not make.

33. ABC 997, 519r [November 14, 1761]; "use diligence" and "describe," 519v. Lodolini, "L'Amministrazione pontificia del 'Buon Governo,'" 216.

34. ABC 997, 527r. This incident suggests that the observations of the visitors from Buon Governo about the level of record keeping in the villages may need to be reconsidered. Were certain records carted away in order to keep things from the papal visitors? "a monstrous," ibid., 527r–528r.

35. "Induce them" is a paraphrase of a statement by Giulio Cesare, ABC 997, 513r. On enforcing the nobleman's grazing laws, see ABC 991, 591v [October 22, 1746]; on the priors' response, see ABC 991, 602v [November 19, 1746]. Giulio's political "analysis" of the village is in ABC 991, 661r [December 3, 1746]. The consiglieri's refusal is in ML, Consiglio, R.6, 4r [September 1, 1748].

36. ML, Consiglio, R.6, 14r–15v [August 16, 1750].

37. Ibid.

38. Ibid.; ML, Consiglio, R.6, 24r–25r [June 24, 1751]; 25v–26v [August 1, 1751]; 26v–29r [August 22, 1751].

39. ML, Consiglio, R.6, 29r–31r [September 19, 1751].

40. Ibid., 29r–31r [September 19, 1751]; 32v–33v [October 21, 1751]. On raising the money for the surgeon, see ibid., 35v–36r [February 20, 1752]; on the physician, see 37r [March 26, 1752]. On the new Gabella, see 36r–36v [March 5, 1752].

41. On the reissue of the edict on the granturchi, see ibid., 41v–42r [June 11, 1752]. On the edict against extraordinary expenditure, see 43v–44r [August 23, 1752].

42. See ibid., 48v–49v [January 21, 1753], for the failure again to pay the physician and the necessity of paying the surgeon by household. On the lawyer's increasing need for money, see 54r–55r [April 29, 1753]; on the Barberini's silence, see 55r–55v [May 26, 1753]; on the loss in the court of the Segnatura, see 55r–56v [June 21, 1753]; on meeting the new tax demands, 58r–59r [November 29, 1753]; avoiding useless imprisonment, see 65v–66v [September 15, 1754].

43. For Grifonetti's suggestions, see ibid., 64r–64v [June 9, 1754]. On the hiring of the lawyer, see ibid., 71v–72r [March 16, 1755]. For Mattia's speech, see 75r–75v [April 23, 1755].

44. See ABG, Serie II, b. 2622, from the years 1755 and 1756 for an overview of the back and forth negotiations between the Buon Governo and the villagers. On raising more money for the lawsuit and sending villagers to talk to the lawyers, see ML, Consiglio, R.6, 77r–78r [October 19, 1755] and 78r–78v [November 16, 1755].

45. ML, Consiglio, R.6, 75v; 14r–14v.

46. ABCS 247, unnumbered fascicolo, testimony of Matteo Bassei, cavallaro for twenty years in Monte Maggiore, May 1759. On the place of oral testimony in the Middle Ages, see M. T. Clanchy, From Memory to Written Record, England 1066–1307, 35, 42.

47. On the consiglio of Monte Flavio, identified by Giulio Cesare as both too large and too ignorant to ever be sufficiently docile, see ABC 993, 158v (bis) [January 30, 1751]; on similar ignorance in Montorio Romano, ibid., 177r [September 26, 1750]; on

the tumultuous and excessively *animoso* meeting in Nerola, ibid., 129r (bis) [December 26, 1750], 134v (bis) [January 2, 1751]. The vice-governor of each village was supposed to be in attendance at every *consiglio* meeting, although the general governor of the entire *stato* was only obliged to attend when a serious matter was to be discussed. See ABC 992, 246v–247r [April 13, 1748], 341r [September 28, 1748], 564v [November 20, 1748]. For how Giulio Cesare attempted to guide his edicts to acceptance in the *stato*, see his letters to his governor in Nerola, ABC 993, 110r–110v [June 13, 1750]; 114v [June 27, 1750].

48. ABC 997, 509v [October 24, 1761]; 513r [November 7, 1761]. The official to whom Giulio Cesare addressed the advice in this case was the superintendent, the overseer of the Barberini income in the village.

49. ABC, 990, 442v [January 7, 1741]. I am grateful to John Martin and Antonio Calabria for their suggestions about translating this term.

50. E. P. Thompson, *Customs in Common.*, 23, 48, 67, 17.

51. Here I am referring of course to Marcel Mauss, *The Gift*, discussed in chapter 1.

CHAPTER 6

1. For Monsignor Dentice's observations, see ABCS 291, fasc. 29. Copies of the 1704 visit are in ABCS 291, fasc. 27 and ABCS 245, fasc. 30. Giulio Cesare's remarks are in ABC 993, 177r; 169r; 158v (bis).

2. The seventeenth-century description of Monte Flavio is in ABCS 243, fasc. 14, pp. 45–46.

3. Clanchy, *From Memory to Written Record*. Clanchy asserts that "lay literacy grew out of bureaucracy, rather than from any abstract desire for education or literature" (19). "By 1300 even serfs, the more prosperous ones at least, were familiar with documents. . . . Clerks did the writing throughout the Middle Ages; most of the reading was done by them, as the custom was to read out loud. By these means laymen of all classes, who remained technically illiterate, could participate in the use of documents and were encouraged to do business with charters" (53). See also his conclusion, "Practical Literacy," 328–334.

4. Walter Ong, *Orality and Literacy: The Technologizing of the Word*, 79. Steven Justice, *Writing and Rebellion: England in 1381*, uses the terms "insurgent literacy," or "assertive literacy," to describe the skills that made rural militancy possible. He summarizes rural literacy as "the ability to sound out, and therefore recognize, one's name and to know the equivalents of perhaps ten or twenty Latin words . . . and recognize references to their lands in court rolls or extents or to be aware of and articulate about the contents of charters they might hold. And I would suggest that this, not fluency or practice in reading books or writing letters, is the literacy that mattered to the rural communities that rebelled in 1381, the literacy that gave them their sense of familiarity with documentary culture and their determination to make it theirs" (34–35). Among some rebels these skills extended further, to writing abilities, crucial, if not common achievements that I will also argue here take the eighteenth-century villagers beyond the realm of "practical literacy." I rely here on the theorizing of Justice about the political implications of medieval literacy because early modern literary studies are more focused on ordinary people's reading of literary and religious texts. The intersection of literacy

and politics, for instance, receives little treatment in R. A. Houston's recent survey of early modern literacy, *Literacy in Early Modern Europe*, 106–112; 218–225. Writing and rebellion are woven together by the incomparable Peter Blickle, who examines the villagers' resort to scripture during the Reformation in *Communal Reformation*, especially, 45, 86, 188.

5. ABC 993, 72r [April 18, 1750]; see especially 127v (bis) [December 26, 1750].

6. James Scott makes brilliant use of Thompson and other historians of Europe and America, demonstrating the transnational quality of resistance among people suffering political and economic subjugation under a variety of regimes. See especially, "Arts of Political Disguise" and "Infrapolitics of Subordinate Groups" in his *Domination and the Arts of Resistance*. In Thompson, *Whigs and Hunters*, see pp. 200, 245–247. On the importance of the political space of the law court to the development of the state in early modern Italy in particular, see Edward Muir, "The Sources of Civil Society in Italy," 379–406.

7. On the appeal of the villagers to the Congregation of the Buon Governo, see ABG, Serie II, b. 2528, Monte Flavio, 1704–1775, letter of Alessandro Salendi, July 23, 1746 (on the labors of the community); on the Borghese as ally (or instigator) of the legal suit, see ibid., copy of the *consiglio* record, August 10, 1746. Giulio Cesare's letter reminding them to pay up is in ABC 991, 495r [March 14, 1746].

8. On the taxes of the eighteenth century, see Lodolini, *L'Archivio della S. Congregazione del Buon Governo (1592–1847)*, lxvi–lxxiv. Expenses related to war totaled 4,900,000 scudi, 3 million of which was spent in the war of Austrian succession alone. See the Barberini letter that discusses the need for more food, carriages, animals, and latrines while the soldiers passed through the *stato*. ABC 991, 352r [June 5, 1745].

9. In 1745 the village surgeon complained to the Barberini prince that the communal government, which had hired him to work in the village, failed to pay him. See ABC 991, 379r [August 14, 1745]. The protest of the priests over the appointment of a priest to the post of tax collector is mentioned in a Barberini letter to the governor of the *stato*, ABC 991, 610v [December 3, 1746]. The list of debtors and Sciarra's testimony on his own behalf are in ABG, Serie II, 2528, Monte Flavio, 1704–1775, "Nota di debitori residuali da Pagarsi"; critical letters from the governors of the *stato* are in ibid., letter of P. Alari [December 7, 1746]. Alari mentions the Barberini edict prohibiting clerics to serve in the commune and dates the edict September 28, 1698. See a more positive assessment of Sciarra in the letter of Michel'Ang.o Troessi [July 16, 1748]. On the troubles of Sciarra's predecessor, see the letters of the noble family, ABC 991, 303r–304r [March 6, 1745]; 324v–325v [April 10, 1745]. The letter criticizing the villagers' choice of the incapable to serve as tax collector is from some village priests, in an undated letter, corroborated by a letter of January 30, 1776 from the governor, who added "shepherds" to the list of the clearly unqualified.

10. The text of the *statuto* reads, "Tutti li Bestiami, che veramente faranno delli Abbitatori possono stare nel detto Territorio senza pagare Erbatici. E per ricognizione di essi Bestiami siano obligati pagare all'Illustrissimi Signori chi averà il numero di trenta Pecore, un Castrato a Pasqua di Resurrezione, e per altre sorte de Bestiame a Natale un Presciuttto, & una Gallina, a Santa Maria di Agosto un paro di Pollastri a

fuoco l'anno." ABCS 290, Signatura Justitiae, Pro Communitate . . . Summarium [1750], numero 1. On the vineyards, the text reads: "Quando essi Lavoratori cesseranno il Paese per far Vigne, e per seminare," ibid. The expression "per ricognizione di essi Bestiami," seems to suggest that only villagers who owned animals would owe the noble family the *minuti*; see ibid., numero 2, "spesse volte li detti Abitatori non averanno Bestiame a sufficienza per il Pascolo del detto Territorio." The payment of what was called in Germany the "bond-chicken" or symbol of servile status was unique to Monte Flavio. Most of the other villages had had such payments converted to percentages of the harvest paid in cash as recognition of Barberini lordship. See Blickle, *The Revolution of 1525*, 69–70.

On the indebtedness of the communes, see the remarks of the Barberini prince on how to handle the debtors (he thought they should all be given seven years to pay off what was owed). ABC 991, 581r [September 24, 1746]. Records collected on behalf of the Barberini for their legal suit with the villagers show the *minuti* were paid in cash in the eighteenth century. ABCS 290, Signatura Justitiae . . . Pro [Barberini]: Summarium, 1751, numero 3 [Receputa minutorum].

11. ABC 991, 298r [February 27, 1745]; 300r [February 27, 1745]; 355r [June 11, 1745]; 570r [September 3, 1746].

12. ABC 991, 433r [November 13, 1745]; ABC 992, 105r [September 2, 1747]; ibid., 503v [July 26, 1747]. The petition is mentioned in ABC 991, 451r [December 11, 1745]. On the *statuto*, see ABC 991, 491r [February 19, 1746]. Scott, *Domination and the Arts of Resistance*, 63.

13. The citations started around the time of her father's death. See ABC 991, 571r [September 6, 1746]; 596r [October 29, 1746]; ABC 992, 32r [March 18, 1747]; 35r [March 21, 1747]; 36r [March 25, 1747].

14. ABC 992, 96r [August 19, 1747]; 250v [April 20, 1748]; 197r [January 4, 1748], on her hesitancy to renounce; 270r [June 8, 1748]; 65v–66r [June 3, 1747]; 72r [July 1, 1747]; ABC 993, 69r–69v [April 18, 1750].

15. ABC 992, 106r [September 9, 1747]; 32r [March 18, 1747]; ABG, Serie II, b, 2528, letter of Governor Alari [December 7, 1746]; Sciarra's letter is in ibid, letter attached to the "Nota di debitori risduali da Pagarsi, anno 1746"; ABC 992, 321r [September 7, 1748].

16. Clearly, Antonio was mistakenly identified as an enemy of the *minuti* in the Barberini letter, or he had a change of heart facilitated by the income potential of the dues, or there were two Antonio Petriccas in the village, a possible scenario. If he was indeed part of the group agitating against the *minuti* in the 1740s, and then became the renter of those dues, this fact might explain some of the personal hostility of the villagers toward him. ABC 992, 398v [December ?14, 1748] and 352r (bis) [December 14, 1748]; 476r [June 28, 1749]; 476r [June 28, 1749]; 488v [July 12, 1749]; 497r [July 29, 1749]; 536v [August 23, 1749]; 600r [November 15, 1749].

17. ABC 992, 519r [August 16, 1749]; on the accusation of Petricca, 524r [August 16, 1749].

18. Mancini's death is mentioned in ABC 992, 536v [August ?28, 1749]; 566v [September 25, 1749]; 568r [September 25, 1749]; 610v [November 29, 1749]; ABC 993, 27v–28r [February 28, 1750].

19. ABCS 290, Signatura Justitiae, Pro Communitate ... Summarium [1750], numero 9 and numero 10.

20. Ibid., numero 15.

21. See ABC 708, a collection of petitions discussed in "Tending to Words and Other Weapons in the Countryside: A Noblewoman's View of Justice in the Late Eighteenth Century," Caroline Castiglione, unpublished paper; ABC 993, 172r bis [February 20, 1751]; Signatura Justitiae, Pro Communitate ... Summarium [1750], numero 16.

22. ABC 993, 200v–201r bis [September 14, 1750].

23. ABCS 290, Signatura Justitiae, Pro Communitate ... Summarium [1750], numero 25, Benedetto Picchioni publico balio, September 18, 1750; ibid., numero 38, Andrea Petrucci and Filippo Gasparri, December 8, 1750; ibid., numero 39, Excarceratio demandata, December 9, 1750.

24. Giulio Cesare's letter is in ABC 992, 65v–66r [June 3, 1747]; on Giulio Cesare's construction of the witnesses' testimony, see ABC 992, 65v–66r [June 3, 1747]; 72r [July 1, 1747]; 79r [July 22, 1747]; 35r [July 29, 1747]; 536v [August 23, 1747]; ABC 993, 60r–60v [April 4, 1750]; 99v [April 23, 1750].

25. ABCS 247, fasc. 43, letter of 25 March 1741. On the place of oral testimony in the Middle Ages, see Clanchy, *From Memory to Written Record*, 35, 42.

26. Testimony of the priests is in ABCS 290, Signatura Justitiae, pro Communitate ... Montis Flavii, Summarium, num. 4 [1751].

27. ABCS 290, Signatura Justitiae, Pro Communitate ... Summarium [1751], numero 9, Fides Popularis, December 27, 1750; ibid., numero 16 A, "Giovanni Jazzone, Biagio Pettinella, Francesco Stozzi ... ," December 21, 1750. The testimony of the six men is in ABCS 290, Signatura Justitiae, Pro Communitate ... Summarium [1750], numero 43, September 23, 1750, "Marco Antonio Corrieri (70); Giovanni Iezzone (59); Carlo Petrucci (86); Domenico Renzi; Pier Angelo Gasbarri (70)." The protest against its payment suggests that Petricca's predecessor might have looked the other way and not collected the sixth on hemp production, or that in the general upheaval after the pig confiscation, broader resistance to a variety of payments emerged in the village.

28. This particular testimony was signed (with a signature or cross) by twenty-three villagers, two of whom qualified it by adding "asserisco non aver pagato mai *minuti*," as a way (I think) of refraining from comment on what their ancestors did or did not do. ABCS 290, Signatura Justitiae, Pro Communitate ... Summarium [1751], numero 9, December 27, 1751.

29. ABCS 290, Signatura Justitiae ... Pro Barberinis. Summarium [1751]: numero 13: Nicola Ranieri and Antonio Petrucci, March 9, 1751. It is also worth noting that the Barberini relied on a notary from the nearby abbey of Farfa to make the copies of the documents that they needed for the lawsuit. Apparently no notary was trustworthy enough in Monte Flavio for the Barberini, once the controversy of the *minuti* began.

30. Ibid., numero 9: Belardino Paleotti, February 20, 1751.

31. Ibid., numero 10: Giovanni di Merchionne Rosati, February 20, 1751. The testimony of the two villagers who qualified there statement is in ABCS 290, Signatura Justitiae, Pro Communitate, Summarium [1751], numero 9: Fides Popularis, December 27, 1750.

32. Root, *Peasants and King in Burgundy*, 191–204.

33. ABCS 291, fasc. 31. The document refers to the Orsini family, the owners of the territory who sold it to the Barberini in 1644.

34. Ong, *Orality and Literacy*, 78, 106. Walter Benjamin noted that stay-at-home peasants were also great storytellers. The villagers of Monte Flavio (more than the residents of neighboring villagers) seemed to combine the creative potential of wandering and rooted-ness, essential to storytelling. "The Storyteller," chapter in *Illuminations*, 84–85.

35. ABCS 993, 206r [November 21, 1750]; 121v bis [December 26, 1750]; 127v bis [December 26, 1750].

36. E. J. Hobsbawm and Joan Wallach Scott, "Political Shoemakers," 86–114; Liisa Malkki, *Purity and Exile: Violence, Memory, and National Cosmology among Hutu Refugees in Tanzania*, on mythico-history, 52–104, "a deeply moral," p. 56.

37. Walter Ong discusses the role of how *"loci communes . . .* could be worked into one's own speech-making or writing," *Orality and Literacy*, 111.

38. Blickle, *Communal Reformation*, 45, 86, 188. ABCS 248, fasc. 98 (issued 1750, 1751, 1753, 1754, and 1756); ibid., fasc. 107 (issued, 1751, 1761). I have found useful in understanding the "social disciplining" thesis and its qualifications the books and articles listed in note 50 of chapter 1.

39. Penny Lernoux, *Cry of the People*, 41; Ong notes the importance of paradoxes and oral culture (*Orality and Literacy*, 130).

40. Gross, *Rome in the Age of Enlightenment*, 200, 202, 207, 209. Maura Piccialuti's assessment of the centrality of charity to governing in Rome bears out the villagers' calculation of its importance to elites. See her *La Carità Come Metodo di Governo: Istituzioni caritative a Roma dal pontificato di Innocenzo XII a quell di Benedetto XIV.*

41. Scott draws the most attention to this process in the chapter, "False Consciousness or Laying It on Thick?" in *Domination and the Arts of Resistance*, reaching some important conclusions about the extent to which those individuals who develop the greatest allegiance to the ideology of a political or economic regime can easily become its biggest troublemakers. See especially p. 107: "The anger born of a sense of betrayal implies an earlier faith," and the connections he makes to the civil rights movement in the United States. This needs further emphasis in early modern and eighteenth-century Europe, especially given the explosive encounter between the political culture of the villagers and the expanding legal system.

42. ABCS 290, Signatura Justitiae, Pro Communitate . . . Summarium [1751], numero 17: Patrizio Rosati and Andrea Petrucci, February 23, 1751, and numero 17: Boni regiminis, November 28, 1750. The decisions of the Rota are collected in ABCS 294, fasc. 11.

43. ABCS 290, Signatura Justitiae . . . Pro Barberinis. Summarium [1751], numero 7, C: Antonio Petrucci, March 6, 1751 and numero 7: Antonio Petrucci, Nicola Ranieri, and Angelico Caldari, March 1, 1751; ABG, Serie II, 2528, Nota di debitori residuali da Pagarsi, 1746.

44. For the earlier testimony and the decisions of the Rota, see ABCS 294, fasc. 11.

45. ABCS 290, Signatura Justitiae, Pro Communitate . . . Summarium [1751], numero 21: Affictuarii; ABCS 290, fasc. 11, on the Rota decisions, ABCS 294, fasc. 11.

46. ABG, Serie II, 2528, Nota di debitori residuali da Pagarsi, 1746.

47. Once it became clear, however, that the villagers would never be able to convince the magistrates to read the *statuto* in a broader, more creative, and ultimately more just manner, the villagers tried to appeal the case on the grounds that the constitution consulted during the trials was not the original, and that there was an older copy of the *statuto* in the village of Scandriglia. Although the Barberini opposed the consultation of that older constitution, it was eventually secured for review by the magistrates, but it contained the same information about the *minuti* as the later versions existing in Monte Flavio.

48. ABCS 294, fasc. 12, "Istromento di concordia . . . copia della risoluzione consiliare" (1761). The villagers returned to their "adversaries," the Barberini, to request that they "use their paternal clemency" in order to lower the payments of the *minuti*. From the lofty language of social justice just a decade before the villagers returned in the summer of 1761 to the language of deference required of vassals approaching their lord for a favor. But the terms of the settlement offered by the Barberini implies that in fact, the villagers had still yet to pay the *minuti* in 1761, so there was clearly interest in negotiating something acceptable to both sides.

The Barberini offer was discussed in the *consiglio* of May 26, 1761. A copy of that *consiglio* was preserved in the Barberini archive, and it gives us a chance to see what the villagers considered most in need of change in the *minuti* payments. First, the Barberini offered a reduction of the back payments on the *minuti* from 1749 to 1761. They calculated the amount owed was 517 scudi, but they would settle for 365 scudi (a "special grace" granted this one time to the villagers). The commune would still have to pay the 155 scudi the Barberini spent in legal fees, and they would have to renounce forever bringing the matter before papal law courts. The Barberini would allow the villagers to pay off the debt to the noble family in installments of 100 scudi per year. Most importantly for the villagers, the Barberini renegotiated what the villagers would owe the new renter (and all the renters thereafter). Those without animals only owed two chickens per year. Any household with between one and three animals owed the two chickens, and the hen, per year. Any household with more than three animals (but fewer than thirty) owed the two chickens, the hen, and the ham, per year. Those with more than thirty animals owed all of these yearly payments, and one lamb per year.

The objections raised in May 1761 were very detailed and were offered by Giovanni Carlo Rosati, who suggested that the villagers present themselves as the "most obedient sons" of the noble family, but sons with some specific directions. He believed that villagers with only one animal should have only to pay the two chickens, unless the animal was worth more than 35 baoicchi. Rosati's adjustment would differentiate more sharply villagers with only one animal (like a pig) from villagers with two or more. Rosati thought the villagers should approach the noble family "with warmest tears in their eyes," to have the new renter accept these terms. He also suggested that they get a further reduction of the 517 scudi, noting that the new renter only rented the *minuti* for 35 scudi per year. In sum, Rosati counseled a teary-eyed intercession to the noble family to lower the penalty and provide some additional financial relief for the small-time animal owners in the village. (The copy of the *consiglio* of May 26, 1761, is at the very end of the fasc. 12. The *consiglio* that accepted the Barberini offer is dated July 19, 1761.)

Rosati's suggestion won the vote, 95 to 1, although it did not get the Barberini to reconsider. The *consiglio* discussed the merit of an offer from the noble family in July 1761 that was substantially the same as what the noble family had offered in May. This time the *consiglio* accepted the noble family's offer and Giulio Cesare and Cornelia Costanza signed the *concordia* in August 1761, closing the controversy, at least for a few years. Another lawsuit was pursued in 1768 by the clerics of Monte Flavio, who sued over whether the payment of the *minuti* applied to them. See ABCS 294, fasc. 13 and 14.

CONCLUSION

1. ABCS 248, fasc. 7, edicts issued by the *General'Auditore*, Alessandro Gavello, probably in the 1620s, Edicts 95; 90; 91. For the eighteenth-century edicts, see ABCS 248. The example here is fasc. 98 (issued 1750, 1751, 1753, 1754, and 1756). The village assembly led astray in this case was that of the village Monte Libretti, during a conflict with the Barberini over grazing in the village lands. See ABC 991, 611r [December 3, 1746].

2. *Whigs and Hunters*. See also his essay, "The Patricians and the Plebs," in *Customs in Common*. I agree with Wayne Te Brake's definition of politics as a bargaining process. See *Shaping History: Ordinary People in European Politics, 1500–1700*, 6; "their rights" is from Scott, *Domination and the Arts of Resistance*, 190. On the centrality of the state to the development of civil society, see McNeely, *The Emancipation of Writing*. On the state as a broker or mediator between social groups, see especially Marino, *Pastoral Economics in the Kingdom of Naples*.

3. Houston, *Literacy in Early Modern Europe*.

4. ABC 995, 196v [September 14, 1754]; ABC 997, 69v [May 12, 1759]; the letter to the shoemaker's brother is in ABC 994, 61v [March 25, 1752]; "purge the souls," ABC 994, 52r [March 11, 1752].

5. Michael Ignatieff, *The Russian Album*, 16.

6. See ABCS 294, fasc. 11, for a summary of the decisions of the papal magistrates. On the inaccurate assessment of Italian villagers as lacking "any political right," see J. C. L. Simonde de Sismondi's assessment of the peasants of Lombardy in his *History of the Italian Republics: Being a View of the Origin, Progress, and Fall of Italian Freedom* (Gloucester, Mass., 1970; orig. pub. 1832), 257, cited in Grew, "Finding Social Capital," 429. Grew notes that the Revolutionary regimes alienated peasants "through conscription and attacks on religion." They failed to build effectively on the communal legacies of rural Italy, it should also be added. For the parallel process of "juridification" of peasant conflict in the Holy Roman Empire during the early modern period, see Winfried Schulze, "Peasant Resistance in Sixteenth- and Seventeenth-Century Germany in a European Context," 82–85.

SELECTED BIBLIOGRAPHY

MANUSCRIPT PRIMARY SOURCES
AND THEIR ABBREVIATIONS

Archivio Barberini [AB], Vatican Library, Vatican City, divided into Indici I–IV [Ind.] and folios [f]

Archivio Barberini Colonna di Sciarra [ABCS], Vatican Library, Vatican City, divided into tomi and fascicoli [fasc.]

Archivio Barberini Computisteria [ABC], Vatican Library, Vatican City

Archivio del Buon Governo [ABG], Archivio di Stato di Roma, divided into Serie and buste [b.]

Archivio del Comune di Monte Libretti [ML], Monte Libretti, Italy, divided into registri [R.]

Archivio Storico del Comune di Nerola, Nerola, Italy

Barberini Collection [BC], Historical Collections, Baker Library, Harvard Business School, Boston, Massachusetts

Orsini Family Archive [OFA], Special Collections Department, Collection Number 902, University Research Library, University of California at Los Angeles, divided into numbered boxes

PRINTED PRIMARY SOURCES

Adami, Antonio. *Il Novitiato del maestro di casa.* Rome, 1636.

Amayden, Teodor. *A New Relation of Rome as to the Government of the City; the Noble Families Thereof . . . Taken out of one of the Choicest Cabinets of Rome; and English'd by Gio. Torriano, an Italian, and Professor of the Italian Tongue.* London, 1664.

————. *La Storia delle famiglie romane.* Ed. C. A. Bertini. 2 vols. Rome, 1910, 1914. Rome, 1979.

Bartoli, Daniello. *La Povertà Contenta.* Venice, 1658.

De Bonstetten, Charles Victor. *Voyage sur la scène des derniers livres de l'Enéide suivi de quelques observations sur le Latium moderne.* Geneva, 1805.

De Luca, Giovanni Battista. *Il Dottor volgare, ovvero il Compendio di tutta la legge civile, canonica, feudale, e municipale, nelle cose più ricevuted in pratica.* Venice, 1740.

Doria, Luigi. *Elementi della Coltivazione de' Grani.* Rome, 1777.

Frigerio, Bartolomeo. *L'Economo Prudente.* Rome, 1629.

Liberati, Francesco. *Il Perfetto Maestro di Casa.* Rome, 1665.

Montaigne, Michel de. *The Diary of Montaigne's Journey to Italy in 1580 and 1581.* Translated and edited by E. J. Trechmann. London, 1929.

Nicolaj, Nicola Maria. *Memorie, leggi ed osservazioni sulle campagne e sull'annona di Roma.* 3 vols. Rome, 1803.

Regesti di bandi, editti, notificazioni e provvedimenti diversi relativi alla città di Roma ed allo Stato Pontificio. Rome, 1920–1934.

Sperandio, Francesco. *Sabina Sagra e Profana antica e moderna ossia raccolta di notizie del paese Sabino divisa in dieci capitoli con carte corgrafiche.* Rome, 1790.

SECONDARY SOURCES

Ackerman, James S. *The Villa: Form and Ideology of Country Houses.* Princeton, 1990.

Ademollo, Alessandro. *I Teatri di Roma nel secolo decimosettimo.* Rome, 1880; reprint, Bologna, 1969.

Ago, Renata. "Braccianti, contadini e grandi proprietari in un villaggio laziale nel primo Settecento." *Quaderni storici* 46 (1981): 60–91.

————. "Burocrazia, 'nazioni' e parentele nella Roma del Settecento." *Quaderni storici* 67 (1988): 73–98.

————. *Carriere e clientele nella Roma barocca.* Rome, 1990.

————. "Conflitti e politica nel feudo: le campagne romane del Settecento." *Quaderni storici* 63 (1986): 847–874.

————. "Ecclesiastical Careers and the Destiny of Cadets." *Continuity and Change* 7 (1992): 271–282.

————. "Enforcing Agreements: Notaries and Courts in Early Modern Rome." *Continuity and Change* 14 (1999): 191–206.

————. "Farsi uomini: Giovani nobili nella Roma barocca." *Memoria: Rivista di storia delle donne* 27 (1989): 7–21.

————. "Gerarchia delle merci e meccanismi dello scambio a Roma nel primo Seicento." *Quaderni storici* 96 (1997): 663–684.

————. "Gli Storici italiani e le fortune dell'antropologia: Il dibattito sulla storia sociale in Italia." In *Orientamenti Marxisti e studi antropologici,* Renata Ago et al., 223–229. Milan, 1980.

————. *La Feudalità nell'età moderna.* Bari, 1994.

————. "Maria Spada Veralli, la Buona Moglie." In *Barocco al Femminile,* ed. Giulia Calvi, 51–70. Bari, 1992.

———. "Popolo e papi: La crisi del sistema annonario." In *Annali della Fondazione L. e L. Basso*, vol. 7. Milan, 1985.

———. "Ruoli familiari e statuto giuridico." *Quaderni storici* 88 (1995): 111–134.

———. "Un Esempio di Mobilità nell'Ancien Régime': La Diocesi di Sutri nel XVII Secolo." *Mélanges de l'École française de Rome-Moyen Âge, Temps Modernes*, 1974, 345–378.

———. *Un Feudo esemplare: Immobilismo padronale e astuzia contadina nel Lazio del '700.* Fasano, 1988.

Alessandrini, Angelo. *Roma ed il Lazio.* Rome, 1881.

Almagià, Roberto. *Documenti Cartografici dello Stato Pontificio.* Vatican City, 1960.

———. *Lazio.* Le Regioni D'Italia, ed. Elio Migliorini, vol. 11. Turin, 1976.

Andretta, S. "Francesco Colonna." In *Dizionario degli Italiani* 6: 303–304. Rome, 1964.

Andrieux, Maurice. *Daily Life in Papal Rome in the Eighteenth Century.* London, 1968.

Ardant, Gabriele. *Papi e contadini.* Translated from French by Luigi Masson. Siena, S. Bernardino publisher, 1895.

Armando, David and Adriano Ruggeri, "La Geografia feudale del Lazio alla fine del Settecento." In *La Nobiltà romana in età moderna: Profili istituzionali e pratiche sociali*, ed. Maria Antonietta Visceglia, 401–455. Rome, 2001.

Astarita, Tommaso. "The Caracciolo di Brienza in Spanish Naples: A Case-Study in the Continuity of Feudal Power, 1550–1720." Ph.D. diss., Johns Hopkins University, 1988.

———. *The Continuity of Feudal Power.* Cambridge, 1992.

———. *Village Justice: Community, Family, and Popular Culture in Early Modern Italy.* Baltimore, 1999.

Aymard, M. "La transizione dal feudalesimo al capitalismo." In *Annali della Storia d'Italia*, vol. 1. Turin, 1978.

Barbagli, Marzio. *Sotto lo Stesso Tetto.* Bologna, 1984.

———, and David Kertzer. *Storia della famiglia italiana, 1750–1850.* Bologna, 1992.

Barberi, Angela, and Maria Teresa De Nigris, *Comune di Monte Flavio: Inventario dell'Archivio Storico Comunale.* Rome, 1990.

Barberini, Francesca. "La famiglia Barberini ed i suoi rapporti con la città di Palestrina in più di tre secoli di storia." In *I Barberini a Palestrina*, ed. Peppino Tomassi, 5–36. Palestrina, 1992.

Barker, G., and A. Grant. "Ancient and Modern Pastoralism in Central Italy: An Interdisciplinary Study in the Circolano Mountains." *Papers of the British School at Rome* 59 (1991): 15–88.

Bastiaanse, A. *Teodoro Ameyden (1586–1656): Un Neerlandese alla Corte di Roma.* Staatsdrukkerij-'S-Gravenhage, 1967.

Beik, William. *Absolutism and Society in Seventeenth-Century France: State Power and Provincial Aristocracy in Languedoc.* Cambridge, 1985.

Benadusi, Giovanna. *A Provincial Elite in Early Modern Tuscany: Family and Power in the Creation of the State.* Baltimore, 1996.

Beneš, Mirka. "Landowning and the Villa in the Social Geography of the Roman Territory." In *Form, Modernism and History*, ed. Alexander von Hoffman, 187–209. Cambridge, Mass., 1996.

————. *The Papal Villa of Innocent X Pamphilj in Baroque Rome (1644–70): Rus in Urbe and the Roman Contribution to the European Garden and Park.* Cambridge, forthcoming.

————. "Pastoralism in the Roman Baroque Villa and in Claude Lorrain: Myths and Realities of the Roman Campagna." In *Villas and Gardens in Early Modern Italy and France*, ed. Mirka Beneš and Dianne Harris. Cambridge, 2001.

————. "Recent Developments and Perspectives in the Historiography of Italian Gardens." In *Perspectives on Garden Histories*, ed. Michel Conan. Washington, D.C., 1999.

————. "Villa Pamphilj (1630–1670): Family, Gardens and Land in Papal Rome." Ph.D. diss., Yale University, 1989.

Benjamin, Walter. "The Storyteller." In *Illuminations*, 83–110. New York, 1968.

Bercé, Yves-Marie. *Revolt and Revolution in Early Modern Europe: An Essay on the History of Political Violence.* Translated by Joseph Bergin. New York, 1987.

Blickle, Peter. *Communal Reformation: The Quest for Salvation in Sixteenth-Century Germany.* Translated by Thomas Dunlap. Atlantic Highlands, N.J., and London, 1992.

————. *Obedient Germans? A Rebuttal: A New View of German History.* Translated by Thomas A. Brady. Charlottesville, 1997.

————. *The Revolution of 1525: The German Peasants' War from a New Perspective.* Translated by Thomas A. Brady, Jr., and H. C. Erik Midelfort. Baltimore and London, 1981.

————, Hans-Christoph Rublack, and Winfried Schulze. *Religion, Politics and Social Protest: Three Studies on Early Modern Germany*, edited by Kaspar von Greyerz. London, 1984.

Boiteux, Martine. "Carnival Annexé: essai de lecture d'une fête romaine." *Annales: Economies, Sociétés, Civilisations* 32 (1977): 356–380.

Boland, Eavan. *Object Lessons: The Life of the Woman and the Poet in Our Time.* New York, 1995.

Bossy, John. *Christianity in the West.* New York, 1985.

Brake, Wayne Te. *Shaping History: Ordinary People in European Politics, 1500–1700.* Berkeley, 1998.

Braudel, Fernand. *The Mediterranean and Mediterranean World in the Age of Philip II.* Translated by Siân Reynolds. 2 vols. New York, 1972.

————. *The Structures of Everyday Life.* Vol. 1, *Civilization and Capitalism: 15th–18th Century.* Translated. Siân Reynolds. New York, 1981.

Brezzi, P. "Il sistema agrario nel territorio romano alla fine del Medio Evo." *Studi romani* 25 (1977): 153–168.

Brigante Colonna, Gustavo. *Gli Orsini.* Milan, 1955.

Briganti, G., L. Trezzani, and L. Laureati. *The Bamboccianti: The Painters of Everyday Life in Seventeenth-Century Rome.* Rome, 1983.

Brucker, Gene. "Civic Traditions in Premodern Italy." *Journal of Interdisciplinary History* 29 (1999): 357–378.

Bullard, Melissa Meriam. "Grain Supply and Urban Unrest in Renaissance Rome: The Crisis of 1533–34." In *Rome in the Renaissance: The City and the Myth*, ed. P. A. Ramsey, 279–292. Binghamton, N.Y., 1982.

Burke, Peter. *The Historical Anthropology of Early Modern Italy: Essays on Perception and Communication.* Cambridge, 1987.

————. *Popular Culture in Early Modern Europe.* New York, 1978.

Caffiero, Marina. *L'erba dei poveri: Comunità rurale e soppressione degli usi collettivi nel Lazio (secoli XVIII–XIX).* Rome, 1982.

————. "Tradizione o innovazione? Ideologie e comportamenti della nobiltà Romana in tempo di crisi." In *Signori, patrizi, caralieri in Italia centro-meridionale nell'Età moderna,* ed. Maria Antonietta Visceglia, 369–389. Bari, 1992.

Calabria, Antonio, and John A Marino, eds. *Good Government in Spanish Naples.* New York, 1990.

Calindri, Gabriele. *Saggio statistico Storico del Pontificio Stato.* Perugia, 1829.

Canaletti Guadenti, Alberto. *La Politica agraria ed annonaria dello Stato Pontificio da Benedetto XIV a Pio VII.* Rome, 1947.

Caraffa, Filippo. "Vallepietra secondo lo Statuto del 1726." In *Seicento e Settecento nel Lazio,* ed. Renato Lefevre, 345–360. Rome, 1980.

Caravale, Mario, and Alberto Caracciolo, *Lo Stato Pontificio da Martino V a Pio IX.* Turin, 1978.

Carocci, G. *Lo Stato della Chiesa nella seconda metà del secolo XVI.* Milan, 1961.

————. "Problemi agrari del Lazio nel 1500." *Studi storici* 1 (1959–1960): 3–23.

Caroselli, M. R. "Aspects of the Economic History of the Roman Campagna in the Modern and Contemporary World." *Journal of European Economic History* 13 (1984): 591–598.

Carpanetto, Dino, and Giuseppe Ricuperati. *Italy in the Age of Reason 1685–1789.* New York, 1987.

Casagrandi, Oddo. *La popolazione, le nascite, le morti negli ultimi due secoli a Roma: Studio demografico-statistico.* Rome, 1903.

Castiglione, Caroline. "Accounting for Affection: Battles between Aristocratic Mothers and Sons in Early Modern Rome." *Journal of Family History* 25 (2000): 405–431.

————. "Adversarial Literacy: How Peasant Politics Influenced Noble Governing of the Roman Countryside during the Early Modern Period." *American Historical Review* 109 (2004): 783–804.

————. "Extravagant Pretensions: Aristocratic Family Conflicts, Emotion, and the 'Public Sphere' in Early Eighteenth-Century Rome." *Journal of Social History* (forthcoming 2005).

————. "Honor and the Female Self: Olimpia Giustiniani Barberini (1641–1729)." Unpublished paper.

————. "Political Culture in Italian Villages." *Journal of Interdisciplinary History* 31 (2001): 523–552.

————. "Roman Nobles and Rural Communities: The Barberini Family and the Stato of Monte Libretti in Latium." Ph.D. diss., Harvard University, 1995.

————. "Tending to Words and Other Weapons in the Countryside: A Noblewoman's View of Justice in the Late Eighteenth Century." Unpublished paper.

Cedrone, Alberto. "Note sulla Finanza Locale in Regime di 'Buon Governo.'" In *Seicento e Settecento nel Lazio,* ed. Renato Lefevre, 547–564. Rome, 1980.

Celani, E. "Lo Statuto del Comune di Montelibretti." *Studi e documenti di storia e diritto* 13 (1892): 401–417.

Celletti, Vincenzo. *Gli Orsini di Bracciano*. Rome, 1963.

Ceroni, G. *Castelli umbro-sabini*. Rome, 1930.

Chartier, Roger. *On the Edge of the Cliff: History, Language and Practices*. Baltimore, 1997.

Chatelier, Louis. *The Europe of the Devout: The Catholic Reformation and the Formation of a New Society*. Translated by Jean Birrell. Cambridge, 1989.

Chittolini, Giorgio. "The 'Private,' the 'Pubic,' the State." In *Origins of the State in Italy, 1300–1600*, ed. Julius Kirshner, 34–61. Chicago, 1995.

Christian, William. *Local Religion in Sixteenth-Century Spain*. Princeton, 1981.

Cipolla, Carlo. *Before the Industrial Revolution: European Economy and Society 1000–1700*. London, 1976.

Clanchy, M. T. *From Memory to Written Record, England 1066–1307*. 2d ed. New York, 1993.

Clifford, James, and George E. Marcus, eds. *Writing Culture*. Berkeley, 1986.

Coffin, David R. *The Villa in the Life of Renaissance Rome*. Princeton, 1979.

Cohen, Thomas. "A Long Day in Monte Rotondo: The Politics of Jeopardy in a Village Uprising (1558)." *Comparative Studies in Society and History* 33 (October 1991): 639–686.

———, and Elizabeth S. Cohen. *Words and Deeds in Renaissance Rome: Trials before the Papal Magistrates*. Toronto, 1993.

Cohn, Samuel Kline. *Creating the Florentine State: Peasants and Rebellion, 1348–1434*. Cambridge, 1999.

Colonna, Prospero. *I Colonna*. Rome, 1927.

Corridore, Francesco. *La popolazione dello Stato Romano (1656–1901)*. Rome, 1906.

Cortonesi, Alfio. *Terre e signori nel Lazio medioevale: Un'economia rurale nei secoli XIII–XIV*. Naples, 1988.

Coste, Jean. "Castello or Casale? Documenti su Cretone in Sabina." In *Seicento e Settecento nel Lazio*, ed. Renato Lefevre, 361–372. Rome, 1980.

———. "I casali della campagna di Roma all'inizio del seicento." *Archivio della Società romana di storia patria* 92 (1969–1970): 41–115.

———. "La Topographie médiévale de la Campagne romaine et l'histoire socio-économique: pistes de recherche." *Mélanges de l'École française de Rome* 88 (1976): 621–675.

———. "Localizzazione di un Possesso Farfense. Il Castrum Caminata." *Archivio della società romana di storia patria* 103 (1980): 53–77.

———. "Missioni nell'Agro romano nella primavera del 1703." *Ricerche per la storia religiosa di Roma* 2 (1978): 165–223.

Curis, Giovanni. *Usi civici, proprietà collettive e latifondi nell'Italia centrale e nell'Emilia*. Naples, 1917.

Cushman, Ellen, Eugene R. Kintgen, Barry M. Kroll, and Mike Rose, eds. *Literacy: A Critical Sourcebook*. Boston and New York, 2001.

D'Alessandro, Alessandro. "I proprietari delle tenute dell'Agro Romano nel 1783." *Rivista di storia dell'agricoltura* 9 (1971): 363–381.

———. "Le tenute dell'Agro Romano alla fine del secolo XVIII." *Economia e storia* 16 (1969): 27–37.

Dal Pane, Luigi. *Lo Stato Pontificio e il movimento riformatore del Settecento*. Milan, 1959.

———. "Orientamenti e problemi della storia dell'agricoltura italiana del Seicento e del Settecento." *Rivista storica italiana* 68 (1956): 165–185.

D'Amelia, Marina. "La crisi di un mercato protetto: approvvigionamenti e consumo della carne a Roma nel XVIII secolo." *Mélanges de l'École française de Rome: Moyen Âge, Temps Modernes* 87 (1975): 495–534.

———. *Orgoglio Baronale e Giustizia: Castel Viscardo alla fine del Cinquecento.* Rome, 1996.

Davis, Natalie Zemon. *Fiction in the Archives: Pardon Tales and their Tellers in Sixteenth-Century France.* Palo Alto, Calif., 1987.

———. *Society and Culture in Early Modern France.* Stanford, Calif., 1965.

Dean, Trevor, and Chris Wickham. *City and Countryside in Late Medieval and Renaissance Italy.* London, 1990.

De Angelis, Gilberto, ed. *Monti Lucretili.* 3d ed. Rome, 1988.

———, and P. Lanzara, "L'Esplorazione Naturalistica dei Monte Lucretili tra XVI e XVIII secolo." In *Monti Lucretili*, 3d ed., ed. G. De Angelis, 225–256. Rome, 1988.

De Clementi, Andreina, "Individualismo agrario e mentalità comunitaria in un villaggio del Lazio." *Quaderni storici* 63 (1986): 931–950.

———. *Vivere nel latifondo: le comunità della campagna laziale fra '700 e '800.* Milan, 1989.

De Cupis, Cesare. *Le vicende dell'agricoltura e della pastorizia nella campagna romana.* Rome, 1911.

———. *Saggio bibliografico degli scritti e delle leggi sull'agro romano.* Rome, 1903.

———. *Supplemento al saggio bibliografico degli scritti sull'agro romano.* Caserta, 1926.

De Felice, Renzo. *Aspetti e Momenti della Vita Economica di Roma e del Lazio nei secoli XVIII e XIX.* Rome, 1965.

Delano Smith, Catherine. *Western Mediterranean Europe: A Historical Geography of Italy, Spain and Southern France since the Neolithic.* New York and London, 1979.

Del Re, N. *La Curia Romana: Lineamenti storico-giurici.* 3d ed. Rome, 1970.

Delumeau, Jean. *Catholicism between Luther and Voltaire.* Translated by Jeremy Moiser. Philadelphia and London, 1977.

———. "Rome: Political and Administrative Centralization in the Papal State in the Sixteenth Century." In *The Late Italian Renaissance: 1525–1630*, ed. Eric Cochrane, 287–304. New York, 1970.

———. *Vie économique et sociale de Rome dans la seconde moitié du XVIe siècle.* 2 vols. Paris, 1957–1959.

De Mico, Fabio, ed. *IV Centenario della Costituzione del Comune di Monte Flavio.* Monte Flavio, 1978.

De Tournon, Philippe. *Études statistiques sur Rome et la partie occidentale des États Romains.* 2 vols. Paris, 1831.

Dewald, Jonathan. *Aristocratic Experience and the Origins of Modern Culture: France, 1570–1715.* Berkeley, 1993.

———. *The European Nobility 1400–1800.* Cambridge, 1996.

Diefendorf, Barbara, and Carla Hesse. *Culture and Identity in Early Modern Europe (1500–1800): Essays in Honor of Natalie Zemon Davis.* Ann Arbor, 1993.

Di Gessa, Roberto. "Aspetti istituzionali di politica economia nell'esperienza dei Barberini a Palestrina." In *I Barberini a Palestrina*, ed. Peppino Tomassi, 127–151. Palestrina, 1992.

Di Stefano, Tommaso. *Montorio Romano*. Rome, 1991.

Doniger, Wendy. *The Implied Spider*. New York, 1998.

Douglas, Mary. "No Free Gifts." In Marcel Mauss, *The Gift: Forms and Functions of Exchange in Archaic Societies*. Translated by W. D. Halls. New York, 1990.

Elias, Norbert. *The Civilizing Process*. Translated by Edmund Jephcott. Oxford, 1994.

Epstein, Stephan R. "The Peasantries of Italy, 1350−1750." In *The Peasantries of Europe*, ed. James C. Scott, 75−108. New York, 1998.

Ertman, Thomas. *Birth of the Leviathan: Building States and Regimes in Medieval and Early Modern Europe*. Cambridge, 1997.

Ferraro, Richard. "The Nobility of Rome, 1560−1700: A Study of its Composition, Wealth, and Investments." Ph.D. diss., University of Wisconsin, 1994.

Ferratini, A. "Un Censimento Inedito dello Stato Pontificio, 26 Marzo 1769." *Statistica* 8/3 (1948): 280−341.

Fiorani, Luigi. "Le visite apostoliche del Cinque-Seicento e la società religiosa romana." *Ricerche per la storia religiosa di Roma* 4 (1980): 53−148.

Forclaz, Bertrand. "Le relazioni complesse tra signore e vassalli: La famiglia Borghese e i suoi feudi nel Seicento." In *La Nobiltà romana in età moderna: Profili istituzionali e pratiche sociali*, ed. Maria Antonietta Visceglia, 165−201. Rome, 2001

Fosi, Irene Polverini. *La Società Violenta: Il banditismo dello Stato Pontificio nella seconda metà del Cinquecento*. Rome, 1985.

Foucault, Michel. *Discipline and Punish: The Birth of the Prison*, trans. Alan Sheridan. New York, 1977.

Friz, Giuliano. *Consumi, tenore di vita e prezzi a Roma dal 1700 al 1900*. Rome, 1980.

———. "Produzione e commercio dei vini del Lazio nei secoli XVIII e XIX." in *Annales cisalpines d'histoire sociale* 3 (1972): 207−228.

Frutaz, A. P. *Le Carte del Lazio*. Rome, 1972.

Furet, François, and Jacques Ozouf. *Lire et écrire*. Paris, 1977.

Ghetti, Bernardino. "Monte Libretti nella Toponomastica della Provincia Romana." In his *Ricerche Storiche*, 29−37. Fano, 1906.

Giorgetti, Giorgio. *Contadini e Proprietari nell'Italia Moderna*. Turin, 1974.

Giuntella, Vittorio E. *Roma nel Settecento*. Bologna, 1971.

Grew, Raymond. "Finding Social Capital: The French Revolution in Italy." *Journal of Interdisciplinary History* 29 (1999): 407−433.

———. "The Paradoxes of Italy's Nineteenth-Century Political Culture." In *Revolution and the Meanings of Freedom in the Nineteenth Century*, ed. Isser Woloch. Stanford, Calif., 1996.

Gross, Hanns. *Rome in the Age of Enlightenment: The Post-Tridentine Syndrome and the Ancien Regime*. Cambridge, 1990.

Guarini, Elena Fasano. "Center and Periphery." In *The Origins of the State in Italy, 1300−1600*, ed. Julius Kirshner, 74−96. Chicago, 1995.

Hallman, Barbara McClung. *Italian Cardinals, Reform, and the Church as Property*. Berkeley, 1985.

Hammond, Frederick. "Bernini and the 'Fiera di Farfa.'" In *Gianlorenzo Bernini: New Aspects of His Art and Thought*, ed. Irving Lavin, 115−125. University Park, Penn., 1985.

Hardwick, Julie. *The Practice of Patriarchy: Gender and the Politics of Household Authority in Early Modern France.* University Park, Penn., 1998.

Harris, Ann Sutherland. *Landscape Painting in Rome, 1595–1675.* New York, 1985.

Haskell, Francis. *Patrons and Painters: A Study in the Relations between Italian Art and Society in the Age of the Baroque.* London, 1963.

Hibbard, Howard. *Bernini.* London, 1965.

Hirschman, Albert O. *The Passions and the Interests: Political Arguments for Capitalism before Its Triumph.* Princeton, 1997.

Hobsbawm. E. J., and Joan Wallach Scott. "Political Shoemakers." *Past and Present* 89 (1980): 86–114.

Hook, Judith A. "Urban VIII: The Paradox of a Spiritual Monarchy." In *The Courts of Europe: Politics, Patronage and Royalty, 1400–1800,* ed. A. G. Dickens, 213–230. London, 1977.

Houston, R. A. *Literacy in Early Modern Europe.* 2d ed. London, 2002.

Hudon, William V. "Religion and Society in Early Modern Italy—Old Questions, New Insights." *American Historical Review* 101 (June 1996): 784–804.

Hughes, Steven C. "Fear and Loathing in Bologna and Rome: The Papal Police in Perspective." *Journal of Social History* 21 (1987): 97–116.

Hurston, Zora Neale. *Their Eyes Were Watching God.* New York, 1990.

Hurtubise, Pierre. *Une Famille-témoin, Les Salviati.* Vatican City, 1985.

Ignatieff, Michael. *The Russian Album.* New York, 1988.

Imberciadori, I. "Spedale, scuola, e chiesa in popolazioni rurali dei secoli XVI–XVII." *Economia e Storia* 6 (1959): 421–449.

Jones, P. M. "Parish, Seigneurie and the Community of Inhabitants in Southern Central France during the Eighteenth and Nineteenth Centuries." *Past and Present* 91 (1981): 74–108.

Justice, Steven. *Writing and Rebellion: England in 1381.* Berkeley, 1994.

Kessel, Peter van, and Elisja Schulte van Kessel. *Rome, Amsterdam: Two Growing Cities in Seventeenth-Century Europe.* Amsterdam, 1997.

Kettering, Sharon. *Patrons, Brokers, and Clients in Seventeenth-Century France.* New York, 1986.

Kintgen, Eugene R., Barry M. Kroll, and Mike Rose, eds. *Perspectives on Literacy.* Carbondale, Ill., 1988.

Kirshner, Julius, ed. *The Origins of the State in Italy, 1300–1600.* Chicago, 1995.

Kuehn, Thomas. *Law, Family, & Women. Toward a Legal Anthropology of Renaissance Italy.* Chicago, 1991.

La Marca, Nicola. *La nobiltà romana e i suoi strumenti di perpetuazione del potere.* Rome, 2002.

Lavin, Marilyn. *Seventeenth-Century Barberini Documents and Inventories of Art.* New York, 1971.

Leggio, Tersilio. *Da Cures Sabini all'Abbazia di Farfa.* Passo Corese, 1992.

Leoni, Edilio. *La Sabina nella Storia di Roma.* Rome, 1970.

Lepre, Anna. "Agricoltura e manifattura in una rione di Roma nel seicento e nel settecento." *Studi romani* 25 (1977): 353–370.

Lernoux, Penny. *Cry of the People.* New York, 1980.

Litta, Pompeo. *Famiglie celebri italiane.* Milan, 1819–1881.

Lodolini, Armando. "Il tribunale dell'Agricoltura." *Agricoltura* 2 (1953): 79–80.

―――. "L'Amministrazione pontificia del 'Buon Governo.'" *Gli Archivi Italiani* 6 (1919): 181–237; 7 (1920): 3–19.

Lodolini, Elio. *L'Archivio della S. Congregazione del Buon Governo (1592–1847)*. Pubblicazioni degli archivi di Stato Series, vol. 20. Rome, 1956.

Luzio, Leopoldina. "Contributo allo studio dei centri scomparsi o abbandonati del Lazio." *Rivista Geografica Italiana* 60 (June 1953): 134–162.

Magnuson, Torgil. *Rome in the Age of Bernini*. 2 vols. Stockholm, 1982–1986.

Maire-Vigueur, Jean-Claude. "Classe dominante et classes dirigeantes à Rome à la fin du Moyen Âge." *Storia della città* 1/1 (1976): 4–26.

Malkki, Liisa. *Purity and Exile: Violence, Memory, and National Cosmology among Hutu Refugees in Tanzania*. Chicago, 1995.

Manzoni, Alessandro. *The Betrothed*. Translated by Bruce Penman. London, 1972.

Maravall, José A. *Culture of the Baroque: Analysis of a Historical Structure*. Minneapolis, 1986.

Marino, John A. *Pastoral Economics in the Kingdom of Naples*. Baltimore and London, 1988.

Massimiani, Umberto. *Scandriglia*. Rome, 1988.

Mauss, Marcel. *The Gift: Forms and Functions of Exchange in Archaic Societies*. Translated by Ian Cunnison. New York, 1967.

Mazzacane, Aldo. "Law and Jurists in the Formation of the Modern State in Italy." In *The Origins of the State in Italy, 1300–1600*, ed. Julius Kirshner, 62–73. Chicago, 1995.

McArdle, Frank. *Altopascio: A Study in Tuscan Rural Society, 1587–1784*. Cambridge, 1978.

McNeely, Ian F. *The Emancipation of Writing: German Civil Society in the Making, 1790s–1820s*. Berkeley, 2003.

McNeill, William H. *Plagues and Peoples*. New York, 1976.

Merola, A. "Antonio Barberini," *Dizionario Biografico degli Italiani*. Vol. 6: 164–165. Rome, 1964.

Metalli, E. *Usi e costumi della campagna romana*. Rome, 1924.

Mistruzzi, Carlo. "La nobiltà nello Stato Pontificio." *Rassegna degli archivi di stato* 23 (1963): 206–244.

Molho, Anthony. "Patronage and the State in Early Modern Italy." In *Klientelsysteme im Europa der Frühen Neuzeit*, ed. Antoni Maczak, 233–242. Munich, 1988.

Montel, Robert. "Un casale de la Campagne Romaine de la fin du XIVè siècle au début du XVIIe: Le domaine de Porto." *Mélanges de l'École française de Rome: Moyen Âge Temps Modernes* 83 (1971): 31–87.

Muir, Edward. "The Idea of Community in Renaissance Italy." *Renaissance Quarterly* 55 (2002): 1–18.

―――. *Mad Blood Stirring: Vendetta and Factions in Friuli during the Renaissance*. Baltimore, 1993.

―――. "The Sources of Civil Society in Italy." *Journal of Interdisciplinary History* 29 (1999): 379–406.

―――, and Guido Ruggiero. *Microhistory and the Lost Peoples of Europe*. Baltimore, 1991.

Murata, Margaret. *Operas for the Papal Court, 1631–1668*. Ann Arbor, 1981.

Musgrave, Peter. *Land and Economy in Baroque Italy: Valpolicella, 1630–1797*. New York, 1992.

Nader, Helen. *Liberty in Absolutist Spain*. Baltimore, 1990.

Nardelli, Franca Petrucci. "Francesco Barberini Junior e la 'Stamperia Barberina' di Palestrina' di Palestrina." In *I Barberini a Palestrina*, ed. Peppino Tomassi, 179–224. Palestrina, 1992.

Necrologia di D. Francesco Barberini, Principe di Palestrina. Extract of the *Giornale di Roma* (no. 54). Rome, 1854.

Nicolai, Vincenzo Fiocchi. "Montelibretti: Prime Ricerche." *Quaderni del Centro di studio per l'archaeologia etrusco-italica* 3, 265–268, 1979.

Nussdorfer, Laurie. "City Politics in Baroque Rome, 1623–1644." Ph.D. diss., Princeton, 1985.

———. *Civic Politics in the Rome of Urban VIII*. Princeton, 1992.

O'Malley, John W. *Trent and all That: Renaming Catholicism in the Early Modern Era*. Cambridge, Mass., 2000.

Ong, Walter. *Orality and Literacy: The Technologizing of the Word*. New York, 1982.

Pagano, Sergio. "Le visite apostoliche a Roma nei secoli XVI–XIX: Repertorio delle fonti." *Ricerche per la storia religiosa di Roma* 4 (1980): 317–464.

Palmegiani, Francesco. *Rieti e la Regione Sabina: Storia, Arte, Vita, Usi e Costumi*. Rome, 1932.

Parsons, W. B. *Engineers and Engineering in the Renaissance*. Baltimore, 1939; reprint, Cambridge, Mass., 1968.

Partner, Peter. *The Lands of Saint Peter*. London, 1972.

———. "Papal Financial Policy in the Renaissance and Counter-Reformation." *Past and Present* 88 (1980): 17–62.

———. *The Papal State under Martin V*. London, 1958.

———. *Renaissance Rome 1550–1559: A Portrait of a Society*. Berkeley and Los Angeles, 1979.

Passigli, Susanna. *La Pianta dell'Architetto Francesco Peperelli (1618): Una Fonte per la Topografia della Regione Romana*. Rome, 1989.

Pastor, Ludwig von. *The History of the Popes from the Close of the Middle Ages*. Translated by Ernest Graf et al. 40 vols. London, 1891–1953.

Patrizi, Adreana. *Palestrina nel Settecento*. Cava, 1987.

Pecchiai, Pio. *I Barberini*. Rome, 1959.

Pelliccia, Guerino. "Scuole di catechismo e scuole rionali per fanciulle nel Roma del Seicento." *Ricerche per la storia religiosa di Roma* 4 (1980): 237–268.

Persichetti, Niccolò. "La via Salaria nei circondari di Roma e di Rieti." In *Bolletino dell'Imperiale Istituto Archeologico Germanico* 23 (1908): 275–329; 376; 24 (1909): 121–169; 208–255.

Pescosolido, Guido. *Terra e nobiltà: I Borghese, secoli XVIII e XIX*. Rome, 1979.

Petrocchi, Massimo. *Roma nel Seicento*. Bologna, 1970.

Petrucci, A. ed. *Scrittura e popolo nella Roma barocca, 1585–1721*. Rome, 1978.

Petrusewicz, Marta. *Latifondo: Economia morale e vita materiale in una periferia dell'Ottocento*. Venice, 1989.

Piccialuti, Maura. *La Carità Come Metodo di Governo: Istituzioni caritative a Roma dal pontificato di Innocenzo XII a quell di Benedetto XIV*. Turin, 1994.

Pisano, Giulio. "L'Ultimo Prefetto dell'urbe, Don Taddeo Barberini, e le relazioni tra la corte di Roma e la Repubblica Veneta sotto il pontificato di Urbano VIII." *Roma* 3 and 4 (1931): 103–120 and 155–164.

Pocock, J. G. A. *The Machiavellian Moment.* Princeton, 1975.

———. *Politics, Language & Time: Essays on Political Thought and History.* Chicago, 1989.

Prodi, Paolo. *Il sacramento del potere.* Bologna, 1992.

———. *The Papal Prince: One Body and Two Souls: The Papal Monarchy in Early Modern Europe.* Trans. Susan Haskins. Cambridge, 1987.

———. "Popolo e papi: La crisi del sistema annonario." *Annali della Fondazione L. e L. Basso* 7 (Milan, 1985): 18.

Pullan, Brian. *Rich and Poor in Renaissance Venice: The Social Institutions of a Catholic State to 1620.* Oxford, 1971.

Pullè, Giorgio. "La pastorizia nell'Agro Romano." *Bolletino della Società Geografica Italiana* 6 (1929): 570–601.

Putnam, Robert, Robert Leonardi, and Raffaella Y. Nanetti. *Making Democracy Work: Civic Traditions in Modern Italy.* Princeton, 1993.

Raggio, Osvaldo. *Faide e parentele: Lo Stato Genovese visto dalla Fontanabuona.* Turin, 1990.

———. "Norme e pratiche: Gli statuti campestri come fonti per una storia locale." *Quaderni storici* 88 (1995): 155–194.

———. *Strutture di parentela e controllo delle risorse in un'area di transito: la val fontanabuona tra cinque e seicento.* Florence, 1985.

Rappoport, Joanne. *The Politics of Memory: Native Historical Interpretation in the Columbian Andes.* Cambridge, 1990.

Razzicchia, Renata Tomassi. "Fiere, feste e Mercati a Palestrina nei secoli XVII e XVIII." In *I Barberini a Palestrina*, ed. Peppino Tomassi, 225–244. Palestrina, 1992.

Redfield, Robert. *Peasant Society and Culture.* Chicago, 1950.

Reinhard, Wolfgang. "Papal Power and Family Strategy in the Sixteenth and Seventeenth Centuries." In *Princes, Patrons, and the Nobility*, ed. Ronald Asch and Adolf M. Birke, 329–356. London, 1991.

———. "Reformation, Counter-Reformation, and the Early Modern State—A Reassessment." *Catholic Historical Review* 75 (July 1989): 383–404.

Reinhardt, Volker. *Kardinal Scipione Borghese 1605–1633: Vermögen, Finanzen und Sozialer Aufsteig.* Tübingen, 1984.

———. *Uberleben in der frühneuzeitlichen Stadt: Annona und Getreideversorgung in Rom 1563–1797.* Tübingen.

Revel, Jacques. "Le Grain de Rome et la crise de l'Annone dans la seconde moitié du XVIIIe siècle." *Mélanges de l'École française de Rome: Moyen Âge, Temps Modernes* 84 (1972): 201–281.

———. "Les Privilèges d'une capitale: l'approvisionnement de Rome à l'époque moderne." *Mélanges de l'École française de Rome: Moyen Âge, Temps Modernes* 87 (1975): 461–493.

Riccardi, R. "La cartografia della Sabina nei secoli XVI, XVII, XVIII." *Bolletino della Reale Società Geografica Italiana*, serie V, 11 (1923): 210–238 and 340–362.

Rollison, David. *The Local Origins of Modern Society: Gloucestershire 1500–1800.* London, 1992.

Root, Hilton. *Peasants and King in Burgundy: Agrarian Foundations of French Absolutism.* Berkeley, 1987.

Rosati, Alessandro. *Il Castello di Nerola (Ricerca storica sulla Sabina tiberina centrale).* Rome, 1983.

Rossi, Emete. "La fuga del Cardinale Antonio Barberini." *Archivio della Società Romana di Storia Patria* 59 (1936): 303–327.

Rossi, Giorgio. *L'Agro di Roma tra '500 e '800: Condizioni di vita e lavoro.* Rome, 1985.

Rotberg, Robert I. "Social Capital and Political Culture in Africa, America, Australasia, and Europe." *Journal of Interdisciplinary History* 29 (1999): 339–356.

Ruggiero, Maria G. Pastura. *La Reverenda Camera Apostolica e i suoi archivi (secoli XV–XVIII).* Rome, 1984.

Sabean, David. *Kinship in Neckarhausen, 1700–1870.* Cambridge, 1998.

———. *Power in the Blood.* Cambridge, 1984.

———. *Property, Production, and Family in Neckarhausen, 1700–1870.* Cambridge, 1990.

Sabetti, Filippo. *The Search for Good Government: Understanding the Paradox of Italian Democracy.* Montreal, 2000.

Sacchi Lodispoto, Giulia. "Mons. Patti 'Visitore Apostolico' in Provincia di Patrimonio nel 1704." In *Seicento e Settecento nel Lazio,* ed. Renato Lefevre, 129–151. Rome, 1980.

Santoncini, Gabriella. *Il Buon Governo: organizzazione e legittimazione del rapporto fra sovrano e comunitá nello Stato pontificio, secoli XVI–XVIII.* Milan, 2002.

Schiavoni, Claudio, and Eugenio Sonnino. "Popolazione e territorio nel Lazio, 1701–1811." In *La popolazione italiana nel Settecento,* ed. Società italiana di demografia storica, 191–216. Bologna, 1979.

Schiera, Pierangelo. "Legitimacy, Discipline, and Institutions: Three Necessary Conditions for the Birth of the Modern State." In *The Origins of the State in Italy, 1300–1600,* ed. Julius Kirshner, 11–34. Chicago, 1995.

Schulze, Winfried. "Peasant Resistance in Sixteenth- and Seventeenth-Century Germany in a European Context." In *Religion, Politics and Social Protest: Three Studies on Early Modern Germany,* ed. Wolfgang J. Mommsen, 61–98. London, 1984.

Scotoni, Lando. *I Territori Autonomi dello Stato Ecclesiastico nel Cinquecento: Cartografia e aspetti amministrativi, economici e sociali.* Lecce, 1982.

———. "La Campagna Romana in una pittura geografica del 1692." *Rivista Geografica Italiana* 78 (June 1971): 204–214.

———. "Le tenute della Campagna Romana nel 1660: Saggi di ricostruzione cartografica." *Atti e Memorie della Società Tiburtina di Storia e d'Arte* 59 (1986): 185–262.

———. "Raccolta e commercio della neve nel circondario delle 60 miglia (Lazio)." *Rivista Geografica Italiana* 79 (March 1972): 60–70.

Scott, James C. *Domination and the Arts of Resistance: Hidden Transcripts.* New Haven, 1990.

Scott, John Beldon. *Images of Nepotism: The Painted Ceilings of Palazzo Barberini.* Princeton, 1991.

Scott, Tom, ed. *Peasantries of Europe: From the Fourteenth to the Eighteenth Centuries.* New York, 1998.

Sereni, Emilio. *Storia del Paesaggio Agrario Italiano.* Bari, 1972.

Settia, A. A. "Il castello da villaggio fortificato a dimora signorile." In *Castelli—Storia e Archeologia* (Convegno tenuto a Cuneo nel 1981), 219–228. Cuneo, 1984.

Sharpe, Kevin. "Reading in Early Modern England." In *Reading Revolutions: The Politics of Reading in Early Modern England*. New Haven, 2000.

Silverman, Sydel. *Three Bells of Civilization: The Life of an Italian Hill Town*. New York, 1975.

Silvestrelli, Giulio. *Città, castelli, e terre della regione romana: Ricerche di storia medioevale e moderna sino all'anno 1800*. Città di Castello, 1914.

Sombart, Werner. *La Campagna Romana: studio economico-sociale*. Turin, 1891.

Spruyt, Hendrik. *The Sovereign State and Its Competitors*. Princeton, 1994.

Stinger, Charles L. *The Renaissance in Rome*. Bloomington, Ind., 1985.

Stumpo, Enrico. *Il Capitale Finanziario a Roma fra Cinque e Seicento. Contributo alla Storia della Fiscalità Pontificia in Età Moderna (1570–1660)*. Milan, 1985.

Thompson, Edward P. *Customs in Common*. New York, 1993.

————. *Whigs and Hunters*. London, 1975.

Tocci, Giovanni. *Le Comunità Negli Stati Italiani D'Antico Regime*. Bologna, 1989.

Toews, John E. "Intellectual History after the Linguistic Turn: The Autonomy of Meaning and the Irreducibility of Experience." *American Historical Review* 92 (1987): 879–907.

Tomassetti, Guiseppe. "Il Feudalismo romano." *Riv. internaz. di scienze sociali* 6 (1894): 37–58.

————. *La Campagna Romana: antica, medioevale e moderna*. 4 vols., Rome, 1910–1926; 2d ed. 7 vols., Florence, 1979, ed. by L. Chiumenti and F. Bilancia.

————. and G. Biasiotti. *Le Diocesi di Sabina*. Rome, 1909.

Tomassi, Paola. "Istituzioni Assistenziali a Palestrina nei secoli XVII–XIX." In *I Barberini a Palestrina*, ed. Peppino Tomassi, 153–177. Palestrina, 1992.

Tomassi, Peppino, ed. *I Barberini a Palestrina*. Palestrina, 1992.

Torniai, Paola. "Città e 'Campagna': Roma, i Barberini, Palestrina nel Seicento. Modi e tendenze di un progetto di riqualificazione." In *I Barberini a Palestrina*, ed. Peppino Tomassi, 37–58. Palestrina, 1992.

Torre, Angelo. *Il consumo di devozioni: Religione e comunità nelle compagne dell'Ancien Régime*. Venice, 1995.

Tosi, Mario. *La società romana dalla feudalità al patriziato (1816–1853)*. Rome, 1968.

————. "Le clausole cancelleresche del diritto feudale nella diplomatica pontificia, in rapporto ai titoli e ai predicati nobiliari." *Gli Archivi Italiani* 7 (1920): 87–122.

Toubert, Pierre. *Les Structures du Latium médiéval: Le Latium méridional et la Sabine du IXe siècle*. 2 vols. Rome, 1973.

Trifone, R., "A proposito della colonia perpetua 'ad meliorandum.'" *Rivista di diritto agrario* 31 (1952), parte I: 23–28.

Trinchieri, Romolo. *Vita di Pastori*. Rome, 1953.

Tully, James. *Meaning and Context: Quentin Skinner and His Critics*. Princeton, 1988.

Ugolini, Piero. *Un paese della campagna romana: Formello. Storia ed economia agraria*. Rome, 1957.

Valeri, U. *Genti e castelli sabini. (Miscellanea storico-biografica)*. Rome, 1946.

Van Creveld, Martin. *The Rise and Decline of the State*. Cambridge, 1999.

Venturi, Franco. *Italy and the Enlightenment*. Edited and with an introduction by Stuart Woolf. Translated by Susan Corsi. London, 1972.

————. *Settecento Riformatore*. Vol I: *Da Muratori a Beccaria*. Turin, 1969.

————. *Settecento Riformatore.* Vol II: *La chiesa e la repubblica dentro i loro limiti, 1758– 1774.* Turin, 1976.

Villani, Pasquale. *Feudalità, riforme, capitalismo agrario.* 1969.

————. "Ricerche sulla proprietà e sul regime fondiario nel Lazio." *Annuario dell'Ist. Storico Italiano per la Storia moderna e contemporanea* 12, 1960.

Visceglia, Maria Antonietta. *La nobiltà romana in età moderna: profili istituzionali e pratiche sociali.* Rome, 2001.

————, and Gianvittorio Signorotto. *Court and Politics in Papal Rome, 1492–1700.* Cambridge, 2002.

Visconti, Pietro. *Città e famiglie nobili e celebri dello Stato Pontificio: Dizionario storico.* 4 vols. Rome, 1847.

Volpi, Roberto. *Le Regioni introvabili: Centralizzazione e regionalizzazione dello Stato Pontificio.* Bologna, 1983.

Waddy, Patricia. *Seventeenth-Century Roman Palaces: Use and the Art of the Plan.* Cambridge, 1990.

————. "Taddeo Barberini as a Patron of Architecture." In *L'Âge d'ôr du mécénat (1598–1661),* by the Colloque international CNRS, 191–199. Paris, 1985.

Waley, Daniel. "La Féodalitè dans la région romaine dans la 2e moitié du XIIIe siècle et au début du XIVe." *Structures féodales et féodalisme dans l'Occident méditerranéen (Xe–XIIIe siècles) Bilan et perspectives de recherches. Actes du Colloque de Rome, 10–13 October 1978,* 515–522. Rome, 1980.

Wilkinson, R. *Poverty and Progress: An Ecological Model of Economic Development.* London, 1973.

Wolf, Eric, *Peasants.* Englewood Cliffs, N.J., 1966.

Woolf, Stuart. *A History of Italy 1700–1860: The Social Constraints of Political Change.* London, 1979.

Zangheri, Renato. *Agricoltura e contadini nella storia d'Italia.* Turin, 1977.

Zenobi, Bandino. "Feudalità e patriziati cittadini nel governo della 'periferia' pontificia del cinque-seicento." In *Signori, patrizi, cavalieri in Italia centro-meridionale nell'età moderna,* ed. Maria Antonietta Visceglia, 94–107. Bari, 1992.

————. *Le "Ben Regolate Città,": Modelli politici nel governo delle periferie pontificie in età moderna.* Rome, 1994.

————. *Tardo feudalità e reclutamento delle elites nello Stato Pontificio secoli XV–XVIII.* Urbino, 1983.

Zotta, Silvio, "The Agrarian Crisis and Feudal Politics in the Kingdom of Naples: The Doria at Melfi (1585–1615)." In *Good Government in Spanish Naples,* ed. and trans. Antonio Calabria and John A. Marino, 127–203. New York, 1990.

INDEX

accounting practices. *See also* tax collection
  Maffeo Barberini's, 101
  in Monte Flavio, 148, 150
  in Nerola, 95
Ademollo, Alessandro, 194n22
adversarial literacy, 13, 60–62, 176
  and accounting practices, 150
  clerics response to, 169–171
  development of, 62–63
Ago, Renata, 130, 191n21, 193n10, 197n45,
    200n2, 212n34, 214n45, 214n47,
    220n20, 221n22
Aldobrandini family, 22
Amayden, Theodor, 22, 193n12
Andretta, S., 194n17
Angelo, Castel S., 192n8
Angelonio, Mariano, 43
archives. *See* records
Armando, David, 189n11
art, villagers as patrons of, 69
assembly. *See* consiglio (assembly)
Astarita, Tommaso, 189n14
Aurelio, Don, 73

authority
  of nobles, 6–7, 151–159
  of papal government, 4, 6, 15, 62

Bamboccianti (painters), 28
Barberini, Antonio, 26
Barberini, Carlo, 24, 34, 80
Barberini, Francesco Junior, 14, 20, 24–25,
    34, 78, 98
  bureaucracy of, 106
  and *consiglio*, 129
  debt relief efforts of, 99–105
  governing style of, 92–93, 99
  as opera sponsor, 26
Barberini, Maffeo, 4–5, 14, 34, 173. *See also*
    Urban VIII
  accounting practices of, 101
  on administration of justice, 54
  death of, 59, 98
  edicts of, 80–1
  in Eugeni case, 53–54
  governing of, 15, 128
  and hiring of village surgeon, 76, 79–80

Barberini, Maffeo *(continued)*
  and hunting ban, 49, 52, 57, 174
  and inn rental, 83–84
  as mediator, 80
  patronage of, 70–74
  on "public good," 85, 88–89
  and schoolteachers, 74
  and village politics, 15, 43, 66, 89–90
Barberini, Olimpia Giustiniani, 98
Barberini, Taddeo, 24, 33, 197n44
  as opera sponsor, 26
  purchase of Monte Libretti, 18
  rule of, 14
Barberini, Urbano, 14, 59, 99
  death of, 99
  and tax collection, 97
Barberini Colonna di Sciarra, Cornelia
      Costanza, 8–9, 14, 67, 93, 99, 118, 175
  and Buon Governo, 117
  and *consiglio*, 128–129
  on disorder in villages, 121–122
  as heir, 108–110
  rule of, 128
Barberini Colonna di Sciarra, Giulio Cesare,
      8, 175
  and access to education, 127
  and administration of justice, 123–124
  and Buon Governo, 117
  charitable donations by, 125–126
  and collection of *minuti*, 167
  and *consiglio*, 128–129
  edicts of, 121, 135
  governing style of, 128, 145, 177–178
  and grazing rights, 144–145
  as heir, 108–110
  and pasture rights, 139–140
  and payment of *minuti*, 154–159
  and tax increases, 151–153
  and village politics, 115, 131–136
  and village priests, 133–134
  and village sanitation, 123
Barberini family
  acquisitions of, 24–28
  becoming lords, 14
  and Buon Governo, 15, 92–94, 106–107,
      109–110
  edicts of, 122–123
  establishing of, in Roman society, 20–23

fall from power, 32–33
family tree of, 181
financial difficulties of, 22
heirs of, 108–109
impact of Urban's death on, 32
insecurity of, 23
officials of, 108–113
origins of, 21
papers of, 5–6
paternalism of, 124–125
rule of, 15–16, 94, 114–115, 120–121,
      127–131, 173, 175
self-identification of, 168
and tax collection, 97, 113–114, 116–117
territory of, 174
Barbetta, Salvatore, 132–133
Bartoli, Daniello, 28
bell, village, refurbishing, 72
Benadusi, Giovanna, 189n14
Beneš, Mirka, 192n3, 194n14, 196n37, 197n45
benevolence, and obligation, 145–146
Bercé, Yves-Marie, 189n13
Bernini, Dominco, 21, 194n16, 194n23
Blickle, Peter, 12, 167, 190n17, 191n18, 191n20,
      202n16, 205n57, 209n44, 224n10,
      227n38
Boccaccio, 27
Boland, Eavan, 5
Borghese family, 151, 192n5
Bossy, John, 198n50
Braudel, Fernand, 192n4
Bravetti, Giacinto, 75–78
Briganti, G., 195n26
Brucker, Gene, 190n15
budget, communal, 80–81, 114–115
Buon Governo, 117
  archive of, 6
  authority of, 15
  and Barberini family, 92–94, 106–107,
      109–110, 116–118, 120
  expansion of, 106
  and tax collection, 97, 113–114

Calabria, Antonio, 191n20, 223n49
Callisto, Mario, 81, 108
Camilli, Domenico, 101–104, 107, 114–115
Campanelli, Innocenzo, 4–5, 187n1
Caracciolo, Alberto, 193n9, 201n12

Caravale, Mario, 193n9, 201n12

Castigliano, Vincenzo, 57, 211n15

Castiglione, Caroline, 199n54, 205n48, 210n2, 226n11

Celani, E., 201n10

Cesare, Giulio, 67

Chi soffre, speri (Rospigliosi), 26

Chittolini, Giorgio, 190n15

citizens, villagers as, 67–70. *See also* political participation, of villagers

Clanchy, M. T., 222n46, 223n3

Clement VIII (pope), 22, 24, 94

Clement XI (pope), 92, 95

Cochrane, Eric, 193n9

Coffin, David R., 193n11

Cohn, Samuel Kline, 189n14

Colonna, Anna, 25, 33–34

Colonna, Francesco, 24

commodity, villagers as, 14–15

concordia (settlement)
 on hunting ban, 58–59, 61
 on olive oil harvest, 59
 records of, 59

consiglio (assembly), 11
 Barberini's efforts to limit, 127–131
 and communal offices, 81–83
 language used in, 61
 membership in, 128–131
 and the "public good," 87–88
 records of, 12–13, 15, 191n19
 subjects discussed in, 69
 and villagers rights, 142–143

constitution. *See statuto* (constitution)

Corese, 104–105, 185

corn harvesting, conflict over, 140–141

Cornacchia, Nicola, 114, 134, 141

Cortonesi, Alfio, 201n10, 201n11

Coste, Jean, 188n9

"courtesy," *versus* obligation, 38–40

Curis, Giovanni, 9, 188n9–10, 197n45, 201n10, 206n2, 214n47

D'Amelia, Marina, 189n11

Da Cortona, Pietro, 25, 29

De Clementi, Andreina, 200n2

De Cupis, Cesare, 188n9–10, 197n45, 198n46

De Montaigne, Michel, 192n6

De Tournon, Philippe, 188n9

debt. *See also* specific villages (i.e., Monte Flavio, Monte Libretti, etc.)
 and governing, 113–118
 and households, 170
 of Monte Libretti, 99–105
 records of, 104

debt collection, 101–104, 107. *See also* tax collection
 in Monte Libretti, 101–102

Decameron (Boccaccio), 27

Delumeau, Jean, 188n10, 192n4, 193n9–12, 194n21

Dentice, Monsignore, 114, 136, 148

depositario, 81–82, 132

Derrida, Jacques, 191n21

Di Sciarra, Giulio Cesare Barberini Colonna. *See* Barberini, Giulio Cesare

Di Stefano, Francesco, 8, 84–85

disorder in villages, causes of, 121–122, 143

disputes, 10, 14, 151–159. *See also* specific disputes (i.e., hunting ban, *minuti* [annual dues], etc.)

Douglas, Mary, 199n54

Duchy of Castro, 28–30, 32, 174, 195n28

edicts
 Barberini, 122–123, 173, 175
 enforcement of, 55
 Giulio Cesare's, 121, 135
 language of, 221n31
 Maffeo Barberini's, 80–1
 nobles', 50–51, 58
 and *statuto* (constitution), 51–52
 Testa's, 95–96
 villagers on, 51

education, access to, 66, 70–71, 127. *See also* schoolteacher, village

Elias, Norbert, 203n27

elites, village, role of, 60. *See also* villagers

Epstein, Stephan R., 189n14

Eugeni, Domenico, 53–54

everyday life, politics of, 14–15, 67–70

Fabiani, Fabiano, 76

Fair of Farfa, 26–28, 42

Farnese, Odoardo, 29

Farnese, Pierluigi, 30

Farnese family, 28–29, 195n28

nobles
    acquiescing to state, 7
    authority of, 6–7
    disputes with villagers, 6, 10, 14, 151–159
    involvement in village politics, 9–10,
        89–90, 97–98
    power and jurisdiction of, 7–8, 189n11
    typical, description of, 8–9
Nussdorfer, Laurie, 188n6, 190n16,
    195n28–30, 195n33, 203n24, 205n55,
    209n54

obligation
    and benevolence, 145–146
    versus courtesy, 38–40
offices, communal, 81–82
officials, Barberini, roles of, 108–113
olive oil harvest, 48, 59
Ong, Walter, 149, 223n4, 227n34, 227n37,
    227n39
opera productions, 26–28
oral culture, 164–165
Orfeo, Andrea, 53
Orsini, Giovanni Antonio, 50–51
Orsini family, 18, 22, 31, 73–74, 83
Ozouf, Jacques, 205n52

Pagani, Tommaso, 215n49
Paleotti, Belardino, 163
Palestrina, Principality of, 24–25, 98
Palozzi, Luigi, 139
Pamphilj, Giambattista, 32
Pangrazio, Marco, 75
Papal Congregation, 15. *See also* Buon
    Governo
papal government, authority of, 4, 6, 62
papal taxes, 94–95, 113–114, 131, 151–152,
    174–175, 179. *See also* tax collection
Papi, Giocchino, 117
Papi, Salvatore, 103
Partner, Peter, 193n13
Pasquale, Valeriano, 84
Pasqualoni, Antonio, 111
Pastor, Ludwig von, 192n7, 194n17–18,
    195n28–30, 196n36–38, 196n42, 197n44
pasture rights, 137–146
paternalism, 15–16, 124, 127, 136, 145–146, 168
    "paternal tenderness," 122–123

patronage, in Monte Libretti, 70–74
Paulini, Pietro Felice, 8–9
payment
    "gift," 39
    interest, Orsini's, 83
    of physician and surgeon, 77, 79, 224n9
Pecchiai, Pio, 8, 192n8, 194n16, 213n41
Pellone, Giovanni Antonio, 82
Pellone, Mattia, 142
Pellone, Simone, 81–82
Perini, Marco, 37–40, 47–48
Pescosolido, 189n11, 192n5, 210n4, 213n37,
    218n7
Petetti, Petro, 85
Petricca, Antonio, 155–159, 162, 169
Petrucci, Andrea, 163
Petrucci, Antonio, 159, 163
Petrucci, Felice Antonio, 152–153, 159, 170
Petrucci, Satunino, 156, 159
Petrucci, Silvia, 154–155, 169
Pettinella, Giovanni Domenico, 159
Pettinelli, Giuseppe, 161
physician, village, 68, 74–80
Piccialuti, Maura, 227n40
Piergentile, Biagio, 77
poaching, case of, 52–53. *See also* hunting ban
political participation, of villagers, 44,
    49–50, 60–61, 149, 176–180, 190n16.
    See also adversarial literacy
    and reading and writing, 16
Ponticelli
    debt of, 103, 105
    population of, 185
    tax collection in, 96
poor, village, 160–162, 166–168
"*Popolo*," letter from, 102–103, 105, 107
Portasacco, Giovanni Nicola, 49
possesso, 45–46, 188n7
priests, local, 133–134
priors, 45
private interest, *versus* "public good,"
    80–90
Prodi, Paolo, 192n8, 193n9, 199n54
the public, defined, 89
"public good," 86
    defined, 66, 87–88
    versus private interest, 80–90
Putnam, Robert, 10